CANADA

THE STORY OF OUR HERITAGE

SENIOR AUTHORS

Elspeth Deir
Elementary Social Studies Curriculum
Professor, Faculty of Education, Queen's
University, Kingston, Ontario

John Fielding
History and Contemporary Studies Curriculum
Professor, Faculty of Education, Queen's
University, Kingston, Ontario

AUTHORS

Nick Brune
Teacher, Iroquois Ridge High School, Oakville,
Ontario

Peter Grant
Writer, Victoria, British Columbia

Stephanie Smith Abram
Writer, Toronto, Ontario

McGraw-Hill Ryerson Limited

Toronto   Montréal   New York   Burr Ridge   Bangkok
Bogotá   Caracas   Lisbon   London   Madrid
Mexico City   Milan   New Delhi   Seoul   Singapore
Sydney   Taipei

McGraw-Hill
Ryerson Limited

A Subsidiary of The McGraw·Hill Companies

COPIES OF THIS BOOK MAY BE OBTAINED BY CONTACTING:

McGraw-Hill Ryerson Ltd.

WEBSITE:
http://www.mcgrawhill.ca

E-MAIL:
orders@mcgrawhill.ca

TOLL FREE FAX:
1-800-463-5885

TOLL FREE CALL:
1-800-565-5758

OR BY MAILING YOUR ORDER TO:
McGraw-Hill Ryerson
Order Department,
300 Water Street,
Whitby, ON, L1N 9B6

Please quote the ISBN and title when placing your order.

Canada: The Story of Our Heritage

ISBN 0-07-560735-2

http://www.mcgrawhill.ca

3 4 5 6 7 8 9 0 GTC 0 9 8 7 6 5 4 3 2 1

Printed and bound in Canada

Canadian Cataloguing in Publication Data

Deir, Elspeth, date
  Canada: the story of our heritage

Includes index.
ISBN 0-07-560735-2

Canada – History – To 1763 (New France) – Juvenile literature. 2. Canada – History – 1763-1867 Juvenile literature. I. Fielding, John (John F.). II. Title.

FC170.D433. 2000   971   C99-932898-0
F1026.D433 2000

PUBLISHER: Patty Pappas
ASSOCIATE EDITOR: Jocelyn Wilson
SENIOR SUPERVISING EDITOR: Nancy Christoffer
SUPERVISING EDITOR: Crystal Shortt
FEATURE WRITERS: Dyanne Rivers, Trudee Romanek
COPY EDITOR: Kathy Evans
PERMISSIONS EDITORS: Jacqueline Donovan, Mary Rose MacLachlan
PRODUCTION CO-ORDINATORS: Yolanda Pigden, Susanne Penny
EDITORIAL ASSISTANT: Joanne Murray
INTERIOR DESIGN: Word & Image Design Studio Inc.
ELECTRONIC PAGE MAKE-UP: Word & Image Design Studio Inc.
INTERIOR MAPS AND ILLUSTRATIONS: Deborah Crowle, Paul McCusker
COVER DESIGN: Greg Devitt and Dianna Little

REVIEWERS

Michael DeKay

Teacher, John Dearness Public School, London, Ontario

Sandy Dobec

Academic Consultant, Ottawa-Carleton Catholic District School Board, Ottawa, Ontario

Neil Ekels

Teacher, Peel District School Board, Mississauga, Ontario

Michael Taylor

Teacher, Churchill Heights Public School, Scarborough, Ontario

CONSULTANTS

Brenda Ahenakew

Director of Education for Saskatoon Travel Council, Saskatoon, Saskatchewan

E. Jane Errington

Professor and Chair of Department of History, Royal Military College, Kingston, Ontario; Professor of History, Queen's University, Kingston, Ontario

Acknowledgements

To the Deirs, who supported me in this project: Paul, Andrew, Matthew, Peter, and Emily. To my parents, Melba and Bill McKay, who taught me that Canada's history begins with stories of the everyday people who built our country. To all the teachers and students who make Canada's stories come alive in their minds, hearts, and lives. And to my colleague and friend, John Fielding, whose passion for history and sense of fun makes "work" play.

— *Elspeth Deir*

To Dianne for her patience as I embarked on another project. To Ellie Deir, with whom I have co-authored since 1991 — a funny and fine person to work with. To Grade 7 and 8 teachers, who may have the toughest job in education but are great to work with because they always seem ready and willing to learn.

— *John Fielding*

Thank you to Patty Pappas for her confidence in us and for letting us build into the texts much of the kind of learning we know works for students. Thanks to the author team, Stephanie Smith Abram, Nick Brune, and Peter Grant for working within the parameters we created for the texts. Thanks to Jocelyn Wilson for performing the difficult role of editor with good humour, skill, and patience, and to Crystal Shortt and Jacqueline Donovan for their efforts to get these texts into the hands of students. We are also grateful to our reviewers: Michael DeKay, Sandy Dobec, Neil Ekels, and Michael Taylor.

— *Elspeth Deir and John Fielding*

Contents

A Tour of the Text

Welcome to *Canada: The Story of Our Heritage*. This textbook introduces you to people in the seventeenth to nineteenth centuries who came from France and Britain to establish and settle New France and British North America. You will read about their social, financial, and political difficulties as they developed their settlements. You will also learn about the Aboriginal Peoples' interactions with these settlers and the effect this had on their culture. Finally, you will read about the rebellions of 1837 in Upper and Lower Canada and how they led to a unified Canada and responsible government.

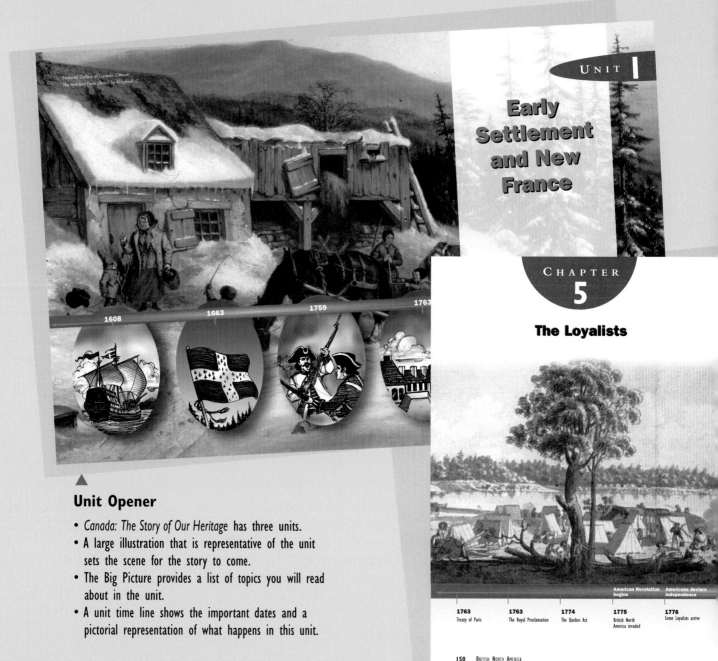

▲ Unit Opener

- *Canada: The Story of Our Heritage* has three units.
- A large illustration that is representative of the unit sets the scene for the story to come.
- The Big Picture provides a list of topics you will read about in the unit.
- A unit time line shows the important dates and a pictorial representation of what happens in this unit.

Chapter Opener

- Each chapter opener includes an illustration that is representative of the chapter.
- An overview of the chapter content is presented under the heading Setting Our Focus.
- Previewing the Chapter lists the specific topics you will be learning about in the chapter.
- Key Words is a list of the important words in the chapter. The words are introduced in boldface type the first time they appear in the text, where they are also defined. They are also compiled and alphabetized in the glossary at the back of the textbook.
- A time line displays the important dates and events highlighted in the chapter.

Madeleine de Verchères
DEFENDER OF CASTLE DANGEROUS

Fourteen-year-old Madeleine Jarret knew the danger she was in. She knew that the French were the enemies of the Iroquois, who had already killed three of her relatives. That is why she was always careful when she was outside the stockade that protected the manor house and habitants' cabins of Verchères, her family's seigneury. Verchères was on the south shore of the St. Lawrence River near the mouth of the Richelieu River. The seigneury was so vulnerable to attack that it was nicknamed Castle Dangerous.

Circumstances were especially dangerous in 1692. Britain and France were at war again. The Iroquois were allies of the British, who were giving them weapons so they could raid French settlements.

Madeleine's parents were away. A single sentry guarded the small fort. Madeleine was in the garden outside the stockade and the habitants were working nearby. Suddenly, a group of Iroquois leaped out of the woods and seized some of the habitants. Madeleine ran for the safety of the stockade. Shots rang out behind her. An Iroquois man caught up with her and grabbed the kerchief that was tied around her neck. Terrified, Madeleine fumbled to loosen the knot and kept running. The man was left with only a piece of cloth in his hand.

Madeleine dashed inside the big gate and struggled breathlessly to close and lock it. Outside, the Iroquois started trying to scale the walls of the fort.

Madeleine ordered the sentry to fire a small cannon from one of the bastions. Luckily, the loud booming noise scared the Iroquois, who retreated to the nearby woods. Madeleine knew that the noise would also tell neighbouring seigneuries that Verchères was under attack. They would pass along word and help would be sent from Montreal, 35 km upriver.

It would take a day for help to arrive. Until it did, the lives of the people of Verchères depended on convincing the Iroquois that the fort was too well defended to attack. Madeleine dashed from bastion to bastion, calling out to make it seem as if many soldiers were stationed inside. She also urged other people to make as much noise as possible. For the rest of the day, the frightened defenders kept up their noisy ruse.

When reinforcements arrived the next day, the Iroquois had already left, taking their prisoners with them. The reinforcements gave chase and caught up to them at Lake Champlain. Two of the habitants had been killed, but the others were released and returned to Verchères. As the story of Madeleine's bravery spread among the settlers, she became the toast of New France.

More people you could research are

Madeleine de Verchères

The Huron
The Iroquois
Father Charles Lalemant
Énemond Massé
Pieskaret

The Colony of New France **71**

Biographies

- Biographies of a famous person and two "everyday" people appear in each chapter. All the people are important players in the story of Canada's past.
- At the end of each biography is a list of other people who also had a part in the story. Their names are provided for you to do further research if you wish.

Reflections

- In these journal activities, you have an opportunity to think about a particular historic event and record how you feel about it.

Reflections

Imagine you are one of the wives about to join her husband at the barracks. Write a journal entry describing your day and how you feel.

Women and the Army

The only women at a barracks were wives of soldiers. A lottery system was used to choose which wives could come.

Life at the barracks was extremely difficult. There was no privacy, and the women were expected to work — as teamstresses, nurses, laundry maids, and cleaners. They also had to look after their own families and not impose on the army in any way.

If her husband died, a woman was allowed three to six months to grieve. She then had to remarry or leave the unit. For the sake of their security, most remarried.

The Volunteer Militia

Aside from the regular trained and experienced soldiers of the British army, the war required additional numbers of volunteers from the citizens of Upper and Lower Canada, New Brunswick, and Nova Scotia. Since most of the battles were in Upper Canada, this was the area most in need of volunteers. What an odd situation these people were — former Americans. How would they feel about active combat against their former comparisons?

There were traitors, and the penalty was death by hanging if caught, but the traitors were not as numerous as some in authority had feared. Even Brock was pleasantly surprised by the small number of actual traitors.

The real stumbling block to acquiring a large volunteer force was the everyday life of the settler. Examine these words from Brock describing volunteers gathered right after the declaration of war:

... So great was the clamour to return and attend to their farms, that I found myself in some measure, compelled by sanction the departure of a large proportion, and I am not without apprehension that the remainder will, in defiance of the law, which can only impose a fine of twenty pounds, leave service the moment the harvest commences.

Web Connection

- These computer research activities appear in every chapter.
- By following the directions, you can use the Internet to find a history topic at school or at home that is related to what you are learning about in the chapter.

Web Connection

http://www.school.mcgrawhill.ca/resources

Go to the web site above to find out more about a soldier's life in 1812. Go to History Resources, then to Canada: The Story of Our Heritage to see where to go next.

196 BRITISH NORTH AMERICA

Lieutenant-Governor Francis Bond Head appointed reformers to the Executive Council, then ignored their advice.

armed conflict within two years. As in Lower Canada, groups of **radicals** broke away from moderate reformers. The moderates believed in the gradual reform of parliamentary institutions, but the radicals wanted to bring in American-style democracy, with elections for many more positions.

A few radicals were prepared to take up arms to change the government. Lieutenant-Governor Head plunged into the election campaign. He branded both radical and moderate candidates as traitors. It worked. The Tory party won.

Snapshot

Voting a Risky Business

In the early 1800s, elections were rough-and-ready affairs. Because there was no secret ballot, bribes, threats, and violence were common. Strict rules governed who could vote. Only men who met certain property qualifications were eligible. Women were not allowed to vote at all. Voting often went on for a week or more. Because only one polling place was set up in each riding, many people had to travel a long way. For some people, voting meant being away from home for days.

On the first day, the candidates gave speeches from rough wooden platforms. These were often conveniently set up outside a tavern. Then the candidate and his supporters mingled with the crowd, trying to win votes. This sometimes meant inviting voters into the tavern and plying them with food and liquor. When a race was close and drink had flowed freely, it was not unusual for the supporters of opposing candidates to end up in wild brawls.

To vote, a man had to show proof that he was qualified. Then he mounted the platform and declared his choice for all to hear. If a man accepted the hospitality of one candidate and then voted for another, he was in for trouble.

318 CONFLICT AND CHANGE

Snapshot

- This feature explores an event, person, or invention that is not part of the central story but was an interesting piece of news during the time period covered.

SETTING OUR FOCUS

In the picture on the left, of a Loyalist settlement near present-day Brockville, Ontario, the year is 1784. You see tents that have been temporarily given by the British government to Loyalist refugee families. Like thousands of other families, these people are waiting, hopefully for only a few months, to be given a land grant so they can start a new life. What does this picture tell us about the newcomer Loyalists? What do you imagine day-to-day life will be like for these families for the next twelve months?

PREVIEWING THE CHAPTER

In this chapter you will learn about these topics:

- the reasons for Loyalist settlements in British North America
- the different groups of people who were Loyalists, and how the groups affected their areas of settlement
- what life was like for those early settlers, for some particular individuals, and how they affected society as a whole
- the contributions of certain individuals, including Sir Guy Carleton and Sir John Graves Simcoe

KEY WORDS

civilians
compensation
elected assembly
Loyalists
migration
military rule
minutemen
Patriots
raids
refugees

American Revolution ends

1783
Loyalists arrive in British North America in large numbers

1791
- The Constitution Act creates Upper Canada and Lower Canada
- John Graves Simcoe becomes first Lieutenant-Governor of Upper Canada

1793
Simcoe founds the settlement of York (later to become Toronto)

The Loyalists **151**

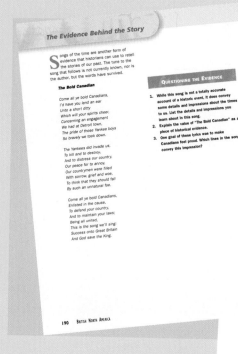

The Evidence Behind the Story

- In each chapter, an item of historical evidence is presented for you to consider.
- Questions and activities are provided to assist you in your assessment of the historical value of the material provided in this feature.

The Story So Far...

- Throughout each chapter, questions and activities are provided to help you recall and explore some of the people and events presented in a section of the chapter.
- The activities are designed to include different learning styles.

Snippet ▶

- This feature appears periodically, in the margin of the text. They are interesting bits of historical information that are relevant to the content.

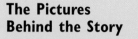

The Pictures Behind the Story ▶

- In this photo essay, you will learn more about Canada's landscapes, cities, towns, countryside, and climate, through the photos and captions.

Stepping Into the Picture

- Two large pictures are presented in each unit. You are asked to step into the role of a person in the picture and imagine what it would be like to be part of the scene.

Stepping Into the Picture

M11588.
Attributed to
Joseph Légaré,
The Burning of the
Parliament Building in
Montréal (detail), ca. 1849, oil
on wood. McCord Museum of Canadian
History, Montréal.

Imagine you are a British Canadian resident of Montréal, loyal to the British Queen. You just heard that the Legislative Assembly has passed the Rebellion Losses Bill. Public money will be given to people who may have participated in the rebellions of 1837 and 1838. You have been waiting for years to see more money spent to improve transportation in Canada.

Or, you could assume you are a Canadien living in Saint-Eustache or Napierville. You had nothing to do with the rebellions but some of your relatives did. For that, General Colborne's troops burned your home.

equipment. You have been waiting for compensation ever since.

Study the people in the foreground of this painting. What do they seem to be doing? Now, step into the picture. You are one of the people in the mob. How do you feel as you watch the Parliament buildings burn? Excited? Angry? Sweaty? Afraid? How do the people around you make you feel? What are you thinking about? Are you glad you participated? Will you get caught? Was it worth it? Talk with ...

Chapter Closer

- At the end of each chapter, there is a summary of the major events in the chapter under the heading Sum It Up!
- A number of questions and activities appear under the headings: Thinking About Your Learning, Applying Your Learning, and Using Key Words, which allow you to put into practice what you have learned from the chapter.
- You and/or your teacher can choose which activities to complete individually or in a group.
- The activities take different learning styles into consideration.

SUM IT UP!

The dominant features of life in Lower Canada, the Maritime Colonies, and Newfoundland at this time are change, contrasts, and struggles. For most inhabitants of these colonies, the struggle to survive was daily and ongoing. Farming was essential, yet difficult. The economy was mostly resource-based; people often suffered from a lack of resources. The population was growing rapidly; most settlers were first- or second-generation immigrants. This early phase of the Great Migration would be devastating to the original inhabitants and put the long-term inhabitants, like the French Canadians, in a difficult position.

Technology was transforming. Steamships and railways were significant advances, yet most people still did everything by hand. Fortunes could be made, and there were aspirations for a more "advanced" society that included universities, public schools, banks, and charitable organizations. On the other hand, sickness and physical injury played a large part in the colonists' lives. So did bad weather, fire, famine, and a host of other unpredictable disasters.

Despite the obstacles, each colony expanded, progressed, and asserted its own particular focus. British North America was still a collection of colonies, but the challenges they faced would ultimately unite them.

This illustration shows a girl miming a colonist at a spinning wheel for activity 3, Thinking About Your Learning, on page 234.

THINKING ABOUT YOUR LEARNING

1. Compare and contrast the early phase of the Great Migration with the Loyalist Migration. Consider why the settlers came, the hardships they faced when they arrived, and the impact they had on the receiving colonies.

2. There is a saying, "history repeats itself." Describe a condition in Canada today that reminds you of something that happened in Lower Canada or the Maritime Colonies in the early nineteenth century.

could include people, dates, places, disasters, and wild cards.

2. Continue to uncover the historical development of your own community. Focus on the developments from 1800 to 1835. Include a graph to show any changes in the population. Categories to research are: immigration, settlers' hardships, sickness, transportation, technology, and institutions.

3. Pick one of the people spotlighted in this chapter and prepare a television talk show interview with him or her. Consider preparation for the host, interview topics and questions, other guests, and possible audience participation.

4. If you could be any person mentioned in this chapter, whom would you be and why? Whom would you least like to be and why?

5. Design a totem pole representing five significant features during the time period of this chapter. (Suggestion: use a paper towel roll or a potato chip tin as a base.)

USING KEY WORDS

1. Make a Word Search puzzle using the key words and at least two other words you think are significant to understanding this chapter.

APPLYING YOUR LEARNING

3. Play Maritimes Charades. Pick a person, place, or thing mentioned in this chapter and have a classmate guess who, what, or where.

1. Create a Trivial Pursuit-type of game in which the questions and answers cover the developments in Lower Canada, the Maritime Colonies, and Newfoundland in th Remember that in Trivial Pursuit t different categories. Perhaps you

Unit Closer

- At the end of each unit, there are two pages of activities called Connecting Your Learning. These encompass Understanding Concepts, Developing Research Skills, Communicating Required Knowledge, and Applying Concepts and Skills.
- You and/or your teacher can choose which activities you will complete individually, in small groups, or in large groups.
- These activities will allow you to apply your learning in a number of ways.

UNIT 3

Conflict and Change

CONNECTING YOUR LEARNING

UNDERSTANDING CONCEPTS

1. Describe the society and way of life of the habitants in Lower Canada in the period 1815–1848. Include details about their environment and surroundings, their property and work, the things they produced, their food, dress, habits, religion, education, and any other notable details.

2. Write a biography of a member of a family settling in Upper Canada, showing why they might have immigrated, how they got there, and what they had to do to get started.

3. In what way(s) did the rebellions of Lower and Upper Canada succeed?

4. How was responsible government different from colonial government? Consider the following points in your answer:
   - the way the ruler was chosen
   - the choice of advisors for the Executive Council
   - the test or proof that Canada's government was responsible

DEVELOPING RESEARCH SKILLS

1. In a democracy, conflicts are resolved by non-violent means. Think about the conflicts you have studied in this unit. In groups, discuss the circumstances when people tried to settle their disagreements by violent means, and those when they used non-violent ways. Report to the class on the conclusions you reached about the causes of violence.

2. The government of Québec staged a referendum on sovereignty, or independence from Canada. The sovereignty side lost, but the result was very close. And the government wants to hold another. In groups, conduct an opinion poll of people living on your street or in your neighbourhood. In your poll, include questions asking people:
   - Should Québec be allowed to separate from Canada?
   - If so, should it be unilaterally or by negotiation?
   - If by negotiation, with what conditions?
   - If not, what measures should Canada take to keep Québec in Confederation? By offering special deals? By the use of force?

Compile the results of your poll and present them to the class with your interpretation of their meaning. Then discuss what it would mean for you and for Canada if Québec separated.

3. Compile a list of street names with historical associations in your community. Trace the origins of the names. Classify them according to origins — people, places, events, or other. Map and display your findings. (It is probably best to choose one neighbourhood.)

COMMUNICATING REQUIRED KNOWLEDGE

1. Write a letter to a sovereigntist student in French Canada, persuading him or her not to separate. Use your knowledge of history to make an argument in favour of co-operation and against separation.

2. Construct a one-page cartoon or storyboard to tell the story of an incident in the rebellions of 1837 or 1838.

3. This cartoon, published in the magazine Punch in Canada, pokes fun at the Rebellion Losses Bill. In 1849, thousands of people flocked to California to pan for gold. Canada was in the depths of a depression, with thousands of people out of work. What is the cartoonist's point of view toward the Rebellion Losses Bill? Translate the dialogue into modern language.

CANADA versus CALIFORNIA.

APPLYING CONCEPTS AND SKILLS

1. On November 11, 1947, Winston Churchill said: "Democracy is the worst form of government except all [the others]." Discuss the meaning of the quotation. Then make a poster or advertisement for democracy that uses the quotation. Include illustrations and text showing the different elements of democracy, such as free elections, representative government, executive responsibility, and so on. Display your work.

2. On a sheet of paper, complete the mind map on the right to show the connections between different forces at work in Upper Canada during the period of 1815 to 1840.

3. In some ways Canada is very similar to the United States; in other ways, it is strikingly different. In groups of three or four, discuss the traits that mark Canadians as different. Create a skit or play that illustrates the differences. Your skit could be about Americans paying a summertime visit to their Canadian cousins, for example.

Canada Is Unique

SETTING OUR FOCUS

Take a careful look at the photograph on the left. These students represent the part of our story that focuses on our people — Canadians from the Atlantic Coast to the Pacific Coast to the Arctic Coast — and the stories they have to tell.

Canada has the most culturally diverse society in the history of the world. That means there are more people from more countries and cultures living in Canada than anywhere else. In the Greater Toronto Area, there are more than 100 different ethnocultural groups that have at least 10 000 people in them. That is certainly a diverse population! How will we uncover their stories that will help us understand more about our country's present and past? We will use the methods all researchers use: collecting, sorting, and interpreting information from many places. Then we will organize and communicate our findings.

In this chapter you will be learning about four ways that our country is unique: our people, our geography, our artists and athletes, and our governments. We will be answering the research question, "What makes Canada unique?"

PREVIEWING THE CHAPTER

In this chapter you will learn about these topics:
- **how personal histories make up part of Canada's heritage**
- **how people from different races and cultures, with different customs and traditions, all live together in one country**
- **how to use different research techniques to obtain information**
- **how Canada is a diverse country because of its various races, cultures, geographical features, cities and towns, and urban and rural settings**

KEY WORDS

archives
autobiography
biography
culture
government document
heritage
interviewee
interviewer
parliamentary system
personal interview
race

WHO LIVES IN CANADA?

Audrey Boros

When Audrey posed for her Grade 8 class picture, she had been in Canada for 13 years — all her life. Audrey, like thousands of Canadians, was born here, the child of first-generation newcomers to Canada. Her parents travelled from two very distant parts of the world to make new lives in Canada. Their stories share similarities with the stories of many Canadians through the ages. These are the stories of refugees, immigrants, and courageous risk-takers — people who made a momentous decision to leave their homelands to settle here. For many, their journey was filled with danger and uncertainty.

Audrey's father escaped from a communist country in Eastern Europe, determined to live in freedom in Canada. Her mother left a troubled and dangerous situation in South Africa to live in Canada. When she arrived here, Audrey's mom wondered if she had made the right decision. Would this country be a welcoming place for her to begin a new life? She would have to learn to be Canadian.

Like many Canadians whose parents are newcomers, Audrey has relatives in other parts of the world. At home, she hears her parents speaking languages that are not heard often in her community, but she is proud that they have learned to live and work using English. She celebrates special family events with the foods her parents enjoyed in their homelands. She plants a maple sapling in Trees for Canada Week and watches fireworks on Canada Day, just like the other teenagers in her neighbourhood. She, like many Canadians, can feel part of more than one **culture**. Culture means the beliefs, arts, customs, and institutions typical of a particular people, community, or nation. Audrey talked about her feelings during an interview in which she shared her family's story. We can use her story to help us understand many things about what makes Canada unique.

What is so special about Audrey's story? Think about how it shows us so many features of our country: many **races** (meaning groups of humans sharing the same biological traits) and cultures; newcomers to Canada; and people learning to live in a new land and help build their communities.

Conducting a Personal Interview

Many researchers use a **personal interview** to obtain basic information. They choose a person to interview, prepare questions, interview the person, organize the information, and then use the information to write a story. An interview is one important way for researchers to collect data. When doing research, or gathering information for any sort of project, be sure to include "people" as one of your resources. Most people are happy to share information and ideas. They are pleased that someone is interested in hearing their story, as Audrey was.

As an **interviewer** you will follow this process:

1 Decide what questions you need to ask. You may need to do some research first, so that you know something about the topic and can ask intelligent questions. Write the questions down in a notebook and leave lots of space for answers.

2 Use the five Ws to help organize your questions. These are questions that begin with <u>Who</u>, <u>What</u>, <u>When</u>, <u>Where</u>, and <u>Why</u>. Questions that begin with <u>How</u> are also useful.

3 Arrange a time to talk with the person you will be interviewing, or the **interviewee**, and be sure the purpose of the interview is clear. Explain your information needs and why you are consulting the interviewee.

4 Take along a notebook, pencil, and small cassette recorder to the interview. Ask the interviewee if you may record the session on tape. Many interviewees agree to talk into a microphone so that others can hear the interview later. However, some people are very uncomfortable with microphones and prefer to have you write down their answers. If you are taping the interview, be sure the microphone is positioned to record both the interviewee's voice and your own. Record a few words, just to make sure the equipment is working properly. This tape will become an important piece of historical evidence, since a moment in history is being captured and can be referred to in the future.

5 When taking written notes, leave lots of room in your notebook to write down questions you may not have thought of during your initial planning, and the answers to them. Make sure not to omit the information these additional answers will provide.

6 Be sure to thank your interviewee and mention that you will provide a copy of your work when it is complete. Everyone wants to know what happens to the information they provide in an interview.

Bill McKay

When Bill McKay had his Grade 8 class picture taken, it was 1927. The story of Bill's family in Canada began more than 100 years before that, in 1813. That is when his ancestors left their Scottish homeland to travel across the Atlantic Ocean and up icy rivers and lakes from Hudson Bay to their new homeland. They were among the tiny group of settlers in the new Red River Colony.

Bill's family lived in a big house near the Red River in Winnipeg, Manitoba. Bill spent every Saturday during the winter stacking wood in the basement, to keep the furnace burning. When he was ten, he began skiing to school, through the backyards of neighbours along the way. Bill's parents would not allow him to go onto the river ice before Christmas. One year, three boys from his school had to be rescued after they went through soft ice. Their friend, the fourth skater, drowned. After that, Bill and his brothers did not need to be reminded to stay off the ice.

Bill and his friends often travelled on snowshoes across Manitoba's deep snow. Sometimes they went out for a walk in the evening, and if the aurora borealis was active, the night seemed magical.

Bill's school was small — just one room for about 44 students and one teacher, along with desks, coat racks, cupboards, a barrel full of water with a ladle to drink from, a few books, and two wood stoves. You may have seen photographs or visited historic sites of schoolrooms like this one. For Bill and his friends, this was no museum. On his very first day at school, Bill's teacher told him that he had pronounced his own name incorrectly. How many of us have had an experience like that with our names? Bill was certainly surprised and confused. But as he wrote in his **autobiography**, "School was not taken too seriously by any of my friends. It was one of the things that happened in life beginning at age six and ending when one was grown up." His autobiography describes his high-school and college days, and all the events that he thought interesting or important enough to write down.

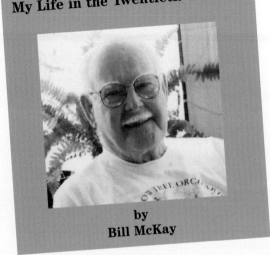

Bill McKay

My Life in the Twentieth Century

by
Bill McKay

USING AN AUTOBIOGRAPHY

A person chooses what to put into an autobiography and what to leave out. Both famous and everyday people write autobiographies so they can share their stories with others. Researchers use autobiographies to help them understand a time period or an important event. We can use Bill's autobiography to find out some details about the story of Canada and to help us understand more about everyday life in the twentieth century. Bill lived through some big events in Canadian history. He worked in a remote Northern community during the Great Depression, flew a bomber aircraft during World War II, and contributed to his community after the war ended. Bill's personal history connects in many ways with events that affected millions of people. However, one person's autobiography does not give us enough information to provide a complete picture of the events.

Hee Sook Lim

"I came to Canada in 1976 from Seoul, South Korea, when I was six years old. My family first lived in a town called Swan Hills. Swan Hills is about 170 km northwest of Edmonton, Alberta, and is famous for its grizzly bears. The town's population was approximately 2500, and I was the only Asian in my elementary school.

The school did not have English as a Second Language (ESL) teaching, and my teacher seemed quite puzzled to have me. What do you do with a kid who does not speak English? Basically, I had to learn English on my own, so that meant picking up words in the classroom and on the playground. I am, however, especially thankful to television. If not for it, I think it would have taken me longer to learn the language. A children's educational television program especially taught me the English alphabet, numbers, and, most importantly, phonics.

A year after arriving in Alberta, my family moved to Mississauga, Ontario, and the school I attended did not have ESL teaching, either. Despite some ethnic minorities in the school, there were few ESL students. Instead of teaching me the English language, the school decided that I should work with the Special Education teacher for pronunciation lessons. As a result, I spent my elementary years learning English by listening to friends and classmates, by watching television, and by reading."

Using a Government Document

Researchers have to gather as much information as they can from as many places as they can. In researching some stories about Canadians to answer our question "Who are Canadians?" we can look at a tool many researchers often use: a **government document**. There are many types of documents provided by our governments, including visas, passports, licences, and many more. Hee Sook's family immigrated to Canada from South Korea. Documents from their long journey help us piece together their story. Other documents are also useful when we investigate the stories of others who have moved here.

Take a look at the sort of information you can obtain from the Canadian Immigration Identification Record reproduced here. How does it help the researcher answer the Who, What, When, Where, Why, and How questions?

A Canadian Patchwork Quilt

We have a great variety of people and places in our country. There are people of many races and cultures who have made Canada their home. They live in parts of a country that have many kinds of geographical features: mountains, valleys, plains, coastal areas, huge cities, towns, tiny villages, and farms. You could think of the people and places of Canada as a patchwork quilt: many different pieces that, together, make the whole. Our country's diversity is shown in the variety of people who are our neighbours and classmates, and in the variety of places where Canadians live and work. Hee Sook's family represents one part of our country's patchwork quilt. She tells a little bit of her story for us in the first person; that is, in her own words. We can use her words as well as government documents to help us understand more about our country's people.

Web Connection

www.school.mcgrawhill.ca/resources

Go to the web site above to find out more about Canadian statistics. Go to History Resources, then to *Canada: The Story of Our Heritage* to see where to go next.

James Sewid

James Sewid never had time to pose for his Grade 8 class picture in 1926. By the time he was 13, James was married and working on a fishing boat near his home in Alert Bay, British Columbia. James was destined to be a leader of his people, the Kwakiutl. Instead of attending school regularly, he learned the ways of his people, as well as how to be a successful captain in the fishery, by watching others and by trying things himself. His parents, grandparents, and other community members taught James the traditions and customs of their Aboriginal ancestors.

You may be surprised to read that James was married at the age of 13. When James heard that his grandparents had arranged for his wedding, he, too, was very surprised. He overheard them talking about his wedding one night after coming in late from a dance. When he asked his stepfather about what he had heard, James discovered he would be married to a girl he did not even know. He soon learned that her name was Flora and that she was 16 years old.

James told his family that he was too young. "It's all right," they said. "We'll look after you." James and his bride had two wedding ceremonies, one in their traditional fashion and one in a Christian church. James was too young to attend his Kwakiutl wedding, since he was not yet old enough to make a speech. Instead the Chiefs and leaders of the local villages carried out the ceremonies and presented the couple with many customary gifts. James and Flora stayed together for many years, and James became a successful fishing captain, businessperson, leader of his community, and builder of the town of Alert Bay.

Research Is Happening Here

USING A BIOGRAPHY

Anybody doing research about Canadians can find information in books. James Sewid's story is told in a **biography**, which is a story about a person, written by another person. These and other books can help us learn the stories of Canadians. Some books are easy to find. Encyclopedias, dictionaries, biographies, textbooks, and general histories are in every school and public library. You may have used encyclopedias to help you answer research questions. History books or biographies are harder to find, but they sometimes provide us with wonderful stories. Look for these in people's private collections, universities, museums, and **archives**. An archive is a place where public records or historical documents are preserved. Researchers love to find that special story in a book that they can share with many readers.

Alexandre Despatie

In September 1998, a 13-year-old boy from Laval, Québec, won a gold medal in men's platform diving at the Commonwealth Games. The gold medal looked immense resting on Alexandre Despatie's chest. His Team Canada uniform looked much too big. The other medal winners looked like giants beside him.

Alexandre Despatie was small in size, with a mass of 45 kg and a height of 155 cm, but he seemed huge because of his spirit, his innocence, and his joy at winning the gold medal. His talent, composure, and enthusiasm made Alexandre a popular figure at the Games' diving pool. When his final marks flashed on the scoreboard, he burst into tears of joy. Other divers gave him big hugs, and the silver medalist raised him high in the air. The student had won his first big international diving event.

During the competition, Alexandre clapped and whistled to cheer on the other divers. He laughed and enjoyed every minute of the event. On the pool deck, he looked small. But way up at the top of the diving platform, Alexandre looked even smaller and much too fragile to be throwing himself into the water from such a height. His scores told a different story. One dive rated a perfect ten. It was a wonderful day for the Canadian from Laval.

Research Is Happening Here

USING NEWSPAPERS AND MAGAZINES

Researchers use newspapers and magazines for finding information about particular people and events. Newspapers have been providing information to Canadians since the 1700s. Stories written by journalists can supply answers to the five Ws. Reporters use these words to help them when writing a story. They also write with the purpose of keeping you reading, with the most interesting or newsworthy information at the beginning of a story. When using newspapers and magazines for research, remember to use more than one source of information. Be sure to note whether the story you are using is a news item, an editorial, or a column. News items are supposed to report the facts of a story. Editorials are opinions expressed by their authors, who are usually not identified. Columns are also opinions, but their authors always identify themselves, often with a photograph. If you are looking for opinions, you might want to use an editorial or column. If you want factual information, a news story should help. You can find newspaper and magazine stories on paper or electronically.

Web Connection

www/school.mcgrawhill.ca/resources

Go to the web site above to find out more about Canadian newspaper web sites. Go to History Resources, then to *Canada: The Story of Our Heritage* to see where to go next.

Mollie Karachunsky Appel

Mollie Karachunsky (now Mollie Appel) did not have time to worry about having a class picture taken. She was too busy caring for her little sister Roslyn. When Mollie was eight, her family made a huge decision. They would sell their belongings, leave their village in Russia, and travel to the port of Antwerp in Belgium. There they would board a ship and cross the Atlantic Ocean to Canada. They would escape the persecution they were experiencing because of their Jewish religion and make new lives there. Mollie's grandfather, who had come to Ottawa in 1923, had sent boat tickets for the family to join him. In 1925 there had been a terrible typhus epidemic in Eastern Europe. Mollie's whole family got sick and, sadly, Mollie's mother died.

When the family arrived at Antwerp, they had to pass a medical examination before they were allowed on the ship. Mollie's oldest sister, Sonia, did not pass the test because she was still weak from typhus. The Canadian immigration officer advised the family to try again in one month — perhaps then the infection would be gone and they could all board the ship. Unhappily, this time Mollie and her little sister Roslyn did not pass the test because of an eye disease.

Now Mollie's father had to make a terrible decision because his tickets and visa would expire if he did not get on the boat. He could go back to Russia and try later to get new tickets to come to Canada or he could leave his young daughters behind for treatment while he and his other three children travelled to Canada to look for a home and work. Her father arranged for a place for his two daughters to stay.

Mollie and Roslyn were on their own for about three months but were helped by a local Jewish immigrant aid society. Eventually they passed the medical examination and walked up the gangplank to a ship on its way to Canada. How would they get along, so young and alone? They made friends with some other immigrants on board who provided some help. It was a rough voyage and Mollie looked after Roslyn, who was very seasick.

What kept Mollie going during that time? She always wore her identification papers around her neck and found courage in thinking that she would soon be reunited with her family.

After the voyage, the two small girls arrived safely in Montréal. Naturally, they expected their father to greet them and take them to their new home in Ottawa. A shock awaited them. No familiar face appeared at the gate! Again, the girls seemed alone in a strange country with two more unknown languages, French and English. Finally, an uncle met them.

Mollie's father had thought that this uncle would be able to
handle the situation better than him, since he spoke English and
knew his way around Montréal. Mollie and Roslyn's adventures
were finally over.

The story of Mollie's bravery became a family treasure as it
was passed down to each succeeding generation in Canada. One
member of Mollie's family shared the story with us more than
70 years after it happened.

Research Is Happening Here

USING FAMILY STORIES

Molly's story is an inspiring tale of courage and determination. She kept going because of one thing:
she wanted to join her family in Canada. Her story has been told and retold to members of her family
and is part of their family's **heritage** — something handed on to a person from his or her ancestors.
Many families have stories of their early days in Canada or of past events that are interesting to
younger family members. You can use oral history to help you understand your family's and your
community's heritage and to learn about the past. You need to be cautious when relying on oral
history, however. Do you think there may be some exaggeration in some of the stories? Do you think
all of the information is reliable? How might you check the accuracy of the information?

Carrington Phillip

When Carrington Phillip had his Grade 8 picture taken, he had been in Canada only three years. He had arrived with his family from the small Caribbean island of Dominica. Carrington, his two sisters, and his mother Joyce had flown to Montréal to meet their dad and husband.

When Joyce got off the plane, she noticed that something seemed strange: the trees in Canada had no leaves. It was October, and the leaves had fallen. This was something that never happened in Joyce's Caribbean homeland. Later that fall, winter showed the newcomers something else they had never experienced before: snow. When Joyce and her little girl looked out one sunny day, they saw that snow had covered the ground. Out they rushed in their sandals. Wow! Snow is cold! Many people who come here from tropical countries are thrilled by their first Canadian snowfall.

Why did Carrington's parents choose Canada? They followed a pattern common to many newcomers. They had a friend working here who encouraged them to move to Canada. Carrington's dad was the first family member to leave the island; then the rest of the family followed. There were few people from the Caribbean living in Kingston, Ontario, when Carrington and his family arrived. It took the family a while to adjust to this new country, but they managed.

Many people who are learning to become Canadian depend on a diary to record their feelings and opinions, and describe events. History students can read diaries as another way to gather information.

Research Is Happening Here

USING A DIARY

Many of you will have a diary: a written account of what you have done, thought about, or felt during the day. Maybe you use it regularly. Maybe you remember to write in it when you have something very important to record. You will find diary entries later in this text. Authors use diaries to keep track of their stories and then share them with all of us so that we can better understand their families' histories. Diary writers can record facts, opinions, and feelings. Researchers then must decide how best to use the information.

The Pictures Behind the Story

From Sea to Sea

The towering ▶ mountains and icy cold lakes and rivers of British Columbia, Alberta, and the Yukon.

Canada stretches from sea to sea to sea, presenting a land of wonder. Use these photographs to help you think about the diversity of this land.

Forget about ice ▶ and snow during the summer in Canada's North.

◀ **Vancouver, Canada's gateway to the Pacific Ocean.**

◀ **Southern Alberta. Did dinosaurs once roam here?**

◀ **A prairie summer. Thirsty cattle need a drink.**

Nearly 4 million people
live within sight of the
CN Tower in Toronto.

A peaceful ▶
winter's day in
southern Ontario.

▼ A spring fog blankets the village
of Peggy's Cove, Nova Scotia.

The glorious
colours of
autumn on
Mount Royal,
Montréal.

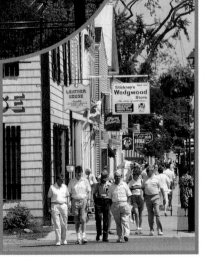

▲ Canadians live, work, and play in
communities large and small, like
St. Andrews, New Brunswick.

FROM NEIGHBOURHOOD TO WORLD STAGE

Canadian artists tell us stories through paintings, songs, plays, novels, and poetry. When your parents nag you to get busy and practise, maybe it is because they want you to be the next Glenn Gould, a celebrated Canadian pianist. Or they want you to be the next Celine Dion, a singer who has won innumerable awards and has international fame. Maybe they are thinking you can be the next Donovan Bailey, Marianne Limpert, or Elvis Stojko: Canadian athletes who broke world records and carried home gold medals.

The famous Canadians in this photo montage are, beginning at the top left and moving clockwise: Donovan Bailey, Susan Aglukark, Marnie McBean, Wayne Gretzky, Sarah McLachlan, Marianne Limpert, and Elvis Stojko.

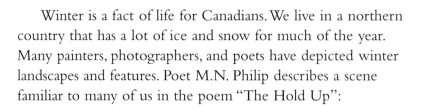

Winter is a fact of life for Canadians. We live in a northern country that has a lot of ice and snow for much of the year. Many painters, photographers, and poets have depicted winter landscapes and features. Poet M.N. Philip describes a scene familiar to many of us in the poem "The Hold Up":

Stripped of leaves,
surprised —
the trees
scrape the grey winter sky
with veined brittle arms.

A. J. Casson 1898-1992, **White Pine** c.1957, oil on canvas, 76.0 x 101.3 cm
McMichael Canadian Art Collection Gift of the founders,
Robert and Signe McMichael 1966.16.119

Susan Aglukark sings about her Inuit culture, family, and friends, accompanied by a mixture of traditional and modern instruments — everything from Aboriginal drums to electronic synthesizers. The song "O Siem" celebrates the joy of seeing friends:

> O Siem, we are all family
> O Siem, we're all the same
> O Siem, the fires of freedom
> Dance in the burning flame.

Sarah McLachlan sent the world of music in a new direction when she organized the highly successful Lilith Fairs. These travelling musical shows featured female artists only and allowed McLachlan and other Canadian women to share their talents and tunes with audiences all over North America.

The Kingston, Ontario, music group *The Tragically Hip* has appealed to young people across Canada for a long time and has won many Juno awards for its music.

Fredericton's Marianne Limpert powered Canada's swimming teams to medals during her Olympic and Commonwealth Games career.

Haida artist Bill Reid's sculptures and jewellery are known around the world for their beauty and images from his Aboriginal heritage.

Donovan Bailey's world record in the 100-m sprint proved he was the fastest man on the planet. Did a serious injury end his career?

How many hockey records does Wayne Gretzky hold? So many that the number may never be matched. The Great One has put more pucks in the net than any other hockey player will ever dream of doing.

Cirque du Soleil, a troupe of acrobats from Québec, has given new meaning to the word *circus*. The innovative and awesome stunts, costumes, music, and settings of their themed shows have amazed audiences worldwide.

Kayaking has been a Canadian pastime for centuries. Canoeist Caroline Brunet captured world championships in her swift kayak.

Elvis Stojko's skates are not for playing hockey. He uses them to win medals at the Olympics and World Figure Skating Championships and to show the world a model of courage and determination despite serious injury.

Marnie McBean rowed her way to greatness, earning a medal in the World Rowing Championships. She is the only rower ever to have won medals in all rowing events: a true Canadian champion.

FROM HERE TO PARLIAMENT HILL

In 1998 Canadians welcomed a hero of the twentieth century to our country and made him a member of the Order of Canada. He was not a sports superhero or a movie star. He spent 27 years in solitary confinement in a South African prison because he opposed a government that denied black people their human rights: justice, equal opportunity, religious freedom, and others basic to human life. When he visited Toronto, President Nelson Mandela greeted and sang and danced with a crowd of 40 000 Canadian children at SkyDome. He told them they were fortunate to live in such a culturally diverse country as Canada. He urged them to carry on the work of building a better world where injustice and racism do not exist.

President Mandela told us that many people do not have the same rights as Canadians have. We are protected by the Canadian Charter of Rights and Freedoms. In some countries, it is illegal to worship, hold meetings, carry a picket sign, live wherever you want to, or protest non-violently against a government's actions. We are free to do any of these things and many more, because some Canadians work to protect the rights and freedoms of all of us and because of our political system.

In Canada, peace, order, and good government are considered very important. Canadians are known to be polite, obedient, non-violent, helpful, and pleasant. They usually vote,

Political protesters also have a place in our democracy. They present opinions that are different from the government's and try to persuade it to make changes in laws. At election time, all citizens help to choose the people who will form their government.

help their neighbours, and pay their taxes. Canadians take part in electing members of local, provincial, and federal levels of government. Democracy begins in the community, and extends to city, provincial, and federal legislative chambers. In our **parliamentary system**, the leader of the political party winning the most seats in the legislature becomes Prime Minister or Premier. Our system of government is part of our British heritage.

Canadians have given their governments the power to provide many services that we use each day: parks, arenas, fire departments, hospitals, police departments, mail service, and even the school where you might be reading this.

THE TORONTO STAR, Tuesday, October 13, 1998

Colombia's kids urge end to civil war

In some countries, peace is only a dream. As the civil war in their country continued, Colombian students aged 5 to 15 worked to convince government and other leaders to end the war that has raged for more than 30 years. The children have tried to involve citizens in actively working for peace.

THE TORONTO STAR, Tuesday, October 13, 1998

French students strike, riot over too few teachers, books

In some countries, governments cannot always meet their basic responsibilities, including providing free education for students until the end of high school. Students in France demonstrated and went on strike to try to convince their government to improve their schools.

Canadian Craig Kielburger (left) has worked with people around the world to prevent child labour. He encourages young people to work to stamp out child abuse and poverty.

The Story So Far . . .

1 Find out the rules for voting in municipal, provincial, and federal elections today. Who is eligible to vote? When did suffrage become universal in Canada?

2 Find your school's list of student rights and privileges. Do any surprise you? Explain why.

The Evidence Behind the Story

As you work your way through the rest of the text, you will read stories, examine photographs, look at maps, and use many other tools to learn. You will be asked to complete various research tasks. What does this mean? Research is the process of asking and answering a question, working in a systematic way. When we say *research*, we mean a thorough, organized way of using many resources to answer a question. We used research methods when we tried to answer the question "What's special about Canada?" You, too, will need to use research methods to complete some of the activities in this book.

With the research process, you will first have a research question — maybe one that can be answered after less than an hour's work. An example is "What is the current population of your community?" Maybe your question is one that you will work on for many hours. An example is "What is the history of your community?" No matter what the research question may be, you can follow the research process in order to answer it appropriately.

STEPS IN THE RESEARCH PROCESS

1 Tuning in

You identify and define the issue or question. Ask:

- Why should I investigate this?
- What do I want to find out?
- What is the issue, if any?
- What do I already know?

2 Deciding directions

You identify a focus and refine your questions. Ask:

- What will I focus on?
- What questions do I need to ask?
- How can I explain. . .?

3 Organizing your work plan

You set up a plan for answering your questions. Ask:

- How will I proceed?
- Will I work in a group?
- What sort of information will we need? Where will we find it?
- Who will complete which tasks in our group?
- When will our work need to be complete?

4 Finding out

You collect information from many sources to help answer your questions.
Ask:

- Where is the information I need?
- How useful is this information?
- How else might I find answers?

5 **Sorting**

You organize the information, discarding what you do not need. Ask:

- **How can I categorize this information?**
- **What similarities and differences can I see?**
- **What connections can I see?**
- **What conclusions can I draw?**

6 **Drawing conclusions and communicating findings**

You express your understandings and communicate them with others. Ask:

- **What have I learned?**
- **Who is the audience for my communication?**
- **What is the best way to share my learning?**
- **What connections can I establish?**
- **What explanations can I offer?**

7 **Reflecting and evaluating**

You reflect on and make judgements about your work and your learning. Ask:

- **What have I learned about the topic?**
- **What have I learned about my skills and work habits?**
- **What skills and work habits do I need to improve?**
- **What do I feel about what I learned and the way I learned it?**

Throughout the research process, you will be dealing with information that you must collect, sort, and use to draw conclusions and show learning. How will you know that the information you have found is accurate? How will you know which of your information sources you can trust? If you rely on a personal history, auto-biography, or diary, how will you know what the author has left out? That is easy: you will be using many other resources, including other textbooks, encyclopedias, government documents, and web sites, so that your story will be more complete. You will be able to fill in gaps, compare opinions, and verify facts. You will never rely entirely on one source, even if it seems to provide a good answer to your question.

As you travel through the pages of this book, you will be given information to help you make decisions about the resources you are using. There will also be infor-mation to help you make the best use of resources that may be one-sided or incomplete. Look for research help in features called *The Evidence Behind the Story* throughout the text.

TIME LINES TO KEEP TRACK

As you look ahead in *Canada: The Story of Our Heritage*, you will have opportunities to use a time line to help you keep track of events. In each chapter, there will be a time line to organize information. These time lines may also be helpful as study guides. Emily's personal time line, shown here, shows the time line format you will see in the chapters in this text. Her time line begins in 1985 and ends with the start of the new millennium. You know that it will go on from there.

Make a time line for yourself, including important events in your own life. You may decide to show your time line on a vertical axis, rather than a horizontal one. Do you find it easier to read? Find some parallels between your own time line and Emily's. Why do you suppose there are no entries for Emily in 1990, 1991, and 1992? How old was she in those years?

1985	1986	1987	1988	1989		1993	1994	1995	1996	1997	1998	1999
Born at Kingston General Hospital	• Learned to walk • Tried to swim by myself	• New puppy	• Nursery school	• Junior kindergarten		• Art classes • Ski trip	• Guide camp at Picton	• Family trip to P.E.I. • Role of major munchkin in Wizard of Oz at school	• Sing with choir at Heritage Fair	• Volleyball champs • Trip to SkyDome	• New teacher	• Grade 8 Graduation Party

SUM IT UP!

At the beginning of this chapter, we took a brief look at some ways in which our country is unique. How did Canada get this way? To answer that question, we need to look at our history. We need to learn about the people, places, and events that have shaped our country, so we can understand how Canada has developed. We will look at the stories of the people who have built our communities, the changing work of our political leaders, the contributions of individuals and groups. We will use the results of other people's research and conduct research into our own questions. We will use many resources and tools as we work to discover the stories of Canada and Canadians.

THINKING ABOUT YOUR LEARNING

1. List three personal benefits of living in Canada. Here is an example:

   Recently, when I travelled to Colombia, South America, and went to a shopping mall, I had to stay inside a high wall with a gate and dozens of armed guards. I had to pass through a guarded checkpoint and sign out when leaving. In Canada, I can travel freely in and out of any mall and will never see an armed guard. I much prefer to shop in Canada. I like the idea of living in a country where "peace, order, and good government" are important.

2. a) Write a letter to the person in your family who was the first to live in Canada, describing what you like about Canada.

   b) If you are an Aboriginal student, you may want to write a letter to an ancestor who lived long ago in what is now Canada. You will have to do some family research to find the name of that person. You will likely have to ask older family members for information. If you cannot complete this activity with family members, use another family, such as your teacher's, a neighbour's, or a friend's. You could even write your letter to someone from Canadian history, such as Samuel de Champlain, Sir John A. Macdonald, or Laura Secord.

3. Make your own *My Canada Includes* collage of photographs, words, sketches, cartoons, and poetry.

   a) Show things that *you* think make Canada a special place.

   b) Include things *you* do not like about Canada.

4. Work together with your classmates to construct a large mural showing what *My Canada Includes* for members of your class.

5. Design a souvenir of Canada: a T-shirt, mug, place mat, or other souvenir. Explain your design.

APPLYING YOUR LEARNING

1. Using the research guidelines as a guide, begin a family research project. Use your own or another family, and try to find as much information as you can about them. Then produce a project to communicate your findings. Be sure to include information you have gathered through a personal interview.

2. Take some photographs and make a *photo essay* about your community, province, or Canada.

3. Collect the stories of the students in your class photograph. Find out about their family heritage and create a class family heritage album.

4. On July 1, 1998, *Maclean's* magazine published ten *Top 10* lists of Canadians. Create your own *Top 10* lists. Decide on categories, provide a rationale for that category and for selections, create your lists, and include descriptive information. You might want to make *Top 10* lists of Canadian animals, places, books, music, art, food, wildflowers, birds, national parks, dancers, hockey players, actors, or whatever. Or you could make a Wall of Fame, a Walk of Fame, or a Hall of Fame that shows examples of your *Top 10* and explains your choices. Do not forget to ensure that all entries on your lists are Canadian.

5. Collect newspaper or magazine articles (paper or electronic) showing examples of aspects of Canadian life that need improvement (poverty, crime, injustice, racism, pollution). What actions might you or your class initiate in order to improve the situation described in one of the articles?

USING KEY WORDS

Match the words on the left to their definitions on the right.

1 culture

2 personal interview

3 interviewer

4 interviewee

5 autobiography

6 government documents

7 biography

8 archives

9 parliamentary system

10 archives

11 race

12 heritage

a the person being interviewed

b a story about yourself, written by you

c a place where public documents and historical records are kept

d a story written about someone's life

e the person who asks the questions

f the way Canadian laws are made

g a prearranged meeting in which personal questions are asked of the person present

h legal papers provided by the government

i human beliefs, arts, customs, and institutions typical of a particular people, community, or nation

j a place where public records or historical documents are preserved

k something handed on to a person by his or her ancestors

l groups of humans sharing the same biological traits

National Gallery of Canada, Ottawa
The Habitant Farm (detail) by Krieghoff, C.

1608   1663   1759

Early Settlement and New France

1763

THE BIG PICTURE

These are some of the stories you will read about in this unit:

- the early European settlement patterns in North America
- the interactions between the French and the Aboriginal Peoples
- the reasons people came to live in New France and what life was like there
- the rivalries between the French and the British
- the Seven Years' War in North America
- the Battle of the Plains of Abraham
- the Expulsion of the Acadians
- the impact of the Treaty of Paris and the Quebec Act on the British and the French

First Settlements

1534

Cartier lands at Gaspé Bay and claims it for France

1535

Cartier sails up the St. Lawrence to Stadacona (Québec City) and Hochelaga

1541

Cartier explores the Saguenay

1604

Champlain and De Monts settle at the mouth of the Saint-Croix River (New Brunswick) over winter

1608

Champlain and De Monts land at Cap-Diamant, Québec, and build the habitation

SETTING OUR FOCUS

The Aboriginal Peoples taught the French many lessons about survival. Perhaps one of the most important was a remedy for the deadly disease of scurvy. The Huron crushed the bark and needles from the white cedar tree and boiled them in water. They drank this mixture as a cure. Many of Cartier's men had already died from the disease but many more were saved by drinking this "tea."

In the picture on the left, what people do you see? What do they appear to be doing? Why might they be doing that? What do you think the picture reveals about the conditions in early New France? What does it reveal about the relationship between the French and the Aboriginal Peoples?

PREVIEWING THE CHAPTER

In this chapter you will learn about these topics:
- **the reasons that led to the European exploration and settlement of New France**
- **the struggles endured by European explorers**
- **the rivalry between Britain and France over expanding their empires in North America**
- **the legacy of New France and its contribution to Canada's history**

KEY WORDS

castor gras
Confederacy
coureur de bois
entrepreneur
habitation
metissage
monopoly
mutiny
rivalry
voyageur

1609	1627	1670	1776	1821
Champlain, the Algonquin, and the Montagnais defeat the Iroquois in battle	Company of One Hundred Associates formed	Hudson Bay Company set up by Royal Charter	North West Company established as Hudson Bay Company rival	Hudson Bay Company and North West Company merge

THE AGE OF EXPLORATION

Around 1298, Marco Polo raised Europe's interest in the gold, silk, and spices of China, India, and Persia by publishing a book of his travels to the Far East. The merchants of Venice, Italy, controlled the European supply of Chinese silks and spices. Partially to break that **monopoly**, or control by one group, countries like Spain and Portugal began to seek new routes to the Far East. Land routes were too difficult, so they began to look for a water route from Europe to China and India.

European nations began an imperial competition. Initially, Portugal, Spain, France, Italy, and England took the lead. Each new voyage of discovery was able to improve on earlier ones. At first the European explorers considered their voyages unsuccessful, since they were unable to find the passage to the Far East. However, as time passed, they realized what material and strategic advantages the "new" continent of North America had to offer. They began to concentrate their efforts on claiming greater areas of land for the sovereign under whom they sailed.

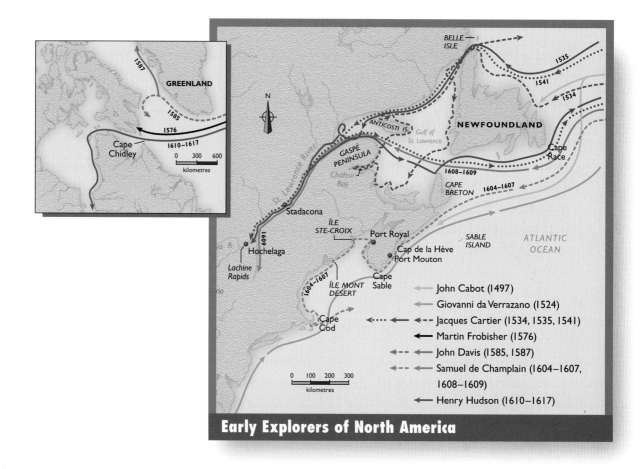

Early Explorers of North America

The following chart summarizes the major European explorations of what would become Canada.

Early Explorers of North America				
Explorer	**Explored For**	**Year**	**Explored/Settled**	**Fate**
John Cabot	England	1497	• Cape Bauld, Newfoundland	Disappeared in 1498 on second voyage
Giovanni da Verrazano	France	1524	• First to explore North American Coast from Florida to Nova Scotia	Died in battle with West Indies Aboriginal Peoples in 1528
Jacques Cartier	France	1534 1535 1541	• Gulf of St. Lawrence • Québec and Montréal • Québec City	Died of natural causes in 1557 at his manor in Limoilu, France
Martin Frobisher	England	1576	• Searched for a Northwest Passage and found Frobisher Bay on Baffin Island	Killed in battle against the Spanish Armada off the French coast, 1594
Henry Hudson	England	1610	• Made four attempts to find a Northwest Passage • Explored Hudson Bay	Cast adrift in Hudson Bay when his crew mutinied in 1610
John Davis	England	1587	• Charted Greenland, Baffin Island, and the Labrador Coast	Shot and killed by Japanese pirates in 1605
Samuel de Champlain	France	1604 1608	• Port-Royal, Bay of Fundy • Québec City	Died of natural causes on December 25, 1635, in Québec

1 Classify the above information by country. Where was each country's area of concentration and focus? Suggest reasons for this.

2 Create a time line for the above information.

Giovanni da Verrazano

France entered the European competition to claim parts of the "new world" in 1524 when a well-travelled Italian explorer, Giovanni da Verrazano, sailing under the French flag, proved that the east coast of North America was not a series of islands. Journeying from what is now Florida to Nova Scotia, he determined that North America was a large, connected land mass. Initially, he named the land *Francesca* in honour of the French King, Francis I. However, when Da Verrazano's brother later drew a map of the area, he renamed the area *Nova Gallia*, which means New France. So New France was born, and it would be known by that name for the next 250 years.

Jacques Cartier

Cartier's First Voyage

In 1534 King Francis I commissioned Jacques Cartier, an experienced French navigator, to explore the Newfoundland coast and the waters to its immediate west. The aim, still, was to find a route to the gold and spices of the Far East. Cartier sailed from St. Malo, France, on April 20, 1534, with two ships and a crew of 20 — several of whom were pardoned lawbreakers. Cartier first sighted what is now Labrador and, in awe of its barren and rough appearance, he called it *the land that God gave to Cain.* He then sailed southward, following the west coast of Newfoundland, and on to the south shore of the Gulf of St. Lawrence. Arriving there at the height of summer, he called the bay through which he sailed *Des Chaleurs,* which means *of warmth* or *of heat.* From Chaleur Bay, Cartier sailed on to Gaspé. There he raised a 9-m cross and claimed the land for his King, Francis I. An important point in history had been reached. By going beyond the ancient Maritime route of the Vikings and the casual commerce of the European fisheries off the Grand Banks of Newfoundland, Jacques Cartier founded New France and the great imperial **rivalry**, or competition, that would overtake North America.

This painting shows Jacques Cartier and his crew raising a cross at Gaspé in 1534. Why did they do that?

An excerpt from Cartier's diary describes the scene:

The chief, dressed in an old black bear-skin, arrived in a canoe with three of his sons and his brother. . . . Pointing to the cross he made us a long harangue, making the sign of the cross with two of his fingers; and then he pointed to the land all around about, as he wished to say that all this region belonged to him, and that we ought not to have set up this cross without his permission.

Cartier found no gold and spices, nor a passage to the Far East. But he wrote that the land he discovered was "as fine as it is possible to see, being fertile and covered with magnificent trees." At Gaspé, he met a group of Iroquois and their Chief, Donnacona. Despite the language barrier, it was not long before the Iroquois began to trade with the French. In exchange for furs, the Iroquois received kettles, coloured beads, tobacco, fish hooks, and other items from the French. Cartier took two of the Chief's sons, Domagaya and Taignoagny, back to France, promising to bring them back. They impressed the French with tales of the "Kingdom of Saguenay where lay infinite gold, rubies, and other riches." Francis I thought of the riches that had been acquired by the Spaniards in Mexico and Peru and dispatched a second voyage the following year on May 19, 1535.

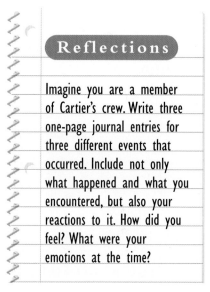

Reflections

Imagine you are a member of Cartier's crew. Write three one-page journal entries for three different events that occurred. Include not only what happened and what you encountered, but also your reactions to it. How did you feel? What were your emotions at the time?

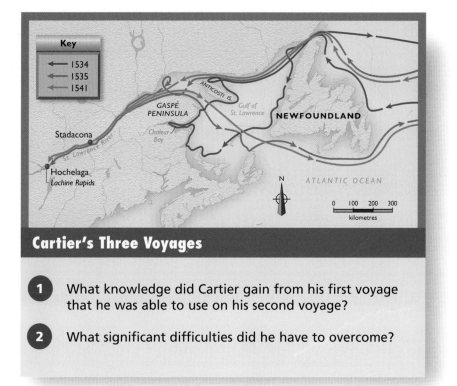

Cartier's Three Voyages

1. What knowledge did Cartier gain from his first voyage that he was able to use on his second voyage?

2. What significant difficulties did he have to overcome?

Donnacona
A TALE OF TREACHERY

Donnacona, Chief of the Iroquois at Stadacona, was fuming because Agona, upstart leader of a rival clan, was challenging his leadership. The village had been plunged into turmoil. To counter the threat, Donnacona hatched a plan. It was spring, the ice on the great river was breaking up, and the French were preparing to leave. Perhaps these treacherous newcomers might be of some use, after all. If he could persuade them to kidnap Agona and take him to France, a rival would be eliminated.

Donnacona was delighted when his messengers returned with the news that Jacques Cartier had agreed to join the plot. Cartier devised a simple plan. A few days before his ships were to sail, he would invite the Iroquois to help celebrate a religious festival. That is when Agona would be taken prisoner. What Donnacona did not know was that Cartier planned to turn the tables on him. It was Donnacona, not Agona, who would be kidnapped. Why? Cartier sensed Donnacona's distrust. The explorer hoped to return to this land and believed that Agona would be friendlier than Donnacona. Besides, he was sure that if the King heard about the fabled Saguenay from the Chief himself, the King would give Cartier money for another expedition.

As planned, Donnacona and the villagers gathered on May 3, 1536, for the celebration. The Chief was not sure the French would keep their word — a suspicion that was well-founded. When Donnacona's party entered the fort, Cartier shouted an order.

The French seized the Chief, his two sons, three other men, and four children. That night, angry villagers milled around outside the fort, loudly demanding the release of their Chief. Inside, a nervous Cartier was doing some fast talking. If Donnacona agreed to tell his story in France, he said, the King would reward him handsomely. He also promised to return the captives the next year. In the end, Donnacona agreed to go peacefully and announced his decision to his people.

On May 6, 1536, the French ships weighed anchor and headed down river toward the Atlantic Ocean. As Stadacona faded from view, Donnacona and the other Iroquois caught their last glimpse of home. None would ever return. All would die in France.

Cartier did not return for five years. When he did, Agona was Chief at Stadacona. Cartier admitted that Donnacona had died, but said that the others were living luxuriously in France. At first, the lie worked. Gradually, though, the Iroquois' belief turned to disbelief and suspicion. The seeds of hatred between the Iroquois and the French had been sown.

More people you could research are

Jacques Cartier

Giovanni da Verrazano

Jean-François de la Rocque
   de Roberval

Domagaya

Donnacona

Taignoagny

Cartier's Second Voyage

This time Cartier had three ships and 110 men, along with Chief Donnacona's sons. On this voyage, he sailed up the St. Lawrence River and cautiously reached the Aboriginal village of Stadacona (Québec City) on September 7, 1535, after criss-crossing from shore to shore. From there, he set out on the smaller of his two ships and in 13 days reached the Aboriginal village of Hochelaga, which had a population of about a thousand. Cartier climbed the hill overlooking the encampment and named the elevation Mount Royal. Even though it was turning cold, he ventured farther west. With the aid of his Aboriginal guides, he was able to travel as far as the rapids at Lachine. He then headed east and wintered at Stadacona.

Cartier and his crew were not prepared for the Canadian winter. The St. Lawrence River froze and snowdrifts were shoulder high. Their hastily constructed fort offered little comfort or warmth. Their diet lacked fresh fruits and vegetables, resulting in many of Cartier's men dying of scurvy. When spring came and the ice broke, Cartier prepared to return to France.

Cartier's second voyage turned out to be more important than the first because he located the St. Lawrence River, the great interior waterway. Travelling up the river, he passed many other rivers that later explorers would use as water "highways." His crew were the first Europeans to survive a northern winter in what was to become Canada. On his return voyage, Cartier came upon the strait that separates Newfoundland from Cape Breton. Thus, map makers were able to conclude that Newfoundland was an island.

Aboriginal map makers used Aboriginal place names which Cartier took back to France. The name *Kanata*, meaning *village* or *meeting place*, began to appear on European maps to identify the lands explored by Cartier. *Kebec*, meaning *a place where the river narrows*, also came from the Aboriginal Peoples' language. Place names, information about the land, and a cure for scurvy were not the only Aboriginal things that Cartier took back to France, however. Cartier kidnapped several Iroquois, including Donnacona himself.

Snippet

Scurvy

Scurvy is a disease caused by a lack of vitamin C in a person's diet. Vitamin C is important for maintaining healthy connective tissues (which support body structures), bones, and teeth. The symptoms of this disease include weakness, gums that bleed easily, loosening teeth, and bleeding scars and nose. In severe cases, scurvy causes death.

Snippet

Aboriginal Map Makers

Europeans were not the only map makers. Map making was also an important skill for Aboriginal Peoples. Because their maps were often drawn in the dirt or snow, they had to be memorized. Children were trained to do this from an early age. Their survival might have depended on it.

Cartier's Third Voyage

In France in October 1540, King Francis I gave Cartier a commission for a third voyage to "Canada and Hochelaga, and as far as the Saguenay." However, on January 14, 1541, he changed the commission and appointed Jean-François de la Rocque de Roberval as Lieutenant-General in the country of Canada. The King commissioned him to establish a permanent colony in New France and to spread the Roman Catholic faith. Cartier was to serve as Roberval's guide. But Cartier set out in May 1541, a year ahead of Roberval. He arrived at Stadacona, where he and his crew endured another harsh winter. The Iroquois increasingly distrusted Cartier and his men and were far less helpful than in the past.

Abandoning the settlement that he had named Cap-Rouge, the following year Cartier and his crew explored part of the *Kingdom of the Saguenay*. They thought they had struck it rich! They found large quantities of what they believed were gold and diamonds. They journeyed to Newfoundland where they met Roberval and his ships arriving from France. Roberval ordered Cartier to winter at Cap-Rouge. However, under cloak of darkness, Cartier slipped away and sailed back to France, depriving Roberval of experienced crew.

In France the "diamonds" proved to be nothing more than quartz, and the "gold" to be only pyrite or *fool's gold*. Cartier's disappointment was huge. Roberval's attempt to establish the permanent colony ordered by the King was defeated by the cold, famine, and sickness that had earlier overwhelmed Cartier, as well as by his own poor administrative skills. Fifty years would pass before France renewed its interest in Canada.

Despite the failures and disappointments that marked Cartier's experiences, he established an important step in the formation of New France. He was the first European to survey the coasts of the Gulf of St. Lawrence and to explore the St. Lawrence River. He established that Newfoundland was an island. He inspired in the French a greater interest in New France. Finally, he was the first to attempt to establish a permanent colony. Although it failed, it paved the way for future developments.

This map, drawn by Nicholas Vallard in 1546, shows the arrival of the colonists brought by Cartier and the Sieur de Roberval to Canada in 1541 and 1542. Note the presence of women among the French party, the fur-clad Iroquois, and the bears and deer in the forest.

The Granger Collection, New York

Snippet

Famous Sayings

Cartier's embarrassing mistake about his "treasure" lived on in some colourful expressions. When the French wanted to emphasize that something had no value, they would say that it was "as false as Canadian diamonds" or "as worthless as Canadian gold."

1 Write a one-page script and role-play the following:
- the initial meeting between Cartier and Donnacona
- the meeting between Cartier and Francis I after Cartier's first voyage
- the meeting between Cartier and Roberval as Roberval is arriving at Newfoundland and Cartier is leaving
- a group of Huron explaining the cure for scurvy to Cartier's crew

2 Most of Cartier's crew were pardoned lawbreakers. Suggest reasons that was the case. Would this kind of crew have made Cartier's job easier or more difficult? Give reasons for your answer.

3 Trade took place between the French and the Iroquois. What did each side trade? Do you think the trading was fair?

4 One of the major sources of conflict between the Aboriginal Peoples and the Europeans was land ownership. As far as the Aboriginal Peoples were concerned, a person could no more "own" the land than they could "own" the air. The Europeans, on the other hand, were exploring this "new world" and "claiming" land for their respective monarchs. Role-play a discussion between the two sides when Cartier was raising the cross at Gaspé. (Refer to the illustration on page 32.) Which argument do you agree with? Why?

THE BIRTH OF NEW FRANCE

Champlain at Port-Royal

In 1603 Samuel de Champlain made the first of an incredible 23 voyages across the Atlantic Ocean. Travelling up the St. Lawrence and passing the area where Stadacona and Hochelaga had once stood, he reported that "You could hardly hope to find a more beautiful country."

In France, King Henry IV did not want to spend large sums of money on the risky prospects of settlement. Instead he decided that he would grant exclusive rights to trade in furs to individuals. In return, those people would agree to bring over a specified number of colonists per year. Pierre du Gua de Monts was one of the very first to receive such a monopoly. So, in 1604 De Monts set sail, with Champlain as his map maker. They

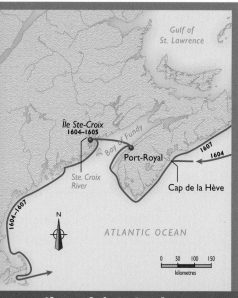

1. From viewing the map, what advantages of the location of Port-Royal do you see?

2. Identify all the bodies of water important to Port-Royal.

chose a small island at the mouth of the Saint-Croix River on the Bay of Fundy as the site for their settlement (in what is now New Brunswick).

Well over a third of these original 100 settlers died during the first winter of 1604 from cold or scurvy. What looked like an inviting location in summer became unbearably harsh in the winter, as the winds and snows ravaged the unprotected island. Unfortunately, in their haste to build shelters, the settlers chopped down most of the nearby trees, forcing them to travel great distances for firewood.

The following excerpt from Champlain's diary comments on his new-found knowledge of Canada:

> *It is impossible to know this country without having wintered here for in arriving in autumn everything is very pleasant owing to the woods, the fine landscape, and the good fishing for cod and other species which are found. But winter in this country lasts for six months.*

Champlain drew this picture of Port-Royal in 1606, to help in the building of the first settlement in Canada.

De Monts was not one to give up easily. Despite the initial disaster, he decided to move the settlement across the Bay of Fundy to the more favourable site at Port-Royal (in what is now Nova Scotia). Acadia was born.

De Monts and his crew learned their lesson from the past. They located close to an abundant forest, built a large weatherproof building, and planted wheat and vegetable gardens. To keep the settlers' spirits up, Champlain created the *Order of Good Cheer.*

Samuel de Champlain
WAGING A WAR OF WORDS

Samuel de Champlain took an instant dislike to the sophisticated Paris lawyer who stepped off the supply ship in the summer of 1606. The feeling seemed to be mutual. Marc Lescarbot did not like Champlain any more than Champlain liked him. At first glance, the animosity between the two was surprising. They were about the same age and shared many interests. Both were already published writers, for example, and both were keeping diaries of their stay at Port-Royal. Rather than uniting them, though, their interest in writing drove a wedge between them. Their temperaments were also different. Champlain was a self-educated, rough-and-ready man of action who had already spent years in New France. To him, the elegant Parisian who had been educated at the best schools must have seemed like a dabbler and an upstart. Furthermore, as Pierre du Gua de Monts' lawyer, Lescarbot had access to the commander of Port-Royal in a way that Champlain did not.

That fall an expedition sailed from the settlement to explore what is now the Northeastern Seaboard of the United States. Champlain was with the group, but Lescarbot stayed behind. When the adventurers returned, they discovered that Lescarbot had a wonderful surprise waiting. He had created an elaborate theatrical presentation called *Le Théâtre de Neptune.* Staged outdoors, it concluded with trumpet calls, cannon-fire, and a great feast. It was only after Lescarbot presented his play, which was the first European drama staged in North America, that Champlain introduced The Order of Good Cheer. Was it one-upmanship that motivated Champlain's idea for keeping the settlers amused?

When Port-Royal was abandoned in 1607, both Champlain and Lescarbot returned to France. Within a year, Champlain was back in New France. This gave Lescarbot an advantage in the race to publish an account of their Acadian adventure. When his book, titled *Histoire de la Nouvelle-France,* appeared in 1609, it chided Champlain for overlooking Jacques Cartier's explorations and claiming the discovery of the St. Lawrence River for himself. Champlain took some revenge with his own book, *Les Voyages,* which was published in 1613. It barely mentioned Lescarbot or *Le Théâtre de Neptune.* Lescarbot retaliated by revising his book and deleting all flattering references to Champlain. He also poked fun at Champlain for believing in *Gougou,* the feared forest monster of the Mi'kmaq. The rivalry that had begun at Port-Royal became a war of words that lasted for years.

More people you could research are

The Algonquin

Samuel de Champlain

Pierre du Gua de Monts

The Iroquois

Marc Lescarbot

The Montagnais

The Order of Good Cheer

Champlain was as much concerned about his settlers' mental health as he was about their physical well-being. The winters were long, cold, and severe. Physical survival was tough enough, but Champlain reasoned rightly that his people's spirits needed attention as well. To address this, he created the Order of Good Cheer. It was simply an organized way of promoting fun.

Every two weeks a different person acted as host or Grand Master. The person had to plan and cook a great feast. The Grand Master wore a gold chain and led a grand procession of people carrying platters of food into the dining hall. Several days were spent planning, hunting for, and cooking the feast, since the competitive spirit encouraged members of the Order to try to outdo one another. The platters were laden with different delicacies: duck, goose, rabbit, moose, bear, fish, and — the great delight — beaver tail. The tables were covered with fresh-baked breads, drinks, and desserts. The feast was rounded out with music, singing, and plays. Few died that first winter of the Order of Good Cheer. Clearly, Champlain knew one of the secrets to good health!

Mathieu de Coste

One of the members of the Order of Good Cheer was Mathieu de Coste, a slave of African descent. His services were highly prized because he spoke the Mi'kmaq language, a skill he had acquired on an earlier journey to the area with his Portuguese owner. When De Coste fell ill and died during that winter of 1606–1607, the expedition lost its interpreter.

Unfortunately, just as Port-Royal was becoming comfortable, it was closed. Because other merchants wanted access to the fur trade, De Monts lost his monopoly in May 1607. As a result, Port-Royal was abandoned and the settlers returned to France. The colony was re-established three years later, however. It became a farming community and formed the basis of the bilingual Acadian community that still exists in the Maritime provinces today.

The Habitation at Québec

By this time Champlain was an experienced soldier, geographer, and explorer. These attributes enabled him to influence De Monts to return to the St. Lawrence area. Champlain received his first official function in his Canadian career, as lieutenant to the Sieur de Monts. In 1608 he landed at the foot of Cap-Diamant, the great rock that dominates Québec City, and established the **habitation** — a settlement outfitted with a house, warehouse, fort, and trading post. The site was named *Québec*. The location had many good features. It had an excellent harbour and a high cliff behind it for additional defence. Champlain wrote:

I employed a part of our workmen cutting down the trees to make a site for our settlement, another part in sawing planks, and another in digging the cellar and making ditches. . . . The first thing we made was the store-house, to put our supplies under cover. . . . After the store-house was finished I continued the construction of our quarters, which contained three main buildings of two stories. . . .

Québec did not start out well. The men complained bitterly about the back-breaking labour, the heat of the summer, and the mosquitoes. There was talk of a **mutiny**, or an open rebellion against an authority figure. As soon as Champlain got wind of it, he took quick action. Trials were held. One ringleader was condemned to be hanged and the others were sent back to France.

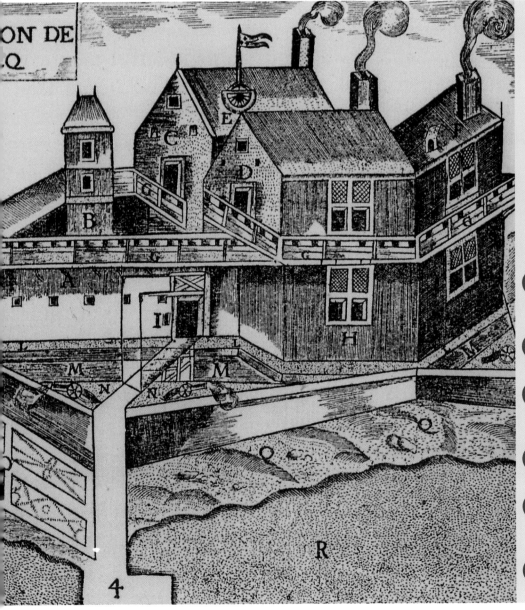

Champlain's sketch of the habitation, 1608
Key: A) Warehouse and storerooms **B)** Pigeon house **C)** Building for weapons and for workers to live **D)** More workers' lodgings **E)** Sundial **F)** Forge and workers' lodgings **G)** Galleries all the way around **H)** Lodging for Champlain **I)** Gate with drawbridge **M)** Moat all the way around **N)** Platforms for the cannon **O)** Gardens

1 What direction do you think the building is facing? Why?

2 What is the purpose of the moat?

3 Why does the location of the building for weapons make sense?

4 What was the purpose of the sundial?

5 What was the pigeon house and what was its purpose?

6 What was the purpose of the galleries?

First Settlements **41**

No sooner had that crisis been resolved than winter struck. Twenty of 28 men died that first winter from cold and scurvy. Champlain learned an important lesson. If the colony were to survive, it needed more support from France. There had to be a steady supply of food, building materials, and, most notably, settlers.

The Iroquois who had previously inhabited this area had disappeared. What happened to them? In the 50 years that passed between the French expeditions made by Cartier and Champlain to North America, historians believe the Iroquois were driven south of the Great Lakes by other Aboriginal groups, such as the Montagnais and the Algonquin. These tribes were enemies of the Iroquois. So when Champlain made friends with the Montagnais and the Huron, the Iroquois' hostility toward the French probably increased.

Champlain played a critical role in determining alliances with the Aboriginal Peoples. He was anxious to befriend the Huron because they could teach the new settlers many important skills. Canoeing, snowshoeing, trapping beaver, and dealing with the elements were all vital to French survival. Champlain also wanted the support of the Huron for another important reason: to expand the fur trade. A significant moment in French-Aboriginal relations came in 1609 when the Algonquin and Montagnais, both allies of the Huron **Confederacy**, asked Champlain to join them in an attack against their enemy, the Iroquois. A Confederacy is when tribes join together under one political structure. Champlain agreed to the Huron request.

The Battle of 1609, near what is now called Lake Champlain, determined the pattern of future alliances between Europeans and Aboriginal Peoples. How do you think the Aboriginal Peoples responded to the French use of the *arquebus*?

The two sides met on what is now called Lake Champlain. The Iroquois had quickly landed and hastily built some temporary forts. The Algonquin and Montagnais, along with Champlain and two other French men, went ashore. The three French men were armed with a type of gun called an *arquebus*. Champlain fired his weapon and killed two Iroquois Chiefs. His two accomplices, hiding in the nearby woods, fired at the Iroquois. Champlain suffered a non-fatal wound when he was hit in the neck by an arrow. That day the Iroquois were defeated. The lines of alliance had been firmly established as the Iroquois turned south and sided with the British.

Champlain made many trips back to France to lobby on behalf of the new colony. However, because both the King and the merchants believed that settlers would diminish the fur trade, only a handful of colonists arrived in New France. In fact, by 1627, almost two decades after its founding, there were only 65 settlers.

Champlain was a remarkable individual and rightly deserves the title *Father of New France*. He wrote six books. He was an accomplished map maker and explorer and an able administrator. He spent the final 27 years of his life devoted to the colony he had founded at Québec. He marked a decisive change in the history of New France with his insistence on settlement and colonization. To a large extent, Champlain created a permanent colony out of a tentative, short-term contact. As historians put it, without Champlain, "there would not have been a New France."

Web Connection

http://www.school.mcgrawhill.ca/resources

Go to the web site above to find out more about Canada's early explorers. Go to History Resources, then to *Canada: The Story of Our Heritage* to see where to go next.

The Story So Far . . .

1 What did Champlain learn from the experience at Port-Royal?

2 Conduct a debate on one of the following resolutions:
   - Champlain deserves the title *Father of New France*.
   - Champlain caused more harm than good.
   - Without Champlain, "there would not have been a New France."

3 In your opinion, what was Champlain's single greatest accomplishment? Provide evidence to support your choice.

THE FUR TRADE EXPANDS

Fur-Trading Monopolies

Following the cancellation of Pierre du Gua de Monts' monopoly in 1608, the fur trade was in an unsettled state. Then, in 1613, merchants from Rouen and Saint Malo in France formed the Canada Company, which existed for the next 12 years. Wanting a more formal system, Cardinal Richelieu, the King's First Minister, organized the Company of One Hundred Associates in 1627. Its purpose was to settle, administer, and develop New France. In return for an exclusive monopoly over the fur trade from Florida to the Arctic Circle, the company was to bring more than 4000 settlers to New France over a 15-year period and provide them with employment, accommodation, and other necessities. They also had to provide three priests for every settlement.

Since colonization cost time, money, and effort, and infringed on fur-trading territory, the company did not pursue it with much commitment. About 20 years later, the Company of One Hundred Associates transferred its monopoly to the Company of Habitants, a group of about a dozen merchants who also had no interest in colonization.

Snapshot

Beaver Fur Becomes European Fashion

The fashion salons of Paris strongly affected the fur trade in New France. They demanded specialty furs, such as ermine, mink, and fox, as trim for wealthy people's garments. However, coinciding with the onset of European exploration, a great demand for beaver fur developed. Fashion dictated that men wear beaver hats. The fashion-conscious were very fussy; not just any beaver pelt would do. The best beaver pelts were those that had been fashioned into clothing by Aboriginal Peoples. And it was only after they had been worn for some time that these pelts, called *castor gras*, or greasy beaver, became really valuable. As the coarse, outer hairs wore away, the oil mixed with human sweat to produce a very soft fur that was especially prized for hat making.

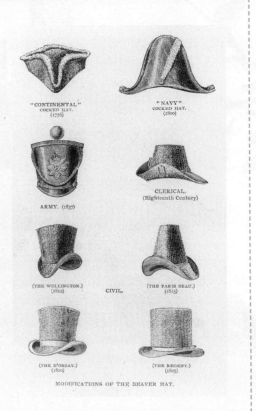

MODIFICATIONS OF THE BEAVER HAT.

In the early days of New France, Samuel de Champlain wisely created a pact with the Huron so that they became the go-betweens for the French. Initially, each spring, Huron traders travelled the waterways in their birchbark canoes filled with furs, arriving at Québec, Trois-Rivières, and, later, Ville Marie (Montréal). It was not unusual for more than 10 000 beaver pelts to be brought down the Ottawa River. In fact, the numbers were staggering, as shown in the chart below, and point to the wealth generated by the fur trade.

Increase in the Beaver Fur Trade	
Date	Beaver Fur (in kilograms)
1675–1685	40 500
1687	63 000
1689	360 000

Traders, however, were almost becoming victims of their own success, since the French market could absorb only about 22 500 kg of fur annually. The tragedy was that year after year, unsold pelts were allowed to rot in stockrooms just to keep the price high.

Initially, one of Champlain's chief aims was to expand the fur trade. He dispatched young men such as Étienne Brûlé and Jean Nicollet to travel to the farthest villages to obtain the best furs. Braving the elements, they and other **coureurs de bois**, or unlicensed fur traders, set out in their birchbark canoes to expand the boundaries of the fur trade and solidify trade alliances. Travelling ever more westward, these self-employed fur traders played many roles: explorer, interpreter, friend, diplomat, businessperson, and soldier. Champlain himself was a dedicated and highly skilled explorer, embarking on a six-year period of discovery after The Battle of 1609 with the Iroquois. "The great love I have always had for making discoveries in New France made me more and more eager to travel this country so as to have a perfect knowledge of it," he wrote as an introduction to a book describing the year he spent living with the Huron.

Étienne Brûlé

FIRST COUREUR DE BOIS

By early June 1611, Samuel de Champlain was starting to worry. For more than two weeks, he had been camped with his men and a young Huron named Savignon near the Lachine Rapids. They were waiting for the Algonquin and Huron to return from *le pays en haut*, the northernmost areas of Canada, with 18-year-old Étienne Brûlé. Champlain was fond of this young man with a thirst for adventure.

At 16, Brûlé travelled to New France with the expedition of 1608 and had been one of the few to survive the first brutal winter at Québec. Fascinated by the Aboriginal Peoples he met, Brûlé had asked to go live with them. His plan made sense — if he learned the languages of the French allies, he could act as an interpreter. Champlain liked the idea.

To guarantee Brûlé's safety, Champlain had taken Savignon to spend the winter in France in a kind of exchange. A year later, it was time to return the two young men to their people. The French were at the appointed meeting place, but where were the Huron and Algonquin?

The next day the Huron and Algonquin were spotted paddling their canoes toward Champlain's camp. Among them was Brûlé, dressed in the style of the Huron. Relieved, the French launched their own boats to welcome them.

Savignon and Brûlé were the centre of attention. Each excitedly told of his adventures. Then Brûlé surprised everyone. He said he had enjoyed his stay so much that he had decided to return to the Huron country. The decision set the young man's life on a course that would include many firsts. Travelling with the Huron on regular trading expeditions to Québec, he became the first coureur de bois. Over the next 22 years, he was probably the first European to see the Great Lakes and to stand on the sites of the present-day cities of Ottawa and Toronto. Yet these accomplishments are overshadowed by a fateful act of disloyalty for which Brûlé would pay dearly.

Many years later, in 1629, he betrayed Champlain to the British traders who had arrived to seize Québec. After that, he was shunned by the French and even by his adopted people, who considered Champlain a great friend.

An even worse punishment was in store for Brûlé, however. In 1633, after the French had regained control of Québec, the Huron killed and ate their former friend. No one is sure just why they did this, but historians suspect that it was to avenge the betrayal of Champlain.

As for Champlain, he took his own revenge. In his journals, he barely mentioned Brûlé. As a result, the exploits of Canada's first coureur de bois were nearly erased from history.

More people you could research are

Étienne Brûlé

Pierre Duquet De La Chesnaye

Médard Chouart des Groseilliers

Frances Ann Hopkins

Jean Nicollet

Savignon

Take a good look at this scene of Samuel de Champlain meeting Étienne Brûlé. Brûlé has lived with the Huron for over 20 years, while Champlain has spent many months exploring the wilderness. Step into the picture. Imagine you are one of the Huron. How are you feeling — hot? Cold? Hungry? Nervous? Excited? How do you feel as these two "white men" greet each other? What are they saying? As the party breaks up, you follow the group.

Where are you going? What kind of celebration is planned back at the village to recognize this important meeting? Are you concerned about the effect these "white men" might have on your way of life? Why are you feeling that way?

Share your thoughts and feelings with a partner, assume the characters of two people in the illustration, and then present a dialogue between them to the rest of the class.

Coureurs de Bois

The lives of the coureurs de bois have been glorified and romanticized. These fur traders are usually portrayed as daring and independent individuals who ventured fearlessly into uncharted territory. There is some truth to the image, but the reality was somewhat different. Often they were men who wanted to escape from the boredom of the daily routine of family and farm. The call of the wild frontier was very enticing. They withstood the challenges of nature — harsh winters, uncleared forests, mosquitoes, and swamps — through their own self-reliance and the aid of the Huron. It was not uncommon for the coureurs de bois to live with the Huron for months at a time. They were fortunate that the Huron were so generous in teaching them important survival skills, such as trapping, snowshoeing, handling a canoe, and building temporary shelters.

As exciting as the lives of the coureurs de bois may have appeared on the surface, they were also filled with considerable danger, loneliness, and, sometimes, boredom. They had to contend with rivals, unfriendly Aboriginal Peoples, harsh climate, rough terrain, and great distances. Toward the end of the seventeenth century, almost a tenth of the entire French population of 9000 were coureurs de bois. Jacques Duchesneau

This painting, *Evening Camp*, by Frances Hopkins, shows what awaited the fur traders after hours of strenuous paddling. Their supper was usually dried meat. Their bed: the rocky ground. Their ceiling: the night sky. What do you think the coureurs de bois talked about around the campfire? What else might they have done around the campfire?

said in 1679, "There is at least one coureur de bois in every family." For the Church and the administrators, they posed a serious problem. They were a symbol of rebellion and lawlessness that did not fit the image the authorities had of the ideal settler. They left their wives and children behind and neglected their farms. They were blamed for corrupting morals and displaying the kind of free spirit that many people associated with lawlessness. The fur-trading companies also bristled at the activities of the coureurs de bois since they were unnecessary competition and were not as controllable as the companies would have liked.

To resolve the problem of the growing number of independent fur-traders, the government passed a law stating that fur traders had to hold a permit and that only a limited number of permits would be issued. Permit holders were classified as **voyageurs**. They did much the same thing as the coureurs de bois had done. Despite the government's attempt to regulate the fur trade, the coureurs de bois, although fewer in number, still continued to operate. In fact in 1716, the coureurs de bois were once again legalized and a second generation of them went out to ply their trade.

Fur-Trade Rivalry

In the 1620s, war between the Iroquois Five Nations and the Algonquin and Huron tribes made it difficult to transport furs on the Ottawa River. Increasingly, both sides, the British and the French, sent their traders along the northern canoe route via the Mattawa River to Lake Nipissing and the French River to Lake Huron.

The competition in the fur trade heated up considerably when the British became involved in 1670. By a Royal Charter of that year, the British Crown gave the Hudson's Bay Company an exclusive fur-trading monopoly in "all the lands that drained into Hudson Bay." The British merchants had been alerted to the wealth to be obtained in these more northern reaches by two coureurs de bois, Pierre Esprit Radisson and Médard Chouart des Groseilliers. In 1682 the British built York Factory and several other smaller posts. In response, the French attacked the British forts and were able to control the area's trade for over the next thirty years. Daniel Duluth's earlier construction of a French trading post on Lake Nipigon had been significant in attracting close to 2000 Cree, Ojibway, and Assiniboine fur traders to the French side.

Reflections

Create a storyboard, cartoon strip, written diary entry, or any other form you choose to depict *A Day in the Life of a Coureur de Bois*.

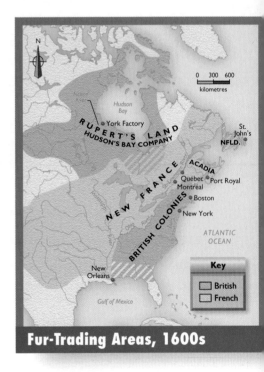

Fur-Trading Areas, 1600s

Denis Riverin, a New France settler, wrote the following description of coureurs de bois in 1705:

The coureur de bois are Frenchmen who were either born in Canada or who came to settle there. They are always young men in the prime of life, for old age cannot endure the hardships of this occupation.

Since all of Canada is a vast forest, it is impossible for them to travel by land. They travel by lake and river in canoes ordinarily occupied by three men. These are made of very light and thin cedar wood.

A canoe skillfully manned can cover 120 miles [193 km] in one day in still waters and still more in swift waters and rapids. When impassable cascades or waterfalls are encountered, the men put ashore, unload the bundles and transport them with the canoe on their backs and shoulders through the forest for a half mile [0.8 km] up to 16 miles [28 km]. . . . They go sometimes 3200 miles [5150 km] to search for beaver among the [Aboriginal People] whom they have frequently never seen. . . .

They carry as little as possible. . . . If they have nothing to eat on their return journey or on their travels from one tribe to another, they will resort to their moccasins or to a glue they make from the skins they have bartered. . . .

Baron Lahontan, a French nobleman living in New France, described the coureur de bois in the following way:

The traders called Coureur de Bois send out many canoes filled with goods to be traded to the [Aborginal Peoples] of this continent. They trade these goods for beaver skins. About a week ago, I saw 25 or 30 of these canoes return to Montreal. They were filled with heavy cargoes. Each canoe was paddled by two or three men and carried one ton [1.02 t] of beaver skins. This load is worth 4000 crowns. The canoes had been away for more than two years. You would be amazed to see how these men act when they come to the city. They feast and gamble and spend a lot of money on clothes. . . . They eat and drink, and play until they run out of money.

Colonist Jean-Baptise Patoulet had an even more negative view.

These men are tramps who never marry and settle down. They never work at clearing the land as good colonists should do. They commit many sins. . . . They go three to six thousand miles [4800–9600 km] from Quebec. . . . They are eager for riches but they have nothing to show for it. . . . They ruin the good image of France in the eyes of the [Aboriginal Peoples]. They get in the way of the missionaries. . . .

QUESTIONING THE EVIDENCE

1. In your own words, briefly summarize the three different views of the coureurs de bois presented here.
2. What might account for the different views of the coureurs de bois?
3. Which of these primary sources do you think is the most reliable? Why?
4. Do you think that the coureurs de bois were good or bad for New France? Why?
5. Can you think of other individuals like the coureurs de bois who have existed in other periods of history?

Because there were fortunes to be made from the fur trade, it produced a tremendous amount of competition. Individual coureurs de bois and voyageurs saw themselves as **entrepreneurs,** or individuals who organized and operated their own businesses, engaged in a fierce economic struggle. Initially they had to compete with one another to obtain the best and most furs. Then they clashed with one another in trying to obtain the best price for those furs.

The North West Company was established in 1776 by a number of rival trade groups who realized that continued competition against one another would be destructive. The North West Company was regarded as extremely efficient, effective, and ruthless. In taking on the Hudson Bay Company, the Nor'Westers would stop at nothing. They built more distant forts, utilized spies, and encouraged intermarriage with Aboriginal Peoples to enhance their business opportunities.

By the turn of the nineteenth century, with the outposts of the Nor'Westers reaching beyond the Athabasca River and into the Rockies, the Hudson Bay Company was feeling the pressure. In 1821 the two organizations put their differences aside. They realized that both would suffer if they continued to compete, so they joined.

York Factory, a busy Hudson Bay Company complex, as sketched by A. H. Murray in 1853.

The Fur Trade's Impact on New France

The fur trade had a critical impact on the development and growth of New France. The conflict between the Iroquois (British allies) and the Huron (French allies) was spread over a larger area. The fur trade provided a considerable source of wealth, and helped create what at one time was known as the *beaver aristocracy*. It led to the exploration and mapping of much of the interior of the continent.

As the fur trade moved westward, it had a dramatic impact on relations both with the Iroquois and Huron and with the land and wildlife. The fur trade led to substantial change in Aboriginal lifestyles. Traditionally, Aboriginal Peoples had a spiritual connection with the animals they hunted. They had a conservationist lifestyle. No part of an animal they killed was wasted. They regarded themselves as *keepers* and *preservers* of the land. These values eroded and were gradually replaced with a dependence on Europeans. Over-killing saw the near extinction of several animals: the beaver in the St. Lawrence area, the moose in Mi'kmaq territory, and the bison on the plains.

This painting, called *The Trapper's Bride*, provides evidence of the custom of *metissage*. How realistic do you think the portrayal is?

The government of New France encouraged *metissage*, or intermarriage between the coureurs de bois and Aboriginal women, although marrying outside the faith was not permitted by Roman Catholic doctrine. The government hoped this would increase the population of New France, build friendly relations with the Aboriginal Peoples, and ultimately absorb the Aboriginal culture.

Since the fur-trading companies controlled the fur trade, they slowed down the population growth within New France severely. Their concern was profit, not colonists. Since the government did not monitor whether or not the companies followed the terms of their monopoly, the fur-trading companies ignored the part of the agreement that dealt with increasing the population of New France.

The Story So Far . . .

1 Imagine that in a Québec courtroom during the late seventeenth century, a group of coureurs de bois is being tried for "discrediting the image of New France" and "hurting the present and future of the colony." Working in teams of two, write a strongly worded opening statement for the prosecution and one for the defence. If time permits, present the statements to the class.

2 Two major issues in the fur trade were the use of brandy in bartering with the Aboriginal Peoples and the custom of *metissage*. In both cases, after considerable debate, the authorities of New France decided to permit both practices. Suggest advantages they saw in allowing both brandy and *metissage* in the fur trade.

3 The exchange of Étienne Brûlé for Savignon offered an interesting situation. List the problems that each of them might have experienced.

4 Create a colourful and creative advertising poster for one of the two rival fur-trading companies.

SUM IT UP!

Explorers left the familiarity of Europe and ventured out across the Atlantic Ocean. Contact had been made with the Aboriginal Peoples of the "new" continent, and alliances and rivalries had been formed. An important economic staple — fur — had been found and developed. Finally, after slow beginnings, a permanent French settlement had been founded, one that would be the basis for future growth and expansion. Much had been achieved, yet much still had to be done.

THINKING ABOUT YOUR LEARNING

1. If the Aboriginal Peoples and the French were to develop a positive and productive relationship, what kinds of difficulties would they have to overcome? Which one of these difficulties do you think would have been the most difficult to master? Why?

2. Compile a list of the problems that Cartier's men would have encountered on their transatlantic voyage. Include six to eight problems. Which of these would you personally have found the most difficult to deal with? Why?

3. Examine the legacy of Jacques Cartier. Do you think he succeeded or failed? To evaluate the historical legacy of any individual, you must do a number of things:
   • have specific criteria for judging that individual
   • consider what the person set out to accomplish and compare it with what was achieved
   • consider the costs involved in the achievements
   • analyze the number of people they affected and how long the legacy was felt

Judge Cartier by these or other criteria and decide whether or not he succeeded or failed.

4. Assume that you are one of the following settlers in New France: explorer, fur trader, or craftsperson. Make a balance sheet of the advantages and disadvantages of living in New France.

5. Create a slogan and a logo for either the Hudson Bay Company or the North West Company. Explain why both your slogan and logo would be effective.

APPLYING YOUR LEARNING

1. Write a diary entry for one of the following:
   • a sailor on board one of Cartier's ships in 1534
   • a member of the party that survived the first winter
   • King Francis I on the eve of Cartier's departure in 1534
   • one of Donnacona's sons who was kidnapped and taken to France
   • Donnacona at various times: after first meeting Cartier, when his sons were in France, and when he was in France

2. Put yourself in the role of one of Champlain's crew and write a letter to your family in France. Describe what your new life is like as well as your feelings about it.

3. A *eulogy* is a speech of praise given for a person at the time of his or her death. Write a eulogy for Cartier or Champlain.

4. Provide three historical and three modern examples of the following: *economic competition, companies,* and *advertising.*

5. Write a newspaper headline for each event included in the time line on pages 28–29.

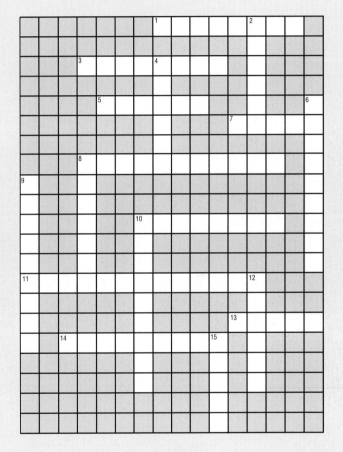

THE TORONTO STAR, Tuesday, October 13, 1998

Rival Fur Trading Companies Merge!

USING KEY WORDS

Complete the following crossword puzzle, using the clues provided, to discover some key words.

Across

1. The name of the firearm used by Champlain at The Battle of 1609 against the Iroquois
3. When a business has exclusive control of a given market
5. The mineral, rather than actual diamonds, that Cartier discovered
7. He is considered to be the first coureur de bois
8. The name for Aboriginal tribes joining together
10. Licensed fur trader
11. Unlicensed fur trader
13. The main rivals of the Iroquois
14. Champlain's chief French rival for power and influence in New France

Down

2. The most-sought fur-bearing animal
4. The real name for the "fool's gold" discovered by Cartier
6. The name given to intermarriage between French fur traders and Aboriginal women
8. The Bay into which Cartier sailed or the French word for *heat*
9. The Aboriginal Chief whom Cartier met on his first voyage of discovery
10. In 1524 he discovered that North America was a large, connected land mass
12. A disease that Cartier's and Champlain's crew suffered from
15. The number of voyages Cartier made

The Colony of New France

National Gallery of Canada, Ottawa. Purchased, 1971. Berczy, William Bent, *Canadian Harvest Festival C. 1840-1850*

1615

The Recollets arrive

1625

The Jesuits arrive

1632

Treaty of St. Germain-en-Laye returns New France to France

1635

Cardinal Richelieu expels the Recollets

1639

- Construction of Sainte-Marie among the Hurons begins
- The Ursuline nuns arrive in Québec

1649

Sainte-Marie among the Hurons destroyed by the Iroquois, the Jesuits leave, the Huron are defeated

SETTING OUR FOCUS

New France was a colony that enjoyed a century-and-a-half existence. Being far removed from Europe and populated almost exclusively by French-speaking Roman Catholics, it developed its own distinct customs and practices. The picture on the left reveals two of the most important aspects of New France. It was a rural society in which more than three-quarters of the population were farmers, and a society in which the influence of the Roman Catholic Church was strong. Where are the people in the picture heading? Why do you think they are going there? Describe how the people are dressed. Can you suggest reasons for that kind of attire? What time of year is it in the picture? How do you know?

PREVIEWING THE CHAPTER

In this chapter you will learn about these topics:
- **the reasons people came to New France**
- **the rise of farming as an industry in New France**
- **the establishment of a Royal Government to take control of New France and develop its population, economy, and industry**

KEY WORDS

census

engagé

les filles du roi

habitant

intendant

Jesuits

martyr

mercantilism

mercenary

missionary

Recollets

Royal Government

tithes

1659	**1663**	**1665**	**1667**	**1672**	**1701**
Bishop Laval arrives	Start of Royal Government	Intendant Jean Talon arrives	French force the Iroquois to sign a peace treaty	Governor Frontenac arrives	French and Iroquois conclude peace treaty after almost a century of war

AT A CROSSROADS

Colonists came to New France for a variety of reasons. Everyday people came to farm and to better their lives or to experience the rugged life of the coureurs de bois. Administrators came to improve the organization of the colony. Priests came to uphold the power of the Roman Catholic Church and to bring comfort to the lives of the struggling colonists. **Missionaries** came from their churches to bring "the word of God" to the Aboriginal Peoples and convert them to Christianity.

Despite colonists' efforts, New France experienced very slow growth throughout its history. By 1620 there were only 60 people in the colony. By 1635 the population numbered only 150 settlers. Even by 1663, more than half a century after its founding, the population of New France was barely 3000 people. This constituted a crisis for the new French King, Louis XIV, especially when he compared his colony's population to the British colonies of North America, where more than 100 000 people lived.

Fort Remi, a *seigneury* in Lachine, 1689. What buildings can you identify within the walls?

By 1663 New France was at a crossroads. Either the development of the colony would continue to play second fiddle to the fur trade because of the fur-trading monopolies that ran the colony, or the French government would have to take a more active role in directing and guiding its affairs and future. Louis XIV's decision to establish a Royal Government in New France in 1663 marked a decisive turning point in the colony's history. For the next century, New France would grow slowly but steadily. By the eve of the Conquest of New France and the birth of the province of Québec in 1759, when the British defeated the French during the Seven Years' War, about 70 000 people lived in New France.

FARMING IN NEW FRANCE

Building the Farm

By far the greatest percentage of immigrants came to New France after 1663 to become farmers. Some had this purpose firmly in mind as they set out on their journeys. Many others, such as the *engagés*, who were hired to work for three years in return for a plot of land, came to farming as a second career. No matter how they came to farming as their way of life, most of New France's colonists were **habitants** — French Canadian farmers. They were the stable foundation on which New France came to depend. It is no wonder that governors admired them greatly and held them up as the "ideal" colonist that others should imitate.

Such admiration did not make the habitants' lives any easier. Their tasks were overwhelming. First, the habitant families had to clear the land of trees, rocks, and boulders. In the following generations, their families did the same.

It was an extremely slow process. The habitants chopped down trees by axe and used the timber for buildings, furniture, and firewood. They removed tree stumps with a team of oxen if the family owned one, or burned the stumps, or simply planted around them. The family cleared the stones and rocks from their land by hand. They kept suitable rocks for buildings, fireplaces, and fences. Some habitants drained marshes. They dug a series of drainage canals to allow the water to flow out or they carried the water out by hand, bucket after endless bucket. Once the land was sufficiently cleared, the habitants tilled the soil to get it ready for seeding. In time, they built roads so they could take their produce to market — when they finally produced a surplus.

Louis XIV was the embodiment of *absolutism*, a political system in which the monarch has supreme and complete power. Why do you think he called himself *The Sun King*?

Reflections

What are your observations of a habitant's life? Record your thoughts in your journal, in an illustration, or in another form of your choice.

Clearing the land and building a homestead like the one in this painting called *Settlers' Log Cabin* was a difficult task given the dense forest and rocky terrain. Once established, the habitant family remained relatively isolated and became self-sufficient out of necessity.

The habitants had to build a shelter before the snow and bitter winds of winter set in. Because the house had to be built quickly, it was usually a small, two-room dwelling. Using materials that were at hand, the settlers constructed simple, functional homesteads. Often, the house raising turned into a communal event as family, friends, and neighbours became part of the backbreaking work. They built most houses from wood because it was cheap and readily available. It was also a better insulator against the cold than stone was. Like clearing the land, constructing the house was very hard labour. The habitants had to choose the site carefully, giving consideration to drainage, level, exposure, and access to water. The family hauled stones from the fields to build the house's foundation. The builders squared the timber and laid the logs one on top of the other. Finally, they put mortar between the logs to hold them in place. They constructed a high, steep roof of overlapping planks so the heavy snow would slide off. The habitants added shingles later if their farm became prosperous.

Habitants used field stones, squared logs, and wooden planks to build their first house.

Planting Crops

Since bread was the staple of the habitants' diet, wheat became the most important crop. The wheat was fairly hardy but the habitants still had to tend it carefully. They also grew corn, oats, barley, and some tobacco. Families often supplemented their diet with vegetables from their gardens. They used livestock as a source of both food and labour.

The habitants' lives were hard and their workdays were long. They rose at dawn and worked until nightfall. Winter or bad weather brought little relief, since that was the time to repair tools and look after household chores. Initially entertainment and pleasures were scarce. The habitants considered themselves fortunate if they could cultivate a dozen or more hectares of land, see their children married, and subdivide the farm for their children.

Louis Hébert was the first habitant in New France. What would be different about farming in New France compared to France?

The Story So Far . . .

1 From one of the following perspectives, write a letter back home to a friend or relative in France after your first six months in New France. Describe what is new in your life, perhaps part of your daily routine, things you like and dislike, and, finally, your overall feelings.
   • a mother of a habitant family
   • a father of a habitant family
   • a twelve-year-old daughter of a habitant family
   • a twelve-year-old son of a habitant family
2 Create a list of jobs that would have to be done on a habitant farm and assign the person(s) who would do them. What conclusions can you make about work on the farm?
3 Why do you think that many of the colonial administrators saw the habitant as the ideal settler?

THE MISSIONARIES

Not everyone came to New France to trade furs or to farm. A very different motive for both exploration and settlement came with the work of a small but influential band of missionaries. They faced many of the same kinds of obstacles and dangers as

A Jesuit, or a *Black Robe*, preaching to the Huron. How would you describe the facial expressions of the Aboriginal people in this illustration? In what language do you think the discussion is taking place? What symbols are evident?

the coureurs de bois faced, but had fewer resources. The missionaries set out to "bring the word of God" to the Aboriginal population of early Canada. Armed with their spiritual strength, they sought to convert the Aboriginal Peoples to Christianity.

Reasons for Conversion

Just as there were different reasons for various groups of settlers to come to New France, there were different reasons for missionaries to try the process of conversion. For some, there was a sincere desire to bring Christianity to the Aboriginal Peoples. Others were caught up in a competitive race to gain more followers for their religion. This was important in light of the struggle between Catholics and Protestants that was raging in Europe at the time.

Religion was the most dominant institution in people's lives at this time. In the early sixteenth century, a kind of religious revolution took place in Europe. Up to that time, the Roman Catholic Church controlled the spiritual world of Christian Europe. However, in 1517, a German monk named Martin Luther criticized the corruption and decadence of the Roman Catholic Church. His publication of his *95 Theses* sparked what is now known as the Protestant Reformation.

The Roman Catholic Church did not take this opposition lightly. They launched the Counter-Reformation, in which they attempted to win back their followers. By 1560 France was torn apart by religious wars. This intense religious rivalry affected early Canada indirectly. Because most of France's energy and resources were committed to winning this religious war, it did virtually nothing about colonization in New France for half a century after Cartier's final voyage in 1543.

Early Missionaries

The earliest missionaries were the Catholic **Recollets**. As early as 1615, they sought to convert both the Montagnais who lived around the St. Lawrence River, as well as the Huron who lived much farther away. The Recollets' poverty and the indifference of the fur traders made it impossible to maintain the mission in Huronia. The Society of Jesus, more commonly known as the **Jesuits**, replaced the Recollets. In 1625 Fathers Charles Lalemant, Jean de Brébeuf, and Enemond Massé joined the

Recollets at Québec and Huronia. Like the Recollets before them, Champlain invited the Jesuits to New France because he saw benefits to be derived from converting the Aboriginal Peoples. France would gain more followers and would therefore have more power.

Founded by Ignatius Loyola in 1534, the Jesuits were more aggressive than the Recollets in their missionary zeal. They would come to be the dominant order within the colony. This was particularly the case after the mid-1630s, when Cardinal Richelieu, the King's First Minister, expelled the Recollets.

Snapshot

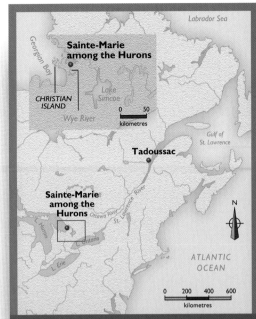

Jesuit Missions in 1640

The Jesuit *Relations*

The Jesuit *Relations* (1632–1673) are an invaluable primary source about Canada's early history. They cover forty years and provide a rich commentary on the history of the time. The Jesuit Paul le Jeune at Québec composed the first *Relation* on August 28, 1632. Written to his superior in France, Father Barthelemy Jacquinot, it was an extraordinary account of his trip to New France. Originally it was intended simply as a personal communication. However, Father Jacquinot was so taken with the lively and perceptive account, that he had it printed and circulated. It became an overnight bestseller! French readers were captivated by the insightful observations of a well-spoken and perceptive person who lived in this foreign land. Two other famous authors of the *Relations* were Jerome Lalemant and Father Jean de Brébeuf. An excerpt from De Brébeuf's account follows.

The Huron Relation of 1635
By Father Jean de Brébeuf

Reverend Father, I write this to give you an account of our trip to the land of the Hurons. It was indeed tiring, and cost us a great deal more than my first trip. But it has been filled with blessings and God willing will be followed by many more.

Last year, 1634, when we reached Three Rivers, the now established trading post, we were beset with some difficulties and perplexities. In the first place, there were only 11 Huron canoes to accommodate 10 extra of us, who were planning to go with them to their home. And we were in serious doubt about any other [Huron] coming down this year because of the great defeat suffered last spring in battle with the Iroquois....

Finally after full deliberation, we decided to try our luck, judging it to be vitally important to set foot in the country in order to open the door now so firmly closed to the faith. It was easier to make this resolution than to carry it out....

I therefore did everything I could. We doubled our presents. We reduced the amount of our baggage and took only what was needed for Mass, or what was absolutely necessary for life.... There were times when I was completely baffled and hopeless, until I turned in a very special way to Our Lord Jesus, for Whose Glory alone we were undertaking this arduous journey....

1 What difficulties would the Roman Catholic Church have in maintaining these missions?

2 Identify the different languages that would have to be learned for missionaries to be effective in all these places.

3 If you were a Catholic missionary in the middle of the seventeenth century, where would you have most liked to have been sent? Why? Where would you have least liked to have been sent? Why?

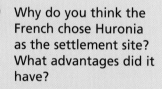

How would you react to being in a Jesuit mission in the 1600s? Write a journal entry, either for the summer or the winter, expressing your point of view.

The Black Robes and the Aboriginal Peoples

The first French Roman Catholic mission was built at Tadoussac, on the Saguenay River in Québec. The Jesuits built a tiny, wooden chapel there for the Montagnais and the fur traders.

The missionaries, priests, and lay people travelled deep into uncharted territory. They initially lived among the Montagnais and Huron and later with many more tribes. They observed Aboriginal customs, ate their food, and learned their languages. In return, they baptized the Aboriginal Peoples and tried to teach them the ways of Christianity.

1. Why do you think the French chose Huronia as the settlement site? What advantages did it have?

2. How would it have been supplied with provisions or would it have been self-sufficient?

3. In kilometres, approximately how far is Huronia from the main settlements of New France?

4. If you were in Huronia, what direction would you have to go to arrive at the following places: Québec, Lake Ontario, Lake Huron, the Thirteen Colonies?

Huronia, 1639–1649

At best, it was probably a tense relationship given the great difference in background. Father Brébeuf, for example, lived among the Huron for more than 15 years, much of it in the Jesuit settlement at Sainte-Marie among the Hurons, near what is now Midland, Ontario. From the Huron point of view, the Jesuits must have appeared curious at best and threatening at worst. They dressed strangely, had facial hair, spoke in a strange tongue, and, perhaps most importantly, they talked of a strange God and believed in very different values.

In the beginning, Brébeuf was shocked by some of the Huron habits, most notably their food: "The ordinary meal is only a little Indian corn, crushed rather crudely between two stones, or sometimes left whole, and then taken with fresh water. This is not very appetizing." Although Brébeuf came to learn and admire many aspects of their culture, he was neither totally accepted by the Huron nor did he completely accept their ways.

Like many other missionaries, Brébeuf died when the Iroquois defeated the Huron in one of the many wars they waged throughout the seventeenth century over land claims. Some Jesuits chose to be **martyred** — to die or suffer greatly rather than give up their religion. The martyrs were burned at the stake, because Aboriginal Peoples either opposed the Jesuits' attempts to convert them or saw the Jesuits as "evil spirits" who brought deadly diseases, such as smallpox, typhus, and the plague. These diseases greatly harmed Aboriginal communities because the Aboriginal Peoples had little or no natural immunity to them. Once the Europeans brought the diseases to North America, they spread rapidly. Between one-third and one-half of early Canada's Aboriginal population died in the first waves of these epidemics.

(Above) Father Jean de Brébeuf at an Aboriginal council. How are the attendants responding to his words? (Below) The construction of Sainte-Marie was begun in 1639 by Father Charles Lalemant. The mission housed well over 100 French priests and lay people.

Marie-Madeleine de Chauvigny de La Peltrie

MAKING DREAMS COME TRUE

One French reader whose imagination was fired by the *Relations* of Father Paul Le Jeune was a spirited young widow named Marie-Madeleine de Chauvigny de La Peltrie. In fact, Father Le Jeune's plea for the "Ladies of France" to devote themselves to founding a convent school in Québec seemed to speak directly to her. It would give her life purpose and, she hoped, stave off her father's attempts to find her another husband.

Much to her regret, she had bowed once to her father's wishes. Setting aside her desire to become a nun, she had given in and married a rich older man when she was 17. When that man, the Chevalier de Gruel, Seigneur de La Peltrie, died, the young woman became a wealthy 22-year-old widow. She longed to devote her inheritance to a life of service in New France.

Her relatives were against her plan, however. They wanted her to remarry. This time, though, De La Peltrie refused to give in. To get around her family's wishes, she talked an acquaintance into marrying her. Both understood that it was a marriage of convenience.

Soon afterward, she met an Ursuline nun — Marie de l'Incarnation — who told De La Peltrie of her dream of founding a convent school in Québec. Excitedly, the two made plans to travel to New France. On May 4, 1639, they sailed from France.

Arriving in Québec, the two women opened their school for Aboriginal and French girls. Two years later, they were on hand for the arrival in the colony of another young woman with a mission. With the help of a rich benefactor, Jeanne Mance hoped to open a *Hôtel-Dieu* at the new settlement of Ville-Marie, which was still in the planning stages.

That winter, Mance and De La Peltrie spent a great deal of time together and formed a lasting friendship. When spring arrived, De La Peltrie travelled to Ville-Marie with Mance and worked alongside her for 18 months before returning to Québec.

Though the names of Marie de l'Incarnation and Jeanne Mance are deeply etched into the history of New France, that of Marie-Madeleine de Chauvigny de La Peltrie is less well-known. Yet this dedicated woman played a pivotal role in ensuring that the dreams of both her friends came true.

More people you could research are

Marguerite Bourgeoys

Jean de Brébeuf

Marie-Madeleine de Chauvigny de La Peltrie

Marie de l'Incarnation

Paul de Maissoneuve

Jeanne Mance

Marie de l'Incarnation was one of the first women to live in New France. After her husband died, she decided to become a nun. Much is known about her life and the conditions of New France through her many letters. Following are excerpts from two of these letters, written 30 years apart.

September 4, 1640
My dear sister [a younger nun], it is a great pleasure to be with this group of [Aboriginal] women and girls. They dress in old blankets or scraps of fur — not the perfumed silks of the ladies of France. But they are open and simple spirits. The men are also. I have seen brave chiefs go down on their knees at my feet. They beg me to help them say grace before they eat. They hold out their hands like children and say everything I ask. . . . The people of Québec give us vegetables and other foods — in some ways we are too well off. We spent the winter as happily as in France. While the hut is small and stuffy, we have not been sick and I have never felt so well. If people in France ate only bacon and salted fish as we do here, they would be sick and not be able to sing. We are in good health and sing better than they do in France. The air is excellent — this is heaven on earth, even the thorns are full of love.

Summer 1670
All of the winters are very cold in this country, but the last was unusually severe. It was both very cold and very long; we have not known a worse winter. All the pipes froze and springs and ponds were dry. At first we melted snow to get water, both for us and the animals. . . . There was still ice in the garden in June. Our fruit trees, which gave lovely fruit, are dead of the cold. All of the country suffered loss. . . . God wants us to

suffer here and live in sweetness in heaven later. After 32 years in this country we are used to the hard life and have had time to forget the easy life in our old home in France.

■ **Marie de l'Incarnation**

QUESTIONING THE EVIDENCE

1. **What is the tone of the first letter? The second letter? Can you account for the difference? Find specific evidence from Marie de l'Incarnation's first letter that life in New France was "heaven on earth."**

2. **Marie de l'Incarnation was a keen observer of her surroundings. What evidence can you find to support that statement?**

3. **What do you think her attitude is toward the Aboriginal Peoples? Do you think she views them the same as or different from the people back in France? Provide evidence for your view.**

4. **What does she mean by the line at the end of her first letter that "even the thorns are full of love"?**

Schools, Convents, and Hospitals

Another of the missionaries' motives for settlement was the development of schools, convents, and hospitals. Marie de l'Incarnation had a vision that she should leave the comforts of Europe and educate young girls in New France. She did just that, even though the son she had borne prior to becoming a nun cried, "Give me back my mother!"

In 1639 a group of Ursuline nuns arrived in Québec and opened a convent school for Aboriginal and French girls, where they were taught religion, housekeeping, reading, and writing. Jeanne Mance, the co-founder of the small settlement of Ville-Marie (later Montréal) along with Paul de Maisonneuve, also opened one of the colony's first hospitals. Calling her hospital *Hôtel-Dieu* — "the house of God" — she worked there tirelessly for over three decades, treating Aboriginal and French people.

Marguerite Bourgeoys, like Mance, was in her thirties when she came to New France in 1653. Five years later, after taking care of the sick and elderly in the colony, she opened the first domestic training school in early Canada.

Protector of Ville-Marie

Many of the early settlers at Ville-Marie owed their lives to a dog named Pilote. Pilote patrolled the woods around the tiny settlement and howled an alarm whenever she sensed that Iroquois were near. At the sound of her warning, settlers working the fields outside the stockade would drop their tools and race to safety.

In 1639 the Ursuline nuns arrived and opened a convent school called Ville-Marie. In the illustration, what are the children doing? Why might they be doing that?

Web Connection

www.school.mcgrawhill.ca/resources

Go to the web site above to find out more about one of the religions mentioned in this section. Go to History Resources, then to *Canada: The Story of Our Heritage* to see where to go next.

The Story So Far . . .

1   If you were a missionary going to an Aboriginal village for the first time, what things would you bring and what would you say first to get the tribe to listen to and accept you? If you were a member of the Aboriginal village, what would you say to the missionary?

2   As an ongoing class project, build a scale model of Sainte-Marie among the Hurons. Begin by thoroughly researching the dimensions of the site and the buildings within it. Then draw a blueprint. Select the most appropriate materials and then construct the scale model.

3 Historical analogies occur when two events, usually one historical and one current, are seen as similar. Explain the historical analogy between the way in which the Jesuits and the Huron viewed one another in the seventeenth century and the way in which, today, newly arrived immigrants to Canada and established Canadians view one another. What are the differences? What are the similarities? In each case, suggest reasons for their viewpoints.

OBSTACLES TO GROWTH AND DEVELOPMENT

Some of the factors that hindered the growth and development of New France are as follows.

First, New France was open only to "natural-born French Catholics." That meant that all other nationalities and religions were excluded, unlike the Thirteen Colonies, which were a magnet for many different groups.

Second, the French government did not do very much to promote the colony. Before 1663 New France was basically run by the fur-trading monopolies and, as we have seen, they were indifferent about fulfilling their colonial responsibilities.

Third, very few Europeans were willing to undertake the great risk of giving up everything and travelling to a remote colony 4000 km away.

Fourth, the shortage of women in New France, particularly before the 1670s, severely reduced any natural increase in population that might have come about. Often there were twice as many men as women in the colony.

Finally, the image that most people had of New France as a barren, forbidding place did not attract immigrants.

Relations Among the Aboriginal Peoples

Another limitation to European population growth in New France was relations with the Aboriginal Peoples. Part of potential colonists' reluctance to settle in New France stemmed from concerns about the danger posed by the Iroquois. In part because the Iroquois greatly outnumbered the French Canadian population, Champlain was eager from the very beginning to keep on good terms with the Huron. Not only were they invaluable in teaching the French Canadians survival skills, but they also played a crucial role in the fur trade. In addition, the

Joseph Légaré painted *The Massacre of the Huron by the Iroquois*. How would you describe his interpretation?

Huron were of great assistance as guides. They led the French through the waterways to the headwaters of the Great Lakes. Largely because of Champlain's early decision to become allied with the Algonquin and the Montagnais in The Battle of 1609, the future pattern of French Canadian relations with the Aboriginal Peoples was set.

By the 1640s, the once proud Huron Nation was in dire straits. Not only were they being relentlessly pursued by the Iroquois, but various tribes within the Huron Confederacy were competing for supremacy. Unfortunately that internal division could not have come at a worse time. The Iroquois Confederacy was eager to take advantage of the situation. In addition, the Huron community was devastated by epidemics of smallpox, brought to them by the missionaries. About 20 percent of their population was wiped out.

In 1649 the Iroquois launched an all-out assault by invading Huron territory. The attack was short, swift, and brutal. The initial Iroquois attackers sacrificed themselves so that the larger forces behind them could enter Sainte-Marie among the Hurons by clambering over the palisades. Their larger numbers allowed them to defeat the Huron defenders.

The Iroquois decided to burn the settlement both in revenge for earlier acts committed by the Huron and as a vivid symbol of their victory. Sainte-Marie among the Hurons was burned to the ground. Virtually every other major Huron settlement met a similar fate. During this Aboriginal war, hundreds were killed on both sides and thousands were taken prisoner, though most were Huron.

Sainte-Marie among the Hurons was burned down by the Iroquois. Why?

Iroquois raids on settlements were frequent occurrences. The fur-trade wars were brutal as both sides, Huron and French, Iroquois and British, competed to gain the advantage. Not only was there considerable wealth to be gained, but the rivalry also involved competition over land. There were strategic advantages that stemmed from holding, or not holding, certain land.

Madeleine de Verchères
DEFENDER OF CASTLE DANGEROUS

Fourteen-year-old Madeleine Jarret knew the danger she was in. She knew that the French were the enemies of the Iroquois, who had already killed three of her relatives. That is why she was always careful when she was outside the stockade that protected the manor house and habitants' cabins of Verchères, her family's *seigneury*. Verchères was on the south shore of the St. Lawrence River near the mouth of the Richelieu River. The *seigneury* was so vulnerable to attack that it was nicknamed *Castle Dangerous*.

Circumstances were especially dangerous in 1692. Britain and France were at war again. The Iroquois were allies of the British, who were giving them weapons so they could raid French settlements.

On the morning of October 22, Madeleine's parents were away. A single sentry guarded the small fort. Madeleine was in the garden outside the stockade and the habitants were working nearby. Suddenly, a group of Iroquois leaped out of the woods and seized some of the habitants. Madeleine ran for the safety of the stockade. Shots rang out behind her. An Iroquois man caught up with her and grabbed the kerchief that was tied around her neck. Terrified, Madeleine fumbled to loosen the knot and kept running. The man was left with only a piece of cloth in his hand.

Madeleine dashed inside the big gate and struggled breathlessly to close and lock it. Outside, the Iroquois started trying to scale the walls of the fort.

Madeleine ordered the sentry to fire a small cannon from one of the bastions. Luckily, the loud booming noise scared the Iroquois, who retreated to the nearby woods. Madeleine knew that the noise would also tell neighbouring *seigneuries* that Verchères was under attack. They would pass along word and help would be sent from Montréal, 35 km upriver.

It would take a day for help to arrive. Until it did, the lives of the people of Verchères depended on convincing the Iroquois that the fort was too well defended to attack. Madeleine dashed from bastion to bastion, calling out to make it seem as if many soldiers were stationed inside. She also urged other people to make as much noise as possible. For the rest of the day, the frightened defenders kept up their noisy ruse.

When reinforcements arrived the next day, the Iroquois had already left, taking their prisoners with them. The reinforcements gave chase and caught up to them at Lake Champlain. Two of the habitants had been killed, but the others were released and returned to Verchères. As the story of Madeleine's bravery spread among the settlers, she became the toast of New France.

More people you could research are

Madeleine de Verchères

The Huron

The Iroquois

Father Charles Lalemant

Énemond Massé

Pieskaret

Snapshot

The "Saviours of New France"

Adam Dollard des Ormeaux was born in 1635, probably in France. He travelled to New France in 1658. There Dollard witnessed first-hand the incessant fighting between the Iroquois and the French. Dollard served as the military commander at the small settlement of Ville-Marie.

In late April 1660, Dollard, along with 16 French, 40 Huron, and 4 Algonquin, left Ville-Marie in search of Iroquois. Rather than encountering a small raiding party, Dollard and his group met an Iroquois force of over 500. Remarkably, Dollard and his men were able to hold out for about a week by barricading themselves in an abandoned fort.

However, Dollard and most of his party were killed by the Iroquois at the Long Sault. They became a legend to the French and were regarded as the "saviours of New France." It was believed that their heroic action probably prevented an intended Iroquois attack on Ville-Marie and Québec.

Adam Dollard des Ormeaux, along with some Huron, Algonquin, and French, defend themselves from an Iroquois attack.

After defeating the Huron, the Iroquois decided to attack the centres of New France to force the French out of the country. They cut off the fur trade coming into Québec. Iroquois groups attacked Montréal and Québec. A sizable group of settlers gave up and decided to return to France.

The colony of New France was at the point of collapse. At one of the darkest hours in New France's history, a ray of light in the person of King Louis XIV broke through. In 1663 he was just beginning his long reign in France as *The Sun King* and he refused to abandon New France. Instead he took the bold step of creating a system of **Royal Government**, which took the responsibility of running the colony from the fur-trading companies and put it directly in the hands of France itself. That was to be a fateful and positive decision.

The Story So Far . . .

1 Which of the obstacles to the growth of New France do you feel was the most significant? Justify your choice with evidence.

2 Do one of the following creative activities:
  - Imagine you are Adam Dollard des Ormeaux holding out against the Iroquois in the abandoned fort. Write a letter to the people of New France on the eve of what you know will be your death.
  - Imagine you are an Iroquois or Huron person ready to defend your land and rights. Write a speech that you will present to your tribe before a major battle.
3 After researching one of the incidents involving Adam Dollard des Ormeaux or Madeleine de Verchères, role-play it for the class. Include appropriate dialogue as well as your own choreography.
4 The word *heroic* appears in this chapter. What do you believe the requirements of a hero are? Identify five people, living or dead, that you believe deserve the title *hero*.

GROWTH AND DEVELOPMENT

Louis XIV's decision to take a direct interest in New France was crucial to its future development. No longer would New France be ignored by the fur-trading monopolies that were supposed to develop it. No longer would the obstacles to growth be ignored. No longer would the economy be totally dependent on the fur trade. Rather, with France's direct involvement in the day-to-day operations and the overall plan of New France, the colony would begin to prosper. This time period marked a century of slow but steady growth, until yet another war would alter the future of New France radically.

Laying the Religious Foundation

Much of the turnaround of New France's development occurred just before 1663. The first colonial bishop, François de Montmorency-Laval, arrived in New France in 1659. Laval's vision was to create a theocracy: a society based on religious principles and administered by the Roman Catholic Church. Through the Seminary of Québec, he aimed to control all parish appointments and finances. For the next dozen years, Bishop Laval would play an important religious and political role in the colony. He strengthened the position of the Church by demanding that it be allowed to collect **tithes**, or taxes. By organizing the colony into parishes — areas that had their own church and priests — he streamlined the delivery of religious

François de Montmorency-Laval, first bishop of New France.

services. He was also a strong believer in education for priests and the general population. Finally, he had a major impact on colonial values by strongly criticizing the use of brandy in the fur trade as well as supporting the family as the foundation of New France.

King Louis XIV wanted to transform New France into a thriving and growing colony. He was driven by two impulses: to gain wealth and to increase France's power and status. France would supply the settlers, the administrators, and the overall vision. The plan was largely conceived by Jean-Baptiste Colbert, Minister of Marine and Colonies.

Snapshot

The Brandy Dispute

Fur traders had been using brandy as a trading item almost from the first days of the fur trade. Bishop Laval believed that it was immoral. He argued that its use took advantage of the Aboriginal Peoples, who had never experienced the effects of alcohol before. Further, he saw that the continued use of brandy would endanger Aboriginal societies. Finally, he believed that the use of alcohol would interfere with the Church's missionary attempts.

The Reserve Law empowered Laval to remove Church privileges from those who engaged in what he regarded as "the disgusting practice." Governor Frontenac, anxious to maximize the profits from the fur trade, wanted no such punishment. The Brandy Parliament of 1678, carefully orchestrated by Frontenac so that no clergy were in attendance, approved the use of brandy in the fur trade.

Mercantilism

Jean-Baptiste Colbert introduced mercantilism to New France.

Colbert's plan was based on the idea of **mercantilism**: a certain type of trade involving a parent country and a colony, whereby the colony exists for the financial gain of the parent country. The colony provides a guaranteed source of raw materials and a ready market for the manufactured goods produced by the parent country. The parent country, by purchasing raw materials cheaply and selling the finished products at a high price, builds up a supply of money. That money was then used to buy supplies or, in times of war, **mercenaries**: soldiers who serve in a foreign army for pay.

Mercantilism built up the economy of New France by attracting immigrants to new jobs, thereby increasing the population and the consumption of goods and extending business into different areas. France was assured that there would always be an available market for the products. The only negative aspect was that mercantilism prevented New France from trading with anyone else, something they would have liked to have done when they had a surplus of fur.

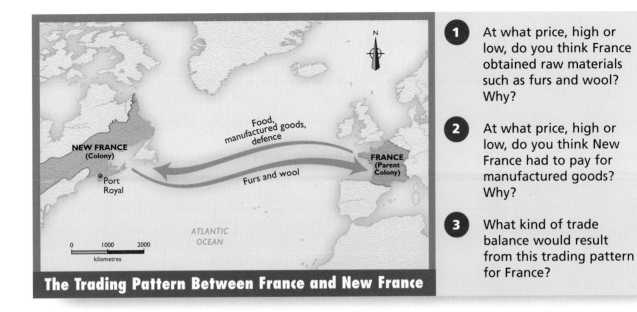

1. At what price, high or low, do you think France obtained raw materials such as furs and wool? Why?

2. At what price, high or low, do you think New France had to pay for manufactured goods? Why?

3. What kind of trade balance would result from this trading pattern for France?

The Trading Pattern Between France and New France

The Sovereign Council

Under the revamped system of government in New France, the Sovereign Council became the dominant political instrument. At the top of the hierarchy was the monarch, in this case Louis XI, who ruled by divine right. Divine right was the belief that the monarch was God's direct descendant on earth and therefore could not be challenged, questioned, or criticized. Louis XIV took a vital interest in the the affairs of New France.

The Sovereign Council was the foundation of Royal Government. Which of the officials is the governor, bishop, and intendant? What evidence can you provide to show that this group was highly important?

The Colony of New France   **75**

As the King's chief representative, the governor was entrusted with the overall running of New France. Like the other chief officers, the governor reported directly to the King while also working with the lesser officials of the Sovereign Council. The governor's specific duties included looking after defence, overseeing relations with the Aboriginal Peoples, and maintaining the overall safety of the colony. The bishop was in charge of churches, hospitals, schools, and missions. The **intendant** was responsible for the day-to-day running of the colony. He also controlled the fur trade, industry, and justice within New France.

The governor, bishop, and intendant, along with appointed councillors, comprised the Sovereign Council. The Council sat in Québec and enforced royal edicts and acted as a court of law. Assisting the Council were various other bureaucrats: the captains of the militia, town governors, and high-ranking priests and *seigneurs*.

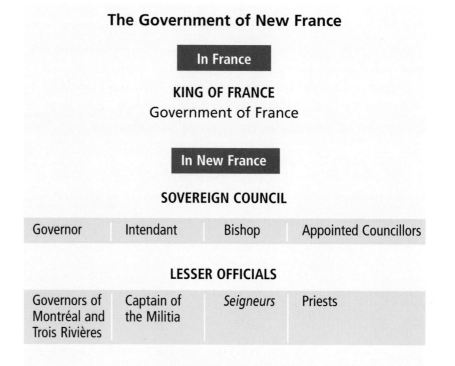

The Government of New France

In France

KING OF FRANCE
Government of France

In New France

SOVEREIGN COUNCIL

Governor	Intendant	Bishop	Appointed Councillors

LESSER OFFICIALS

Governors of Montréal and Trois Rivières	Captain of the Militia	*Seigneurs*	Priests

CITIZENS OF NEW FRANCE

These colonial officials often exercised quite a bit of independence. Sometimes they chose not to enforce a directive from France. Other times, they suggested policies that were relevant to the local circumstances. In both cases, they were fairly confident of getting away with these decisions simply because of the distance between themselves and France. Also,

Louis XIV had stated in 1663 that "the general spirit of government ought to lean in the direction of gentleness" in order to encourage settlement and local initiative.

Because of the responsibilities and the individuals who held the position, the intendant became the most powerful figure in the history of New France. His staff increased over time as clerks, bookkeepers, store owners, bailiffs, local agents, and various administrative agents were added. Also, the introduction of Royal Government meant that religious leaders had less power. This further increased the intendant's power.

The Defence of New France

The military defence of New France was improved in a number of ways after 1663. Thousands of French troops were sent to New France to help defuse the threat of Iroquois attack. They were soldiers from the *Troupes de Marine*, a kind of naval guard in France. They were organized into companies of 50 men commanded by a captain. Careers as marine commanders were pursued eagerly by sons of the local nobility of New France. Their knowledge of local conditions made for a more efficient defence system.

Another important contribution to the improved security of the colony was a decree in 1669 forcing all men between 16 and 60 to serve in the militia. (Those who were physically disabled, or members of the nobility and clergy were exempt.) The citizens accepted this military duty with a high degree of patriotism, and very few deserted.

The Story So Far . . .

1 Explain in your own words why the introduction of Royal Government marked a decisive turning point in the history of New France.

2 In groups of three, debate one of the controversial issues affecting New France, such as the use of brandy in the fur trade.

3 In your opinion, which of the three highest officials within the system of Royal Government had the most important job? Provide evidence to support your choice.

4 Over time, the power exercised by the bishop declined while that of the intendant increased. Give reasons for this.

THE ROYAL PLAN TAKES SHAPE

The End of the Iroquois Wars

After dissolving the financially troubled Company of One Hundred Associates (the association of fur-trading companies) and establishing the Royal Government, Louis XIV took steps to prevent the immediate threat of a large-scale attack by the Iroquois. By the 1660s, the Iroquois were in a fairly commanding position, while the power of the Huron was greatly reduced after their defeat by the Iroquois in 1649. The Iroquois prospered from the fur trade as well as from their military conquests. They had altered their strategy. Rather than engaging in guerrilla warfare tactics, they were contemplating a massive assault on the French centres of power.

Louis XIV dispatched the Carignan-Salières Regiment, a group of 1300 French soldiers, to assist the local volunteer army in protecting the colonists from the Iroquois. Together they invaded Iroquois territory and burned their crops and villages. These attacks, coupled with devastating losses from epidemics, forced the Iroquois to sign a treaty in 1667, which ushered in 20 years of peace. Thus, an important obstacle to the growth of New France was removed. The resulting peace, safety, and security ensured the future development of the colony.

An officer of the Carignan-Salières Regiment. Members were instrumental in ending the Iroquois threat. They would later become important in increasing the population of the colony. How?

Increasing the Population

The Carignan-Salières Regiment provided help in resolving the old problem of New France's small population. To augment the population, Louis XIV offered the soldiers free farm land if they remained in New France for three years. Close to 500 members of the regiment accepted the offer. Other military corps followed the Carignan-Salières to New France and also decided to remain there.

Civilian artisans and tradespeople were also recruited. As many as 500 arrived over a few years. These people were important in a variety of ways. They helped build many of the roads, buildings, forts, and homes that began to dot the landscape. They contributed money to the domestic economy. Finally, with the colony at peace, an ever-growing number decided to reside permanently in New France.

However, this positive turn emphasized a continuing problem that had plagued New France's population from the very beginning. Not only was the colony's population small and growing very slowly, but there was an imbalance within that population: men outnumbered women by almost two to one. That imbalance was the main reason for New France's slow population growth.

New France Takes Its First Steps

Having Jean Talon as the first intendant proved to be highly beneficial for New France. Not only was he highly capable but he was also sensible in addressing the short-term needs of the colony and providing a plan for its long-term development. Realizing that he needed accurate information upon which to base his plans for reform, he had the 1666 census conducted. A **census** provides important information about trends in population growth or decline, population shifts, and breakdowns of that population (age, religion, nationality, spending patterns, and so on).

Population of New France, 1666		
By Gender	Males	2034
	Females	1181
	Total Population	3215
By Age	Under 16	1250
	Over 81	4
By Occupation	Servants	401
	Seigneurs	63
	Carpenters	36
	Stone masons	32
	Tailors	30
	Joiners	27
	Ship captains	22
	Shoemakers	20
	Storekeepers	18
	Weavers	16
	Millers	9
	Coopers	8
	Gunsmiths	7
	Ropemakers	6
	Armourers	4
	Teachers	3

1 Draw a pie graph to indicate the gender breakdown of the population. What important conclusions can you draw from this information? What factors might have caused this imbalance in the population? What impact might it have had on New France?

2 Suggest why there were so many more young people than seniors in New France. What effects might this have had on the colony's history after 1666?

3 Overall, do you think these figures would make France optimistic or pessimistic about its colony's future? Provide reasons for your point of view.

Note: The occupational breakdown does not include farmers, clergy, nobles, or government workers.

Jean Talon
THE GREAT INTENDANT

Jean Talon was brimming with ideas. As the first intendant to arrive in New France, his mission was to boost the growth and prosperity of the remote colony by making it self-sufficient. It was a responsibility that the brilliant bureaucrat, who had already begun forging a successful career in France, accepted enthusiastically.

Talon believed that attracting settlers and promoting industry and trade were the keys to creating a thriving colony. Standing in the way of settlement, though, were some *seigneurs* who were content to own huge tracts of land without clearing or farming them. Also, *seigneurs* often had trouble attracting settlers because the design of the *seigneuries* left people isolated and vulnerable to attacks by the Iroquois. Staying in Québec was much safer, but the city was starting to burst at the seams. When families grew or new immigrants arrived, there were few places for people to live.

Within months of his arrival in 1665, Talon had already come up with a scheme to help solve all these problems. To get his plan off the ground, he took over part of a Jesuit *seigneury* in the Charlesbourg area outside the city. There, he founded three new villages called Bourg-Royal, Bourg-la-Reine, and Bourg-Talon.

The design of the villages was quite different from that of the old-style *seigneuries*. Each was divided into 40 pie-shaped lots. The homes were built at the narrow tip of each wedge. They were grouped around a piece of land set aside for a church that would form the heart of each community. With the houses close together, the villages could be readily defended. The design also meant that people were less isolated and could help one another more easily. Settlers who applied for the lots were paid a small amount and given tools and enough food to keep them going until they could harvest their own crops. In return, the new landowners were required to clear a certain amount of their own land and help clear other lots in the community.

To show how much he believed in the plan, Talon bought one of the lots himself. Like most of Talon's plans for New France, the scheme was an instant success. Settlers flocked to the villages, which soon became thriving communities.

Unfortunately for New France, Talon was as ambitious as he was clever. For him, serving as intendant was merely a stepping stone to greater things. That is why he leaped at the opportunity to become an important official in the court of Louis XIV in Paris. Talon's departure from New France in 1672 was a great loss for the colony. No other intendant ever came close to matching his vision or ability. He was, indeed, the Great Intendant.

More people you could research are

Jean-Baptiste Colbert

Louis de Baude, the Comte de Frontenac

King Louis XIV

Joseph Antoine Lefebvre de La Barre

François Montmorency-Laval

Jean Talon

Talon quickly saw that one of the greatest shortcomings was the small population. He believed that the main cause was the small number of women in New France. To address that problem, Talon established **les filles du roi**, or *the King's daughters*.

Snapshot

Les Filles du Roi

Perhaps the most innovative idea instituted by Talon was bringing more than 1200 *filles du roi* to New France. They were a special group of young women who emigrated from France between 1663 and 1673. Their specific purpose was to come to New France, marry quickly, and bear children. They received their name from the fact that all their expenses were paid for by the Crown.

The government's commitment to them was serious. Agents were hired to find ideal young women. Thirty livres was given for a wardrobe of two sets of clothes and 60 livres for their transport. Les filles du roi received room and board after their arrival in New France. Many received a dowry of 50 livres at the time of their marriage. On many occasions, the colonial government did not have the necessary money and provided the dowry in the form of useful household articles. However, sometimes the dowry was not paid at all. Les *filles du roi* accomplished Jeau Talon's plan by tripling the population of New France within 15 years.

Talon also created a system of incentives that increased New France's population. There were financial rewards for those who married early and for those who had more than ten children. There were penalties for those who turned 20 and were still single and for parents whose daughters had reached the age of 16 and were still unmarried. Talon was eminently successful in increasing New France's population. Most of the increase was a natural one as immigration to the colony declined significantly after 1700.

Talon made other significant improvements. He wanted to reduce New France's dependence on the fur trade. He accomplished that by encouraging the habitants to spend more time farming and clearing the land and less time hunting and trapping. To make New France more self-sufficient, Talon experimented with hardier strains of wheat to improve the wheat crops and brought over large numbers of livestock. Cows and oxen became far more numerous. Talon had a grand scheme

Blacksmiths and armourers are shown going about their typical work day. What are the two men in the picture doing? If you were doing this job, what working conditions would you dislike? Identify six products that blacksmiths would make that would be useful for the people living in New France.

for creating a shipbuilding industry as well as related marine manufactures such as sails and ropes. In addition, he established a number of other industries: iron works, a brewery, and shoemaking.

Governor Frontenac and Expansion

Just as Laval was the most important bishop and Talon was the most significant intendant, Louis de Baude, the Comte de Frontenac, was the foremost governor. He served his first term from 1672 to 1682, was reappointed in 1689, and served until his death in 1697.

The Governor continued Talon's major reforms: increasing the population, diminishing the influence of the Jesuits, and continuing westward expansion. To enrich both himself and New France, Frontenac decided to build a fort at Cataraqui on the eastern end of Lake Ontario. To command that post, later named Fort Frontenac (present-day Kingston), the Governor choose Sieur de La Salle. La Salle would prove a worthy choice.

The construction of Fort Frontenac had another purpose. Governor Frontenac realized that any future growth and development in New France would depend on maintaining peace with the Iroquois. To that end, he met with their Chiefs at the newly built fort and exchanged gifts and promises of friendship. He convinced the Iroquois to travel to Fort Frontenac with their furs, rather than going to the British at Fort Albany, on the west side of James Bay. Further, he persuaded the Iroquois to meet him annually at Fort Frontenac to renew their vows of peace and friendship.

France began to hear criticisms from the clergy and the fur traders. In addition, Talon disagreed with Frontenac's extension of the fur trade into the Ohio country. Both Talon and Laval strongly opposed Frontenac's encouragement of the use of brandy as an item of exchange in the fur trade. In 1682 Louis XIV recalled Frontenac to France.

Frontenac's successor was Joseph Antoine Lefebvre de La Barre, a member of the nobility. New France prospered for a time under a group called *the beaver aristocracy*. La Barre encouraged great expansion of the fur trade in a number of ways. He granted far more licences. He attempted to bypass the Aboriginal go-betweens. He continued Frontenac's construction of forts as French outposts spread westward from the Great Lakes to the Ohio and Mississippi Rivers. Finally, La Barre organized La Compagnie du Nord to compete with the recently formed British Hudson Bay Company.

However, New France's fragile relations with the Iroquois broke down and war ensued. When the Iroquois learned that another war between France and England had started in Europe, they gave up all thought of peace and decided to attack New France with all their might. In August 1689 the Iroquois and their British allies attacked and wiped out the French settlement at Lachine. Louis XIV called on Frontenac to rescue the colony. He arrived to survey the damage. He saw that while the Iroquois had struck an important blow, they had failed in their more important attempt to isolate the island of Montréal.

After several years of guerrilla campaigns conducted largely by the Iroquois, in 1696, Frontenac organized a large force of over 2000 French soldiers along with their Aboriginal allies for a final assault on Iroquois territory. Finding little but deserted villages, the French force burned everything in its path. Fighting continued for five more years until a peace treaty was signed in 1701. That agreement marked a climactic victory for the French in both the war with the Iroquois and the fur trade.

A sculpture of Louis de Baude, Comte de Frontenac, an important governor of New France.

The Story So Far . . .

1 What problems led to the creation of the Royal Government, and how effectively did it solve those problems?

2 What major problem revealed in the 1666 census did Talon seek to solve, and how effective were his reforms?

3 Do you think that Frontenac was an effective governor of New France? Provide supporting evidence for your answer.

SUM IT UP!

People came to New France for different reasons: to become coureurs de bois, to start a new life, to help establish the colony, and to convert the Aboriginal Peoples to Christianity. As colonists began to settle in New France, they faced the arduous task of clearing the land. Thus, farming became the second economic staple of the colony after fur trading.

However, the growth of New France was extremely slow. As a result, in 1663 France took the operation of the colony out of the hands of the fur-trading companies and established a Royal Government. The newly created Sovereign Council would promote growth and development in New France by encouraging greater immigration and creating income from diverse sources. For its final century of existence, the fortunes of New France were controlled directly by France.

THINKING ABOUT YOUR LEARNING

1 Working in groups, create a chart like the one below. Fill in the information in order from the greatest number and type of immigrants first to the least number and type last.

Settlement of New France			
Type of Immigrant	Reason for Immigrating	Positive Contributions to New France	Problems Posed for New France

2 One of the most controversial issues of early New France was the use of brandy in the fur trade. Laval and Talon opposed it while Frontenac favoured it. Divide the class into thirds and conduct a debate on the issue, with one person from each group representing one of the three chief administrators.

3 Missionaries had to cope with a very difficult existence. Explain, in one or two sentences, how each of the following added to that difficulty:
- adjustment to the environment
- lack of support
- rivalry with political administrators
- language barrier
- differences between their beliefs, religions, and customs and those of the Aboriginal Peoples

- their religious and cultural biases
- being caught in the middle of the Huron-Iroquois rivalry.

4 Which types of personalities, characteristics, and traits were needed to be a successful colonist? Do you think you have that type of personality? Why or why not?

APPLYING YOUR LEARNING

1 Imagine you are a struggling seventeenth-century French farmer with a family of seven. You are thinking about emigrating to New France. Compile a *balance sheet* that shows the advantages and disadvantages of leaving Europe. Then, write a summary paragraph about your final decision.

2 Draw a picture showing the early period of adjustment for one of the types of settlers: fisher, coureur de bois, *fille du roi*, farmer, missionary, soldier, craftsperson, or administrator.

3 Write three days of diary entries for any person mentioned in this chapter or select someone more anonymous. As a suggestion, you might write an entry for the arrival period, one for the middle period, and one for toward the end of the person's life in New France.

4 Write a meaningful and catchy headline for all the events listed in the time line at the beginning of the chapter.

USING KEY WORDS

1 Unscramble the following words to discover some of the key words used in the chapter:

a) htstie — taxes collected by the Church

b) ggeean — a worker who signed a three-year work contract

c) taiahbtn — the name the *censitaires* preferred to be called

d) esl lifesl ud oir — unmarried young women sent to increase New France's population

e) eaiimmsrlctn – economic trading system designed to enrich France

Daily Life in New France

National Archives of Canada/C-011225. Québec 1854

1608

Champlain founds Québec

1614

The British burn Port-Royal to prevent French expansion south. No new settlers arrive in Port-Royal until 1623.

1621

The British attempt to establish a Scottish settlement in Acadia

1626

Louis Hébert becomes the first habitant of New France

SETTING OUR FOCUS

Although New France was a relatively small society, there was considerable diversity within it. You will learn about some of the features of life in the colony, such as holidays, entertainment, transportation, diet, and dress. You will appreciate the vital role played by the *seigneurial* system, the family, and the Roman Catholic Church. These were the three foundations of everyday life for the people of New France.

Cornelius Krieghoff was a nineteenth-century artist who painted many rural scenes. In the one on the left, members of a habitant family are involved in various activities on their farm. What tasks can you identify? Who is doing them? What does this tell you about life on a habitant farm?

PREVIEWING THE CHAPTER

In this chapter you will learn about these topics:

- **the lifestyles of the settlers in New France and the factors that created these lifestyles**
- **the features of colony life**
- **the roles played by the *seigneurial* system, the family, and the Roman Catholic Church**
- **the evolution of the colony of Acadia**

KEY WORDS

aboiteau

calèche

carriole

cens

censitaire

corvée

curé

dowry

lods et ventes

maritime

parish

seigneur

seigneurial
  system

1632

The Treaty of St. Germain-en-Laye returns New France and Acadia to France

1634

Jean Juchereau and Robert Giffard become the first *seigneurs* of New France

1654–1670

The British and French switch ownership of Acadia several times

THE SOCIAL FOUNDATION

The *Seigneurial* System

Since the majority of the people in New France were rural (80 percent were farmers and their families), one of the foundations of daily life was the ***seigneurial* system**, a method of land distribution. It was copied from the French feudal system but was adapted to suit conditions in New France. It involved a set of duties for those who owned the land and for those who rented it. The system was important for determining the pattern of development and for providing the basis of the social system of New France. The first individuals to hold the title ***seigneur***, or lord, were Jean Juchereau and Robert Giffard of Percé, Québec, in 1634.

All the land in New France belonged to the King of France. His representatives divided it into lots called *seigneuries*, which varied in size from 12 km² to over 150 km². By 1740 over two hundred *seigneuries*, which were self-contained communities, extended outward from both sides of the St. Lawrence River and its tributaries.

The King granted a tract of land to a *seigneur* on condition that he or she find settlers to occupy and develop it. *Seigneurs*

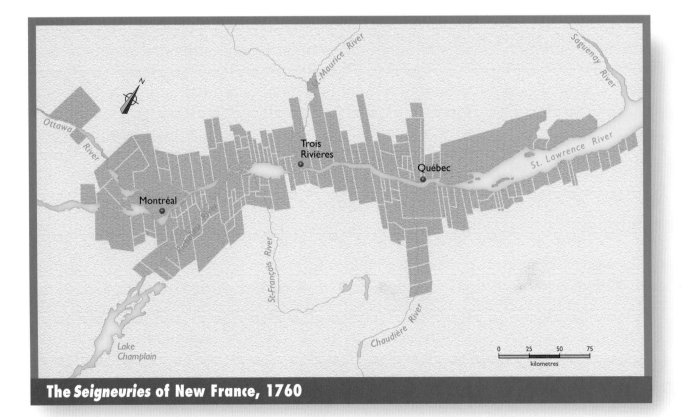

The *Seigneuries* of New France, 1760

were also obligated to build a house, a mill, and a chapel for their habitants. In addition, they were obligated to clear the land, look after defence, and act as judges in disputes. Finally, the *seigneurs* were responsible for maintaining a manor house. They could either reside in it themselves or hire a responsible person to live in it throughout the year.

Seigneurs at first were usually male, and prominent military, political, or religious figures. However, by 1663, over half the *seigneuries* were owned by women. This situation was the result of a number of factors. One was the French system of inheritance. Unlike the British system, in which land, title, and wealth were passed on only to the eldest son, the French system divided an estate equally among all children, including daughters. Thus, many women acquired their *seigneury* through inheritance. Another reason was that many men joined either the military or the fur trade and left their farms for their wives and children to operate. Some women obtained their land due to the death of their husbands. Remember that this was a fairly violent society so many men died as soldiers in battle or while living the lives of coureurs de bois.

National Gallery of Canada, Ottawa
Davies, Thomas
Canadian; British
A View of the Château-Richer, Cape Torment, and Lower End of the Isle of Orleans near Quebec
C.1787 Purchased, 1954

This painting, *A View of the Chateau-Richer,* shows a typical *seigneury.*

The Habitant's Duties

An *engagé*, or hired hand, who wanted to remain in New France after completing a three-year labour requirement for a merchant, relative, farmer, or the Church, usually became a tenant-proprietor of about 60 *arpents* of land. (One *arpent* equals about 3 ha.) Beginning in about the middle of the seventeenth century, the government in France sent over several hundred *engagés* annually. Most of them rented the land from *seigneurs* and became known as **censitaires** because one of the taxes they had to pay was called a **cens**. The *cens* was a small annual cash payment. The *rentes* was a similar payment. The two taxes combined were less than one-tenth of the habitant's annual income.

Lods et ventes were like today's inheritance taxes. A habitant's land was not taxed if it were directly given to surviving children. However, when the person disposed of the land either as a gift or by sale, it was subject to *lods et ventes*. This tax was normally one-twelfth of the price of the land.

The *censitaire*, or habitant, as he or she preferred to be called, first had to clear the land of trees and rocks and build a house. There were also other duties. The habitant had to pay the *seigneur* a share of the crops. There was also a work duty, called a ***corvée***. Three days a year, usually during planting and harvesting, the habitant had to work the *seigneur's* land. In addition, the habitant was obliged to work one or two days a year for the government, or the Crown. The work often involved clearing and repairing local roads. The habitant was obliged to use only the *seigneur's* mill for grinding wheat into flour. Whenever it was used, the habitant had to pay with one-fourteenth of the flour. The habitant also had to hand over a portion of the fish caught and wood cut down within the borders of the *seigneury*.

Finally, after churches were built, the habitant had to pay a tithe to support the priest and church. Initially, the tithe was one-thirteenth of the crop. However, because this was deemed excessive, at the turn of the seventeenth century it was reduced to one twenty-sixth of the crop. Normally, if the habitants met all these obligations, they became the virtual owners of the land and could pass it on to their heirs.

This drawing by C.W. Jefferys shows a habitant paying his taxes to his *seigneur*. Habitants paid the taxes in either money or produce. From the facial expressions, what do you think is going through the mind of the habitant and of the *seigneur*?

Louis Hébert

A MAN OF MANY FIRSTS

Louis Hébert was born in Paris, France, around 1575, to apothecary (or druggist) Nicholas Hébert and his wife. Louis had a dream of owning land and becoming self-sufficient. His interest in cultivating the soil and his relation to Jean de Biencourt de Poutrincourt on his mother's side enabled Hébert to accompany Samuel de Champlain on both his voyages, in 1606 and 1610, to New France. At Port-Royal in 1610, he acted as apothecary and tended both the French and the Aboriginal Peoples. In November 1614 Hébert was forced to return to France when Port-Royal was destroyed by American pirates.

In the winter of 1616–1617, Champlain encouraged Hébert to return to the colony at Québec by offering him a contract from a fur-trading company in control of the St. Lawrence region. With a promise of 200 crowns a year for his services as an apothecary, plus food and shelter for his family while their land was cleared, Hébert sold his house in Paris. He and his wife Marie Rollet and their three children, Anne, Guillemette, and Guillaume, were ready to embark at Honfleur when he discovered that the company did not intend to honour its agreement with him. He was forced to strike a new contract for half the pay, half the land, and one extra condition: his family and servant were to be in the company's service without pay. Having no choice, he accepted the offer and the family set sail on March 11, 1617.

In Québec, Hébert managed to minister to the sick as well as clear some land and plant it. When Champlain visited him in 1618, his fields were "filled with fine grain" and his gardens were brimming with a variety of vegetables. However, the restrictions the fur-trading company placed on the distribution of Hébert's produce prevented him from enjoying his success.

In 1620 Champlain relieved Hébert's discontent by appointing him the first King's attorney, giving him the power to administer justice in the colony.

In February 1623 Hébert received title to his land, the estate called Sault-au-Matelot. In 1626 he acquired the estate de Lespinay. These lands enabled Hébert to achieve his lifelong dream. He became the first habitant. Besides the grain fields and vegetable gardens the Héberts started with, they also had an apple orchard and a pasture dotted with cattle. They accomplished all of this using hand tools, and despite the fur-trading company's opposition!

In the winter of 1626, Louis Hébert had a bad fall on the ice, eventually leading to his death on January 25, 1627. His body was the first to lay in a vault of the newly erected Recollet Chapel in Québec.

More people you could research are

Marguerite Couillard

Jean de Biencourt de Poutrincourt

Robert Giffard

Louis Hébert

Jean Juchereau

Jean Nicollet

The Habitant's Life

The habitant's battle in life was, in many ways, as important as that of the soldiers and leaders of New France. The habitants played an essential role in creating a permanent, settled population along the St. Lawrence River. But it was not an easy life. As one historian noted:

At his death, thirty years after he received his concession, he possesses thirty arpents of arable land, a bit of meadow, a barn, a stable, a slightly more spacious house, a road by the door, neighbours, and a pew in the church. His life was passed in clearing and building.

The habitants had to clear the land, build a homestead, and plant and harvest a crop. The first task was never-ending, while the last one was annual. Building and repairing the house and barn were continual tasks. So were cutting and hauling firewood. The habitants had to be largely self-reliant in looking after all routine tasks such as cooking, baking, making furniture, and repairing tools. They had to attend to the educational and medical needs of the family. They had to endure the harsh physical climate and rough terrain, largely unaided by government support. The habitants had to pay taxes to the *seigneurs* and the Church. On top of all this, the threat of an Aboriginal raid was never far away.

The Land Pattern

Because the habitants divided their land among their children, over time a series of long, narrow lots running in neat rows were developed so that everyone would have frontage on the river. Access to water was important for both transportation and irrigation. Later that pattern would allow everyone to have access to roads built farther back in the *seigneury*. However, it made for an inefficient agricultural system, as lots became further and further subdivided and narrower and narrower with each passing generation. The habitants' lots were rectangular and normally had a ratio of width to length of about one to ten.

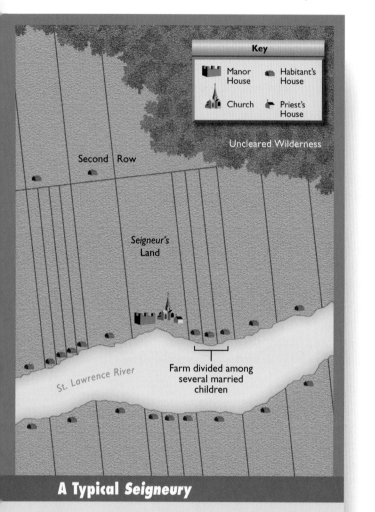

A Typical *Seigneury*

1 This is a map of the seigneuries in New France in 1760. Note the thin, rectangular plots of land arranged in rows farther and farther away from the river. Why do you think some of the rectangles are thinner than others?

Was the System Fair?

The *seigneurial* system provided a fair distribution of the land in New France. If it seems overly harsh for the habitant, remember that it was a vast improvement on the European feudal system in a number of ways. First, although many *seigneurs* were prominent members of society, they did not amass the kind of fortune that the European lords and nobles did. There was not the social gap between *seigneurs* and habitants as there was between lords and serfs in Europe. Second, the habitants could always augment their income by cutting down trees or trapping furs. Third, whenever the *seigneur* tried to enforce "bonus" taxes, the authorities would prevent it. Fourth, there were fewer annual taxes for the habitants than there were for their European counterparts. Finally, if life ever became too hard, there was always the lure of the frontier. The habitant could leave family and farm behind and become a coureur de bois, which as much as ten percent of the population did.

In this painting, a habitant is hauling lumber, possibly to sell for extra money.

The Story So Far . . .

1 Why was the habitant of New France better off than the serf of Europe?
2 The *seigneurial* system and the French inheritance system combined to make for an inefficient agricultural system. Give reasons that was the case.
3 If you were living in New France at this time, would you prefer to have been a *seigneur* or a habitant? Provide reasons to support your choice.
4 By 1663, over half of the *seigneuries* were held by women. Identify two ways women could acquire their *seigneuries*.

FAMILY LIFE IN NEW FRANCE

Another pillar of daily life in New France was the family. It was a closed, self-supporting group, particularly because children usually remained with the family until they married. This was different from the custom in France. The French, at that time, did not believe in the period of carefree innocence known as childhood. Rather, children at that time were seen as young adults. They were expected to do their chores unquestioningly and to contribute to the household. Often children were apprenticed at a young age and had to leave the family home.

It was quite common in New France to have large families.

In eighteenth-century New France, almost 250 of 1000 children died in infancy. In other words, one out of every four babies died before reaching his or her first birthday. Today in Canada less than 20 of 1000 die during infancy.

One household could include parents, children, grandparents, and even aunts, uncles, cousins, nieces, and nephews. Over 16 percent of eighteenth-century families had between 10 and 14 children. Almost 3 percent had more than 15 children. The habitants needed extra hands for the endless tasks on the farm. Many hands lightened the load, especially when the father was absent while on a hunting trip, or if he decided to become a fur trader, or join the military.

Increasing the Population

Priests of the Roman Catholic Church encouraged habitant families to have many children. The Church subscribed to the Biblical teaching of "go forth and multiply." More children meant more followers of the Roman Catholic religion. A childless marriage was deemed to be the work of evil spirits and the Church was known to dissolve such a marriage.

In addition, intendants such as Jean Talon, who were government officials who ran the colony, further encouraged large families by rewarding those with more than ten children and those who had children who married at a young age. Legally, a girl could marry at the age of twelve. The explorer, Jean Nicollet, caused a sensation in 1637 when he married eleven-year-old Marguerite Couillard, who was Champlain's goddaughter.

Finally, because there was no such thing as pensions, as we have today, people had many children to provide them with some security of being cared for in their old age.

For more than the next two centuries, New France (Québec, after 1759) would win the so-called "battle of the cradle" by having one of the highest birth rates in the world. People who study population patterns estimate that New France's birth rate was between 55 and 65 births annually per 1000 people. By comparison, the birth rate in Canada today is about 15 births annually per 1000 people. The following table presents the population growth of New France.

This painting shows the inside of a settler's home in New France. What could you say about the family from the details in the picture?

Population of New France, 1608–1765

Year	Number of People*
1608	28
1641	240
1653	2 000
1667	3 918
1668	6 282
1680	9 677
1685	10 725
1692	12 431
1698	15 355
1707	17 204
1720	24 438
1734	37 716
1754	55 009
1760	70 000
1765	69 810

1 Graph the information from the table.

2 What reasons would account for the slow growth at the beginning?

3 What factors caused the large population increase between 1653 and 1685?

4 What was the only period of population decline in New France? Can you suggest why the population decreased at this time?

* These figures do not include the Aboriginal population.

Family Roles

Families in New France were self-sufficient in the same way that farms were — each provided almost everything that was required. The farm provided food, opportunity, and employment. The family provided guidance, skills, income, and a sense of belonging. Relatives helped one another to obtain jobs and promotions.

Most of what transpired within the family farmhouse — cooking, serving, preserving, tending the sick, and cleaning — was the mother's responsibility. Also, she would instruct her daughters in those essential domestic skills. Daughters were expected to care for younger siblings. However, this traditional view of the role of women on the *seigneury* does not do justice to their true contribution. Besides attending to what is viewed as the "domestic" side of their role, women did much more. Current historians have pointed out that many women worked in the fields side by side with their husbands and sons. In

A habitant family gathers around the stove to while away the winter months. What is the mother doing? How are the children being entertained?

addition, women often looked after the business side of the *seigneury* by keeping the financial books and records and being responsible for purchases and sales.

In New France, a far greater proportion of women were literate compared with men. Thus, the mother often taught her children and her husband to read. The father taught his sons how and where to plant, how to look after tools, animal husbandry, hunting and fishing, and how to make furniture.

Children were expected to do exactly what their parents told them. They rarely would question, complain, or disobey them. Disregarding one's father was punishable by law in New France. For example, French law dictated that a son had to receive his father's approval of whom and when he wanted to marry. If the father objected to his choice, the son drew up three *respectful applications* at a lawyer's office at intervals of a few weeks. Following is the letter of 30-year-old Jean-Claude Louet to his father, written in January 1733. The tone conveys children's place in society at that time.

> *My Very Dear Father,*
>
> *I am in the throes of misery at finding myself deprived of the kindness that I was used to receiving from you. I am extremely pained that your tender impulses which have moved me so often and so deeply are entirely extinct. However, dear Father, if I withdraw the obedience and submission that I owe you it is out of an indispensable obligation to restore the reputation of the one whom I have lost, without which there is no salvation for me.*
>
> *Finally, dear father, I entreat you in your paternal love, and by all that is dearest to you of your own blood, to let yourself be touched and persuaded by the pitiable fate of the poor girl and the lamentable state to which I have been reduced for so long. You have spoken; I have obeyed. You have sent me away to a place where I have nothing but tears and sighs to console me and keep me company.*
>
> *I believe, however, that today you will be moved by my woes and grant me the favour I am asking you.*
>
> *From he who is,*
> *My Dear Father,*
> *your humble and most submissive son,*
> *C. Louet*

From a very young age, children would assume responsibility for a number of daily chores, such as fetching water, milking the cows, collecting eggs, churning cream into butter, cutting kindling and firewood, cleaning and washing dishes and clothing, and helping to clear the land by picking up stones.

Daily and Seasonal Cycles

Usually families went to bed early, right after the evening meal. Families crowded into their small, two-room farmhouse. A wooden ladder led to one large room upstairs, where more than a dozen children might sleep. Heated only by a single fireplace, the children could huddle together in bed to keep one another warm.

This is a typical habitant's home built on Ile d'Orléans, New France, around 1825–1850.

Just as the daily schedule was dictated by nature, the habitants' work was related to seasonal cycles. After the habitants completed the initial task of constructing the family home and clearing the first tracts of land, they erected other buildings, such as a barn, shed, and a stable and dairy barn if the family became prosperous enough.

Habitants spent the wintertime cleaning and repairing tools and tending the animals. In spring they planted crops, took animals to pasture, and fixed fences. They ploughed the land with a team of oxen, then seeded it. They also cultivated a vegetable garden. In summer the entire family worked in the fields from sunrise until sunset. In late summer, they harvested grain crops and took them to the *seigneur's* mill for grinding. In the autumn, they put up preserves, chopped and stacked firewood, brought in animals, butchered and salted the meat, which they put into barrels, and prepared the soil for next season's crop. Their lives, both in the short run of days and in the long run of years, had a very natural rhythm.

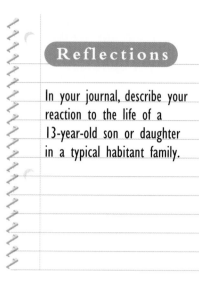

Responsibilities

When parents became too old to take care of the farm, the eldest son or sometimes the daughter assumed responsibility for it as well as for taking care of the parents. The cycle was repeated for generations. Although both husband and wife played very important roles, in the final analysis, the family of New France was very much a patriarchal institution. The father's word was final, whether in giving a daughter's hand in marriage, managing the finances, or allowing a son to venture into the nearest town.

Families in New France were vital for another reason. Through hard work and careful saving, the family collected a **dowry** for each daughter. A dowry was an essential gift in money, goods, or produce given to a prospective bridegroom from the family of the girl he was about to marry. This was a mammoth undertaking, since there might be more than six daughters in the family. The necessity of a dowry also caused women to marry later than they might have wanted. Even though some married in their early years, by 1700 the average age of marriage for women in New France was 21. Without a dowry, a girl's prospects of marriage were very doubtful.

Essentially, success for the typical habitant was based on bringing more land under cultivation and marrying off their daughters. If a son or a daughter married up the social ladder, it was the height of success for the family.

Snapshot

A Two-Way Street
Though a bride was expected to bring a dowry to a marriage, it often worked both ways. The groom had to show that he, too, would make a good partner. In fact, the families of the two often tried to match offers. Furthermore, if the bride were coming from France, the groom was expected to provide more. Why else would parents permit their daughter to leave the comfort of French society for a hard life in a remote colony?

This is exactly what happened when Françoise-Marie Jacquelin of Paris agreed to marry Charles de Saint-Étienne de La Tour of Acadia in 1640. La Tour had sent an agent to France to ask Jacquelin to join him at his trading post. The marriage contract was all in Jacquelin's favour. No dowry was required, though her parents agreed to supply her clothes and linens. La Tour, on the other hand, offered cash so Jacquelin could buy rings, jewels, and other things before she left France. He promised a generous inheritance if he died. He also agreed to provide her with three servants and to follow a Paris custom that entitled a wife to a half-share of everything acquired during a marriage. Jacquelin followed another French custom of the time: she did not take her husband's last name.

Marie-Marguerite d'Youville
A SAINTED SISTER

Everyone who was anyone in New France attended the wedding in 1722 of Marie-Marguerite Dufrost de Lajemmerais and François-Madeleine d'Youville. The 20-year-old bride belonged to one of the great families of the colony, and the groom was also from a wealthy background.

Unfortunately, the marriage did not live up to everyone's expectations. Cruel and selfish, François spent money like water. To get more money, he started illegally trading furs and liquor with Aboriginal Peoples. His bad reputation grew even worse. This was hard for his young wife to bear. Even harder to bear, though, were the deaths of three of their five children. Still, when François fell ill, D'Youville nursed him devotedly until he died in 1730. Soon after her husband's death, she gave birth to a sixth child. Tragically, this child also died.

Saddled with her husband's huge debt and desperate for money, the 28-year-old widow opened a store in her Montréal house. Times were tough, but D'Youville refused to pity herself. Instead, she focused on helping others who were down on their luck. As she comforted the poor and sick, she gradually realized that she had found her calling. She and three other like-minded women took a pledge to devote their lives to helping others.

D'Youville's relatives were scandalized. They believed that it was improper for a woman from a good family to associate with the poor. Even worse, people jeered at the women as they carried out their work. Despite everything, the women kept their pledge.

Gradually their good works began to win people over. Other women joined the group, and D'Youville was appointed director of Montréal's *Hôpital Général*. There, she and her helpers sheltered the poor and cared for the sick. Finally, the French King and the Roman Catholic Church officially recognized the work of these remarkable women. They allowed the women to create a new religious community called the Sisters of Charity of the *Hôpital Général*.

D'Youville chose a grey fabric for the nuns' habits. From then on, the sisters were known as the Grey Nuns.

Though D'Youville died in 1771, the memory of her good works lives on in the religious community she founded. In 1959 she became the first Canadian-born person named as a candidate for sainthood in the Roman Catholic Church. In 1990 she was declared Saint Marguerite d'Youville.

More people you could research are

William Alexander

Samuel Argall

François-Madeleine d'Youville

Marie-Marguerite d'Youville

Cornelius Krieghoff

The Mi'kmaq

The Evidence Behind the Story

Following are three contemporary descriptions of the French Canadian habitant.

French army officer, 1757:
They are not thrifty and take no care for the future, being too fond of their freedom and their independence. They want to be well thought of and they know how to make the most of themselves. They endure hunger and thirst patiently, many of them having been trained from infancy to imitate the [Aboriginal Peoples], whom, with reason, they hold in high regard. They strive to gain their esteem and to please them. Many of them speak their language, having passed part of their life among them at the trading posts.

Intendant Gilles Hocquart:
The Canadians are husky, well built, and vigorous. The country people handle the axe very skilfully. They make themselves most of the tools and utensils needed for farming and build their own houses and barns. They love honours and praise, and pride themselves on their courage.

Colonel Bougainville:
The ordinary habitants would be insulted to be called peasants. In fact, they are of a better stuff, have more wit, more education, than those of France. This comes from their paying no taxes, that they have the right to hunt and fish, and that they live in a sort of independence.

QUESTIONING THE EVIDENCE

1. Using a dictionary, define any of the words from these quotations that you are uncertain about, such as *thrifty, vigorous, peasant, wit*.
2. What similarities can you detect from all three observers? Are there some differences among them? If so, what are they? Suggest reasons for the differences.
3. What skills did the habitants possess according to these commentators? Can you suggest reasons the habitants were better off than the serfs in France were?

The Story So Far . . .

1. Whose life do you think was harder in the days of New France: a girl's or boy's? Give reasons to support your choice.
2. Compare your chores to those of a typical 13-year-old girl or boy in New France.
3. Suggest factors that would account for the daily cycle of getting up at sunrise and going to bed at sunset.

THE HABITANT DIET

Food

You might consider the diet of the people of New France fairly plain and simple. Their concerns were not nutrition, cost, nor variety. Rather, because people worked at physically demanding jobs for long hours, they needed food that would give them a great deal of energy. The farmers produced enough food for their own families' needs. By the turn of the eighteenth century, they grew enough to sell to the townspeople.

The most important part of the habitants' diet was bread. The average person ate about 1 kg of bread a day, which is roughly equal to two full-size loaves today. They produced the bread from the grain they grew. After milling the grain into flour, the habitants baked the kneaded dough in the ovens located in their farmyards, usually once or twice a week. They brought out large, round, crisp loaves, left them to cool, and then eagerly devoured them.

The habitants kept cows for their milk, which they made into butter and cheese, and chickens for their eggs. They obtained other sources of protein from the cattle and pigs that they raised, as well as from animals such as rabbits and deer that they hunted. Because of religious rules requiring meat-free days, fish was another important part of their diet. The most popular vegetables grown in the family plot were peas and fèves, or large beans. Hearty soups were a fairly regular feature of evening meals. While the wealthy drank tea and coffee obtained from traders, the average person drank the more plentiful milk and cider.

This drawing shows a habitant mother and daughter baking bread in an outdoor oven. Why do you think the oven is located outdoors?

Meal Times

Typically, most habitants continued the European tradition of eating four meals a day. Rising at or before dawn, the family attended to lighter household chores, which were followed by a filling breakfast of pancakes, bread, and milk.

The noon lunch and an afternoon snack at around four o'clock were usually carried out to the field so family members would not have to walk to the house and back again. Both meals usually consisted of bread, cheese, and cold meats, with lunch being the more substantial meal.

Interestingly enough, the habitant rarely, if ever, ate potatoes. The habitants regarded them as scarcely fit for animals. This was strange because at that time in Europe, the potato was becoming popular. It could be grown in almost any kind of soil and it produced the highest caloric yield per hectare. These two advantages allowed the potato to become a food staple in the coming Industrial Revolution.

The habitant family ate the main meal around eight o'clock in the evening after the day's work had been done. It normally included soup, meat or fish, and a vegetable, which they washed down with milk, cider, or homemade beer. The supper normally ended with some kind of sweet, such as maple syrup pie, fruit pie, sugared fruit with cream, or something as simple as bread soaked with syrup and cream.

Although families of New France had very few of the food choices we have today, they added variety to their diets in a number of ways. Most habitants kept a small vegetable garden close to their house. They picked berries and, later, fruit from the trees they planted. Maple syrup was a special springtime treat.

On festive occasions, such as Christmas, Easter, weddings, and birthdays, the families ate more sumptuous meals, including ham, goose, duck, or even bear, moose, or porcupine. Salted eels and beaver tails were two favourite delicacies in New France.

Although the habitants' diet was plain, it served their purposes. It had enough variety to make it interesting, and was hearty enough to provide for their needs.

Snapshot

Habitant Pea Soup

A typical habitant dish was pea soup. Below is the recipe.

> 500 g dried green peas
> 1 large onion, chopped
> 1 carrot, grated
> 500–1000 g salt pork
> 1 bay leaf
> sea salt
> 4 L water

1. Wash peas.
2. Soak overnight.
3. Add 4 L water.
4. Mix in onion and salt pork.
5. Bring to a boil.
6. Simmer for 2–3 hours until peas are tender.
7. Remove pork after 1–2 hours.
8. Crush peas against side of pot.
9. Add salt to taste.

Serve with bread, pickles, and cheese.

The Story So Far . . .

1 What were the reasons for the types of food the habitants ate?

2 Why did the habitants eat four meals a day?

3 Whose diet, that of the typical habitant or your own, is healthier? Suggest reasons to support your view.

SELF-SUFFICIENCY ON THE FARM

The habitant was very much on his or her own. There was no corner store for food, no repair person to fix broken machines or tools, no government to provide services such as road building and maintenance, firefighting, or policing. These sturdy settlers tried to provide for themselves and their families in an often harsh environment. They learned to become self-reliant.

Clothing

The women and girls in the family made almost all of the clothing. They spun yarn and wove cloth. They sewed, knitted, and darned. The clothes had to be practical and durable. If the family were fortunate, every member had two sets of clothing, one for everyday and one for special occasions.

The majority of habitants had a fondness for quite fancy and colourful clothing. As one person from that time observed about the typical French Canadian habitant, "He cuts down on food in order to be well dressed." The ladies fashioned their clothing out of brightly coloured cloth and adorned the finished product with ruffles. Because they lived in a country with long, bitterly cold winters, women wore a *pelisse*, a fur-lined coat. They also wore homemade beaver-lined mittens and moosehide boots.

A habitant woman at her spinning wheel. How would you describe the dress she is wearing? Identify five items in the room and what they may have been used for.

Household Items

Women also crafted useful household items such as rugs, curtains, blankets, and towels. They made additional household articles, such as candles, soap, and paint, that could not be obtained elsewhere.

The family crafted almost all the household furniture — tables, chairs, desks, bed frames, and armoires — usually out of pine, maple, or oak. The habitants are considered to have been master furniture makers and their custom-crafted pieces fetch the highest prices at auctions today.

This photograph shows hand-dipped candles drying on a rack. In the fall when the farm animals were butchered and there was a large supply of animal tallow or fat on hand, women in New France made candles. The women prepared numerous candle rods, each holding six cotton wicks that were tied and suspended from the rod. Each set of wicks was dipped smoothly into a pot of hot, melted tallow, then set on a rack to dry. The rack was made by laying two long poles over the backs of chairs or benches. This process was repeated until tapered candles formed.

Snippet

Playing Cards

Besides their use in games, playing cards were Canada's first home-grown money. The custom started in 1685, when a ship carrying the soldiers' pay was late arriving from France. The intendant gave the troops playing cards instead. On the back of the cards, he wrote a value and signed his name. For more than 50 years after this, cards were used whenever there was a shortage of coins or paper currency.

Recreation

At first the habitants had little leisure time, since they spent much of their days working. What recreational pastimes they did have were dictated by the amount of light in the evenings, finances, and their own inventiveness.

It was fortunate for the habitants that the *seigneurial* system produced a group of farms located fairly close together, especially compared with other North American settlements. This was important in the colony's early days because roads were few in number, were of poor quality, and travel to visit friends or family was limited. However, the habitants looked forward to the winter, when there were no crops to tend and when sleighs made the trip to a neighbour's home quick and easy.

After 1663, when the population expanded and New France became more settled, the habitants proved to be a very social and festive people. They had so many celebration days that the authorities began to complain that not enough work was being done! Aside from religious holidays, there were a variety of communal events that allowed neighbours to get together: barn raising, harvesting, flax beating, corn husking, weddings, and *sugaring off* (making maple syrup).

One of the biggest annual celebrations took place on November 11, when all the habitants gathered at the *seigneur's* manor to pay their rent, settle their accounts, and mark the end of the harvest. There was music, dancing, and storytelling. Six months later, on May Day, a colourful maypole dressed with streamers was put on the *seigneur's* lawn to welcome the coming of spring.

The habitants invented simple games, or if they were lucky enough to have a few books, they read and reread them. When candles became more widely used, evening entertainment and family get-togethers became more common. Older family members would delight their audiences by recounting fabulous tales from the past.

Parlour games, such as *galet*, tric-trac (a forerunner of backgammon), and checkers later became popular. Card games were by far the most popular form of family amusement. Evening gatherings, called *veillées*, would consist of parlour games as well as singing and dancing, though the Church frowned on the latter activity.

Outdoor activities were almost as popular. In winter, the habitants skated, tobogganed, or went for sleigh rides. In summer they hunted, fished, and canoed. These were a hardy, industrious people who could be highly self-sufficient and highly social as the occasion demanded.

The Story So Far . . .

1 Discuss why habitants had to be as self-sufficient as possible.
2 Sometimes people speak or write of "the good old days." Do you think the early days of New France represented "good old days" for most of the families? Why?
3 What "old-time values" did the habitants display?
4 What occasions brought the habitants together for celebrations? What did these occasions have in common?

THE CHURCH IN DAILY LIFE

Another pillar of New France was the Roman Catholic Church. Remember that virtually all the settlers in New France were Roman Catholics so the religion dictated the people's spiritual lives. The religion supported and guided them at all the important stages of their lives: baptism, confirmation, marriage, and death. The priests performed important rituals such as confession, mass, prayer, and thanksgiving, and held ceremonies to mark significant holidays, such as Christmas, Easter, and Lent.

New France was organized into religious areas called **parishes**. There were about 100 of them by 1760. The church the habitants built in each district became the heart of their religious life. They, in turn, supported it through their tithes. Parish priests were rare in the beginning; smaller communities might see one only every few months. However, as New France grew, more and more parish churches sprang up, each with its own priest. The parish priest, or *curé*, became the centre of community life.

In many ways, the Church was the heart of French Canadian culture. It provided a strong sense of morality and values. The people were expected to be obedient and to follow the Church's instructions. The Roman Catholic Church instilled a sense of right and wrong in the colonists, both in terms of "big issues," such as the use of brandy in the fur trade, and in day-to-day actions.

Not only did the Church provide spiritual and moral guidance, it also offered a great deal more: It founded and ran many schools. It provided a place for celebrations and festivities. It served as a patron of the arts by employing dozens of artists and musicians. It established and maintained hospitals within the colony. It was a charitable agency for those in need, especially the newly arrived.

As a major landowner, the Roman Catholic Church exerted considerable economic influence. For example, the Sulpician Fathers owned all of Montréal as a *seigneury*. About two-thirds of all the land in New France was controlled by the Roman Catholic Church and tithes further enriched it.

Through the work of people such as Bishop Laval, the Church had significant political impact as well. His dream was that the Roman Catholic Church would define both the present and future reality of life there. He contributed largely to the organization of a parish system.

A hand-crafted chalice and paten made by a French-Canadian artisan.

A major goal of Roman Catholic missionaries was to convert the Aboriginal Peoples. They were also engaged in a fierce struggle against the Protestants to win over more followers to their religion.

The Story So Far . . .

1. List the sources of the Roman Catholic Church's power in New France.
2. In both villages and towns, visitors would immediately know that the Church was the centre of the social life in the community. Why?
3. Describe what you think was the most important role of the Church. Justify your choice.

TRANSPORTATION IN NEW FRANCE

The Water Highway

Transportation and security had been forefront in the mind of Samuel de Champlain when he originally chose Québec City as the site of the new colony. Its location high above the sheer cliffs where the St. Lawrence River narrows gave the site immense defence advantages. The river quickly became a natural "water highway" as well as a vital supply of water for irrigation, washing, and drinking.

The situation and the pattern of development for the *seigneuries* of New France again confirmed the importance of transportation. All lots fronted the St. Lawrence River or one of its tributaries. The St. Lawrence River was, in fact, the water highway that linked the settlers clustered in the *seigneuries* around Québec City and Montréal. It also connected them to the colonists in Acadia (present-day Nova Scotia) and with Europe. In many ways, the St. Lawrence River was the very lifeline of New France.

The Aboriginal Peoples taught the settlers how to get around. They instructed the French Canadians how to paddle a canoe and how to use snowshoes in the deep snow.

Birchbark canoes became the favoured method of transportation throughout the spring, summer, and fall. They conveyed heavy loads in a *cajeu*, a raft-like structure that had both oars and sails. A *cajeu* might be as large as 20 m by 15 m. The habitants used them to carry farm equipment, furniture, building materials, or grain. Because a *cajeu* was far too heavy and cumbersome to be portaged around rocks or rapids, it was simply left behind and whoever came along in the opposite direction could use it.

Even in winter, the French Canadians still used the St. Lawrence River for transportation. Being able to travel on it was important because it would sometimes freeze over for up to five months a year. **Carrioles**, or sleighs with runners, were pulled by horses for the wealthy or by dog teams for the poor. Because the sleighs had no covering, travellers had to be bundled beneath several layers of blankets and furs. They placed heated rocks on the floor of the sleigh to heat their feet.

The wealthy townspeople of New France preferred the **calèche** as a means of conveyance. It was a light, two-wheeled carriage with large wheels. The wheels allowed both for speed on smooth surfaces and for pulling power through the mud.

Both rich and poor travelled in *carrioles* during winter.

National Gallery of Canada, Ottawa
Todd, Robert C., Canadian
The Ice Cone, Montmorency Falls   c.1850
Purchased, 1957

M13712 Isaac Weld, Canadian Calsh or Marche-Donc.
McCord Museum of Canadian History, Montreal

The First Roads

Roads came late to New France, partly because the natural waterways served the French Canadians so well and partly because of the backbreaking labour that went into even the most primitive road's construction. However, by the turn of the eighteenth century, French Canadians began building roads toward the back of the long, narrow *seigneuries*. This allowed the habitants to get to their neighbours or to the nearest town more quickly. Much of the time these roads were impassable because of the mud or ice. The French Canadians did not complete a full road connecting Québec City and Montréal until 1734.

The Story So Far . . .

1 Explain how geography determined the methods of transportation in New France.
2 What did the colonists learn from the Aboriginal Peoples that helped them get around?

Calèches carried the wealthy to destinations around town.

Snippet

The First Speed Limit

Intendant Michel Bégon introduced Canada's first speed limit on April 29, 1716. This notice was posted on the door of every church in New France:

We forbid all persons, drivers of carrioles as well as those on horseback, to allow trotting or galloping while the congregation leaves the church, until they are 10 arpents [58 m] from the church; afterwards they may give their horses their heads provided there is no one ahead of them on the road.

Françoise-Marie Jacquelin
HEROINE OF ACADIA

Françoise-Marie Jacquelin was a prisoner. Her hands were tied. A heavy rope cut into her neck. Charles de Menou d'Aulnay, the sworn enemy of her husband, Charles de Saint-Étienne de La Tour, was making her watch as the loyal friends who had fought at her side were hanged one by one. Their crime? They had battled too fiercely in defending Fort La Tour. When Jacquelin finally surrendered, D'Aulnay had promised to show mercy. Then he went back on his word. He decided that the fort's defenders must pay for their gallantry with their lives.

The brutal mass hanging on that cold April day in 1645 marked the end of a deadly struggle for control of Acadia. It had all started innocently. Ten years earlier, La Tour had commanded Fort La Tour, a small trading post at the mouth of the St. John River in present-day New Brunswick. D'Aulnay had been in charge of a settlement at La Hève on the Atlantic Coast of present-day Nova Scotia. D'Aulnay was greedy, though. He wanted total control. First, he moved his settlement to Port-Royal. Then he started lobbying his contacts at the court of the French King. His goal was to be appointed governor of the entire colony.

La Tour used contacts at court to try to maintain his command. Unfortunately, the political feud turned violent. People were killed in clashes between followers of the two men. With D'Aulnay gaining the upper hand and threatening to take his fort by force, La Tour sailed to Boston in the British colony of Massachusetts. His plan was to drum up support for his cause. While he was gone, Jacquelin was in command of the fort.

D'Aulnay saw this as the perfect chance to destroy Fort La Tour. With a force of about 200 men, he sailed up the Bay of Fundy and demanded Jacquelin's surrender. Though badly outnumbered, Jacquelin and the 45 defenders fired their cannons and ran up a red flag, a signal that they would not give up.

Furious, D'Aulnay ordered a bombardment. Then, his men stormed the walls. Jacquelin valiantly led the few remaining defenders in hand-to-hand combat. She surrendered only when D'Aulnay promised mercy. In the end, D'Aulnay spared Jacquelin's life. When she was caught trying to smuggle a message to her husband in Boston, she was locked up in a small room, where she fell ill and died.

Five years later, La Tour got his revenge. When D'Aulnay drowned in the bay at Port-Royal, La Tour was appointed governor of the colony. In a strange twist, he ended up marrying D'Aulnay's widow. It was the name of his first wife, though, that will be remembered as the heroine of Acadia.

More people you could research are

Jean de Biencourt

Nicolas Denys

Isaac de Razilly

Charles de Saint-Étienne de La Tour

Pierre du Gua de Monts

Françoise-Marie Jacquelin

LIFE IN ACADIA

A Troubled History

There was another part of the French Empire in North America that is sometimes overlooked. *Acadia* was used to designate the eastern part of the French Empire, as opposed to the valley of the St. Lawrence, which was called *Canada*. For the sake of convenience, think of Acadia as comprising the present-day provinces of New Brunswick, Nova Scotia, and Prince Edward Island.

New France originated in Acadia at the beginning of the seventeenth century when Pierre du Gua de Monts and Samuel de Champlain spent three years exploring the area. They established the colonies of Ile Sainte-Croix and later Port-Royal. In 1604 and in 1611 French nobleman Jean de Biencourt, Sieur de Poutrincourt tried to establish a permanent settlement. However, he failed after the pirate Samuel Argall launched an attack from Jamestown, Virginia, in 1613 and chased away the colonists of Port-Royal. French investors in De Biencourt's settlement were ruined and French interest in the area disappeared until the 1630s. However, in 1621 the British government changed Acadia's name to Nova Scotia and moved in the Scottish settlers of Sir William Alexander.

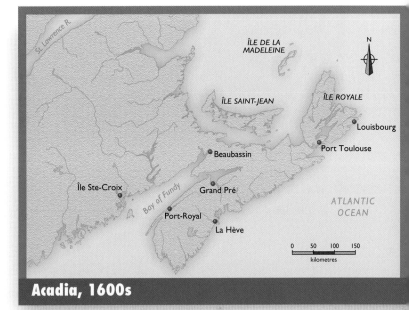

Acadia, 1600s

In 1632 the Treaty of Saint-Germain-en-Laye returned Acadia to France, ending Alexander's attempt at Scottish expansion. Isaac de Razilly was appointed governor and he began the next attempt at colonization. First he moved the capital from Port-Royal to La Hève, in present-day Nova Scotia. Most of the new settlers immigrated from the French port of La Rochelle, so they were used to the environment they encountered.

Several hundred colonists attempted to clear the land, drain the marshes, and harvest salt from the low-lying areas. They built dikes to reclaim fertile marshland that the powerful tides of the Bay of Fundy flooded twice a day. They developed an ingenious device called an ***aboiteau***, which acted as a hinged valve. It permitted fresh water to run off the marshes at low tide but

prevented salt water from flowing onto the diked farmland at high tide.

In 1635 Governor de Razilly died. Confusion and chaos followed. Three men, Charles de Saint-Étienne de La Tour, Charles de Menou d'Aulnay, and Nicolas Denys struggled for control of Acadia.

Acadians built dikes and drained marshes to create fertile farmland.

From 1654, Acadia became a pawn in the French-British colonial rivalry. It would be raided and looted several times, and peace treaties would switch its ownership from one side to the other.

The British finally captured and held Acadia until 1670. Under the British for the first time, most Acadians attempted to find a path of reconciliation. Some learned to speak English. But the tension between the victorious British and the defeated French was evident and the pattern for uneasy relations was set for the next century.

Population

In half a century, the population of Acadia had increased from a few hundred to several thousand. A tightly knit community was developed in part because intermarriage was allowed. Also, the absence of war, famine, and epidemics led to rapid population growth. Families usually consisted of 10 to 12 children. Rather remarkably, 75 percent of the population reached the age of 21. (In France, less than 50 percent of the population did so.) Not surprisingly, the population doubled every 20 years, a rate much faster than New France. In the following table, notice how quickly the number of people increased.

Web Connection

http://www.school.mcgrawhill.ca/resources

Go to the web site above to find out more about an aspect of Acadian lifestyle or culture that you find interesting. Go to History Resources, then to *Canada: The Story of Our Heritage* to see where to go next.

Population of Acadia, 1670–1755	
Year	Population
1670	500
1711	2 500
1750	10 000
1755	13 000

A Maritime Lifestyle

The daily life of an Acadian was somewhat different from that of a typical habitant on a *seigneury* along the St. Lawrence River. Much of the Acadian lifestyle was more **maritime**. There were far more people engaged in fishing — either catching, salting, transporting, or selling.

As a result, Acadia had far fewer farmers. However, the farmers were, for the most part, better off than their counterparts to the west. Wheat and peas were the principal crops. Nearby orchards, rooted in richer soil, produced bountiful harvests of apples, cherries, and pears. They normally kept cattle, sheep, and pigs. Many Acadian farmers were able to supplement their incomes with proceeds from the lucrative cod trade. Because they used the tidal flatlands, areas of little interest to the Mi'kmaq in the area, they developed good relations with the Aboriginal Peoples.

Acadians developed a unique lifestyle. Their language, French combined with some English and Aboriginal words, was different. Ties of kinship and necessity formed a unique system of harmony and mutual support. As powerful as the Roman Catholic Church was in the St. Lawrence region, it was even more so in Acadia. Along with the same religious, political, social, and educational functions that priests performed in Québec, religious officials in Acadia also acted as judges in legal disputes.

The Story So Far ....

1 Draw a time line identifying the key dates and events of Acadia's history from 1604 to 1670.
2 Identify the reasons for Acadia's rapid population growth in its early years.

SUM IT UP!

Many different aspects of society contributed to the evolution of a distinctive lifestyle in New France. Religion, language, the *seigneurial* system, the family, the roles of men and women, diet, and celebrations all made for a lifestyle that existed nowhere else: neither in France nor in the Thirteen Colonies.

Acadia had a troubled upbringing, being ruled alternately by the French and the British. Despite this problem, it developed its own maritime lifestyle and culture. It was similar to, and yet different from, New France in several ways. The Acadians established a mutually supportive relationship with the Mi'kmaq in the area. They also developed a strong trading tie with the New England colonies.

THINKING ABOUT YOUR LEARNING

1. The family, the economy, the Roman Catholic Church, and the government all affected the daily lives of the people of New France. Which do you think had the greatest impact? Justify your choice.

2. Using a Venn diagram, identify the features of daily life in New France and Acadia that are distinctive and that are shared. What made each of them distinctive?

Daily Life in New France and Acadia

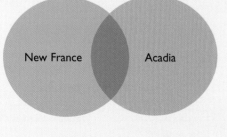

3. Would you prefer to have lived in the St. Lawrence area or in Acadia? Provide reasons to support your view.

APPLYING YOUR LEARNING

1. Conduct a debate on the following resolution: The habitants' lifestyle is proof of the existence of New France's distinct society.

2. Create a graphic organizer to compare the possessions of a typical family today with those of a typical habitant family. What does each have in common? What are the differences?

3. What are your forms of entertainment? In what ways are they similar to a habitant's forms of recreation? How are they different?

4. As a class, prepare a habitant lunch, including cheese, wholesome bread, cold meats, and apple cider. If the weather permits, eat it outdoors, as the habitants would have done.

5. In the early days, the habitants had to create games for their own amusement. Design and invent an interesting game from the materials available in your house.

6. Illustrate a scene of some aspect of habitant or Acadian lifestyle.

USING KEY WORDS

 1 Match the term from Column A to the appropriate definition in Column B.

Column A

a) *seigneurial* system

b) *carriole*

c) *censitaire*

d) *calèche*

e) *cens*

f) *maritime*

g) *corvée*

h) parish

i) *lods et ventes*

j) *curé*

k) *aboiteau*

l) dowry

Column B

i) a gift of cash, land, or goods given at the time of a daughter's marriage

ii) a type of inheritance tax paid by the habitant

iii) sleighs pulled by horses or dog teams

iv) a hinged valve used by the Acadians

v) a religious administrative district

vi) the less popular term for a habitant

vii) a small annual cash payment made by a habitant

viii) a method of land distribution based on European feudal system

ix) a work duty, usually three days a year, done by a habitant

x) a type of carriage

xi) religious official in charge of a local area

xii) a lifestyle revolving around the sea

The Fall of New France

1663	1670	1713	1748	1755
Creation of Royal Government in New France	Formation of Hudson's Bay Company	Treaty of Utrecht ends War of Spanish Succession	Treaty of Aix-la-Chapelle ends King George's War	Expulsion of the Acadians

SETTING OUR FOCUS

Perhaps the most significant battle in Canadian history occurred on September 13, 1759. The Battle of the Plains of Abraham marked the major turning point in the Seven Years' War. Five days later, Québec surrendered to the British. The French-British war in the Americas was an extension of a conflict in France and England. The British victory gave them control of all of North America. With the Treaty of Paris in 1763, which ended the Seven Years' War, New France no longer officially existed. From then on it was referred to as the *Colony of Québec* and was the only French, Roman Catholic colony within the British Empire. Its future was going to be very different from its past. What do you think Britain's chief goal was, regarding their newly acquired colony of Québec? What do you think the chief goal of the Québec colonists was?

PREVIEWING THE CHAPTER

In this chapter you will learn about these topics:
- **the expansion of the fur trade into the Hudson Bay, Rocky Mountains, and Ohio Valley areas**
- **the expulsion of the Acadians**
- **the causes, results, and key individuals of the Seven Years' War**
- **the impact of the Battle of the Plains of Abraham**
- **the impact of the 1763 Treaty of Paris on British Canadians and French Canadians**

KEY WORDS

assimilate
capitulation
conflict
congés
decapitation
deportation
expel
guerrilla warfare
guild
martial law
oath
la survivance

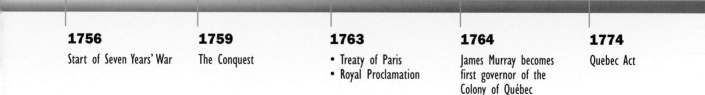

1756
Start of Seven Years' War

1759
The Conquest

1763
• Treaty of Paris
• Royal Proclamation

1764
James Murray becomes first governor of the Colony of Québec

1774
Quebec Act

GROWTH AND EXPANSION OF NEW FRANCE

Expansion of the Fur Trade

Because of overtrapping, both French Canadian and British Canadian fur traders began to exhaust the supply of fur-bearing animals near settled areas. Consequently, both sides sought to push the boundaries of the fur trade farther out. Toward the end of the seventeenth century, a number of French Canadian adventurers expanded New France's land claims.

In 1652, while on a duck shoot, Pierre-Esprit de Radisson was ambushed by a band of Mohawks. They took him back to their village on the shores of Lake Champlain, where he was adopted by a Mohawk family. In essence, he became a "white Mohawk," learning their language, customs, and ways of life. However, fond memories of his life as a French colonist inspired several escape attempts during his stay with the Mohawks.

Médard Chouart des Groseilliers (his last name literally means *gooseberries*) emigrated from North-Central France in his late teens. He joined the Jesuits and served as a lay assistant at their Huron mission near Georgian Bay. After a brief return to Québec, Groseilliers journeyed back to the land of the Huron to persuade them to bring more furs down the St. Lawrence.

Groseilliers led the French exploration into the upper Great Lakes area in 1656. He was joined by his brother-in-law, Radisson, three years later. By 1663 the pair had travelled as far as Lake Superior country and possibly as far north as James Bay. They met the Cree, who were the main suppliers of furs. The Cree explained that the prime fur country lay far north of Lake Superior. When the Cree spoke of a "frozen" northern sea, the two men believed they were referring to Hudson Bay.

Groseilliers and Radisson travelled beyond Lake Superior to trade directly with the Cree for furs.

Pierre-Esprit de Radisson
A PERSUASIVE PERSONALITY

In the mid-1600s, the fur trade in the colony of New France was thriving. Few of the men who traded for its plentiful beaver pelts had as much success as one named Radisson.

Pierre-Esprit de Radisson was born in France in 1636. He followed his half sister to New France, arriving in Trois Rivières in 1651 when he was just 16. If he had crossed the sea looking for adventure, he certainly found it.

The next spring, Radisson and two friends went duck hunting, despite warnings that angry Mohawks were about. After a squabble with his friends, Radisson separated from them. Imagine his horror when, hours later, he came across their mutilated bodies. He was quickly surrounded by Mohawks. Instead of killing him, however, they took him back to their village, where a Mohawk family adopted him.

Radisson lived for several months in their village until he and an Algonquin captive killed three sleeping Mohawks to escape. As they made their way back to Trois Rivières, the two were recaptured by the enraged Mohawks. The Algonquin was killed, but when it was Radisson's turn to die, his adoptive family argued for his release. Within a year he had completely regained the trust of the Mohawk community. He escaped a second time and successfully made his way back to Trois Rivières.

By then Radisson's knowledge of the land and the Aboriginal people was considerable. He teamed up with his brother-in-law, Médard Chouart des Groseilliers, and the two began exploring the interior, meeting new Aboriginal groups and trading for many pelts as they went.

In 1759, Radisson and Groseilliers had their furs confiscated by the governor of Québec. The partners then turned to the British. They easily lined up financial backers for their trip to find a northern route into this rich land. That voyage resulted in the founding of the Hudson's Bay Company in 1670. Between 1674 and 1687, Radisson switched allegiances twice more, even though he had previously destroyed the forts of those who were rehiring him. When the French offered a reward for Radisson's capture, he wisely retreated to England where he died in London in 1710.

A man of questionable loyalties, Radisson must have possessed considerable charm. At each critical point in his life, he managed to talk his way back into the good graces of those he had betrayed. More historically significant, though, he fueled the competition for furs that eventually opened up the unexplored territories of what is now Canada.

More people you could research are

Charles Aubert de La Chesnaye

Antoine de Lamothe-Cadillac

René Robert Cavelier de la Salle

Pierre de la Vérendrye

Pierre-Esprit de Radisson

Louis Jolliet

Charles II signing the charter of the Company of Adventurers

Recognizing that it was easier to ship furs via Hudson Bay rather than through Montréal, Radisson and Groseilliers altered the dynamics of the fur trade. They would ignore the Montréal merchants and instead appeal to London promoters. In 1670 King Charles II of England gave his cousin Prince Rupert and "a company of adventurers" a royal charter, shown here:

> *Wee Doe Grant —*
> *Unto the said Governor and Company and theire successors the sole Trade and Commerce of all those Seas Streightes Bayes Rivers Lakes Creekes and Soundes — that lie within the entrance of — Hudsons Streightes — and make create and constitute (them) — the true and absolute Lordes and Proprietors of the same Territory —*

The Hudson's Bay Company, a Canadian institution that still exists today, was born. Originally, it was given a monopoly to trade in furs in all the lands draining into Hudson Bay. The creation of the Hudson's Bay Company heated up the competition between the French and British in the fur trade.

The French did not stand idly by after the British began moving aggressively into the more northerly areas. French traders such as Charles Aubert de La Chesnaye established a *Company of the North* in 1682 to compete with the British. Daniel Greysolon Dulhut built a French fur-trading post on Lake Nipigon and successfully took from the British the trade with more than 1500 Cree. In the 1690s, the French attacked several Hudson's Bay posts and took York Factory. As a result, they dominated the region's fur trade until 1714.

1 Looking at the French and British Forts, which side had the advantage? Militarily? Strategically? In terms of the fur trade? Explain your answers.

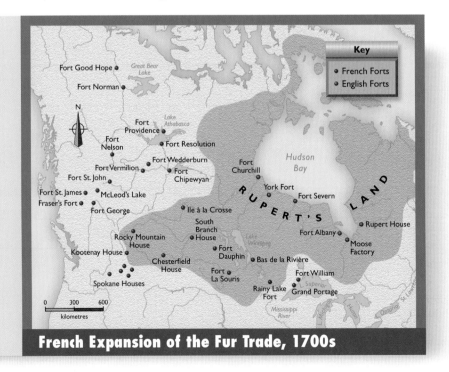

French Expansion of the Fur Trade, 1700s

While the explorers and traders were pushing west and north, the thought ever present in the back of their minds was that they might yet find a western ocean. Many undertook the search. Perhaps no one took it further than Pierre de La Vérendrye.

La Vérendrye commanded a trading fort on Lake Superior. In 1729 he and his sons began an arduous trek to discover that ocean. Exploring the waterways west of Lake Superior, they spent years travelling across the Great Plains. They never got to the ocean and, in fact, never even reached the foothills of the Rocky Mountains. However, they did extend French influence. They built several trading posts on the plains, the one farthest west being at the present-day site of Portage La Prairie in Manitoba. They were responsible for a rich new supply of furs as hundreds of canoes came back annually to Montréal filled with beaver pelts from the places they had explored.

M993.154.75/John David Kelly, "Pierre de la Verendry, on the Upper St. Maurice River, 1725." McCord Museum of Canadian History, Montreal

Pierre de La Vérendrye and his sons expanded the fur trade west into present-day Manitoba.

The Empire of New France

France was extending its influence in other areas as well. In fact, as New France's frontiers grew in the early decades of the eighteenth century, the colony was transformed into an extensive, though sparsely settled, continental empire. It had grown into much more than the original settlements in Acadia and along the St. Lawrence. It now stretched west to the Great Plains and south through present-day Ohio and present-day Illinois country, even as far as the Gulf of Mexico.

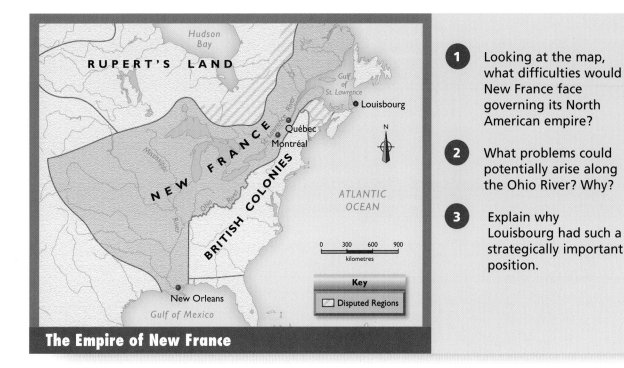

The Empire of New France

1 Looking at the map, what difficulties would New France face governing its North American empire?

2 What problems could potentially arise along the Ohio River? Why?

3 Explain why Louisbourg had such a strategically important position.

Marquette and Jolliet exploring the Mississippi River

Louis Jolliet and René Robert Cavelier de La Salle explored the South along the Mississippi River. Journeying through present-day Ohio and Illinois, they eventually reached the Gulf of Mexico. In the process, they befriended the Sioux and paved the way for significant growth in the fur trade. Pierre Le Moyne d'Iberville founded a colony in Louisiana (named in honour of the French King) in 1699. Two years later, in 1701, Antoine de Lamothe-Cadillac established Detroit, a strategically important colony since it controlled travel and commerce between Lake Erie and Lake Huron.

New France Protects Itself

Between 1701 and 1713, France and England were once again at war. The War of the Spanish Succession was a European struggle that indirectly affected North America. French leaders became convinced that New France could act as a barrier to British westward expansion into the heartland of the continent. To implement that policy, French authorities had a series of forts constructed from Montréal to Detroit, in the Ohio and Illinois country, even as far away as Louisiana.

The territorial make-up of New France changed considerably in 1713 when the War of the Spanish Succession ended with the signing of the Treaty of Utrecht.

Britain re-acquired the Hudson Bay forts as well as all of Newfoundland and parts of Nova Scotia. France retained its cod fisheries, Île Royale (Cape Breton), Île St. Jean (present-day Prince Edward Island), and the area west of the Bay of Fundy (present-day New Brunswick). It was essential for New France to have a naval base on the Atlantic Ocean to prevent a possible British blockade of the entrance to the St. Lawrence. If the British navy did put up a blockade, New France would be completely cut off from supplies and reinforcements and therefore would be an easy target for takeover. Such a base would help New France maintain contact with Île Royale and protect its Atlantic fisheries as well. As a result, in 1720, France began construction of the Fortress of Louisbourg. The French spared no expense on the fortress. It took 25 years to complete and included massive stone walls and dozens of imposing cannons. The French believed it would be impossible for any enemy to take this *Gibraltar of North America*.

Web Connection

http://www.school.mcgrawhill.ca/resources

Go to the web site above to find out more about the Hudson Bay and Northwest companies. Go to History Resources, then to *Canada: The Story of Our Heritage* to see where to go next.

Peace and Economic Growth

After a long period of war, New France enjoyed a relatively long era of peace from 1713 to 1744. France and Britain maintained a tense peace, and Aboriginal groups remained faithful to their alliances with the French or the British. Even the Iroquois, who had waged a century-long fight with the French, followed the terms of the treaty they had signed in Montréal in 1701. As a result, France continued its fort-construction program.

New France grew in several areas: the economy, immigration, and population. The fur trade also enjoyed something of a rebirth. In 1716 the government reintroduced the *congés*, a system of permits that provided annual official trips for licensed fur traders, or voyageurs. The voyageurs could journey west to trade goods for beaver pelts. Montréal merchants prospered from the *congés* system because they supplied the voyageurs with the trading goods. The system also gave post commanders in the northern country control over local trade and made many of them wealthy.

Other areas besides the fur trade were also developing. A considerable number of small-scale industries grew up in the early eighteenth century. Naval shipyards were built in Québec and iron foundries in Trois Rivières. Small communities of artisans and skilled craftspeople sprang up in the three main towns of Québec, Montréal, and Trois Rivières. Numerous **guilds**, or societies that offered support for particular crafts, began about this time, including guilds for carpenters, furniture makers, and silversmiths.

A view of Trois Rivières in 1759. What impressions do you get of the city?

A view of Louisbourg from the Lighthouse in 1758, when that city was beseiged by the British.

A Population Boom

The population of New France reflected the overall growth in the economy and the fur trade. In 1663, at the start of Royal Government, the colony numbered just a little over 3000 people. By the end of the seventeenth century, it had increased more than five times, to about 16 000. A steady growth of almost 10 000 people every ten years increased the population of New France to about 70 000 colonists by the Conquest of 1759. (The Conquest refers to the military defeat suffered by the French at the hands of the British on the Plains of Abraham in Québec.) That population growth occurred because of a number of factors:

- the successful implementation of Intendant Jean Talon's plans
- economic development
- natural increase
- the maintenance of peace
- immigration

The Story So Far . . .

1 List some areas of growth and development in New France during the first half of the eighteenth century. Give reasons to explain that growth and development.

2 Working with a partner, draw a plan for a French fort to be constructed in the Ohio Valley. Before drawing your plan, compile a list of things a fort should contain.

3 Imagine you are a carpenter who helped build the fort you designed in question 2. Give yourself a name and an age, and write a letter to a friend or relative in either Québec or Paris.

4 Another reason for the growth of the fur trade was the decision to use brandy and other alcohol as an item of exchange. Assume one of the following identities and write a paragraph on your view of the practice: a priest, fur trader, Aboriginal person, government official, or businessperson. Provide specific support for your position.

5 Explain why the construction of the fortress at Louisbourg was vital for French strategic interests.

THE FRENCH-BRITISH CONFLICT

Historically, it may appear that the French and the British were always fighting. In fact, they once clashed in perhaps the longest **conflict** ever, the Hundred Years' War, which actually lasted one hundred and sixteen years! They were constantly competing against each other throughout this era of New France. They argued over land, over alliances, over fisheries, and over the fur trade. There is still considerable conflict between the two sides even today in Canada. To better understand and appreciate the reasons for this conflict, you have to go back in time.

One cause of conflict is differences. This does not mean that whenever there is a difference between two parties, there will automatically be a conflict. But when differences exist, there is a higher possibility of conflict. The French and the British were historically very different people. They spoke different languages. They developed different legal and political systems. The French were mainly Roman Catholic while the British were mainly Protestant. This religious difference was important because it gave the two groups some different values, beliefs, and attitudes. The two groups developed very different customs and lifestyles. The French tended to live in rural areas and based their economy on agriculture, while the British began to move to cities and become involved in commerce and industry. Because of these differences — and many others — each side came to view the other's actions with suspicion and distrust.

In this illustration of Acadia, farmers are cutting saltmarsh hay.

The Acadians

One group caught in the middle of the French-British conflict was the Acadians, who lived in what is now Nova Scotia. By the 1713 Treaty of Utrecht, France agreed to hand over Acadia and Newfoundland to Britain. The French, Roman Catholic Acadians faced a difficult decision. They could either remain on their land in Nova Scotia and become British subjects or sell what could not be transported and move to other French colonies. French authorities instructed the Acadians to relocate to Île Royale or Île St. Jean. After hearing gloomy reports about the barren and rocky land of Île Royale, all but a few hundred Acadians decided to remain in Nova Scotia. Their attachment to their land was greater than their loyalty to their former ruling country, France.

The Treaty of Utrecht included a provision that permitted the Acadians to retain their Roman Catholic religion. With their religion, land, and strong sense of family, they resisted the subtle British attempts to **assimilate** them, or absorb them into the British culture. They continued to speak their unique dialect of French, and very much went about their lives as they had in the past. They avoided Annapolis Royale, where the British congregated, and maintained their traditional ways. As a result, they prospered. Their numbers doubled to 5000 by 1730 and to 10 000 by 1750. Their rulers may have changed, but that made scarcely any difference to the Acadians.

The Oath of Allegiance

Still, the British-French conflict was always lurking in the background. It was customary in seventeenth- and eighteenth-century Europe to require citizens to swear an **oath**, promising to serve the monarch and to help defend the country. The oath was, in some ways, similar to the oath that new Canadian citizens swear today. However, the issue of the loyalty oath caused trouble.

The British demanded repeatedly that the Acadians swear the oath of allegiance. The Acadians did not object to promising to serve the monarch and to be good, obedient subjects. They even agreed to remain neutral in the event of a conflict. However, they strongly refused to take up arms. Why? If war broke out, France, their former ruling country, was going to be the enemy. Although the Acadians may not have had either great loyalty or affection for their former ruling country, they would not agree to take up arms against it. They repeatedly refused Britain's demand of them to swear an oath of loyalty. The Acadians even petitioned the British to change the wording of the oath, but to no avail.

Further Conflict

Another French-British conflict broke out in 1744. King George's War was fought over the successor to the Austrian throne. Fighting took place in Acadia because the area was strategically important and was desirable to both sides. In May 1744, a French force under François Duvivier captured and burned Canso, an important fishing port on the northeastern coast of Nova Scotia. In June, the French and over 400 Mi'kmaq allies attempted to take Fort Anne (Annapolis Royale). The Acadians who lived nearby feared Britain would retaliate, so they either hid in the woods or reluctantly provided the French with supplies. A handful of Acadians were involved in a second siege, or lengthy attack, three months later but it failed.

Although the majority of Acadians remained neutral, rumours about their allegiance were growing into fears. Both the governing council of Nova Scotia and the powerful governor of Massachusetts, William Shirley, began suspecting the Acadians of disloyalty. Governor Shirley was concerned that Canadian Maritime privateers would threaten shipping in New England. In the spring of 1745, a combined British-New England force captured the supposedly impregnable Fortress of Louisbourg after a seven-week siege.

The New England militia and the British army attack Louisbourg.

It turned out that the fortress was not nearly as invincible as people thought. The hills behind it were perfect for the invaders' cannons. In addition, the walls of the fortress began crumbling from the vibrations of the fort's own cannons! The French, under the Duc d'Anville, attempted a massive counterattack to take back the fortress. It ended in defeat as many of the French crew were hit by smallpox and other infectious diseases, and the Duc d'Anville died of a stroke. All the while, the Acadians attempted to steer a very uncertain course of neutrality. However, they were trusted by neither side.

King George's War came to an end in 1748 with the signing of the Treaty of Aix-la-Chapelle. In return for regaining holdings in Holland and India that the French had captured, the British government returned Île Royale and Louisbourg to France. Nova Scotia remained in British hands but was populated almost exclusively by Acadians. Both sides had grown weary and wary of the Acadians and their fragile neutrality. The treaty was more like a temporary truce than a permanent peace.

The oath of loyalty was never far from the centre of the controversy between the Acadians and the British government. There appeared to be no way to arrive at a mutually satisfactory compromise. It was just a question of time before the issue exploded. In 1755, the Seven Years' War broke out in Europe between the French and British. And there were growing disputes between the two sides in the interior of the continent. Charles Lawrence, the British Governor of Nova Scotia, was

Charles Lawrence, Governor of Nova Scotia

worried about *the Acadian question*. Acadia had been fought over for the past century and had proven to be a convenient pawn to switch from one side to the other in each successive peace treaty. The 10 000 French, Roman Catholic Acadians living in Nova Scotia, New Brunswick, and Prince Edward Island had refused to swear an oath of loyalty to the British Crown. French-British hostilities were again looming on the horizon. Could the Acadians be trusted in the event of a war? Were they secretly helping the French? Those were the questions that haunted Governor Lawrence.

The Expulsion of the Acadians

For security, Governor Lawrence once again demanded that the Acadians swear the oath of allegiance. Once more, they refused. But this time, the consequence was different. Lawrence decided that there had to be a punishment attached to the Acadians' refusal. He announced that they would be **expelled**, or forcibly removed, from the area and resettled in other British colonies far from potential trouble.

The initial plan was to capture all Acadian males and seize their boats. That way, the women and children would be unable to escape with their possessions, including their livestock. This plan was dropped because it could not be executed quickly enough. British troops moved in swiftly. Homes, property, and possessions were confiscated, and Acadian men, women, and children were forcefully herded onto waiting ships. The British torched many Acadian homesteads; the Acadians could see the destruction of their settlement as they sailed away.

Between 1755 and 1763, about three-quarters of the 10 000 Acadians were forcibly deported, although they did have some choice as to where to relocate.

Location of the Acadians in 1763	
French colonies	2400
France	3500
England	850
Nova Scotia	1250
Other British colonies (Thirteen Colonies, Caribbean)	4600

The Evidence Behind the Story

Four hundred and eighteen men entered the Roman Catholic church in Grand Pré, Nova Scotia, to hear John Winslow, a British government official, deliver the **deportation** order on September 3, 1755.

Gentlemen, I have received from his Excellency, Governor Lawrence, the King's Commission which I have in my hand, and by whose orders you are conveyed together, to Manifest to you His Majesty's final resolution to the French inhabitants of this his Province of Nova Scotia, who for almost half a century have had more Indulgence Granted them than any of his Subjects in any part of his Dominions. What use you have made of them you yourself Best Know.

That Part of Duty I am now upon is what thoh [sic] Necessary is Very Disagreeable to my natural make and temper, as I Know it Must be Grievous to you who are of the Same Species. But it is not my business annimadvert [sic], but to obey Such orders as I receive, and therefore without Hesitation Shall Deliver you his Majesty's orders and Instructions. . . .

That your Land & tennements, Cattle of all Kinds and Livestocks of all Sorts are forfeited to the Crown with all other your effects Savings your money and Household Goods; and you yourselves to be removed from this Province. . . . I Must also Inform you That it is His Majesty's Pleasure that you remain in Security under the Inspection & Direction of the Troops that I have the Honr. To Command.

They were then declared to be prisoners of the king.

QUESTIONING THE EVIDENCE

1. What evidence is there that this document is an example of a primary source?
2. What is the basic message in the document?
3. What is the tone of the message?
4. Imagine that you are one of the 418 people hearing the message being delivered. Write a paragraph about how you feel as you hear the words of John Winslow.
5. Role-play a dinner-table scene of a man who heard the Expulsion Order explaining it to his family.

John Winslow announces the expulsion of the Acadians in a church in Grand Pré.

The Granger Collection, New York

Look at the picture. Focus your attention on the background. What is taking place on the water? Now, slowly move your gaze to the foreground, going from left to right. As your eye falls on the man seated beside his belongings, step into the picture. Why do you think he is seated there, away from the crowd behind him? What do you think he is feeling? What is happening to the people behind him? Who are they? What might they be feeling? Are they saying anything? To whom? What are the men in uniform doing? Are they saying anything? What might they be feeling?

The picture shows Acadians being forced by British officers to leave their homes in Nova Scotia in 1755. With a partner, pick two people from the picture and create a conversation between them. Role-play the scene for the class, including appropriate gestures and any props that might add to the drama.

The Acadians had committed no crime. They were simply in the wrong place at the wrong time. The expulsion of the Acadians had a very negative effect on French–British relations. The British saw the expulsion as a simple necessity of war. The French, on the other hand, saw it as unwarranted, unfair, and unjust.

Snapshot

For the past two decades, the residents of Grand Pré have set aside a weekend each July to celebrate the culture of the Acadian people. It is a relaxed, family event of picnics, entertainment, and activities. Unlike most festivals, it is not even promoted to tourists. It is more like a reunion, a chance for old friends to meet once a year. Festival-goers enjoy traditional Acadian foods such as a chicken stew called *fricot*. On Sunday, they take part in an outdoor Catholic mass at Grand Pré, the historic site of the expulsion.

Each year the festival brings together about 5000 Acadians, descendants of these neutral farmers caught in the middle of a conflict.

The Story So Far . . .

1 What feelings did John Winslow seem to have about his task on September 3, 1755? How do you know this?

2 Role-play a scene about the deportation of the Acadians. Some possibilities are:
- the scene in the church in Grand Pré when the deportation order is first announced
- a family meeting during which plans are drawn up to avoid being deported
- a dinner-table discussion between two Acadians about their reaction to the expulsion order
- a Catholic priest talking to another priest about the sermon that he is going to give the Sunday following the deportation announcement
- the harbour scene when families are dragged onto British ships, in most cases never to return to their native land

3 Provide a breakdown by percentage of the locations the Acadians went to after their expulsion in 1763. Either by hand or with a computer, generate a pie graph to represent this information. What location did the greatest percentage of Acadians choose? Why do you think that was the preferred location?

4 Based upon what you have learned about the Acadians, write a short poem or song about their plight.

THE SEVEN YEARS' WAR

The Seven Years' War began unofficially in 1754 in the Ohio Valley and was later transferred to Europe. This reversed the usual situation; most wars started in Europe and were transferred to North America. The problem was that both French and British settlements were expanding. It was just a matter of time before the two sides would clash over the same territory. In 1749 a group of Virginian businesspeople secured a grant of 200 000 ha of Ohio Valley land from the British for the purposes of settlement — despite the fact that France claimed the same territory! France had explored and traded in the area first, but the British were settling and staying there. To enforce their claim and to protect the fur trade, the French built a chain of forts. These forts were on the same land claimed by the British. It was an awkward and confusing situation, with few possibilities of an easy resolution.

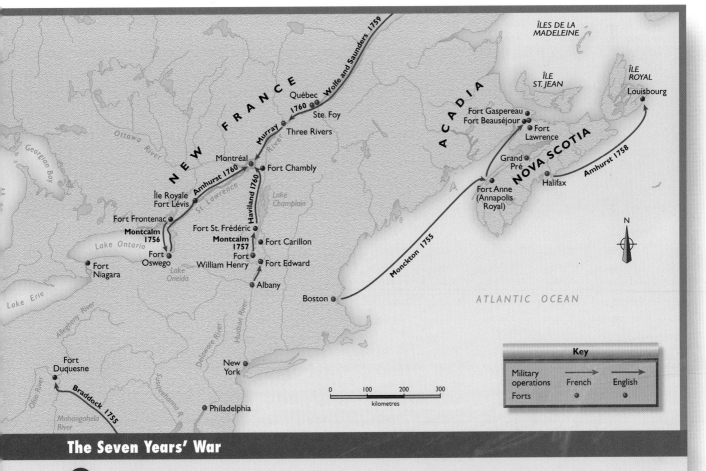

The Seven Years' War

1 Many of the campaigns involved long overland marches or long water voyages.
- How long were some of them?
- What difficulties would there be moving men over these distances?
- When would you want to travel?

In 1754 the French built a larger fort, Fort Duquesne, at the junction of the Allegheny and Monongahela rivers. Virginia's Governor Dinwiddie sent 22-year-old Lieutenant-Colonel George Washington to take back the area from the French. At Great Meadows, just south of Fort Duquesne, Washington attacked a French group, killing ten men and taking 22 prisoner. One of the deaths was that of the French ensign Joseph Coulon de Jumonville. This incident started the war. The French sent 1000 troops, most of whom were Aboriginal People, to avenge the attack. Hearing of their advance, Washington quickly constructed a temporary post, Fort Necessity. It was not enough. The French easily defeated Washington.

In 1755 France and Britain both sent troops to North America. General Braddock and a force of 1500 British soldiers attempted to recapture Fort Duquesne and remove the French from the Ohio Valley. The British employed their usual war tactics. Two long rows of soldiers dressed in bright red uniforms marched ahead. While the back row reloaded, the forward row would kneel and fire. The French and their Aboriginal allies employed no such tactics. Using **guerrilla warfare** — surprise ambushes and hiding behind trees and rocks while shooting — they fired on the ill-prepared British. More than two-thirds of the British force were killed. Although the British had out-numbered the French two to one, the French had won the first decisive victory.

The war continued in France's favour the following year. Then Louis-Joseph de Montcalm replaced Baron Dieskau as leader of the French forces in North America. He was a trained and experienced career soldier. He captured Fort Oswego on Lake Ontario, which secured the French posts in the Ohio Valley. In 1757 Montcalm took Fort William Henry on the Richelieu River. The important city of New York now lay open to the French. However, Montcalm failed to take advantage of the situation and did not press the attack.

Louis-Joseph de Montcalm, leader of the French forces in North America

The British Take the Lead

Up to this point, the Seven Years' War had been going very badly for the British. Several strategic forts had been lost. British leadership and strategy had proven ineffectual and inappropriate. The British colonists, although outnumbering the French 12 to 1, were indifferent to helping the British troops.

The British launched a massive assault on Fort Duquesne. The French lost. Rather than seeing the fort fall into enemy hands, they burned it to the ground. On that site, the British constructed Fort Pitt (the future site of Pittsburgh) in honour of

Joseph Coulon de Jumonville

THE MAN WHO STARTED A WAR

Joseph Coulon de Villiers, Sieur de Jumonville or Joseph Coulon de Jumonville, as he came to be called, was a mere ensign, the lowest level of officer in the infantry. Unlike his brothers, he commanded no troops and captured no British forts. He simply stepped into history at a critical moment in time and was instantly famous.

Joseph Coulon de Villiers was born in 1718 in Verchères, New France, and grew up in Fort St. Joseph. His parents, Nicolas Antoine Coulon de Villiers and Angélique Jarret de Verchères, had two other sons, Louis and François. All three brothers served in the French military.

In 1739 Joseph was sent to Louisiana on an expedition against the Aboriginal Peoples in that area. After that he became an officer who was often used in affairs involving Aboriginal Peoples. He spent a number of years in Acadia but, unlike his brother François, did not make a name for himself there.

Early in 1754, De Jumonville was sent to Ohio with a force commanded by Claude-Pierre Pécaudy, Seigneur de Contrecoeur. Their mission was to inhabit Fort Duquesne and secure the Ohio Valley for the French. In May, with the British under George Washington pushing forward, Contrecoeur decided to send a message to any British troops in the area, warning them to leave or be forced out. To carry his message, he put De Jumonville in command of a group of about 30 others.

De Jumonville located Washington's men and set up camp. For some reason, he decided to stay in that spot for almost two days without attempting to deliver Contrecoeur's message. Washington's allies spotted De Jumonville, however. In spite of the fact that France and Britain were technically at peace, the British attacked the small French company. In 15 minutes they killed ten French, including De Jumonville, and took the rest prisoners.

The French were furious that their soldiers had been killed on what they considered their own soil. The British claimed that De Jumonville was a spy and had fired first. And so began the war.

Although little else is known about De Jumonville, his name is linked inextricably with the Seven Years' War because of this incident. The actions of this rather ordinary soldier will forever mark the beginning of the last major French and British war.

More people you could research are

François Bigot

General Braddock

Joseph Coulon de Jumonville

François Gaston de Lévis

Charles Lawrence

James Murray

Colonel George Washington (centre), of the Virginia militia, raises his hat to the British flag flying over Fort Duquesne in November 1758. From details in the picture, how recently would you say the British captured the French fort?

their Prime Minister, William Pitt. This French defeat was a signal for their Aboriginal allies to desert them. Not wanting to be on the losing side, various tribes in the Ohio Valley either switched sides and joined the British or remained neutral. The French withstood a British attack on Fort Carillon (now Ticonderoga, New York) but suffered heavy casualties. They were less fortunate at Fort Frontenac, at the eastern end of Lake Ontario. The British took over this fort with less of a struggle. The British now had a free hand to plan an attack from the west on Montréal and Québec.

The Siege of Louisbourg

Things went from bad to worse for the French. The climax came at Louisbourg. Two brilliant British commanders, James Wolfe and Jeffrey Amherst, laid siege to the fortress at Louisbourg. "Slow but sure" was Amherst's policy and he applied it both in the thoroughness of his preparations and in carrying out the seven-week siege. The British were unrelenting. Day after day British cannons pounded Louisbourg. The British Royal Navy proved decisive. It blockaded the fortress for seven weeks and at the same time continually bombarded it. As supplies and the morale of the French within the fortress declined, the British landed troops. On July 26, 1758, the French commander at Louisbourg surrendered to the British. The victors demolished the fortress.

For the French, complete defeat in the Seven Years' War was a very strong possibility. With the mouth of the St. Lawrence in the hands of the British, who possessed the world's most powerful navy, the heart of French Canada lay in grave jeopardy.

In the spring of 1759, British General James Wolfe, fresh from his success at Louisbourg, sailed up the St. Lawrence with 40 000 men. Unfortunately for the future of New France, no French reinforcements could get through. What would this mean for the people of New France?

Québec was the heart of New France. Protected by its high walls, imposing cliffs, and massive cannons, it appeared to have the ability to hold out against the strong British forces. After sailing up and down the St. Lawrence, Wolfe decided to camp at Point Lévis, on the south shore across from Québec and on Île d'Orléans, on the north shore below the falls of Montmorency, about 10 km down river from Québec.

From there, the British bombarded Québec for two months, reducing the city to rubble. Québec stubbornly held out. By late summer, General Wolfe was becoming desperate. More importantly, he recognized that he had to force Québec's surrender quickly before the St. Lawrence River froze. Everything hinged on a landing being made on the north shore before the onset of winter drove them back to England.

To further destroy French resistance, Wolfe ordered a massive destruction of the south shore of the St. Lawrence. Sixteen hundred soldiers fanned out, burning farms and destroying crops and livestock along the way. Wolfe wanted to prevent the area's French population from crossing the St. Lawrence River and joining the local French militia. His manifesto left no doubt as to his intention. He warned them that "their habitations [would be] destroyed, their sacred temples exposed to an exasperated soldiery, their harvest utterly ruined" if they resisted the British order. But Wolfe realized that he had to act more decisively.

On the Plains of Abraham

Just before his fleet had to return to England, Wolfe successfully landed 4500 men on the north shore at Anse au Foulon. The element of surprise was all that the bold plan had going for it. The point was guarded by the inept Louis Dupont Du Vergor, who had surrendered Fort Beausejour in 1755. Seventy of Vergor's 100 men were away on harvest leave and the remainder were inattentive or sleeping. British spies had seen women washing clothes there and thought there must be a path nearby. Wolfe ordered his soldiers to scale the steep cliffs above them and attack Québec from the more exposed western side. Silently and surely, during the night of September 12, they carried out their orders. By sunrise, they were in battle formation on Abraham Martin's fields, 3 km from the centre of Québec.

James Wolfe
A MAN OF DETERMINATION

M245, George Townshend (Major General James Wolfe), 1759,
McCord Museum of Canadian History, Montreal

James Wolfe died a hero when he defeated Montcalm on the Plains of Abraham. He was only 32 years old and was already a general. How did such a young man gain command of what some call the most important event of the eighteenth century? Through sheer determination.

Wolfe was born in Westerham, England, on January 2, 1727. He decided early on that he, like his father and grandfather, would become a soldier. With a single-mindedness that became his trademark, he volunteered in his father's regiment at age 13. Within two years, he was an official member of the army, one whose outstanding abilities were soon recognized.

He fought his first battle at 16, followed by many more over the years, and moved quickly up through the ranks. Wolfe worked the soldiers he commanded long and hard. He himself worked twice as hard and took almost no holidays from his duties. He even hired tutors in math and history, and spent his free time on these studies.

In 1758 Wolfe was a senior officer in Amherst's expedition against Louisbourg and led the assault on the landing. He was rewarded for his outstanding service in that battle with a promotion to general and command of the upcoming expedition against Québec.

What eventually happened at Québec has made Wolfe a hero in both Canada and Britain, but some historians question whether he deserves that status. The young general was sick in bed leading up to the final assault against the French. It was his senior officers who had the inspiration for the offensive. Wolfe recognized it to be a sound plan and threw himself into the preparations.

As the British force climbed to the Plains of Abraham, Wolfe was with them. He exposed himself recklessly during the fighting, walking up and down the lines of soldiers to spur them on. Within minutes he had been wounded three times. Even as he lay dying, gasping for breath, he gave further orders in an effort to help seal the victory.

Perhaps Wolfe was not the only hero that day at Québec. His glory should probably be shared with his officers, his critics say. None can question Wolfe's devotion to the cause, however. Throughout his life, he threw everything he had into Britain's victory and, on the Plains of Abraham, paid the ultimate price.

More people you could research are

Jeffrey Amherst

Louis-Joseph de Montcalm

Pierre de Rigaud de Vaudreuil

Baron Dieskau

François Gaston

James Wolfe

This watercolour depicts the Battle of the Plains of Abraham in 1759. What is happening between the two groups of men and horses in the foreground?

Montcalm acted hastily. Rather than waiting for reinforcements, he decided to engage the British on the Plains of Abraham. He thought the best strategy was to try to drive the British from the Heights on the Plains of Abraham as quickly as possibly before they were able to increase their numbers. Montcalm ordered troops from the Beauport lines below Québec to re-form themselves on the Plains of Abraham. When they arrived, Montcalm had a force of close to 4000, mostly colonial militia and some Aboriginal fighters. The colonial militia were local citizens who had little training and experience in warfare. The inexperienced French militia were no match for the seasoned British regulars.

After a brief consultation with his officers, Montcalm ordered his men to attack. They advanced raggedly as the militia dove to the ground to reload rather than hold formation as was the practice with the regular troops. The disciplined British troops fired volley after volley and easily halted the French advance. The main body of French and French Canadian troops broke ranks and scattered. In little more than half an hour, the British defeated the French. Montcalm was fatally wounded and rode, bleeding, into Québec. Wolfe had already been killed on the battlefield. Québec was now in British hands.

The **capitulation**, or official document of surrender, identified the terms: Québec was given to the British, an exchange of prisoners was permitted, and French troops could leave freely. It did not end the war itself. Wolfe's successor, Brigadier Robert Monckton, was forced to be merciful. General Pierre de Rigaud de Vaudreuil was allowed to withdraw his forces to Montréal.

Reflections

Along with the military defeat, the Conquest also refers to the disgrace that was attached to the French defeat on the battlefield. Imagine you are a regular in the French army. Write a letter to your relatives in France after the Conquest of 1759, explaining why you think you lost the war, what your future prospects are, and how you feel.

The British Conquest of New France left The Place Royale in Québec City in ruins.

Before the winter set in, the British forces sailed back to Britain, leaving a garrison in Québec.

The French were able to mount a brief comeback in the spring of 1760. Their forces, under the command of François Gaston, Chevalier de Lévis, mounted an offensive which climaxed with the British being forced out of Ste. Foy. The British retreated behind the walls of Québec. This was the last time the French tasted victory in North America.

The British planned an invasion from three different directions at Montréal, using close to 20 000 troops. On September 8, 1760, a week before the first anniversary of the fall of Québec, Governor Vaudreuil signed the Articles of Capitulation. These surrendered all of France's North American empire to Britain. The era of New France was over.

The Story So Far . . .

1 Americans rarely, if ever, refer to this war as the Seven Years' War. They call it the *French and Indian War*. Research why this is the case.

2 Imagine it is immediately before the start of the Seven Years' War. Assess which side has the advantage. Factors that you could consider are: the population of New France versus the population of British Canada, forts, willingness of home country to provide assistance, leadership, army, navy, allies, economy. Put these criteria in order of importance.

3 Write one of the following about the fall of New France: a eulogy, a series of newspaper headlines, an editorial.

AFTER THE CONQUEST

The Colony of Québec

For the first three years, the newly named Colony of Québec was administered under **martial law**, a system of temporary rule by the army, usually with special military courts instead of civil authorities. Several of the key terms of the articles affecting the French Canadians were incorporated in the Treaty of Paris:

- There would be no punishment for the French Canadian militiamen.
- The people could still worship the Roman Catholic religion.
- The clergy and *seigneurs* retained their rights and privileges.

Military rule ended in 1764 with the appointment of James Murray as the first civilian governor.

The defeated French Canadians searched for answers. Why had they lost? How would they survive under their new rulers? How would their lives change? What was going to happen to their culture? Some claimed that France had abandoned them, both on the battlefield and at the negotiation table. They were angered by the French decision to sacrifice the perceived cold, inhospitable colony of New France for the warm Caribbean island of Guadeloupe where sugar was produced. Others charged that French leadership, including Montcalm's, was incompetent. Still others claimed there was internal corruption and division within the upper society run by Intendant François Bigot.

James Murray, the first Governor of the Colony of Québec

Whatever the cause of their defeat, the French Canadians had to get on with their lives. Fearing life under British rule, many of the wealthiest educated French Canadians decided to leave. Some of them went to the Thirteen Colonies, some to the Caribbean, and some back to France. That left the clergy and the *seigneurs* as the only leaders left from the old regime. Historians have referred to this occurrence as the **decapitation**. The natural leaders of New France disappeared, leaving only the Roman Catholic Church and the new British conquerors in a position of authority. The financial void left by their departure was filled by British merchants and traders. As they settled in Montréal and Québec, the British took over industry, commerce, and, perhaps most notably, the fur trade.

La Survivance or Assimilation?

Most of the population was simply concerned with the everyday matters of feeding their families and tending their farms. But they had to address the dishonour of being a defeated people.

What they fell back on was the tradition of *la survivance*, or cultural survival. They realized that they were a tiny island of people in a sea of British Protestants and an even larger body of British Americans. The French Canadians came to believe that the triple pillars of land, religion, and family would ensure the survival of their culture. They were now being governed by a foreign people, the British, who not only spoke a different language but also practised a different religion. They had to guard against assimilation.

The British also had a problem. How were a few hundred of them going to rule over 70 000 French Roman Catholics? Their first answer was a policy of assimilation. The Royal Proclamation of 1763, which substantially shrunk the boundaries of Québec, was actually intended to solve a number of problems for Britain.

After fighting with Aboriginal Peoples in their uprising called Pontiac's War in 1762, the British government believed that the best way to avoid future conflicts with the Aboriginal Peoples and the settlers was to create a huge reservation for the

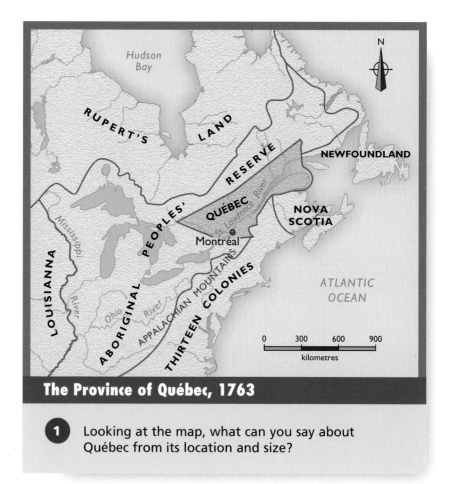

The Province of Québec, 1763

1. Looking at the map, what can you say about Québec from its location and size?

at that battle. Which decisions do you think were effective and ineffective?

3 The expulsion of the Acadians has sometimes been compared to the internment of the Japanese-Canadians during World War II. As a research activity, examine the similarities and differences between these two events.

4 Debate the following resolution either in small groups or as an entire class: Resolved that the British were wise in passing the Quebec Act of 1774.

5 In the role of a priest, teacher, habitant, merchant, artisan, government administrator, soldier, lawyer, or fur trader, write a letter to a relative in France about your reaction to the Conquest of 1759.

6 Draw an x and y axis as shown below. Include a scale of 1-10 on the y axis and the dates and events on the x axis. Plot the degree of conflict or co-operation between the French and the British on a scale of 1 to 10, using the events on the horizontal axis as a guide.

USING KEY WORDS

1 Provide a synonym for each of the words listed below.

assimilate	decapitation	guild
capitulation	deportation	martial law
conflict	expel	oath
congés	guerrilla warfare	*la survivance*

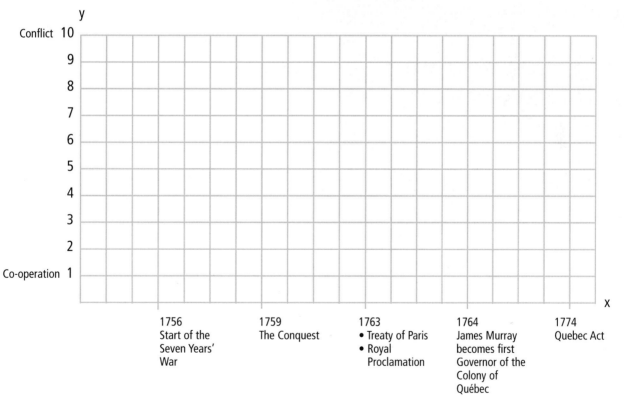

French-British Relations

y
Conflict 10
9
8
7
6
5
4
3
2
Co-operation 1

x

1756
Start of the
Seven Years'
War

1759
The Conquest

1763
• Treaty of Paris
• Royal
  Proclamation

1764
James Murray
becomes first
Governor of the
Colony of
Québec

1774
Quebec Act

Early Settlement and New France

CONNECTING YOUR LEARNING

UNDERSTANDING CONCEPTS

1 Was New France a distinct society? Write a list of reasons that did or did not make it so.

2 Create a report on the most significant changes that occurred in New France over the century and a half of its existence.

3 Put yourself in the role of a historian and write a position paper entitled, "The Greatest Individual in the History of New France."

4 Design a collage that gives a sense of "The Legacy of New France."

DEVELOPING RESEARCH SKILLS

1 Develop at least six questions to guide your research into the life of one of the people you read about in this unit. The person you research might be female, male, everyday, or one of the leaders of the colony of New France. Use the five Ws to help you write your questions. Find the answers to your questions using as many of the following resources as you can: a textbook, the Internet, a CD-ROM encyclopedia, a paper encyclopedia, a video. Present your findings using an oral report, video, or newscast.

2 Find two different sources that describe the Battle at Québec. One source might be this textbook. Make a list of five facts and three opinions about the battle. Next, make a Venn diagram to show the facts and opinions about the battle that you find in the two sources. Which facts and opinions do the sources have in common? Which do they seem to disagree about? Why do you think there might be this disagreement?

3 Historians use sketches, maps, paintings, and drawings for information. Take a good look at the illustration of the Battle of the Plains of Abraham on page 116. See how much information you can gather from this picture. Draw imaginary lines across the illustration to divide it horizontally into three equal sections. The bottom section is the foreground; the middle section is the middle ground; and the top section is the background. The focal point is the part of the picture the artist considers most important.

Describe what you see in the foreground, middle ground, background, and focal point. Write a title for the picture and explain why it is appropriate. Make some inferences (educated guesses) about what you see in the foreground, middle ground, background, and focal point.

COMMUNICATING REQUIRED KNOWLEDGE

1 Compose a song or write a poem about one of the significant events in the unit.

2 Draw an advertising poster that would have encouraged people to emigrate to New France.

3 Research one person of interest to you in the unit and write a one-page biography about him or her.

APPLYING CONCEPTS AND SKILLS

1 Add to the mind map below words for each category that describe those aspects of New France.

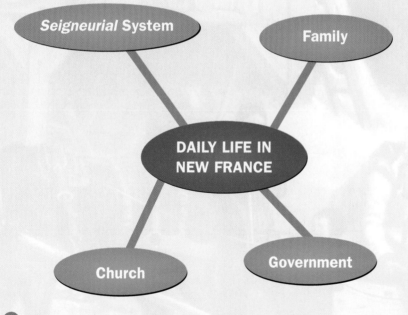

2 Suppose that the result of the Battle of the Plains of Abraham were reversed and the French won. Write an alternative ending for the battle from the perspective of a 13-year-old French resident of Québec.

3 Assess what kind of conquerors the British were and what kind of conquered people the French Canadians were.

1775

1784

NEW
BRUNSWICK

NOVA SCOTIA

1791

LOWER CANADA

UPPER CANADA

J.D.Kelly

148

British North America

THE BIG PICTURE

These are some of the stories you will read about in this unit:

- War has far-reaching consequences.
- Loyalty is a very complicated issue, sometimes a life and death issue.
- Struggle and sacrifice were two things all immigrants to British North America had in common.
- Discontent, especially with the government, was an outgrowth of all of the above.

1812

1815

CHAPTER 5

The Loyalists

American Revolution begins

Americans declare independence

1763
Treaty of Paris

1763
The Royal Proclamation

1774
The Quebec Act

1775
British North America invaded

1776
Some Loyalists arrive

SETTING OUR FOCUS

In the picture on the left, of a Loyalist settlement near present-day Brockville, Ontario, the year is 1784. You see tents that have been temporarily given by the British government to Loyalist refugee families. Like thousands of other families, these people are waiting, hopefully for only a few months, to be given a land grant so they can start a new life. What does this picture tell us about the newcomer Loyalists? What do you imagine day-to-day life will be like for these families for the next twelve months?

PREVIEWING THE CHAPTER

In this chapter you will learn about these topics:
- **the reasons for Loyalist settlements in British North America**
- **the different groups of people who were Loyalists, and how the groups affected their areas of settlement**
- **what life was like for those early settlers, for some particular individuals, and how they affected society as a whole**
- **the contributions of certain individuals, including Sir Guy Carleton and Sir John Graves Simcoe**

KEY WORDS

civilians
compensation
elected assembly
Loyalists
migration
military rule
minutemen
Patriots
raids
refugees

American Revolution ends

1783
Loyalists arrive in British North America in large numbers

1791
- The Constitution Act creates Upper Canada and Lower Canada
- John Graves Simcoe becomes first Lieutenant-Governor of Upper Canada

1793
Simcoe founds the settlement of York (later to become Toronto)

CHALLENGES IN BRITISH NORTH AMERICA

After the Seven Years' War in Europe finally ended, the 1763 Treaty of Paris officially transferred all land claims in British North America to Britain. While there were some people, especially within the British government, who were not impressed by this gain, most people felt that it was a favourable outcome. One British statesperson, William Pitt, summed up what seemed to be the majority's view. He said that North America was an extremely valuable asset because "it is a double market, the market of consumption and the market of supply." There were, however, challenges to be met while holding on to this desirable market.

Military Rule

Although Britain won the Canadian colonies from France in 1760, no civilian government was established. The area was governed by British **military rule**. Military rule means that the people are under the control of the army. The commander-in-chief, General Jeffrey Amherst, headquartered in New York, became responsible for the area. To administer it as smoothly as possible, the areas of Montréal, Trois Rivières, and Québec each reported to its own general for local concerns. Military rule is not necessarily unjust or oppressive, but it must have seemed a constant reminder to French Canadians that they were now a conquered people. Britain wanted to avoid an uprising, so military rule was fairly lenient, allowing French Canadian laws, religion, and language to continue as before. By 1763, however, a small British population, mostly merchants and traders, settled in the French region of Lower Canada. They wanted an official British government — even though there were only approximately 500 British Canadians compared to 80 000 French Canadians. After all, Britain would have to establish a non-military rule eventually, and they wanted a government that would favour its interests. Also, since most of the recent British arrivals were from the Thirteen Colonies, they sought the type of elected government they were used to.

French Canadians under British military rule, in Québec, after the Conquest

Aboriginal Relations

There was general unhappiness among several Aboriginal groups, especially those around the Great Lakes, after the British takeover of the British North American colonies. These groups included the Algonquin, the Nipissings, the Ottawas, the Chippewa, the Huron, and the Six Nation Iroquois. Since there was no longer any competition for fur, the British had been steadily lowering the price they would pay Aboriginal hunters and traders for it. In addition, the American colonies seemed to be continually expanding west, and settlers were simply taking the Aboriginal land. Chief Pontiac of the Ottawas created a coalition of several tribes and launched a successful attack against these most western British settlements throughout the upper Mississippi and Ohio River Valley area. Every British post west of Niagara, except for Detroit, was captured by Pontiac and his confederacy. The British government responded to this crisis with the Proclamation Line of 1763. This was an emergency measure meant to pacify Pontiac and his alliance by forbidding settlers from moving west of the Allegheny Mountains. It eventually became a policy for boundaries to be established, though often moved, to prevent too rapid an expansion westward.

American Expansion

1 Imagine you are an Aboriginal person affected by American expansion. How would you want your Chiefs to react?

Chief Pontiac in council. What might he and his council be discussing?

The Thirteen Colonies

The Thirteen Colonies were well-established and flourishing, even expanding. British settlements had existed along the Atlantic Coast since 1607. The first British settlement in North America, in Jamestown, Virginia, boasted a representative government — a government elected by the people — by 1624. In 1763 the British observed, however, that the colonies were expensive to run. This and the Aboriginal People's uprising were signals to Britain that expansion needed to be controlled for more than one reason.

The Story So Far . . .

1 List, in point form, the variety of concerns Britain faced while ruling North America in 1763.
2 Imagine you are a recent British arrival in Québec. You have migrated north from New York because you have heard there is money to be made for enterprising merchants such as yourself now that Britain controls the area. Write a letter to a relative in New York explaining what you think the British government should do now that the Seven Years' War in Europe is over and the territory of Québec is a British colony.
3 Imagine you are a third-generation French habitant in what is now British North America. What are your priorities? List at least four.
4 How would you describe the situation for the Aboriginal Peoples around the Great Lakes before 1763?

THE ROYAL PROCLAMATION AND OTHER UNPOPULAR ACTS

The Royal Proclamation of 1763 was Britain's first attempt to establish a non-military government for Québec and to deal with some of the other problems in North America. A Governor General was appointed, and the territory of Québec was limited to a small area along the St. Lawrence River.

The Royal Proclamation was somewhat unclear, but it was understood that, sometime in the future, there would be an **elected assembly** that would represent the people's view on government policies. This did not make either the French or the British very happy. The French did not like their new boundary and, since Catholics were not allowed to run for office, they knew that any future elected assembly was not likely to be

Snippet

Aboriginal Ownership of Lands

The Royal Proclamation of 1763 was the first Act to recognize Aboriginal ownership of lands in North America. It set a precedent and was the foundation of treaties to come.

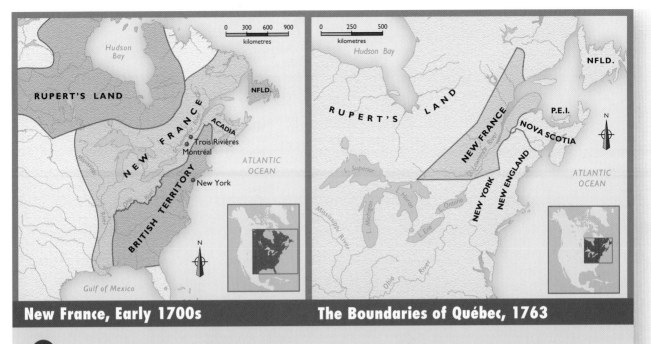

New France, Early 1700s

The Boundaries of Québec, 1763

1 Compare the boundaries of New France in the early 1700s, shown on the map on the left, with the boundaries of Québec in 1763, shown on the map on the right. What is the difference?

representative of the population. They were also nervous about the future of the Roman Catholic Church. The British settlers in Québec were not satisfied by the mere promise of an elected assembly. They also did not like the restrictions that the Proclamation placed on the fur trade. The limited territorial border that the Proclamation placed around Québec was like a noose around the neck of its economy. The best fur areas were south and west of the Great Lakes, through the Ohio River Valley area. With the Proclamation, those areas were out of bounds. People in the Thirteen Colonies were particularly upset by the limit that the Royal Proclamation placed on expansion to the west.

So, while no British North American colony was content with the Royal Proclamation, Britain went ahead and passed other acts that were even more controversial. The Seven Years' War had been a huge drain on the British economy. For the first time, the British government decided that colonies should, somehow, contribute to paying part of the cost of their defence. Little did Britain know that their economic experiments would end in revolt. For the Thirteen Colonies, the British government's attempts to extract money from them were in stark contrast to what they were used to. Dissatisfaction with the new policies inevitably led to discontent with the British government. At this time, Québec had no experience with British rule, so it had no points of comparison.

The Stamp Act of 1765 was a way for the British government to make money. All newspapers and legal documents were required to display a government stamp. The stamp was seen as an unjust tax, especially in the Thirteen Colonies. Protesters there refused to buy British goods. The phrase "No taxation without representation" became popular. This phrase reflected the Americans' general dissatisfaction with the British parliament that governed things from afar without representation from the Thirteen Colonies.

The Granger Collection, New York

Do you detect any bias in this painting of the Boston Tea Party? Who do you think painted it — someone for or against the British government?

The Townshend Acts of 1767 negated the Stamp Act but imposed new taxes on goods entering North America by ship. Protesters in the Thirteen Colonies again refused to buy British goods. Eventually Britain withdrew these taxes, except the one on tea. This remaining tax would eventually become a symbol for American dissatisfaction with Britain. In 1773 the "Sons of Liberty" dumped tea into the Boston Harbour in protest. This event became known as the Boston Tea Party.

Convinced that there would be a revolt in the Thirteen Colonies, Sir Guy Carleton, the Governor General of Québec, was instrumental in the creation of the Quebec Act of 1774. It was an attempt to maintain and build on the support of the French Canadian majority in Québec for the British. To accomplish this, the government expanded the territory of Québec to include all the land around the Great Lakes and the Aboriginal reserves to the west, including the Ohio Valley. Also, the government allowed the French Canadians to maintain language rights and French civil law. It officially recognized the Roman Catholic Church and allowed it to collect taxes. However, it specifically denied an elected assembly. The appointed council was open to both French and British landowners.

Reflections

Write your view on whether or not an elected assembly would be a good thing in Québec in 1774.

The majority of French Canadians were not landowners, so while they were relieved to maintain their language and church, they were not won over by the Quebec Act. The British in Québec were openly hostile to the Quebec Act. They objected to legal recognition of the Roman Catholic Church, French law, and French customs. They were, however, satisfied with the advantages they gained in the fur trade because of their increased territory.

The British Americans saw the Quebec Act as even more reason to rebel against Britain. They resented the restrictions placed on their expansion west, and they were shocked by the denial of an elected government. British Americans nicknamed the Quebec Act an "Intolerable Act" and saw it as a betrayal.

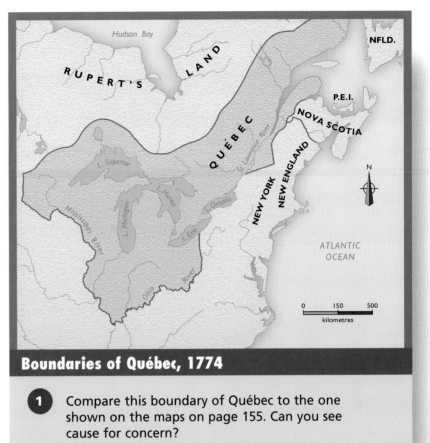

Boundaries of Québec, 1774

1 Compare this boundary of Québec to the one shown on the maps on page 155. Can you see cause for concern?

The Story So Far . . .

1 William Pitt said that North America was an extremely valuable asset because "it is a double market, the market of consumption and the market of supply." Place that quotation in the middle of a web and relate to it, with some explanation, the Royal Proclamation and the other unpopular acts.

2 Imagine you are a third-generation colonist in one of the Thirteen Colonies. Write a letter to the editor of a newspaper expressing your dissatisfaction with Britain's recent colonial policies.

3 Compare the French and British colonists' response to the Royal Proclamation by creating a list of reasons each group was against it.

4 Using a graphic organizer, outline the pros and cons of the Quebec Act for the French Canadians and the British Americans.

THE AMERICAN REVOLUTION AND THE LOYALIST MIGRATION

Partly in response to the Boston Tea Party, partly due to concerns about the volatile mood of discontent in the Thirteen Colonies, Britain decided to punish Boston. King George III applied policies only against Massachusetts — seemingly the centre of resistance and revolt. The Boston Port was closed, its elected assembly was suspended, no meetings were allowed, and the original charter that had established Massachusetts was cancelled. Eventually the hostilities intensified. In 1775 a clash broke out between British soldiers and a citizens' militia at Lexington and Concord. The American Revolution had begun.

For months before the incident at Lexington and Concord, farmers and townspeople had been gathering guns and ammunition and training to fight on a minute's notice. These rebel soldiers would become known as **minutemen**. No one knows for sure who fired the first shot, but we do know that the American rebels were ready. John Adams, who would be elected President of the United States, said, "The Revolution was effected before the war commenced. The Revolution was in the minds and hearts of the people." On July 6, 1775, delegates from every colony except Georgia signed a Declaration of Causes that said the American people had been left only two alternatives: "unconditional submission to the tyranny of irritated ministers or resistance by force."

Not even half the American people were in favour of this revolt, but for the first time in the history of war there were many **civilians** who were not in the army who were willing to take up arms for their cause. Very quickly, thousands of rebel American colonists rallied to that cause.

The American Revolutionary army, under the command of George Washington, took the offensive and began a series of attacks, including some along the border of Nova Scotia and Québec. They planned to capture Québec so the British could not conduct their military operations from there. Montréal and Québec City were both occupied and held by the Americans over the winter of 1775-1776.

American **Patriots** — those who supported the war for independence against Britain — were sure that they would have no trouble convincing French and British citizens in Québec and Nova Scotia to join them in their fight against England.

Much to their surprise, they found virtually no support. The British war with the American colonies would be, for the most part, fought by regular British troops assisted by **Loyalists**: people who supported the British. Except for **raids**, which are swift and sudden charges made by one military group against another, the rest of the revolution was fought to the south of Québec. By May 1776, British ships approached with reinforcements and supplies. The Americans, sick, tired, and short of ammunition and provisions, retreated.

Americans invading Québec City on New Year's Eve, 1775. How did the citizens react to their fight for independence from Britain?

Loyalists, Patriots, and Others

As mentioned, the British did not have much success convincing civilians in Québec or the Maritimes to join their fight against the rebels. However, there were many actively loyal people living in Québec and the Maritimes who were willing to place their allegiance with the British and serve in the military. Consider the example of John Macdonald. He had come to North America in 1772 with a large wave of Scottish immigrants. Though he owned and operated a large piece of land in Tracadie, Island of St. John (later Prince Edward Island), the pension provided to a British officer was an attractive enticement for serving the British. Also, as a Catholic, he believed American colonists wanted to wipe out his religion. For these reasons, he became an officer of the Royal Highland Emigrants and a Maritime Loyalist.

The Evidence Behind the Story

There are many pieces of evidence we can examine to uncover events, and people's feelings about them, from the past. Consider, for example, the poem that follows. "The Pausing American Loyalist" appeared in the *Middlesex Journal*, a newspaper of the day, on January 30, 1776. The poem is based on Shakespeare's famous "To be or not to be" speech in *Hamlet*.

At the time, residents of the Thirteen Colonies were pressured to sign oaths swearing their allegiance to the American Continental Congress. Although you may need to read this poem carefully and more than once, it should add to the picture you are forming about those times and the actions of the people living then.

To sign, or not to sign? That is the question,
Whether 'twere better for an honest man
To sign, and so be safe; or to resolve,
Betide what will, against associations,
And, by retreating, shun them. To fly — I reck
Not where: And, by that flight, t' escape
Feathers and tar, and thousand other ills
That loyalty is heir to: 'Tis a consummation
Devoutly to be wished. To fly — to want —
To want? Perchance to starve: Ay, there's the rub!
For, in that chance of want, what ills may come
To patriot rage, when I have left my all —
Must give me pause: — There's the respect
That makes us trim, and bow to men we hate.
For, who would bear th' indignities o' th' times,
Congress decrees, and wild convention plans,

The laws controll'd, and inj'ries unredressed,
The insolence of knaves, and thousand wrongs
Which patient liege men from vile rebels take,
When he, sans doubt, might certain safety find,
Only by flying? Who would bend to fools,
And truckle thus to mad, mob-chosen upstarts,
But that the dread of something after flight
(In that blest country, where, yet, no moneyless
Poor wight can live) puzzles the will,
And makes ten thousands rather sign — and eat.
Than fly — to starve on loyalty. —
Thus, dread of want makes rebels of us all:
And thus the native hue of loyalty
Is sicklied o'er with a pale cast of trimming;
And enterprises of great pith and virtue,
But unsupported, turn their streams away,
And never come to action.

QUESTIONING THE EVIDENCE

1. Make two lists based on this poem: one stating the reasons a person should sign the oath and another stating the reasons a person should not sign. Which list seems the most persuasive to you?
2. How do you know if this poem was written by a Loyalist, a Patriot, or someone who was neutral?
3. Explain which is a more reliable piece of historical evidence, news or art? How would you rate "The Pausing American Loyalist" as a piece of historical evidence?

The Loyalist settlers who fled to British North America from the Thirteen Colonies were certainly not the only **refugees** from the American Revolution. There were some people who were forced to flee from British North America to the Thirteen Colonies for treason against Britain. In fact there were at least three or four whole townships set aside in New York State for British North American refugees after the war. Moses Hazen is an example of one of these refugees. He was a resident of Québec and had been recommended for a commission by Sir Guy Carleton. At the start of the war, Hazen served the British but was convinced by Americans that he would be richly rewarded if he served them instead.

By offering a joining bonus and a small monthly payment, Hazen recruited a regiment of about 250 habitants. In 1776 they were forced to leave British North America with the retreating American army. At the end of the war, Hazen, and what was left of his regiment, were stateless and dependent on the mercy of the American government for protection.

Not all citizens of the Thirteen Colonies supported the war with Britain. Samuel Adams estimated that only one-third of the people in the Thirteen Colonies supported the quest for independence. He believed that one-third was probably neutral while the other third supported Britain. Many families were torn apart by the pressure of choosing their position.

Unfortunately the atmosphere even after the revolution was unruly. Many people, whether they were actively Loyalist or not, were persecuted by the Patriots. Individuals were harassed and physically assaulted, homes were looted, and property was destroyed or stolen. This treatment was given not only to those who seemed actively Loyalist but to others who did not seem Patriot enough; for example, the families of anyone who held an official position before the revolution and the families of those who were in the British military.

A British Loyalist who has been tarred and feathered by American colonists. Why do you think the colonists are pouring tea into the Loyalist's mouth?

The Story So Far . . .

1 Do you agree with John Adams's statement, "The Revolution was in the minds and hearts of the people"? Why or why not?

2 Make a list of the various reasons some citizens had for becoming Loyalists.

LOYALIST ROUTES AND SETTLEMENTS

Some Loyalists came to British North America early in the revolution. Many came by sea. Overall, Nova Scotia received the largest number of Loyalist refugees: 35 000–40 000! Another 15 000 to 20 000 settled in Québec and along the north shores of lakes Ontario and Erie.

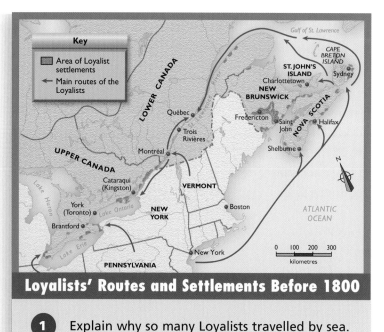

Loyalists' Routes and Settlements Before 1800

Key
- Area of Loyalist settlements
- Main routes of the Loyalists

1 Explain why so many Loyalists travelled by sea.

"Escorted" Loyalists

Not all refugees' stories were the same. Let us piece some parts together and see if we can understand the migration.

Richard Cartwright was a wealthy landowner, innkeeper, and deputy postmaster of Albany. He was a Patriot and had given money to them to help finance the military. His daughter, Elizabeth, was marriedElizabeth, was married to a British soldier. When it was learned that Elizabeth still communicated with her brother, Richard Jr., a local committee forced Richard Jr. to pay a security guaranteeing his patriotism. This occurred in February 1777. By October of that year, Richard Jr. did not feel he could or should continue to give his guarantee so he fled through New York to British North America.

The senior Cartwrights were harassed, their property was confiscated, and within a year they were taken under guard to the border. Not exactly Loyalists, the Cartwrights are an example of those who were forced to assume that identity as a consequence of family actions or beliefs. Their story was not unusual.

Many women found themselves in difficult circumstances. If their husbands, fathers, brothers, or sons served with the British, held positions of authority, or were even suspected of being sympathetic to Britain, they were harassed and abused as if they were Loyalists too. Often when men served in the British army, the women were left to run households and face the consequences on their own. Some women fled, but the hardships of making their way to safety, usually with children, and very few supplies, was too much for many of them. Many women sought permission to leave their communities and the

Snippet

Women Fool Raiders

In 1782 a group of women in Chester, Nova Scotia, scared off a raid by reversing their scarlet-lined skirts and appearing, from a distance, as a regular British troop.

Thirteen Colonies. Patriot committees were established to grant this right. If permission was obtained, then the women were escorted to the border. This may have been a safer arrangement for many women. The escort was not free, however, so only women with some means of paying could arrange this. In addition, all their property was taken by the Patriots. Also, sons aged 12 and over had to be left behind.

Many women did not have the resources to keep themselves and their families going and were exchanged for Patriot prisoners being held in British North America. By the late 1770s, several locations had adopted the practice of simply removing families of men who had joined the British. The Patriots did not want these families to be in any way supported by the community. They also feared that these families were supporting the Loyalists with food, shelter, or military information.

Loyalists leaving New York in the 1780s. Some women fled with their children to avoid persecution.

© Collection of the New-York Historical Society, negative number 59064

George Carscallen
BRAVE YOUNG LOYALIST

In 1776, 13-year-old George Carscallen was no stranger to hard work. As his family struggled to carve out a new life on a farm in the British colony of New York, George helped out where he could.

The Carscallens had more to worry about than just making their farm succeed though. For years anger at Britain had been simmering among many American colonists. But George's family, like many of their neighbours in the Camden Valley, had tried to remain neutral.

When fighting broke out in 1775, though, the Camden Valley settlers were forced to take sides. "If you're not with us, you're against us," the rebels told them. Some neighbours did join the rebels, but George's father refused. Twice he was arrested and twice he escaped and returned home. Fearing a third arrest, he packed a few belongings and went into hiding, along with his three older sons. This left George, his mother, his older sister, Elizabeth, and his younger sister, Ann, to look after the farm by themselves.

Not long afterward, a gang of rebels arrived at the farm. When they could not find his father, they grabbed George and threatened to hang him if he did not reveal his father's hiding place. George's response? "Hang away!"

Three times, the rebels placed a noose around the teenager's neck and hoisted him up at the end of a rope. Three times, George refused to betray his father and brothers. Some of the rebels were neighbours who knew George and his family. Finally, when they realized that he was going to stand firm no matter what, they stopped.

After this it was too dangerous to stay on the farm. The rebels who arrived next time might not be so merciful. Besides, the family could no longer survive. The rebels had stolen all the livestock — a yoke of oxen, a yoke of steers, three horses, one cow, and 11 hogs — as well as tools, utensils, clothes, and furniture. Along with his mother and sisters, George joined a stream of Loyalists from the area who were fleeing to Québec as refugees.

In the meantime, George's father and older brothers had signed up to fight for the British. Three years later, as soon as he was 16, George did the same. He joined the King's Royal Regiment of New York. After the war, in return for the losses they had suffered, the entire family received grants of land near what is now Napanee, Ontario. Once again, they started farms from scratch.

This time the Carscallens prospered. Three descendants of the family have served as members of the Ontario Legislature, and one of these also became a federal member of Parliament. As for George, his name lives on in the story of bravery that is told in the family to this day.

More people you could research are

Daniel Begal

George Carscallen

Mary Hoyt

Alexander and Suzanna MacDonald

Rev. James Nichols

Thomas Peters

Richard Pierpoint

African-American Loyalists

Soon after the start of the American Revolution, the British authorities, anxious to enlarge their armies, offered freedom to any slave who would join British troops. This offer of freedom led thousands of African Americans to join the British army. There were, however, some African-American soldiers who were there as property seized by the British. In total, about 3500 free African Americans were moved, mostly to Nova Scotia, at the end of the war. Several also came to British North America as slaves of white families who were part of the Loyalist **migration**, which is a mass movement of people who leave as a group.

Aboriginal Loyalists

The British military quite actively looked for allies among the Iroquois nations. Not all Aboriginal people were interested in becoming involved in the American Revolution, and there were probably many Aboriginal families that were as divided as many Patriot and Loyalist families.

The British Americans did gain a large group of Iroquois supporters, however, because many Iroquois were afraid that if the Patriots won, more Iroquois land would be lost. The Aboriginal Peoples were very aware that the inhabitants of the Thirteen Colonies wanted to expand west, through the Ohio Valley, farther into Aboriginal land. Most Aboriginal support of the British came from the Six Nations of the Iroquois Confederacy. They knew from past experience that American settlers would simply take the land they wanted. Experiences during the American Revolution justified their fears. Many Iroquois people suffered the same consequences as other Loyalists. In 1779, for example, a Patriot raiding expedition destroyed several Iroquois villages along the Genesee River in New York. This forced hundreds of Aboriginal Peoples to seek refuge with the British in Fort Niagara, making them part of the early Loyalist migration.

In the end approximately 5000 Iroquois settled in British North America. Many of them settled on a land grant in what is now Southern Ontario, along the Grand River, running south into Lake Erie.

The Cape Breton council meets to discuss the hordes of Loyalist refugees arriving from America.

Joseph and Mary Brant

TORN BETWEEN TWO WORLDS

(detail) Romney, George, 1734-1802, British, Joseph Brant (Thayendanegea), 1776, oil on canvas, Transfer from the Canadian War Memorials, 1921. National Gallery of Canada, Ottawa.

Like the European settlers, the Iroquois of the Six Nations were divided when the colonists rebelled. Some sided with the rebels. More sided with the British. Most, however, wanted to remain neutral.

Into this conflict stepped Joseph Brant (Thayendanega in Mokawk) and his sister, Mary (Konwatsi' Tsiaienni in Mohawk). The stepchildren of an important Mohawk *sachem* — a hereditary Chief — they had grown up in the longhouses of the Mohawk River Valley of New York. But they had also spent a lot of time with Europeans and had adopted many of their ways. Each had one foot in the Mohawk world and another in the European world.

Recently widowed, Mary had been married for years to William Johnson, a wealthy and powerful Irish trader who had been in charge of Aboriginal affairs for the British. Johnson had arranged for Joseph to attend a special school. There, the young man had learned English and trained as an interpreter.

The Brants were firmly pro-British. They believed that the British would stop settlers from taking over Aboriginal lands and persuaded their people to fight for the King. This would have lasting consequences for the people of the Six Nations — and for the Brants.

When the tide of war turned in favour of the rebels, the people of the Six Nations were forced to flee northward. Mary and some of the Mohawks settled at Cataraqui, now Kingston, Ontario. After the war, much of what had been their homeland was granted to American soldiers. What is worse, the treaty that ended the war did not even mention the Aboriginal nations. The people of the Mohawk Valley were now exiles. Many felt betrayed by the British — and by the Brants. To make the best of things, Joseph Brant persuaded the British to grant the Six Nations land along the banks of the Grand River in Southern Ontario. When they moved there, the ford across the river at his farm was called Brant's Ford. Today it is the site of the city of Brantford. Mary stayed at her new home in Cataraqui.

For the rest of their lives, Joseph and Mary Brant tried to help their people. But the Mohawks could not agree on the kind of help they wanted, and many blamed the Brants for their troubles. In the end, Joseph decided to move away. He built himself a mansion overlooking Burlington Bay on Lake Ontario.

Still, he never forgot his heritage. When he died in 1807, his last words to the friend at his bedside were, "Have pity on the poor Indians. If you can get any influence with the great, endeavour to do them all the good you can."

More people you could research are

Mary Bliss

Colonel Stephen Blucke

Joseph and Mary Brant

John Deserontyou

General Haldimand

William Johnson

Russell Pitman

Was There a Typical Loyalist?

Many Loyalists probably had things in common with one another, but there was no typical Loyalist. Close to half the Loyalists were connected to the military, as part of a Loyalist or a British regiment that was disbanded after the war. Just over half were civilian refugees. As you have already learned, there were African-American, Aboriginal, English, Scottish, and Irish Loyalists. There were also paid soldiers from several countries who had served in the British army, so the Loyalist migration also included Germans, Swiss, and Dutch.

Several Acadians took this opportunity to return to their former homes. Quakers and Mennonites had refused to fight in the American Revolution due to their religious beliefs. They found themselves in an awkward position when the war ended, so some migrated.

In 1783, when Britain announced its willingness to award land grants as **compensation**, or repayment, for Loyalists' losses, there were probably many "instant" Loyalists, attracted more by offers of land than by beliefs. It must be acknowledged, however, that a great number came without thought of payment. The compensation of land grants ended in the late 1790s, but self-proclaimed Loyalists continued to trickle into Canada after that.

Aside from the military service, Loyalists came from all walks of life. There were shopkeepers, sailors, doctors, blacksmiths, lawyers, politicians, farmers, carpenters, and servants, to name a few. Some Loyalists were able to bring possessions, but many had lost everything and had to start over with very little.

The Story So Far . . .

1 If you had to leave your home tomorrow with just a bag full of your possessions, what would you take? Think in terms of physical survival.
2 Besides land, what else did the Loyalists need to start a new life?
3 The Loyalists faced both physical and emotional hardships in their new home. Make a list of challenges you think the Loyalists might have experienced.

DESTINATION WILDERNESS

While many Loyalists migrated at the beginning of, and during, the American Revolution, thousands migrated as the war was ending. Most of them travelled by ship to Nova Scotia. There were private organizations of Loyalists who made arrangements with the British government. The British covered the expense of the passage and supplied food and tools as long as their supplies lasted. No land was given in advance.

Some Loyalists, as you have already learned, travelled overland. Aside from those who had been escorted to the border, many made their way by foot and wagon.

The Loyalists who came before the war ended were largely dependent on the military leaders in charge to help them as much as they could, given the circumstances. From 1784 to about 1786, most Loyalists could expect to receive: a two-year supply of food; a year's supply of clothing; two scythes, two spades, three hoes, a chisel, a handsaw, a hammer, and a plough; one axe and gun for every male over age 14; and boards, nails, shingles, and window glass.

Land was also granted, though it was not distributed evenly. This was an extremely slow process that created discontent for many Loyalists waiting in tents in the wilderness. Since land grants were intended for adult males, women Loyalists who were left without a husband, father, or brother had to make claims for compensation. Usually the women received less than the men.

From a hat, a Loyalist picks a certificate that identifies what will be his plot of land. How will he know where this plot is located? Do you think there could have been a better way to assign land?

This painting, by Reverend Bowan Squires, shows Loyalists arriving on the shore of the Bay of Quinte in present-day Ontario. You see one tent set up. British army officials rationed tents to each family waiting to be granted land so they could start their new life. As you can see, this group of Loyalists arrived by boat. Step into the picture. There now, aren't you glad it stopped raining? How did you like being cooped up with the whole family in the tent all day because of the pouring rain? Do you miss home? Do you think you'll ever meet up with your old friends again? Who do you think is arriving in that boat? When do you think you'll get your land allotment? Do you know how to clear land and build a cabin? What do you think you'll do for food this winter? It's already August, so you won't be able to plant much. Do you think the newcomers will share some of their food? Maybe you should talk to one of the others.

With a partner, present the conversation you would have with one of the Loyalists just arriving.

Rose Fortune, Canada's First Policewoman

Rose Fortune came to Annapolis in 1783 at the age of ten, as part of the African-American Loyalist movement. She had her own business as a baggage handler and served as a police officer. Apparently she was also known for a unique style of dress. Seven generations later one of her descendants, Daurene Lewis, became the first African-Canadian mayor in Nova Scotia and the first African-Canadian mayor in Canada in 1984.

This formula was not strictly followed, though. Some officers received much larger grants. The quality of the land granted was not of equal value either. The Loyalists drew paper from a hat, lottery style, to receive their piece of land. Some had better luck than others. In all cases, good land or not, all the Loyalists who received land had a big job ahead of them. To receive the official deed certifying that the property was theirs to keep, they had to clear the land, build a house, and start farming.

The African-American Loyalists were not as well compensated as the white settlers. Of the 3000 African-American Loyalists in Nova Scotia, just over a third actually received land grants. Also, their average grant was slightly less than 5 ha each. The African Americans who did not own land took work wherever they could find it. All faced discrimination.

One problem was in finding jobs. After the war was over there were many disbanded soldiers and other Loyalists looking for work. In July 1784, for example, disbanded white soldiers chased African-American workers from the town of Shelburne and burned their homes. This was Canada's first race riot. There were other problems too. Even if they held land and paid taxes, the free African Americans were not entitled to trial by jury, nor could they vote. So in 1792, with no land and few job prospects, nearly half of the African-American Loyalists in Nova Scotia accepted a British anti-slavery society's offer of free passage to Sierra Leone, a small country on the west coast of Africa. On the other hand, more than half stayed and nurtured what have become the oldest African-American settlements in the country.

The migration of African-American Loyalist pioneers established towns in Nova Scotia like Shelburne, Birchtown, Brindleytown, Tracadie, and Preston. Birchtown grew to be the largest settlement of free African Americans in North America by 1784.

The African-American settlements in Nova Scotia are the oldest in the country. This illustration is of Shelburne in 1788, where one was located nearby.

Aboriginal Loyalists had their own reasons for discontent. In Canada most of them came from the Iroquois Confederacy. They were given two land grants in what would become Southern Ontario. It hardly made up for the huge mass of their land, south of the Great Lakes and as far west as the Mississippi River, that their British allies had transferred to the Americans after the war ended. The British built a church, school, sawmill, and flour mill on the new reserves, and paid the salary of one teacher for each Aboriginal settlement. These were not necessarily projects the Aboriginal Peoples were interested in, but when they decided to sell some of the land to get money for their own projects, the British government would not allow it.

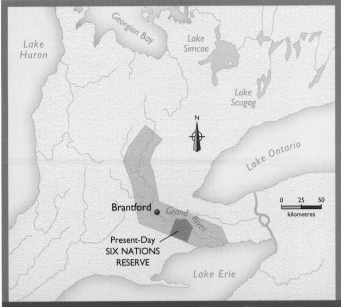

Land Granted to Aboriginal Loyalists

1 Notice the difference between the original Aboriginal land grant on the Grand River and the present-day reserve.

Snapshot

A Mohawk Village

This painting by Elizabeth Simcoe shows a Mohawk Village on the Grand River, where the Six Nations Reserve was established in 1785. The church in the foreground still exists and is the oldest house of worship in Ontario.

Loyalist Hardships

Most people cannot imagine living in the circumstances faced by so many Loyalist refugees. Some people had to eat leaf buds, roots, tree bark, and beech leaves to survive. In 1788 there was a crop failure, a severe winter, and no more British aid. It is recorded that one family lived on beech leaves for more than a week. Some people died after eating poisonous plants or roots. Skunk (musk glands removed) skinned and baked was considered a tasty treat. This was known as the "hungry year." One eyewitness in 1789 wrote that wild leaves and starved domestic animals were rationed "one spoonful of meal per day, for one person." This same witness also reported that one family "leaped for joy at one robin being caught, out of which a whole pot of broth was made."

Clothing was another challenge. Whatever clothing the Loyalists had brought was quickly worn through. The Aboriginal Peoples gave them the idea of using deerskin. It was warm in the winter and very durable. Almost every family grew flax and kept sheep to make cloth at home by hand.

The Loyalists used handwoven cloth and deerskin to make their clothing. What were the advantages of these materials?

Toward a New Society

Many Loyalists shared a feeling of discontent. The length of time it took to get a land grant and the poor quality of some of the land were their first problems. Poor land created an additional migration, as many Loyalists moved shortly after they arrived at their original destination.

Discontent among the Loyalists soon became political. In Québec they were dissatisfied with the lack of a representative government. In Nova Scotia they were perturbed that the government was dominated by older inhabitants and they blamed it for their inadequate compensation. It must have been frustrating to come from one of the Thirteen Colonies, where political involvement was expected, to a situation that was much less participatory. Many Loyalists felt, justifiably, that they had suffered a lot for their allegiance to the British crown. When land grants and government compensation were slow in coming, the Loyalists blamed those who were closest. Some of the older inhabitants found the Loyalist newcomers irritating in their demands.

The British government's first response was to divide Nova Scotia in 1784 and create the new colonies of New Brunswick and Cape Breton Island. This pleased the Loyalist settlers who had located in large numbers there, especially since elected assemblies would be allowed. By dividing the area and allowing the Loyalists a measure of control over their everyday life, Britain hoped to avoid the kind of civil unrest that had led to the American Revolution.

The Loyalist population in Québec was not as large as in Nova Scotia, yet the problems there were greater. The Quebec Act of 1774 had been designed to govern a French, Catholic population and allow them to carry on with their traditions. Although the 10 000 Loyalists were still the minority, it was, after all, a British colony. The Loyalists in Québec expected representative government, especially after the New Brunswick solution.

In 1791 the Constitutional Act attempted to satisfy the requirements of both the Loyalists and the French in Québec. Using the solution that worked in Nova Scotia, Québec was divided into Lower Canada and Upper Canada. The terms *lower* and *upper* were used to indicate each colony's position on the St. Lawrence River. Lower Canada, the eastern area, contained most of the French inhabitants with a small number of British. Upper Canada, the western area, was home to the majority of British Loyalists.

The division of Québec formally separated British North America on the basis of two distinct societies. Loyalist demands were satisfied, but not at the expense of French Canadian traditions.

Snippet

The First City in British North America

In 1795 Saint John, New Brunswick, became the first official city in British North America. Thomas Carleton, Lieutenant-Governor of New Brunswick, incorporated Saint John to placate residents. They became angry because, after briefly naming Saint John capital of the new colony, he had transferred this honour to Fredericton, a much smaller community.

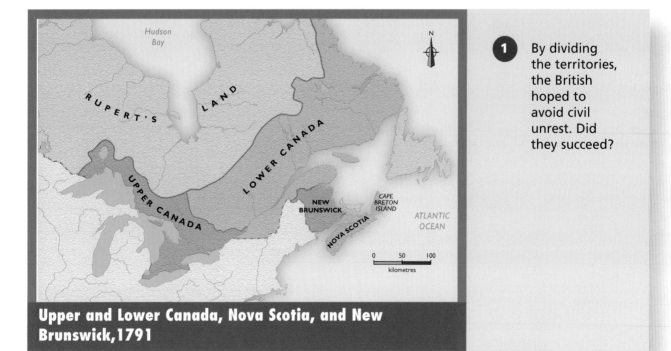

Upper and Lower Canada, Nova Scotia, and New Brunswick, 1791

1 By dividing the territories, the British hoped to avoid civil unrest. Did they succeed?

The Loyalists **173**

John Graves Simcoe
REDCOAT WITH ATTITUDE

John Graves Simcoe founded the settlement at York over the objections of his superior, Governor General Guy Carleton. This was not unusual for Simcoe. He was often at odds with people who did not share his vision.

The son of a Royal Navy captain, Simcoe was born in England and joined the British army when he was 19. When the American colonists rebelled, his regiment was sent to help crush the revolt. He soon realized that something was wrong. The military tactics that had made the British so successful on European battlefields did not work in the North American bush.

When he was placed in charge of a regiment called the Queen's Rangers, Simcoe had a chance to put some of his own ideas into practice. He outfitted his troops in green uniforms because he believed that the red coats of many British soldiers made them easy targets. Rather than practising marching, he drilled his men in handling their muskets and bayonets. He also did something even more unusual: he ordered the Rangers to bathe as often as possible, since he believed it was healthier to be clean.

Under Simcoe, the Rangers became a crack fighting force, able to move quickly and strike suddenly. Their reputation of being gallant meant that they were chosen to fight in many battles. As a result, Simcoe was wounded several times. In 1779 he was taken prisoner, but managed to escape.

When the British surrendered, Simcoe's first thought was for the safety of his troops. Most of them were Loyalists rather than British soldiers. He was sure the Americans would treat them as traitors, not prisoners of war. He was right. Though Simcoe helped many Rangers escape, some were left behind. These men were executed.

Because of his experiences with the Queen's Rangers, Simcoe had great affection and respect for the Loyalists. When he returned to England, he did not forget those who had served under him. He arranged for them to be granted land in Nova Scotia. He also played an active role in the debate about the future of Canada, speaking out for all Loyalists.

More people you could research are

Sir Guy Carleton

Thomas Jefferson

Chief Pontiac

Elizabeth Simcoe

John Graves Simcoe

George Washington

Simcoe Establishes Upper Canada

When John Graves Simcoe was offered the post of Lieutenant-Governor of the new province of Upper Canada, he jumped at the chance to help create a new colony. He wanted it to be a refuge for everyone who shared his belief that British institutions were the best. One of his ideas was to re-establish the Queen's Rangers as a military force and to help build the necessary roads and bridges.

On September 26, 1791, Simcoe sailed for Upper Canada. With him were his wife, Elizabeth, and his two youngest children. For the next five years, the Simcoes would make Upper Canada their home.

Simcoe hoped that Upper Canada would show Americans what they were missing. He hoped to attract more settlers to the area and create a model community based on British government and law. He quickly set about surveying land, creating positions of authority, and passing laws to keep order. Land grants of about 75 ha were available to settlers who would swear loyalty to the King, serve in a militia for the defence of Upper Canada, and improve and farm their land. As a result of the grants, thousands of *Late Loyalists* arrived from America.

Barely ten years after the war with America ended, Simcoe sensed that there might soon be a need for a strong military defence position for Upper Canada. Conflicts between Aboriginal groups and American settlers in the Ohio Valley and south had been escalating steadily. This was complicated by the fact that the British had not totally withdrawn from the area the way they were supposed to after the war.

Simcoe thought that of all the sites in Upper Canada, York (now Toronto) would make the best base for controlling Lake Ontario. He moved the capital of Upper Canada from Newark to York and planned to build Fort York. The development of the fort never did match Simcoe's grand plan for it, but York was established as a populated settlement.

Snippet

Upper Canada First to Limit Slavery

Thanks to John Graves Simcoe, Upper Canada became the first place in the world to limit slavery. Simcoe wanted to abolish the practice completely, but many government members owned slaves. To win their support, he had to water down the anti-slavery law introduced in 1793. People were allowed to keep slaves they already owned, but no more could be imported. Children born to slaves were to be set free when they turned 25.

Web Connection

www.school.mcgrawhill.ca/resources

Go to the web site above to find out more about an aspect of the Loyalist experience that interests you. Go to History Resources, then to *Canada: The Story of Our Heritage* to see where to go next.

The Story So Far . . .

1 Design a coin to commemorate the Loyalist migration.
2 Explain how the hardships were different for African-American Loyalists.
3 Britain did not want "history to repeat itself." Explain.

SUM IT UP!

When we set our focus for this chapter we acknowledged that the Loyalists were one of the most significant groups to settle in Canada. Driven here by reasons mostly connected to the American Revolution, the sheer change in population alone could not be ignored. The Loyalists created a spirit of allegiance to the British crown and its institutions that we see around us even today.

By reading about a variety of individuals, we have observed that no two Loyalists were alike. There were common problems for all, though. Most started their lives in British North America with very little, and their lives were very challenging. We saw how quickly the arrival of these Loyalists forced the government to meet the newcomers' demands and to protect and maintain the British colonial system. Lands and people were divided.

The interconnectedness of Britain, France, the Aboriginal Peoples, French North America, and British North America would continue for quite some time. Simcoe knew that they would clash again so he established York and created a military base and settlement there.

THINKING ABOUT YOUR LEARNING

1 Choose one of the different groups of people who took part in the Loyalist migration. From the point of view of a child in a Loyalist family from that group, write a children's story that highlights some of the challenges the family met both getting to British North America and after their arrival. Make the details as authentic as you can.

2 Create a mural to depict the Loyalists' experience. You could choose to:
a) depict one group involved in the Loyalist migration, or
b) concentrate on one aspect that affected all the Loyalists, or
c) create a montage to highlight several aspects of the Loyalists' situation.

APPLYING YOUR LEARNING

1. Go back to the introductory chapter and review *Steps in the Research Process* on pages 21-22. Following the steps shown there, begin a project to uncover the historical development of your own community. This project will be ongoing throughout this unit. For now, complete steps 1 to 3. In your planning be sure to consider origins, key personalities, and the contributions of all the cultural groups involved.

2. Refugees still look to Canada as a place to make a new life and, like the Loyalist refugees, most still face problems.
   - What problems would refugees in Canada face today?
   - How are the problems of today's refugees similar to or different from the Loyalists' problems?
   - Make a plan to investigate what type of assistance Canada offers refugees today.

3. Loyalty is a very complicated concept. Jot down a list of people, places, and ideas to which you feel loyal. Try to decide just how loyal you think you would be and what you would be willing to do to prove it.

4. Protests against taxes are not just a thing of the past. Ask your parents or other family members if they can remember some recent protests against taxes. Piece as much of the story together as you can. What was being taxed? How did people protest? What happened to the tax?

USING KEY WORDS

1. Look up the following words in a dictionary:
   - compensation
   - elected assembly
   - migration
   - military rule
   - Loyalist
   - Patriot
   - refugee

   Given what you have just learned about these words, what would you add to the definition in your dictionary?

CHAPTER

6

The War of 1812

1794	1803	1811	1812
Jay's Treaty	War resumes in Europe	Battle of Tippecanoe	• United States declares war on Britain • Battle of Michilimackinac, July 17 • Battle of Detroit, August 16 • Battle of Queenston Heights, October 13

SETTING OUR FOCUS

In the picture on the left, British troops burn Washington in 1814 in retaliation against the Americans who burned York in 1813. Examine the picture and discuss what reasons a military leader would have for destroying a capital city's buildings, whether or not this type of destruction should be allowed, and what consequences might result from the destruction of a capital city.

In this chapter you will be learning about the War of 1812, in which British North American and British soldiers fought against American soldiers. The War of 1812 was ended by an armistice, The Treaty of Ghent, on December 24, 1814. Since the war did not end as a result of a decisive defeat or retreat, this war is described as the war that both sides won. It also provided British North Americans with a sense of military glory and, more importantly, a sense of identity. The War of 1812 was the last time British North America had to defend itself against American military invasion. Policies since then have been based on an underlying desire to maintain friendly relations.

PREVIEWING THE CHAPTER

In this chapter you will learn about these topics:
- **the major causes of the War of 1812**
- **the different groups of people, and some specific individuals, who were significant to the War of 1812**
- **the impact the War of 1812 had on the development of Canada**
- **the tendency of past events to affect future events**
- **the achievements and contributions of Sir John Graves Simcoe**

KEY WORDS

armistice
coalition
displaced
greatcoat
mess
treaty
War Hawks

1813
- Battle of Stoney Creek, June 5–6
- Battle of Beaver Dams, June 24
- Battle of Moraviantown, October 5
- Battle of Châteauguay, October 26
- Battle of Crysler's Farm, November 11

1814
- Washington burns
- Battle of Chippawa, July 5
- Battle of Lundy's Lane, July 25
- Battle of Plattsburg, September 11
- The Treaty of Ghent

1815
Battle of New Orleans

1817
Rush-Bagot Agreement

In the early 1800s, roads in Upper Canada were under the control of special supervisors called *pathmasters*. One of a pathmaster's jobs was to ensure that settlers obeyed the law requiring them to work 3 to 12 days a year on the roads. This system did not work very well, however. The dreadful state of the roads was a source of endless complaint by travellers and settlers alike.

REMEMBERING SIMCOE AT YORK

When Sir John Graves Simcoe was appointed the first Lieutenant-Governor of Upper Canada in 1792, his main goals were to attract more settlers, survey the land, and create a model community. Simcoe was, first and foremost, a military man, and like many British military authorities of the day, he was governed by a sense of the inevitability of war. In 1795 travel writer La Rochefoucault-Liancourt wrote of Simcoe that, "No hillock catches his eye without exciting in his mind the idea of a fort."

During his time in Upper Canada, Simcoe always directed settlement with an eye to military movement. Roads, for example, were laid out to provide military routes and speedy communication paths, should the need arise. Probably the most famous example of Simcoe's plans for York is Yonge Street. At 1885 km, it is still the longest street in the world, stretching far north from Lake Ontario. Two other significant routes that were a result of Simcoe's planning and surveying were Kingston Road and Dundas Street.

By the time he left in 1796 to be governor of Santo Domingo, Haiti (now the Dominican Republic), Simcoe had also managed to direct populations toward a string of settlements, east, west, north, and south that later became, and still are, important urban centres.

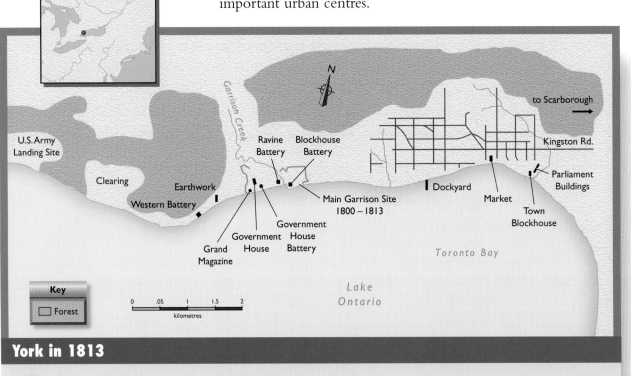

York in 1813

1 Relate the landmarks on the map of York in 1813 to the landmarks that are there today.

Snapshot

The Governor's Roads

Worried about another war with the United States, Lieutenant-Governor John Graves Simcoe had envisioned two important military roads in Upper Canada. The first was Dundas Street, named after Henry Dundas, British colonial secretary. It was to stretch more than 800 km between the boundary of Lower Canada and present-day Windsor. The second was Yonge Street, named after Simcoe's friend, George Yonge, the British minister of war. Running north from York to Lake Simcoe, the road was intended to help move troops and supplies to the Upper Great Lakes.

Work on Dundas Street started at present-day Dundas in 1793. Following an old fur-trading route, *the Governor's Road*, as it was called, had been extended to La Tranche, near present-day London, by 1794. A year later, an American road builder named Asa Danforth had cleared the leg linking Dundas and York. Danforth later won the contract to build the section between York and Kingston, shown in the picture, a stretch that became known as *the Kingston Road*.

By 1796 the Queen's Rangers and settlers had cleared Yonge Street as far as Holland Landing, about 53 km north of York.

Though they were called streets and roads, they were little more than trails through the woods. They were often blocked by fallen trees and brush that threatened to grow back as fast as they were cleared. Wagons and coaches had to dodge tree stumps and often became mired in mud when it rained. For years winter was the best time to travel in Upper Canada because the roads were frozen solid.

British-American Relations

A **treaty** that ends a war is a negotiated, signed, and approved agreement between the countries that had been at war. In 1763 the Treaty of Paris was signed by France, Britain, and Spain to end the Seven Years' War. That treaty transferred Québec from France to Britain, giving Britain control of almost all of North America. In 1783, another Treaty of Paris marked Britain's signed acknowledgement of the independence of the United States.

This acknowledgement of American independence was supposed to usher in a new age of cordial relations between the new nation and the parent country. The British government was tired of war, so the treaty was negotiated in such a way as to avoid future friction between the United States and Britain. One of the causes of the American War of Independence had been the expansion of the territory of Québec in 1774, to include all the land around the Great Lakes, the Aboriginal reserves to the west, and the Ohio Valley — the area around the Mississippi River.

Hoping for a lasting peace, the British negotiators were anxious to make almost any boundary arrangements. According to the Treaty of Paris in 1783, Britain was supposed to give the Ohio Valley to the American government. Expansion west was extremely important to the newly formed United States. In return, America was to compensate Loyalists for land and property that had been taken during the war.

More than ten years later neither side had fulfilled the treaty's requirements. Britain hesitated to turn over the Ohio Valley for a few reasons. The colonists in Lower Canada, especially the merchants in Montréal, were extremely unhappy about losing access to an area that they had come to call their own. The Quebec Act of 1774 had made the Ohio Valley part of Québec to maintain French Canadian support of Britain by increasing their advantage in the fur trade. The merchants in Lower Canada did not want to lose this advantage and urged Britain to hold on to this area.

Joseph Brant and other Aboriginal leaders of the Six Nations encouraged an alliance of tribes to recover land south of the Ohio River.

Aboriginal Peoples' Concerns

Another great concern for Britain at this time was retaining the Aboriginal Peoples as allies for British North America. The Treaty of Paris did not consider Aboriginal concerns at all.

Fearing continual westward expansion into their land, some Aboriginal groups carried out a series of raids in an attempt to regain and hold their land.

Since the British had not released their hold on the Ohio Valley, Americans believed that the British were behind these raids. In fact, they were not. The British feared that if they pushed too far, those Aboriginal groups who had been displaced by the Treaty of Paris might attack Québec too. Sir Guy Carleton, Governor of Québec, urged Britain to hold onto the Western area in order to regain Aboriginal confidence. Many Americans wondered why the British would not leave, since the land was not theirs anymore.

Tecumseh, Chief of the Shawnee, his half-brother, known as The Prophet, and Joseph Brant of the Six Nations were some of the leaders who encouraged an alliance of tribes, especially south of the Great Lakes. Between 1786 and 1791 this confederacy of Aboriginal nations successfully recovered some land south of the Ohio River.

Jay's Treaty

By 1794 the Americans were ready to take a stand. They had defeated the Aboriginal confederation led by Tecumseh in a battle at Fallen Timbers, close to the Maumee River on the west coast of Lake Erie. Many Americans seemed ready to take up all grievances on a battleground. Britain was at war with France and so was anxious to avoid a war with the United States. By signing Jay's Treaty, Britain agreed to surrender the Western Ohio area by 1796. This treaty did not, however, resolve a border dispute that existed between Maine and New Brunswick.

The Story So Far . . .

1 Think about the quotation on page 180 describing Sir John Graves Simcoe. State the reasons a military man like Simcoe might feel the need to worry about forts and transportation during this time period.

2 Compare Simcoe's impact on British North America in the 1790s with Talon's impact on New France in the 1660s.

3 Think about the Treaty of Paris of 1783. Create a chart showing the reasons for dissatisfaction for Americans, Aboriginal Peoples, and British North American colonists.

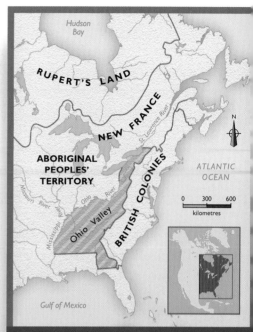

American Expansion

1 How would you feel if American settlements displaced you from where you live?

CONSEQUENCES OF WAR IN EUROPE

From 1803 to 1809, Britain and France were at war with each other. They established trade blockades that prevented enemy and neutral ships from entering their ports to exchange goods. The British navy also searched ships for deserters. Many of the ships were American. These incidents provoked the United States into considering a war against Britain. The **War Hawks** were vocal advocates for a war with Britain, but the majority of people in the United States did not agree with them.

The British North American colonies benefited from the situation in Europe and from all the trade blockades. The colonies soon became a major supplier of goods that Britain had previously purchased from the United States, like timber, wheat, fish, and fur. The ports in Nova Scotia and New Brunswick, especially Saint John, became important bases and shipping centres. At the same time, there was a fair amount of trade between Nova Scotia and the Eastern United States.

Halifax was a busy harbour during the time of the trade blockades in Europe.

By 1812 the population of British North America had increased quite dramatically, to nearly half a million. Though settling the land was hard work, colonists could prosper, largely because Britain provided them with a ready market during the war. For the average person, though, survival and advancement depended on one's own efforts. Interest in world affairs was far from many people's minds.

War Hawks, Tecumseh, and Tippecanoe

The Granger Collection, New York

The War Hawks attacked Tecumseh and the Aboriginal coalition at Tippecanoe. What were they fighting over?

During his presidency, Thomas Jefferson had initiated a policy of the removal of Aboriginal Peoples. His plan was to either convert the Aboriginal Peoples to become settled farmers or force them to move west of the Mississippi River. Tribe after tribe were forced to move, or were **displaced**, this way. The individual tribes had not been able to thwart the American force. After Tecumseh created an Aboriginal **coalition**, or union, they were able to fight back. They attacked several American posts and settlements all along the western frontier from Michigan to Mississippi. The War Hawks focused their efforts on this development and launched a large attack against Tecumseh at Tippecanoe, just south of Lake Michigan, in 1811.

Many were killed on both sides and Tecumseh's coalition was defeated. However, various Aboriginal groups continued to attack American settlements, especially in the West. The War Hawks claimed that Britain was providing the attackers with guns and ammunition.

Tecumseh

WARRIOR WITH A DREAM

The Granger Collection, New York

Tecumseh had a dream. The great Shawnee Chief, who lived south of Lake Erie in the present-day state of Ohio, wanted to unite his Aboriginal neighbours and establish a separate territory. He had seen what happened when settlers took over Aboriginal lands. With no place to hunt or grow crops, his people became sick, or starved. They had to beg for food. All his life, Tecumseh had fiercely resisted this.

When war broke out in 1812, Tecumseh knew his people were threatened. Shawnee territory lay between the American states and Upper Canada. If American troops marching to attack Upper Canada overran Shawnee land, settlers would not be far behind. He decided his only hope was to side with the British.

After the capture of Detroit, Major-General Isaac Brock immediately returned to oversee the defence of the Niagara frontier. He left Colonel Henry Proctor in charge at Detroit. Tecumseh did not like this man. He thought Proctor was a coward. Shortly afterward, Brock died at the Battle of Queenston Heights. By the fall of 1813, the Americans had recaptured Detroit and were again preparing to invade Upper Canada.

Against Tecumseh's advice, Proctor ordered a retreat up the Thames River. Tecumseh felt as if he had been betrayed. Still, he was not willing to give up his dream. When Proctor said that his plan was to stand and fight at Chatham, Tecumseh persuaded his followers to stay with the British.

When Tecumseh arrived at Chatham, however, he discovered that no preparations had been made. In fact, Proctor had split his force, leading some of them up the Thames to a Delaware mission at Moraviantown, now called Thamesville. The situation was getting worse. Tecumseh's spies reported that American troops were hot on his heels. Furthermore, the Americans seemed to be ignoring the British and following Tecumseh's band.

Proctor and Tecumseh met and decided to make a stand. When the attack came, though, Proctor fled, leaving about 300 of Tecumseh's men to face 3000 American soldiers. Tecumseh refused to give up. Above the noise of battle, his war cry could be heard: "Be brave! Be brave!"

Then his voice fell silent. The great Chief had fallen. Without their leader, his men scattered.

When Tecumseh died, his dream died with him. American settlers moved freely onto Shawnee land and, over the next 20 years, nearly all the Shawnee were driven out of Ohio.

More people you could research are

John Douglas

Felix Grundy

The Prophet

John Randolph

The Shawnee

Tecumseh

America Declares War on Britain

The British were aware that many officials and representatives in the American government were ready for war. Recognizing the validity of some of the American complaints, especially the violation of American waters, interference with trade, and the blockade, the British decided to discontinue the Orders-in-Council that had been the cause of those areas of conflict. This decision was reached on June 17, 1812.

News did not travel quickly. There were no phones, conference calls, faxes, or e-mails. All news from Britain travelled in the same way: by ship, across the Atlantic Ocean. Typically, this trip took six to eight weeks.

Unaware that Britain was suspending the Orders-in-Council, the United States declared war on June 18, 1812. Many have wondered if the Americans would have cancelled their war effort if they had received the news from Britain sooner. What do you think?

The Canadas in the War of 1812

There were many Americans who believed that Upper and Lower Canada would be won easily. Former American President Thomas Jefferson had said it would be "a mere matter of marching." There were even those who believed that the American army was not invading British North America, so much as liberating the people there.

Consider the following facts. It is little wonder that some Americans envisioned a swift victory.

- The population in British North America was 500 000, compared to 8 000 000 in America.
- The population in British North America included a huge number of former American Loyalists, generally situated together, many in Upper Canada. The Americans believed they would support their cause.
- Britain was engaged in a fierce war with France.
- The people of Lower Canada had not been particularly active during America's War of Independence.

Former American President Thomas Jefferson believed Upper and Lower Canada would be easily won by the Americans.

The Story So Far . . .

1 Predict the reaction of the following groups to America's declaration of war against Britain:
- Loyalist settlers in Upper Canada
- European or British settlers in Upper Canada
- French Canadians in Lower Canada
- Aboriginal Peoples
- settlers in the Maritimes

2 Choose one of the above groups and imagine you are one of that group. Either write a diary entry that expresses your feelings and how you think you will react to the outbreak of war, or work with two or three others to develop a short skit that portrays people's feelings at the time.

3 Explain why many Americans were infuriated by the French and British trade blockades.

WAR IN PROGRESS

Much to the surprise of many people on both sides of the border, British North America was not simply "there for the taking." Many citizens really did not wish to be "liberated." A few different factors contributed to this resistance.

Loyalty Revisited

Since so many citizens in Upper Canada were recent arrivals from America, Americans hoped that citizen support would be swayed easily. While some former Americans did switch their allegiance back to their old homeland, most did not. Their lives were developing in Canada. There were some people who were not particularly loyal to Britain, but who had left the United States for a fresh start in British North America after the War of American Independence. Most of these former Americans did not want to be treated like traitors or forced to flee like refugees again. For the settlers struggling to make a life for themselves, war was an unwelcome interruption. Remember, too, that many Loyalists had been forced to flee America, so it is unlikely that they would ever consider supporting their old home country.

In America there were many people who did not want to go to war. Many families had just recovered from the War of Independence. The blockades had created further economic hardships. The New England states were able to avoid an economic Depression because of the overland trade with British

Snippet

North America. They, in particular, were against the war, and a truce was arranged between the Eastern states and the Maritime Colonies.

War is not usually an appealing option for most people. Think about your own life here in Canada. Would you want it interrupted by war?

The Aboriginal Peoples around the Great Lakes had several grievances with the Americans over securing or regaining their land. They did not see the Americans' war with Britain as an outbreak of war for themselves. Many welcomed the British-American conflict as an opportunity to join forces with the British against their long-time foes. The British had managed to maintain relatively friendly relations with the Aboriginal Peoples and these were swiftly put to good advantage by Major-General Isaac Brock.

Brock Leads the Way to Victory

In 1802 the British military sent Isaac Brock to British North America. Although he was in command of all its British naval forces, he viewed his next ten years as uninteresting and uneventful. The War of 1812 thrust him into a leading role.

Looking at the situation around him in 1812, Major-General Isaac Brock believed that swift and aggressive action was required in order to frustrate the Americans and inspire optimism in the British North American people. He did not believe that the Americans had strength merely because of their numbers.

Brock was an inspiring and charismatic leader. Those around him were encouraged by both his actions and his words. Brock himself said, "Most people have lost all confidence. I however speak loud and clear." Brock was also adept at negotiations with Aboriginal Peoples. Having seen him in action and listened to him speak, Tecumseh gave Brock his highest praise, saying simply, "Here is a man." Tecumseh formed an alliance with Brock and encouraged other members of the Aboriginal alliance to do so. Hundreds of Aboriginals joined Tecumseh in this alliance.

Chief Tecumseh and Major-General Brock met as peers, leader to leader. This artist's rendering of the scene is not true to life, because Tecumseh refused to be painted by a European. Why do you think he did this?

The Aboriginal Peoples helped a relatively small British force sent by Brock to capture Michilimackinac. The force's surprise attack on and capture of this major fur-trading post helped convince Upper Canadians that they could defend themselves.

Brock knew that years of conflict between American posts and a variety of Aboriginal nations, especially in the Ohio Valley, had created an American fear of Aboriginal warfare. He also knew that the American army, while larger, was mostly volunteer. His forces were both volunteer and regular British troops, and the British army still maintained a reputation of being fierce. So despite having fewer troops, guns, and equipment, Brock set about making the best of his circumstances.

- He made sure that every available regular-army red coat was passed out among both regular troops and the volunteers. This would make the Americans think that there were more regular soldiers than there actually were.

- He sent a courier to Michilimackinac with a message stating that his forces had been joined by 5000 Aboriginal people, so he needed no further reinforcements before an attack. His hope was that the courier would be captured by the Americans and the message would fool them into believing that his force was mightier than it was. In reality there were only about 600 Mohawks with him.

- He devised this plan: the night before he took his troops across the Detroit River, Tecumseh and his followers would paddle across in the dark and spread themselves out. On the day of the attack, their sudden appearance would be even more threatening.

Emboldened by the initial victory, Brock swiftly moved his combined forces of regular British soldiers, civilian volunteers, and Aboriginal allies toward Fort Detroit in August 1812. The American commander at Detroit, Brigadier-General William Hull had just crossed the border into Upper Canada. He issued a proclamation stating, among other things, "You will be emancipated from tyranny and oppression and restored to the dignified state of freedom. . . . I come prepared for every contingency. I have a force which will look down all opposition." Hull surrendered Detroit virtually without a fight, frightened by both Brock's strategy and his Aboriginal allies.

Snippet

Baker Rifles

Some lucky soldiers were armed with the latest in weaponry: Baker rifles. Designed and made by an English gunsmith named Ezekiel Baker, these guns were different from muskets because the inside of the barrel was *rifled*, or engraved with fine spiral grooves. Rifling made bullets spin when they were fired. As a result, rifles could shoot farther and more accurately than muskets.

Brigadier-General Hull surrenders Detroit to Major-General Isaac Brock. How is the surrender symbolized in the picture?

The Evidence Behind the Story

Songs of the time are another form of evidence that historians can use to retell the stories of our past. The tune to the song that follows is not currently known, nor is the author, but the words have survived.

The Bold Canadian

Come all ye bold Canadians,
I'd have you lend an ear
Unto a short ditty
Which will your spirits cheer,
Concerning an engagement
We had at Detroit town,
The pride of those Yankee boys
So bravely we took down.

The Yankees did invade us,
To kill and to destroy,
And to distress our country,
Our peace for to annoy,
Our countrymen were filled
With sorrow, grief and woe,
To think that they should fall
By such an unnatural foe.

Come all ye bold Canadians,
Enlisted in the cause,
To defend your country,
And to maintain your laws;
Being all united,
This is the song we'll sing:
Success onto Great Britain
And God save the King.

QUESTIONING THE EVIDENCE

1. While this song is not a totally accurate account of a historic event, it does convey some details and impressions about the times to us. List the details and impressions you learn about in this song.
2. Explain the value of "The Bold Canadian" as a piece of historical evidence.
3. One goal of these lyrics was to make Canadians feel proud. Which lines in the song convey this impression?

Snapshot

Brown Bess

Most Canadian and British soldiers carried a flintlock musket nicknamed the *Brown Bess*. Loading a Bess was a long process that required endless drill. Missing a step in the heat of battle could get a soldier killed.

With a sergeant bellowing a command for each step, the soldiers began by setting the musket's firing hammer at the half-cock. This opened the priming pan. Next, they pulled a paper cartridge from a pouch at their waist. Wrapped in the cartridge was gunpowder and a musketball, or bullet. The soldiers bit off the bullet and held it in their mouth while they trickled a pinch of gunpowder into the gun's priming pan. The rest of the powder was poured down the muzzle. Then the cartridge paper, called wadding, was pushed into the muzzle and the ball was popped in on top of this.

The soldiers then used the long metal ramrod, which was stored under the barrel of the Bess, to push the wadding and ball into the powder. The gun was ready to fire. Pulling the trigger sparked the flint, which set off the powder and fired the bullet.

After all this, the chances of actually hitting a target were poor to non-existent. The Brown Bess was notoriously inaccurate. Still, when a line of redcoats pointed their muskets in the general direction of the enemy and fired together, the effect could be deadly.

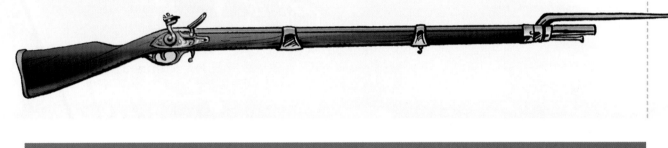

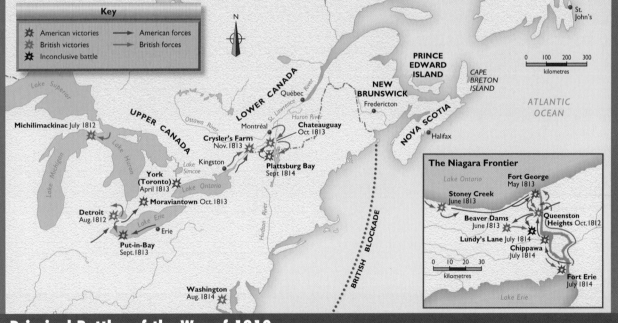

Principal Battles of the War of 1812

1. What observations can you make about the war by looking at this map? Brainstorm and list as many ideas as you can.

2. There do not seem to have been any battles in the Maritime Colonies or Eastern states. How would you account for this?

This is a painting of the Battle of Queenston Heights. What impressions do you get from the drawing?

On October 13, 1812, a large American force was again frustrated by a smaller British force led by Brock and was forced to retreat at Queenston Heights on the Niagara Peninsula. After his escapades at Detroit, Brock took up a position of defence and strung his troops out along the Niagara frontier. When 3000 American troops crossed from Lewiston, New York, into Queenston, there were only 300 British soldiers to oppose them. Brock himself was at Fort George. When he heard the firing, he ordered reinforcements and sped off on horseback to rally the troops.

Brock arrived and was leading the British forces up the hill when he was shot. Legend has it that he urged his followers on even after being shot. Judging by the evidence, experts have decided that Brock died instantly, though his powerful leadership certainly spurred the British on to victory that day.

African-American Pioneers

Recalling a tactic from the American War of Independence, Britain attempted to cause disruption in the United States by offering freedom to anyone of African descent who left the United States and joined the British. From 1812 to 1816 approximately 1600 African-American pioneers were transported on ships from Chesapeake Bay to the Maritime Colonies. As the Loyalists before them were promised, they were to receive free passage, rations, land, and freedom. Unfortunately, fulfilment of these promises did not always occur. Ironically, most African-American settlers at this time took over the land that had been abandoned previously by the African-American Loyalists who had left for Sierra Leone, Africa.

Snippet

Captain Robert Runchey's Company of Blacks

Among the civilian volunteers who served with Brock was Captain Robert Runchey's Company of Blacks. This company was made up of former American slaves. As a group, they were commended for their bravery at the Battle of Queenston Heights.

Isaac Brock

MODEL OF A MODERN MAJOR-GENERAL

For 118 days in 1812, Major-General Isaac Brock gave hope to the hopeless. When war was declared, the people of British North America had despaired. How could the small British colonies stand up to the mighty United States? Brock showed them how.

Brock was born October 6, 1769, on the island of Guernsey, the eighth son in a wealthy family. At 15, he joined the British army. Like many officers, he worked his way up by buying most of his promotions. Unlike many of his fellow officers, however, he was a gallant soldier and brilliant strategist.

Brock spent several years fighting battles overseas in the West Indies and in the Netherlands. By the age of 28, he was making a name for himself as a soldier and had become lieutenant-colonel of his regiment. Mostly because of Brock's skills and ability to motivate his soldiers, his unit went from being one of the worst to one of the best in the overseas service.

In 1802, when the fighting in Europe had abated, Brock and his regiment were sent to British North America. His postings in Montréal, York (or Toronto), Fort George at Niagara, and Québec gave him a chance over the next few years to become familiar with the land and its people. He worked constantly to improve the colony's defences and train militia units in case of a war with the United States. By 1811 he had reached the rank of major-general and was appointed commander-in-chief of Upper Canada.

In Brock's first battles of the War of 1812, his clever planning and bold actions led to speedy victories over the American invaders at Michilimackinac and Detroit. His accomplishments did not go unnoticed back in Britain. For the Detroit victory, Brock was made a Knight of the Bath. Unfortunately, the news of this honour did not reach Upper Canada in time for Brock to hear it.

On October 13, 1812, while leading a bold attack in the battle of Queenston Heights, this war hero was shot and killed by an American sniper. Brock's exploits captured the imagination of British North America. He instilled bravery and confidence in his troops and provided the Upper Canadian people with a hero. Even more important, he gave Upper Canada hope that it was possible to resist the Americans.

More people you could research are

Isaac Brock

Henry Dundas

William Hull

James Madison

George Yonge

EVERYDAY LIFE IN THE BRITISH ARMY

We can probably never imagine how difficult life must have been for soldiers in 1812. Let us examine a few pieces of evidence to further understand their experience.

The Elements

Aside from actual battle with the enemy, one of the greatest challenges to soldiers was the weather, especially in winter. There were no heated vehicles for transportation. Regiments marched. Also, there were few roads, except where men like Simcoe had the foresight to construct them.

Winter was probably their worst adversary, but soldiers marching at other times of year also faced challenges. One group of soldiers, for example, found themselves marching to the Battle of Lacolle in Québec in the spring of 1814. The snow had melted, but this meant they were forced to make their way through mud and water up to their waists for many kilometres.

Flannel Shirts and Greatcoats

The British army did make efforts to provide their soldiers with some suitable clothing. Wool flannel shirts became the norm in British North America as opposed to the white linen shirts that were issued elsewhere. As a cloth, wool flannel is warmer than linen and is also more absorbent and comfortable. Each recruit was provided with two flannel shirts. In fact the two flannel shirts were featured in recruitment advertising for the War of 1812.

The **greatcoat** had been a required part of a soldier's clothing in British North America by the end of the eighteenth century. Each coat weighed 2.5 kg and was made of dark grey wool, lined, with an attached cape that reached to the elbow for extra warmth. Though each soldier was to be given a new one every two to three years, this was not always the case. The coats came from contractors in England who did not always fill complete orders, and occasionally entire orders were lost at sea.

The greatcoat became particularly scarce during the war of 1812, just when it was most needed. At the capture of York, for example, hundreds of greatcoats were lost to the Americans since the men were ordered to leave their coats in their barracks before the battle. Hundreds were lost in other battles.

A greatcoat was provided to most soldiers in British North America to help keep them warm.

Food Allotments

Each company or group of soldiers was divided into smaller groups known as **messes**. In each mess the men combined their rations and took turns cooking. It was hoped that this organization would prevent individuals from selling or exchanging their rations for alcohol or gambling.

Typically the soldiers were provided with a breakfast of bread, milk, and tea. Sometimes there was soup and occasionally there was butter. At midday there was a dinner served with meat (usually beef), vegetables, bread, rice, and salt. The unmarried soldiers were not allotted a supper. Sick soldiers were given tea for supper. Married soldiers probably did have a supper but this would mostly have been purchased as their own supplies. Only six wives were permitted per every 100 soldiers, and the army allotted them only a half-ration of food, a quarter-ration to children. If it appeared that a wife was not providing for herself and her children, then she was not allowed to stay with her husband.

British soldiers in camp. What activities are the soldiers involved in?

© Collection of The New York Historical Society, negative number 2377, accession Number 1919,4

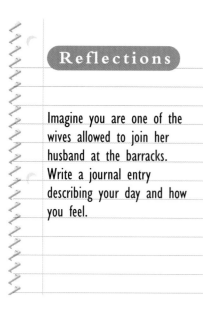

Reflections

Imagine you are one of the wives allowed to join her husband at the barracks. Write a journal entry describing your day and how you feel.

Women and the Army

The only women at a barracks were wives of soldiers. A lottery system was used to choose which wives could come.

Life at the barracks was extremely difficult. There was no privacy, and the women were expected to work — as seamstresses, nurses, laundry maids, and cleaners. They also had to look after their own families and not impose on the army in any way.

If her husband died, a woman was allowed three to six months to grieve. She then had to remarry or leave the unit. For the sake of their security, most remarried.

The Volunteer Militia

Aside from the regular trained and experienced soldiers of the British army, the war required additional numbers of volunteers from the citizens of Upper and Lower Canada, New Brunswick, and Nova Scotia. Since most of the battles were in Upper Canada, this was the area most in need of volunteers. What an odd situation these settlers found themselves in! Many of the people were former Americans. How would they feel about active combat against their former compatriots?

There were traitors, and the penalty was death by hanging if caught, but the traitors were not as numerous as some in authority had feared. Even Brock was pleasantly surprised by the small number of actual traitors, considering the large number of American settlers in Canada.

The real stumbling block to acquiring a large volunteer force was the everyday life of the settler. Examine these words from Brock describing volunteers gathered right after the declaration of war:

> . . . So great was the clamour to return and attend to their farms, that I found myself in some measure, compelled to sanction the departure of a large proportion, and I am not without apprehension that the remainder will, in defiance of the law, which can only impose a fine of twenty pounds, leave service the moment the harvest commences.

Web Connection

http://www.school.mcgrawhill.ca/resources

Go to the web site above to find out more about a soldier's life in 1812. Go to History Resources, then to *Canada: The Story of Our Heritage* to see where to go next.

Snapshot

Whistle Signals Used in the War of 1812

In the days before more advanced communications technology, officers trained their troops to respond to specific whistle signals. This ensured their actions were uniform on the battlefield. Here are some of the more common whistle signals used.

The enemy is discovered

This signal warned the platoon or company that the enemy was near. If the enemy were within musket range, then the signaler would also have clapped his hands afterward.

Advance

This signal ordered a line of soldiers to move forward.

Retreat

This signal ordered a line of soldiers to withdraw or move backwards.

Commence firing

This signal ordered the soldiers to aim and fire at the enemy. When working in pairs, the men spotted targets for each other. When in extended ranks, they may have been given specific instructions or they may have chosen their targets. When given after the order to *Advance*, it meant to advance rank through rank, and fire as each rank reached its position in front of the other.

Cease firing

This signal ordered the soldiers to stop firing. If a soldier had just finished a shot, he would have automatically reloaded his musket and waited for the next order.

The Story So Far . . .

1 List the physical difficulties soldiers faced during the War of 1812.
2 If you had to make a list of things to worry about while fighting as a soldier in the War of 1812, where would a greatcoat appear on the list?
3 Besides food and clothing, what else did soldiers need?
4 Identify the pros and cons of being chosen as one of the soldiers' wives who could live at the barracks.
5 Discuss in small groups whether it would be an easy or difficult choice to remarry if your soldier husband died.

THE DURATION OF THE WAR

After Brock's initial victories, the battles went back and forth. In April 1813 American troops briefly occupied York and destroyed much of it with fire. On June 24 at Beaver Dams, Iroquois from the Montréal area and the Six Nations territory on Grand River ambushed the Americans. Credit for discovery of the location of these American troops went to Laura Secord, a 37-year-old settler who walked a considerable distance to warn British forces that American forces were on the way.

Americans managed to destroy a British fleet on Lake Erie in the fall of 1813. This led to a British retreat east, away from Detroit, and then a defeat at Moraviantown on October 5. Tecumseh was killed in this battle and the British lost a great ally. Tecumseh's death also meant the end of the Aboriginal coalition. Later that fall, before the winter set in, the British were victorious at Châteauguay and Crysler's Farm.

This is a painting of the Battle of Lundy's Lane. The Americans lost 833 soldiers; the British lost 876 soldiers.

The Granger Collection, New York

In 1814 there were American victories at Chippawa and Fort Erie, but then the tide turned. On July 25, 1814, the war in Europe was over. The British had defeated the French and were able to direct their attention to the situation in British North America. They transferred thousands of experienced soldiers and a large number of ships.

Laura Secord

HEART OF A HERO

Laura Secord's heart was pounding when the American officers hammered on her door in late June 1813. In the weeks since the fall of Fort George, American soldiers had been buzzing around Queenston. Their mood had not improved with their recent defeat at Stoney Creek. Had they come to seize her husband, James?

Secord's fear was understandable. The Americans had already imprisoned several men from the village. James might be next on the list. A sergeant in the Canadian militia, James had been badly wounded defending Queenston Heights the previous fall and was still recovering at home. When the officers demanded billets — a place to stay — Secord breathed a sigh of relief. Billeting soldiers was an added burden for someone who was already looking after a sick husband and seven children, but at least James was still safe.

On the evening of June 21, Secord served the officers supper. After the meal, they talked of their plans to launch a surprise attack on the small British outpost at Beaver Dams, site of present-day Thorold. Secord listened carefully. She knew someone had to warn Lieutenant James Fitzgibbon, commander of the outpost. But who? Her husband could barely walk. She would have to carry the message herself.

She set out at dawn the next morning. By road, Beaver Dams was about 20 km north of Queenston. But following the road was just too risky. If the Americans caught her, she would be shot as a spy. So Secord took a roundabout route through the woods. The scariest part of the journey was through an area called Black Swamp. With every step, her feet sank into the wet, black bog. She was soon soaked, filthy, and covered in mosquito bites. Exhausted, she finally reached her destination and delivered her message.

Two days later, 500 American soldiers were moving stealthily toward the outpost at Beaver Dams. Suddenly, they were ambushed from behind by about 300 Iroquois warriors under the leadership of Captain Dominique Ducharme.

Ducharme and the Iroquois had travelled from Québec to reinforce the troops in Upper Canada. As they fought, they were joined by about 100 Mohawks from the Six Nations territory. By the time Fitzgibbon arrived with his entire force — 46 soldiers — the Americans were ready to surrender.

Though the Americans had a toehold in Upper Canada, a hero like Laura Secord was teaching them that taking over the rest of the colony was going to be an uphill battle.

More people you could research are

Robert J. Barrett

Dominique Ducharme

James Fitzgibbon

Billy Green

Francis Scott Key

Laura Secord

In July 1814 the British defeated an American attempt to capture Upper Canada at Lundy's Lane in Niagara. The British then developed a strategy of aggressive counterattacks on America. Not all of the British attacks were successful, but they were wearing on the Americans in more ways than one. Interestingly, a diversionary battle at Chesapeake, also known as the Battle of Bladensburg, was so easily won that the British were emboldened enough to march into Washington, DC. Burning down the public buildings in America's capital seemed to them a fitting revenge for America's destruction of York.

The British invasion and burning of Washington in August 1814 represented the limit on American public support for the war. In fact support for the war was so shaky that opponents of the war from New England were seriously considering the prospects of separation from the United States. The British victory at Washington was halted at Fort McHenry in Baltimore.

On September 11, 1814, the British planned an attack into the United States from Montréal. This was not successful, however, and they lost the naval Battle of Plattsburg (Lake Champlain) to an American fleet. On the other hand, the British kept up a tight naval blockade along the east coast of the United States that threatened to destroy the almost exhausted American economy. By the end of 1814, both sides were ready to negotiate an end to the war.

The Treaty of Ghent

On December 24, 1814, Britain and the United States both signed the **armistice**: a formal agreement between governments to stop fighting on all fronts. This ended the War of 1812. Oddly, nothing had really changed. Both sides agreed to a mutual restoration of property and America did not push for recognition of neutral rights. The war ended as it began. Since news of the armistice could not be sent across the Atlantic Ocean quickly, The Battle of New Orleans went ahead after the armistice had been signed. The American forces won this battle, and the victory led many Americans to believe that they had won the war. A new surge of patriotic nationalism was created throughout the United States.

News of the signing of the
Treaty of Ghent did not reach
America in time to stop the
last battle.

The Story So Far . . .

1 Explain why the death of Tecumseh was so harmful for the
   Aboriginal coalition and their British allies.
2 When the British burned down Washington, Dolly Madison,
   President James Madison's wife, thought to rescue a few
   national treasures as she fled the White House. Make a list of
   items you would save if your national capital were under
   attack.
3 Define the words *patriotic* and *nationalism*. Explain how the
   War of 1812, which resulted in little change, could have
   inspired so much patriotic nationalism.

WHO WON?

Although neither the Americans nor the British North
Americans won territory or even concessions, both sides gained
a sense of symbolic victory that would help define their nations
for years to come. The popularized American view was one of
military victory and glory, a second successful War of Indepen-

dence against interfering Britain. Great patriotism resulted, symbolized by the official adoption of the stars and stripes pattern for their flag by the Flag Act of 1818. A poem about the flag, Francis Scott Key's "Star Spangled Banner," was an immediate hit, sung frequently until it was finally adopted as the American national anthem in 1931.

Unrestrained westward expansion was also a result for America. The real losers of the War of 1812 were the Aboriginal Peoples. After the death of Tecumseh, the Aboriginal coalition fell apart. They lost their leader and very shortly they would lose their land. American expansion westward was unstoppable. In British North America, the Aboriginal nations made several land surrenders to accommodate the flood of settlers who arrived shortly after the War of 1812.

British North Americans gloried in the successful defence of their country. The War of 1812 represented their second victory against an American invasion. One result was a strong anti-American feeling. It also led to the building of Fort Henry in Kingston. Signalers in these fortifications could send a message by semaphore telegraph to warn of American attack. As well, troops in the forts could defend Upper Canada.

Another result of this anti-American nationalism was the persecution of former American settlers suspected of disloyalty to Britain. There were traitors but, in some instances, those who were persecuted had served in the British North American militia. Loyalty was also an issue in America. Some citizens had again fought on the side of the British in the War of 1812, and New Brunswick was once again the destination for those who chose or were forced to leave.

Ties to Britain in British North America were strengthened, especially in Upper Canada, but also in Lower Canada, New Brunswick, and Nova Scotia. For a time in Upper Canada, only those people who could prove they were British could own land. This quickly helped turn an American population into a staunchly British colony. Since all colonists in British North America at the time could claim to be British or British Loyalists, it was not a huge stretch for colonists to prove their allegiance. As long as they could swear to loyalty and sacrifice during the war, and no one contradicted them, they were safe. This must have resulted in more than a few colonists cutting ties with their home countries in order to appear all the more loyal.

The War of 1812 gave Canadians their first heroes and patriotic symbols: Tecumseh, Brock, Secord, and Brock's Monument. The Prince of Wales, who visited the Niagara region in 1860, observed that Canada's proud monument to Brock was larger than England's monument to Nelson. This same Prince of Wales sent Laura Secord a reward of £100 after he heard about her contributions to the war effort during his visit in 1860. As a result of that reward, the story of her heroism spread and grew. Symbols were among the most significant results of the War of 1812.

Peace

In 1817 peace was finally assured by the Rush–Bagot Agreement. This treaty limited armed vessels on the Great Lakes to avoid an arms race. An arms race occurs when countries assert their military power by acquiring more and more weapons. Eventually border issues were straightened out, and other agreements, like fishing rights, were reached. The Convention of 1818 further clarified the western border between British North America and the United States. The boundary between New Brunswick and Maine, however, was not settled until 1842.

The Story So Far . . .

1   Brainstorm a list of as many national symbols (people and objects) as you can think of for the United States and British North America. Discuss how the symbols are different from one another. What do they have in common?

2   Identify some of the negative results of the War of 1812, both in the United States and in British North America.

3   Explain why the Aboriginal Peoples were the real losers in the War of 1812.

Reflections

Imagine a scenario in which you wake up to a different national flag flying over your school. How did it happen? How do you feel about acknowledging a different flag? Write a journal entry explaining what happened and how you feel.

SUM IT UP!

The history of Britain, the United States, British North America, and France remain intertwined. The war in Europe was a major cause of tension in North America. Its conclusion led to a positive outcome for British North America. The War of 1812, in which the American military fought against the British, would not be repeated. America expanded its borders but did not invade its northern neighbour again. The War of 1812 established the United States and British North America as separate entities.

We have seen how the environment, food, clothing, and technology of the day affected the life of the soldier. In the chapters to come we will see how these factors affected everyday life and what everyday life was like for those who lived in British North America.

THINKING ABOUT YOUR LEARNING

1 You are a reporter for the *Upper Canada Gazette*, assigned to cover the American declaration of war in 1812. Perhaps you were even able to interview Brock or Tecumseh. Write the front page story, using the 5 Ws: who, what, where, when, and why.

2 Imagine you have written a novel about the War of 1812. Make up a title and design a book cover, both front and back. Remember that the back of a book usually gives a short summary of the story or a glimpse of a scene from inside the novel.

3 Create a *Jeopardy*-style of game for the War of 1812. Create at least four different categories and a number of answers within each category. Remember that on *Jeopardy* the contestants must provide a question to the answer that is given. The answers are also of various levels of difficulty. Some categories you could consider are: *Personalities, Heroes, Causes, Significant Events, Dates, and Places*.

APPLYING YOUR LEARNING

1 Aboriginal land claims are still a major concern. Examine a recent land claim and how it was settled.

2 The Canadian army still advertises for recruits, but two flannel shirts are not part of the campaign. How does the army attract recruits now?

3 Copy the web below and write the symbols that are significant to a nation of your choice.

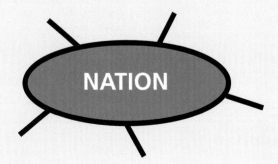

NATION

4 Interview a few members of your community (parents/guardians, teachers, principal, librarian) to get their opinions about Canadian-American relations now and any recollections they have of recent areas of conflict. Keep a written record of your interviews. Prepare a report to explain your understanding of the Canadian-American relationship today.

5 Continue to uncover the historical development of your community. For this section, focus on the developments in and around your area during the time of the War of 1812. Include a map of your area in 1812. If your community was involved in the war, make a note of the places on your map.

6 Go back to the time line on pages 178–179. Pick the three dates and events that you think are most significant to this time period. Explain why you think these are the most important.

USING KEY WORDS

1 About 5000 years ago, Egyptians used picture symbols to write their language. Even after people had letter symbols, pictures continued to be used as shortcuts in communication. Here are three examples:

- This hieroglyph means *water*.
- This hieroglyph means to *overthrow*.
- This is a modern picture symbol that means *elevator this way*.

As you can see, the pictures are very basic yet are quite recognizable.

Use your imagination to create your own picture symbols for the following words:

- armistice
- greatcoat
- treaty
- coalition
- mess
- War Hawks
- displaced

You should be able to explain your picture symbols. Pick your best one and share it with the class.

CHAPTER 7

Lower Canada, the Maritime Colonies, and Newfoundland

1799
St. John's Island is renamed Prince Edward Island

1809
First steamship built in Canada

1812
The War of 1812

1815
Population of Newfoundland reaches 40 000

1817
Bank of Montreal is established

Setting Our Focus

The watercolour *Lumber Mill on the Saint John River* illustrates how crucial timber was to the economy of British North America. In fact, in the early nineteenth century, wood surpassed fur as the main export item. By 1810 three-quarters of Lower Canada's and New Brunswick's exports were wood products. The growth of the timber trade was significant to the people in British North America in a few different ways. It helped farmers make extra money in the off-season. Bonds were formed between settlers and merchants, who would give credit for timber, and then make a profit for themselves. Credit with merchants meant that farmers could buy what the merchants had for sale without having to pay cash. Shipbuilding expanded right along with the timber trade and, in Lower Canada alone, over 3000 people were employed in building ships.

After the War of 1812, when immigration to North America from Britain became more popular, the increasing number of timber ships provided cheap, though uncomfortable, passage to British North America. Timber continues to be a significant industry in Canada today.

Key Words

cholera

depression

economy

emigration

genocide

immigration

Industrial
   Revolution

industry

institution

libel

responsible
   government

Previewing the Chapter

In this chapter you will learn about these topics:

- **the institutional and technological advances, emerging cities, and social concerns in Lower Canada, the Maritime Colonies, and Newfoundland**
- **groups and individuals who were significant to this time and place**
- **the hardships of the day and their impact on Canada**

1820	1824	1825	1831	1832
Cape Breton unites with Nova Scotia	Newfoundland is recognized as a colony	Lachine Canal finished in Lower Canada	60 000 immigrants enter Canada from Britain	• Newfoundland gains representative government • Cholera sweeps through Lower Canada

A water-powered grist mill, illustrated by C.W. Jefferys. What do you think the sled is filled with?

LIFE IN THE CITY IN LOWER CANADA

The major cities in Lower Canada were Montréal and Québec City. Both cities expanded rapidly at this time. Rising birth rates and immigration eventually quadrupled the population. While the population grew, so did both wealth and poverty.

Both cities are situated on water, so there was a lot of hustle and bustle around the ports. Shipbuilding was a booming **industry**, or business. There were at least 80 shipyards along the St. Lawrence River. The biggest ones were located in Québec City. There were also flour mills that ground wheat into flour, sawmills that cut logs into boards, textile factories, candle and soap manufacturers, and an expanding construction industry to accommodate all this growth. About two-thirds of the industrial work force were employed in textile manufacturing, black-smithing, and trades connected to resources, such as timber and ore. Most places of industry were small, employing less than five people and usually manufacturing only enough to supply the local market within the city. There were also markets, shops, and administrative buildings.

Even in the city, most people paid *seigneurial* dues on their lots, like rent. Workers did not make large wages and it usually took at least half that wage to feed a family. There was no way to organize for better salaries since there were no unions and it was against the law to strike. Yet the workers were lucky to be making at least some money. There were some who had no such luck.

Back in the early nineteenth century, people were expected to look after themselves or depend on relatives. Poverty was a serious problem, as it is now. Here is a description of the home of Maria Louise Beleau, a child who died in the winter of 1816–1817:

> *It is open in many parts of the roof, and on all sides. There is no other floor than the bare earth. It is a mere wooden shell; it has no window, nor a chimney. In the middle is a shallow hole made in the earth, in which there are the marks of a fire having been made. . . .*

Imagine living like this in the winter in Canada!

Reflections

Most large cities in Canada have many contrasts. Perhaps you live in a large city or you have visited one. Write a journal entry describing how you feel when you see or hear about homeless people living on the street in a town or city.

The Farmer in Lower Canada

During this time period, the vast majority of French Canadians farmed. They continued to farm in the *seigneurial* tradition. This is not to say, however, that rural areas did not change. From the 1790s to about 1815, many farmers in Lower Canada were able to benefit from their plentiful crops, world politics, and the world's **economy** or financial well-being. They had good harvests, wheat prices were high, and Britain was willing to buy the excess wheat. Many farmers were able to improve their lot in life, at least temporarily.

The War of 1812 disrupted trade. After the war, Britain entered a period of economic **depression**. Economic activity was low and unemployment was high, so prices fell. To protect its own economy, Britain established tariffs — taxes on imported goods — which blocked the purchase of grain from colonies like Lower Canada.

A farmer reaping grain with a cradle scythe. Imagine how long it would take to cut a farm field using this tool!

At the same time, crops started to fail. The soil had been depleted, and without fertilization, the harvests became small again. Insects and crop diseases became more common. Almost all the fertile land in the colony had been claimed. Farms were also stretched to accommodate more than one generation. Some French Canadians even moved to the United States to find farm land.

On top of their problems on the land, the habitants had to deal with the large numbers of people from Britain who were starting to arrive in Lower Canada. Most arrived with very little except a desire for the same thing French Canadian farmers wanted: to own some land and establish a better future. To make matters worse, many British immigrants arrived very ill and needy.

The Story So Far . . .

1 Using a point-form chart, compare life in the city with life in the country in Lower Canada.

2 Reread the description of Maria Louise Beleau's house. Imagine you are the child's mother or father and write a letter to tell a relative about her death.

3 Where do people turn for financial and other help now if they need it?

IMMIGRATION AND THE CITY

Before 1815, when Britain was at war with France and the United States, the British government had not encouraged **emigration** because a stable or growing population base is an advantage when a country is at war. After 1815 the first ripple of what would turn into a tidal wave of **immigration** from Britain to British North America began. War with France was over, the War of 1812 had ended, and the economy in Britain shifted from wartime prosperity to post-war depression. High unemployment, a rising population, and an **Industrial Revolution** created great dissatisfaction, especially among farmers and workers. An Industrial Revolution occurs when a society changes from agricultural to industrial, as it did in England and France between 1750 and 1850.

The British government began to encourage emigration to British North America. Emigration was publicized in pamphlets and newspapers, not to mention in letters from settlers already in Lower and Upper Canada. The British government even assisted some prospective emigrants with paid passage, land grants, and tools for working the land. Many of those assisted in this way were soldiers who were disbanded after the wars. Others were people in Scotland and Ireland who had lost their homes because of new agricultural techniques, or who were known to be from areas of rebellious, anti-British factions.

The majority of newcomers to Upper and Lower Canada, however, were not assisted in this way. There were other developments that encouraged what would become the largest mass movement of population in human history. In some cases, private landowners or land companies attracted settlers by offering free passage and land on credit. In other cases, ship owners or shipping companies recruited settlers by offering low transportation fares so that their ships, most of which normally carried freight from North America, would not be making the return trip empty. These were not good ships to travel on. They were not meant for human cargo, and the ship owners who recruited passengers did not care where the people ended up. They simply dropped them off at a port! It was this last detail that bothered the people in Lower Canada the most. The majority of new immigrants, regardless of where they intended to end up, landed at Québec!

A priest blesses Irish immigrants as they leave their poverty-stricken village for British North America. How would you describe the mood of the people? Why might they feel this way?

No official immigration figures were kept in British North America at this time, so we have to look at the numbers from Britain as they tracked the approximate number of emigrants. Britain's record shows that between 1815 and 1820, 70 000 people left Britain for British North America. Between 1821 and 1830, 139 000 immigrants arrived here from Britain. In 1831 alone, 60 000 people came, with 50 000 of them landing in Québec.

This influx was perceived as a huge problem in Québec. Worse, a **cholera** epidemic swept through Lower Canada in 1832. Cholera is a contagious disease of the stomach and intestines that is often fatal. Many French Canadians believed that with this avalanche of immigration, Britain was deliberately trying to dump its unwanted population and also destroy the French Canadians by infecting them with cholera.

Before the cholera outbreak and for many years after, there were many problems that seemed to be associated with this wave of immigrants. First, the newcomers were all British. This fact alone would change the nature of Lower Canada. Montréal, for example, grew quickly. It became the largest city in British North America. By the 1830s, its French citizens were in the minority.

Many of the British immigrants who stayed in Lower Canada did not have enough money to buy land, so they stayed in the cities or towns as labourers or remained unemployed. For Lower Canada, this wave of immigration was a mixed blessing. There was a demand for labour in shipbuilding, constructing the Lachine Canal, logging camps, and domestic service, but there were more workers available than were required. This placed a huge strain on cities and towns to provide housing and to care for those in need.

1 Based on this graph, explain which city you think faced the most drastic adjustments to population growth during this time period.

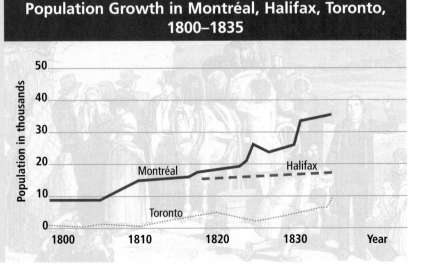

Population Growth in Montréal, Halifax, Toronto, 1800–1835

Stepping Into the Picture

Raphael, William, 1833-1914, Canadian, Behind Beausecours Market, Montreal, 1866, oil on canvas, purchased 1957. National Gallery of Canada, Ottawa

Such a busy port! Everything comes and goes here: people, animals, vegetables, ships. But the people — who could believe how many people? Step into the picture. Feeling a little crowded? Well, don't worry. You're not staying. Montréal is just a stopover for you. You want to get to Cobourg. How far do you think that is? Do you have enough money to buy a house? No? Well, don't worry, maybe you could get a job here for a bit. Now, who should you speak to? What if those stories you heard on the boat are true? What if everyone else here *does* want to steal your stuff? What if the person you pick has that terrible sickness — the disease that killed thousands? Quick — pick someone — you have to get going.

With a partner, present the conversation between the newcomer and someone in the crowd.

Why Cholera?

Disease was a serious threat in towns and cities, even before many immigrants carrying diseases arrived. In 1815 Lower Canada's Assembly created a Vaccine Board to provide public vaccination against smallpox. There was little public support for the program so it ended in 1823. Some say that it was doomed to failure because a favourite doctor of the British establishment was appointed to the Board.

The real problem was sanitation. Cities and towns were filthy and overcrowded. Garbage was piled in every yard and sewers were open. Businesses, including slaughterhouses, dumped their waste directly into the water. The situation was so extreme in 1832 that the board of health in Québec City tried to order residents to "carry away all filth." This order was not followed.

Lower Canada attempted to quarantine immigrants on Grosse Île, but this was not effective. No measure would work until people made the connection between disease and poor sanitation. Between June and October 1832, more than one-tenth of the population of Montréal and Québec City died.

Land of Opportunity

The timber trade flourished in Lower Canada in the 1800s. What do you think the different boats were used for?

In sharp contrast to the daily struggle to survive that many citizens and new settlers faced, there were some people who were able to take advantage of these times and circumstances. Some, like William Price, who came to Lower Canada in 1810, made their fortune in the expanding timber trade. Price's family would remain prominent in the timber trade into the twentieth century. Others who were established in more traditional businesses, like the fur trade, diversified. Peter McGill, for example, had been a fur trader, then switched to timber, ships, and exporting. John Molson made his fortune with a brewery, a distillery, hotels, a steamship line, and banking activities.

The accomplishments of people like John Molson are examples of the opportunities that were possible for hard-working and clever immigrants. Although he came to Montréal with enough money to purchase a small brewery, Molson transformed that first relatively modest purchase into an empire. Not content simply to make money, he also became involved in politics and was appointed a member of the Legislative Council. His political interests were the interests of the British Canadian business people and helped fuel the growing discontent of the French Canadians in Lower Canada.

John Molson

Born in farming country in England in 1763, John was the eldest of five children. Their parents died when John was just eight. He inherited the family farm, including Snake Hall and 16 ha of land in Lincolnshire. His grandfather was appointed as his guardian until he reached adulthood. An uncle and aunt gave him a thirst for industry and profit.

When he was 18, John took a sea voyage as a remedy for ill health. He landed in Montréal in 1782 and decided to stay. When he reached the age of 21, he sold the farm in England and used the proceeds to establish a brewery in Montréal. It was the first brewery in North America. John's life partner, Sarah, worked alongside him in the first winter of operation. They married in 1801 after having three children. The brewery grew by leaps and bounds.

Molson's Brewery is still the biggest brewer of beer in Canada, although it passed out of the hands of the Molson family in 1953, when it became a public company. The brewery still operates out of the same riverfront site where John Molson started it in 1786.

One of John Molson's cleverest schemes was to start a steamboat service on the St. Lawrence River. Molson contracted Canadian craftworkers to build *Accommodation*. When *Accommodation* started operating in 1809, it was the first steamboat to be built outside Britain, and only the third steamboat service in the world. The Molson Company gained sole use of steamboats on the St. Lawrence River between Québec and Montréal. How? John Molson merged other operations with his own until there was no competition. The Molson family also built and operated steam tugs, hauling barges on the river.

Molson went on to become an early president of Canada's first bank, the Bank of Montreal. It was founded in 1817, and John Molson was its president from 1826 to 1830.

About the same time, Molson put up money to build Canada's first railroad, the Champlain and St. Lawrence Railway. The line created a connection between Montréal and the huge port of New York City. It offered proof that Montréal was the city of the future.

More people you could research are

Alexis de Tocqueville

Jean-Jacques Lartigue

James McGill

Peter McGill

John Molson

William Price

In 1831 a young man from France, Alexis de Tocqueville, travelled through British North America and the United States. De Tocqueville would later become famous for his two-volume study, *Democracy in America*. Letters and journal entries from his stay in Lower Canada paint an interesting picture.

When De Tocqueville visited Lower Canada, he was assured by church officials there that French Canadian farmers were happy, contented people who did not mind paying their dues or tithes. In contrast, De Tocqueville reported that he found the farmers worried and resentful about their circumstances. Eyewitnesses do not always share the same point of view.

Journal Entry About Canada, August 25, 1831

External appearance: Canada is beyond comparison, of those parts of America which we have visited so far, that which bears the greatest analogy to Europe and, especially, to France. The banks of the Saint Lawrence are perfectly cultivated and covered with houses and villages in every respect like our own. All traces of the wilderness have disappeared; cultivated fields, church towers, and a population as numerous as in our provinces has replaced it.

The towns, Montréal in particular (we have not yet visited Québec), bear a striking resemblance to our provincial towns. The basis of the population and the immense majority is everywhere French. But it is easy to see that the French are a conquered people. The rich classes mostly belong to the English race.

Although French is the language most universally spoken, the newspapers, the notices and even the shop-signs of French tradesmen are in English. Commercial undertakings are almost all in their hands. They are really the ruling class in Canada.

In this particular journal entry, De Tocqueville went on to mention that he did not think the French Canadians would remain the ruling class, as long as British emigration did not manage to shut the French Canadians into a particular area. Perhaps that was wishful thinking, because he ended this journal entry by stating, "At the present moment the division of the races singularly favours domination by England."

Alexis de Tocqueville was a well-educated man and a lawyer when he made his trip. Later he became highly respected for his ideas about politics, government, and philosophy. The question for historians is whether or not his interpretation of what he saw is a valid one.

QUESTIONING THE EVIDENCE

1. Compare the impression you have about Lower Canada with the impression De Tocqueville conveys in his journal. Are there any areas where you disagree?
2. The opening paragraph of his journal entry is visually descriptive. Make a sketch based on his description.
3. Define the word *bias*. Explain any suspicions you may have about the biases of De Tocqueville as a recorder of history.
4. If De Tocqueville were able to answer, what questions would you ask him about Lower Canada? Compose at least two.

James McGill is another noteworthy person from the time. He was a fur trader, merchant, and magistrate. He was also a member of the first Legislative Assembly of Lower Canada in 1792. Although he, too, found himself in conflict with his French Canadian peers, his marriage to Charlotte Guillimin, a French Canadian woman, helped him make alliances.

McGill is probably the most famous for his will. When he died in 1813, he left an estate and about £10 000 to the Royal Institution for the Advancement of Learning for a college to be built. His stepchildren contested the will but lost, and a charter for the University of McGill College was granted in 1821.

You may have noticed that none of these important men in Lower Canada was French Canadian. This was another source of discontent for the French Canadians. Although the population of Lower Canada was still predominantly French Canadian, the wealth, trade, and even institutions were mainly in the hands of the British Canadian residents.

James McGill left his fortune to the Royal Institution for the Advancement of Learning to build the University of McGill College.

The Birth of Institutions

At the end of the nineteenth century, the Roman Catholic Church was the dominant institution in Lower Canada. An **institution** is an organization established for a public or social purpose. Attendance at church was high and it was the social hub of most communities. Most early Québec churches existing today were built during this time period, including the famous Notre-Dame de Montréal. Within the first quarter of the century, however, other institutions would compete for people's attention and loyalty.

Imagine living in a society with no public schools, banks, and only a few newspapers. Sound tempting? Now try to imagine these institutions suddenly appearing, and the impact they would have. Do you imagine their appearance would happen smoothly, without a struggle?

The Royal Institution for the Advancement of Learning was established in 1801 to create a system of voluntary public education. Today we take public education for granted, but in 1801 it was viewed with suspicion and hostility. Many in the Roman Catholic Church were afraid that public education was a British, Protestant plot to assimilate the French Canadian Catholics. "It is better for them not to have a literary education than to risk a bad moral education," said Jean-Jacques Lartigue, the man who would eventually become the first bishop of Montréal.

A school built in Ontario around 1815. What do you think the outbuildings were used for?

Building schools did not appeal to many farmers because of the cost. They knew the money would have to come from somewhere and they knew they had no more to give. Several schools were built, but there were so many conflicts between school officials and priests that eventually the Elementary School Act was cancelled in 1836. However, the institution of schooling would continue, just in a different fashion.

When the French-language newspaper *Le Canadien* was started in 1806, it took as its motto "Our religion, our language, our laws." Freedom of the press was not as we know it in Canada today. In 1810, for example, the governor of Lower Canada stopped the presses and threw contributing writers and editors in jail because he disliked their criticisms of the government!

Pierre Bedard is an example of French Canadians who had, through education, moved beyond their farming backgrounds. He was born near Québec in 1762, studied at the seminary, and became a lawyer. In 1792 he was elected to the Assembly for Northumberland and continued to be the elected representative until 1812.

When *Le Canadien* was founded, Bedard became a regular contributor and critic of the government in Lower Canada. He was thrown in jail in 1810 for expressing his views. In the face of much criticism and Bedard's re-election to the Assembly, the governor attempted to release him. Bedard refused to leave jail without a regular trial. The governor would not grant one for fear of appearing even more foolish. Bedard finally left after spending an entire year in jail.

The founding of the Bank of Montreal in 1817 signalled a financial coming-of-age: the existence of currency and credit. This institution was also a source of British-French irritation. The bank presidents, John Molson among them, were British Canadian. "In the cities the English make a display of great wealth," observed Alexis de Tocqueville. "Among Canadians there are but fortunes of limited extent."

Other institutions became necessary too. Those created solely to care for dependent or orphaned children began to appear around 1830. Before then these children would have been cared for by other members of the family or the local community. There were also *houses of industry*, which provided needy children and adults with bread and clothing in exchange for labour.

Political Division

Government became a source of increasing irritation. Unfortunately the hostilities were divided along French versus British interests. Most of the elected members in the Legislative Assembly were French Canadians. Usually, however, the governors of Lower Canada acted on the advice of the Executive Council. The Executive Council was appointed and was made up mostly of British Canadian merchants and appointees of the British government. Each group believed the other was blocking its goals.

Transportation and Technology

The early nineteenth century was a time of great technological achievement. The technology that most affected North America had to do with transportation. The first steamship was built in Canada in 1809. Up until this time, ships travelled under power of sail and were at the mercy of the wind.

Reflections

Write a diary entry describing what you imagine it would have been like to see a steamship or hear about a steam engine pulling a train for the first time.

The *Royal William* was the first steamship to cross the Atlantic Ocean. Steamships cut down travel time from six weeks to three weeks. A few years later, faster steamships would make the trip in two weeks.

After the introduction of the steamship, manufacturing steam engines and parts became a major industry. Although they did not replace other boats, steamships became more and more common. Eventually the concept of steam-powered transportation would evolve into the use of steam engines on railroads. In fact, by the mid-1830s, Lower Canada financed Canada's first railway: a 22-km link from La Prairie to St. Jean, southeast of Montréal.

Canals were another important development. Since waterways were plentiful but cleared land was not, it must have seemed logical to link the rivers to make "water highways." Also, the War of 1812 prompted military concern about safer and faster transportation for goods, supplies, and people. The Lachine Canal, west of Montréal, was the first one, finished in 1825. This canal attracted dozens of factories so that by the mid-1850s, Montréal would become the largest manufacturing centre in Canada. As will be seen, the development of canals also created political problems.

1   List the changes that occurred in Lower Canada during the
    early nineteenth century.
2   Create a collage to depict life in Lower Canada during the
    early nineteenth century.
3   With a partner, plan a talk show. The host is Pierre Bedard
    and the two guests are John Molson and Maria Louise
    Beleau's mother. What questions should Bedard ask? What
    responses would the guests give?

THE MARITIME COLONIES

At the start of the
nineteenth century,
four Maritime
Colonies were part of
British North America:
Cape Breton, New
Brunswick, Nova
Scotia, and Prince
Edward Island. Cape
Breton had separated
from Nova Scotia in
1784, but rejoined in
1820. Newfoundland
was recognized as a
colony in 1824.

The population in
each of these areas
grew substantially in
the early nineteenth
century. The Loyalist
migration had
increased the popula-
tion in these colonies
after the American
Revolution. In the
1800s most of the
immigrants arrived
from Britain.

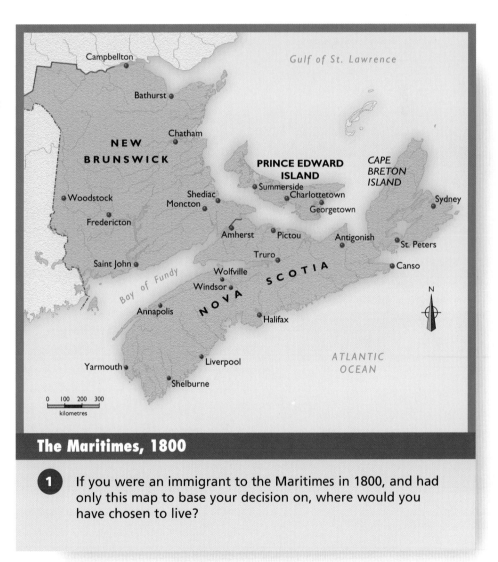

The Maritimes, 1800

1   If you were an immigrant to the Maritimes in 1800, and had
    only this map to base your decision on, where would you
    have chosen to live?

1 Examine the bar graph. Calculate the total increase for each colony.

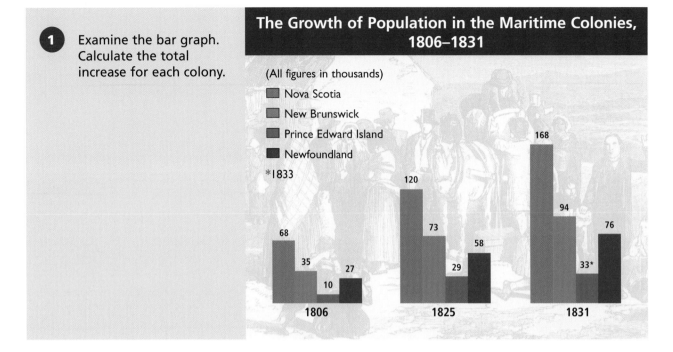

The Growth of Population in the Maritime Colonies, 1806–1831

(All figures in thousands)

- Nova Scotia
- New Brunswick
- Prince Edward Island
- Newfoundland

*1833

1806: 68, 35, 10, 27

1825: 120, 73, 29, 58

1831: 168, 94, 33*, 76

The people who came at this time were part of the Great Migration, mainly trying to escape overcrowding, unemployment, poverty, and famine. By the mid-nineteenth century the numbers above would almost double.

Snippet

Fire!

Wherever there is a forest, there is threat of forest fire, especially during a hot, dry season. In October 1825 there was a devastating forest fire that started around Miramichi, on the East coast of New Brunswick. It eventually destroyed the governor's residence in Fredericton. At least 500 lives were lost and thousands were left wounded and destitute. Disaster relief came from all the British North American colonies, Great Britain, and the United States.

New Brunswick

The timber trade was extremely important to the economy of New Brunswick. However, most workers were not only employed in lumber camps but also ran family farms. Land was cheap and seemingly plentiful, so many settlers owned enough land to grow the necessities for their own families and a little extra to exchange for imported items like sugar, rum, and high-quality cloth. On the coast, fishing families also farmed. Inland, farming families took on other work when it was available. The winter was a good time for farmers to cut timber, since trees are easier to cut when the sap is not running, and there were fewer chores to do on the farm.

The life of the lumberer was not easy, even on a part-time basis. The trees were cut down in winter when it was extremely cold and there were 60-90 cm of snow. In spring the timber would be thrown into icy cold water and floated down a river to merchants. When guiding the lumber down, these workers were often immersed in the water themselves. In his *Historical and Descriptive Sketches* from 1828, John McGregor wrote, "Premature old age, and shortness of days, form the inevitable fate of a lumberer."

Both the climate and the land of New Brunswick were unreliable, so poor harvests were common. In 1816, for example, snow fell in June. The harvest was so bleak that Joel Hill wrote in a letter to his family, "Crops of hay and potatoes are very slim. Cattle are very cheap. Men is plenty and Money was never known to be so scarce."

As the timber trade grew to meet the demand in Britain caused by Napoleon's blockades, so did the shipping industry. In 1807, 156 ships sailed out of New Brunswick carrying 250 000 000 kg of mostly timber to Britain. In 1810, 410 ships left New Brunswick with 800 000 000 kg heading for Britain. At least a hundred shipbuilding villages sprang up along the Maritime coasts.

The timber merchants realized that they could improve their profits if they also built and owned the ships used to transport the timber. One advantage that Maritime shipbuilders had was the relatively low cost of their vessels. Since they built the ships from the wood that was most available, usually spruce, the cost per kilogram was lower than for the American ships built of oak. The lower costs would help keep the Maritime ships popular throughout the 1800s, even after the development of iron steamers that cost four or five times as much.

Saint John, New Brunswick, became the largest shipbuilding and ship-owning port in the Maritime region. About half of the ships built in Saint John were sold to Britain; the other half were owned in and around Saint John.

This picture was one of a series of illustrations designed to attract immigrants to New Brunswick. What does this picture say? How realistic a view does it portray?

Saint John was the largest city in New Brunswick. It controlled the timber trade and the shipbuilding industry in the colony as well as in the other Maritime Colonies. Halifax, Nova Scotia, tried to compete with Saint John, but since it is not on a main waterway like the Saint John River, it was not a natural site. Aside from its function as a port, most merchants and manufacturers gathered around Saint John. Almost half of the goods manufactured in New Brunswick were produced in and around Saint John.

Snapshot

The World's Fastest Ship

In the middle of the nineteenth century, the James Smith Shipyard in Saint John, New Brunswick, created a sensation with a unique ship, the *Marco Polo*. Its design combined features of a sleek clipper ship and a broad cargo carrier with large sail capacity. Its round trip from Liverpool, England, to Melbourne, Australia, cut a week off the previous record for length of time. Although the trip took close to six months, the *Marco Polo* still became known as the world's fastest ship.

New Brunswick's capital, Fredericton, remained smaller than Saint John, largely because it is not a port city. It had been selected in 1785 as the colony's capital partly to encourage inland settlement and partly to provide the British army with a safe haven away from the coast in case of American attack.

Responsible government, government in which elected representatives had the final say, was as popular an ideal in New Brunswick as elsewhere at this time. As early as 1795 a few elected representatives challenged British Governor Thomas Carleton's control over finances.

James Glenie led the elected assembly's challenge of Governor Carleton. Glenie had served as a British officer during the American Revolution and then settled, as a Loyalist, in New Brunswick. He was frustrated by corrupt land deals and Governor Carleton's strict control over finances. Glenie led a coalition of elected representatives against the governor. The government was immobilized for about four years until Governor Carleton finally granted some political authority to the elected assembly.

Thomas Carleton, Governor of New Brunswick

Responsible government was not officially granted in New Brunswick until 1848. By the 1830s, however, a reform movement led by men like Charles Fisher and Lemuel Alan Wilmot had brought about changes so that the appointed Executive Council was responsible to the elected assembly.

One interesting development during this time period was the beginning of a literary history in Canada. In 1824 the first novel by a British North American was published. *St. Ursula's Convent or The Nun of Canada* was written by Julia Catharine Hart (born Julia Beckwith) from Fredericton, New Brunswick. There was also a strong folk culture that depended on the handing down of stories and songs orally. Stories and songs from the lumber camps became increasing popular, especially after about 1850.

Nova Scotia

Nova Scotian settlers faced issues similar to those faced by New Brunswick settlers. The land was not ideal for farming, so many pursued other ways to help make a living. The shipping industry employed several thousand people on a part-time basis. Fishing and lumbering activities employed others.

As you probably noticed on the population graph on page 222, Nova Scotia had the largest population of the Maritime Colonies at the start of the nineteenth century. It more than doubled in less than 30 years.

One distinguishing feature of Nova Scotia during this time was an active interest in literary and intellectual matters. The University of Kings College was established in 1802. By the 1830s there were more colleges and several academies. There were several subscription libraries, and literary and scientific societies attracted followings. Newspapers and magazines also flourished. This is peculiar since it was discovered in 1825 that only about 25 percent of school-aged children outside Halifax attended school! The government acted quickly and provided further access to public schools.

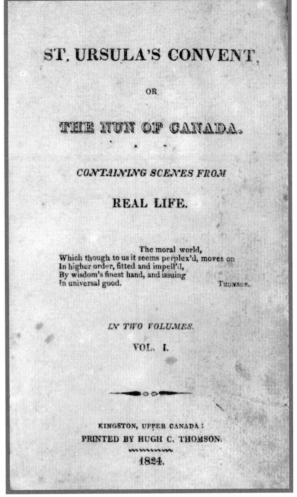

ST. URSULA'S CONVENT,

OR

THE NUN OF CANADA.

CONTAINING SCENES FROM

REAL LIFE.

The moral world,
Which though to us it seems perplex'd, moves on
In higher order, fitted and impell'd,
By wisdom's finest hand, and issuing
In universal good.   THOMSON.

IN TWO VOLUMES.

VOL. I.

KINGSTON, UPPER CANADA:
PRINTED BY HUGH C. THOMSON.
1824.

This was the first novel to be written by a British North American.

An illustration from *The Clockmaker* by Thomas Chandler Haliburton

Nova Scotia was also home to the first writer from British North America to attract international attention. Thomas Chandler Haliburton wrote *The Clockmaker; or the Sayings and Doings of Samuel Slick, of Slicksville*. The story was first published in instalments in the *Nova Scotian*, a weekly paper. It was published as a book in 1836. More than 70 editions of this book have been printed and you can still buy it today!

In early 1848 Nova Scotia became the first British North American colony to win responsible government, though people in the colony had worked toward that goal for quite some time. Joseph Howe was a notable part of the reform movement in Nova Scotia.

Nova Scotia did not know such bitter struggles as those in Upper and Lower Canada. The problem that preoccupied most people was who controlled the government.

Joseph Howe was editor of the newspaper the *Nova Scotian*. In 1835 he was sued for **libel** — publishing a false statement that would damage a reputation. Howe acted as his own lawyer. At one point he addressed the jury for more than six hours! He won his case and was elected to the Assembly the next year. As an elected representative, Howe continued the struggle against control of the government by the elite of society.

Halifax was the dominant city in Nova Scotia. Its harbour was busy with trade. The Halifax Banking Company began trading money in 1825 and the Bank of Nova Scotia was founded in 1832. Halifax was also home to one of the first theatres in the Maritime Colonies. The Grand Theatre opened there in 1789. The New Union Singing Society of Halifax was founded in 1809.

As in other Maritime cities, Halifax was full of contrasts. The seasonal nature of shipping, fishing, and lumbering meant there was a large number of people unemployed or underemployed during the winter. Charitable organizations, mostly organized by women, sprang up to help the poor deal with cold, hunger, and illness. No official government assistance existed until the 1860s.

Halifax was not the only city in Nova Scotia. Windsor, Annapolis Royal, Yarmouth, and Liverpool all existed before 1840. Academies and colleges were also established in the early nineteenth century at Pictou, Wolfville, Windsor, Antigonish, and Halifax.

Joseph Howe exposed corruption in the upper levels of government in the *Nova Scotian* newspaper.

Halifax as it looked in 1819. How would you describe the city?

Minority Groups

The Aboriginal Peoples were in a frustrating position. The Mi'kmaq had never signed any treaties with the British government. They maintained that they should be paid by the British for the land the British settled. The governments of New Brunswick, Nova Scotia, and Prince Edward Island set aside reserves, but this did not stop settlers from encroaching on reserve lands. By mid-nineteenth century, the Aboriginal Peoples accounted for only 0.5 percent of the Maritime Colonies' population.

When describing the Mi'kmaq of Prince Edward Island, John McGregor, who lived in the colony from 1806 to 1827, observed that, "This tribe, like all those in the vicinity of civilization, has diminished in number by two-thirds during the recollection of the present settlers. The wild beasts and game having become scarce, they are subjected to a precarious subsistence; and small pox, fevers. . . have often swept away whole families. . . ."

The African-American population of Nova Scotia and New Brunswick continued to face difficulties. The new wave of immigration from Britain made their lives even harder as cheap labour became plentiful and jobs became harder to find. They also continued to face discrimination and prejudice. Slavery was abolished in British North America in 1834, but this did not mean that African Americans were treated equally or better than before.

Web Connection

http://www.school.mcgrawhill.ca/resources

Go the web site above to find out more about The Underground Railroad. Go to History Resources, then to *Canada: The Story of Our Heritage* to see where to go next.

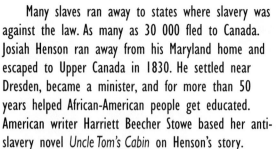

The Underground Railroad

Nearly 2.5 million African Americans were slaves in the United States in 1840, of a total population of 17 million people. Slaves laboured without pay in the fields or as domestic workers. They could be bought and sold, beaten, and even killed by their owners. They were not allowed to marry.

Many slaves ran away to states where slavery was against the law. As many as 30 000 fled to Canada. Josiah Henson ran away from his Maryland home and escaped to Upper Canada in 1830. He settled near Dresden, became a minister, and for more than 50 years helped African-American people get educated. American writer Harriett Beecher Stowe based her anti-slavery novel *Uncle Tom's Cabin* on Henson's story.

Many brave people helped runaway slaves get to Canada by a system that came to be known as "The Underground Railroad." Runaway slaves travelled by night, guided or driven by "conductors," and hid out during the day at "stations" along the way. Because slaves were considered valuable possessions, people who helped them escape risked prison sentences. One famous "conductor" was Harriet Tubman Davis, a fugitive slave from Maryland. Based in Canada, she conducted some 300 others to freedom during the 1850s.

▌ **Josiah Henson**

▌ **Harriet Tubman**

Prince Edward Island

Prince Edward Island was the only Maritime colony with fairly reliable farmland, so agriculture was the biggest source of its economy. Most of the colony was owned by large absentee landholders who were supposed to settle their land. Many promised to sell the land to attract settlers, but they frequently refused to turn the land over, even after the settlers had cleared the lots and erected buildings. Imagine the frustration and dissatisfaction you would feel if you had been lured by the promise of land ownership and then were never able to purchase the land!

Between 1806 and 1831 the population of Prince Edward Island more than tripled. The majority of its nineteenth-century immigrants came from Scotland, while the rest came mainly from Ireland and England. By the 1850s this tiny island was the most densely inhabited colony in British North America. Nicknamed the *Garden of the Gulf*, it exported large quantities of produce from the farms that had taken over at least three-quarters of its land.

Samuel Cunard

SHIPPING MAGNATE AND ABSENTEE LANDHOLDER

Samuel Cunard controlled the most land of any of Prince Edward Island's absentee landowners. His estate of 85 000 ha was more than twice the amount of the lands reserved for the Aboriginal Peoples in the entire Maritime Colonies!

Cunard was born in Halifax on November 21, 1787. His father, Abraham, was a carpenter who worked at the dockyards. Samuel was successful in business from a young age. After school he gathered dandelion greens and sold them door to door. With the money he earned, he bought broken crates of coffee and spices, divided them into small, neat packets, and sold them at a profit.

As a young man, he learned the shipping trade while working in an engineering office, then a shipbroker's office. Just after his twenty-first birthday, Samuel's father led him to a window and pointed out a modest sailing ship in the harbour. Painted on its bow was the name *Margaret*, after Samuel's mother, and in smaller letters "A. Cunard and Son." Few people could have predicted how successful that small shipping business would become.

Following his motto, "Nothing but the best," Samuel ran their business well and it thrived. In 1820, his father retired and Thomas changed the company name to S. Cunard and Company. Around that same time he began to purchase large tracts of land in Prince Edward Island. By 1830 his company owned forty ships and Samuel was a very wealthy man.

Not satisfied to rest on his success, Samuel began to think about the possibilities of steam travel. When a paddle wheeler, the *Royal William*, made the first steam crossing of the Atlantic in 1833, Samuel Cunard's name was first on the list of shareholders. But it was another six years before anyone, including Cunard, attempted to use steam ships for regular transportation.

Then in 1839 Cunard won a bid to provide regular mail service across the Atlantic Ocean between Britain and North America using steamships. Mail that had previously taken up to two months to cross the ocean now arrived by steamer in a mere 12 days.

The Cunard Line grew and Samuel moved to England to supervise his business. And so Canadian-born Cunard became an absentee landlord and remained one until he died in London in 1865. The next year, his lands in Prince Edward Island were sold for some $258 000.

More people you could research are

Pierre Bedard

Samuel Cunard

Charles Fisher

James Glenie

Joseph Howe

Lemuel Alan Wilmot

In the 1830s two-thirds of the island's settlers lived on land owned by absent owners. There was a Reform group, though, that fought against these absentee landowners. Unfortunately many of the landowners were men of great influence in England, so the protests of the land tenants were ignored for a long time. Prince Edward Island was the last of the three Maritime Colonies to be granted responsible government, in 1851. The fact that the people's grievances could be heard did not seem to resolve the absentee landowner problem any quicker. The people living on Prince Edward Island wanted to buy their land at a fair price, but as late as 1873 only one-third of the island was owned by actual residents.

Newfoundland

Newfoundland was originally considered a summer fishery by Britain. Despite a permanent population of about 40 000 in 1815, there was no year-round governor until 1817. Britain recognized Newfoundland as a colony in 1824 and established a representative government in 1832. Labrador had been taken from Lower Canada's control in 1809 and was then restored to Newfoundland.

Fish, especially cod, originally attracted settlers to Newfoundland. Fish would continue to be the colony's economic mainstay for generations to come. As in other colonies, though, fishers farmed and farmers fished and did other odd jobs as the need arose. Newfoundland's nickname is *The Rock*, so you can imagine how difficult farming was. The land partly explains why a permanent population was slow to establish.

The seal industry grew in the early- to mid-nineteenth century. By 1833 sealing accounted for 30 to 40 percent of Newfoundland's total exports. It also employed thousands of people, although over-harvesting would become a problem.

St. John's was always the most densely populated area of Newfoundland. The population rose steadily in the early nineteenth century, but in 1828 John McGregor noted that the population still fluctuated noticeably over the course of a year. In the fall, St. John's was full of permanent residents, merchants, and fisherfolk. In the winter many people left to work in the surrounding colonies. From spring until fall, many would come back to fish while others would go to other fishing spots.

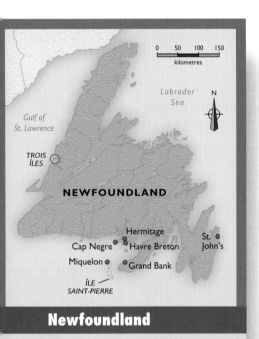

Newfoundland

1 If you had named this land, what name, besides Newfoundland, would you have chosen?

Despite a changeable population base, St. John's became increasingly important. The first governors made their headquarters there and soon the usual markers of a thriving city emerged. By the 1830s there were three weekly newspapers and a book society. The Newfoundland School Society was founded in 1823.

There was a reform movement in Newfoundland, too, but the goals were somewhat different from those in the Maritime Colonies. The first goal was to acquire some sort of governance. From 1811 until 1817, Dr. William Carson led a campaign to have Newfoundland granted a year-round governor. Gradually other reforms followed so that by 1832 there was representative government. Responsible government, though, was a long way off and would not be granted until 1855.

St. John's, Newfoundland, in the 1830s. How would you describe the landscape?

Snapshot

A Divided Colony Newfoundland was populated, for the most part, by Irish Catholics and English Protestants. The Irish immigrants were fleeing famine and religious persecution. They also came with a history of numerous English invasions and land seizures. The English settlers did not think highly of the Irish settlers, so their communities were quite separate. They would not live in the same neighbourhoods, and intermarriage almost never occurred. This split in the population affected Newfoundland's politics, too. In 1842 Britain suspended Newfoundland's Constitution and restructured the government to address a political deadlock that was caused by this split in the population.

Shawnadithit
THE VOICE OF THE BEOTHUK

When Shawnadithit was born in 1800, her people had no way of knowing her importance: in 30 years' time she alone would be left to tell the story of the vanishing Beothuk.

By the time Shawnadithit was eleven, her dwindling tribe consisted of about 70 people. Her family group was one day surprised to find themselves face to face with a troop of European men lead by John Buchan. Buchan's mission was one of goodwill. He intended to find the Beothuk in order to help them. Unfortunately, some of the local men who accompanied him were known murderers of the Beothuk.

The encounter began well, but fear and mistrust won out. The Beothuk, discovering that Buchan had enough armed men to kill their whole tribe, panicked. They murdered two of Buchan's men and fled deeper into the woods. In retaliation, many more Beothuk were shot by settlers in the years that followed.

During the harsh winter of 1823, many of the remaining Beothuk starved. By spring, Shawnadithit was one of only 17 left. She, her sister, and mother were part of a group that went in search of food and crossed paths with some furriers. All three women were captured and taken to St. John's where they were given gifts of food and other supplies for their people.

The three returned to the woods, searching for months without finding any other Beothuk. Shortly afterward, her sister and mother died, and Shawnadithit returned to the British settlers who had captured her.

She lived among them for five years and was described as a tall woman with a musical voice and a gentle, intelligent nature.

In 1828 she was moved to St. John's. There she learned English and was asked to describe her life as a Beothuk. She made sketches of many Beothuk objects including their hunting tools and wigwam-like dwellings, called *mamateeks*. She described the traditional food they ate and the clothes they wore. She told of their normally peaceful way of life and related, from her people's perspective, many important events in the Beothuk's final years.

The information Shawnadithit provided before her death in 1829 comprises almost all we know of these people who once flourished on the coasts of Newfoundland. If not for Shawnadithit's sketches and stories, practically all knowledge of the Beothuk culture and their true, peaceful nature would have died with her.

More people you could research are

William Carson

Frederick Dibblee

Thomas Chandler Haliburton

Julia Catharine Hart (born Beckwith)

John McGregor

Shawnadithit

The Beothuk

The Beothuk, who lived only in Newfoundland, were probably among the first Aboriginal people seen by European explorers. There are many theories as to why their entire race disappeared: disease, starvation, and **genocide** being among them. Genocide is the deliberate destruction of a racial or cultural group. One common thread among theories is their contact with British and European settlers. Unlike other colonies, where settlers established a mutually beneficial relationship with the Aboriginal groups to make life run more smoothly, the residents of Newfoundland did not see a need for friendly relations with the Beothuk. Permanent and non-permanent residents simply took over the coast as they saw fit. They cut the Beothuk off from their food source, the sea. They did not rely on them for furs or military assistance, so almost all contact was hostile. Relations became more and more violent. It was widely known that settlers murdered several Beothuk and that the Beothuk retaliated.

By the early 1800s the Beothuk population had seriously dwindled. In 1829 the death of Shawnadithit, a Beothuk woman, signalled the end of the Beothuk race.

The Story So Far . . .

1 Divide a page into two columns. In one column list the hardships faced by settlers in the Maritime Colonies and Newfoundland. In the other column list the hardships faced by the Mi'kmaq and the Beothuk. What conclusions can you draw by comparing your two lists?

2 Create a flag for one of the Maritime Colonies or Newfoundland at this time. What symbols would you include on the flag?

3 With a partner, role-play a conversation between Samuel Cunard and a tenant farmer in Prince Edward Island.

4 Imagine that, like Shawnadithit, you are the last of your race. What would you want others to remember about your people? Your answer can be in the form of words, an illustration, or a representation, like a collage.

Web Connection

http://www.school.mcgrawhill.ca/resources

Go to the web site above to find out more about the Mi'kmaq or the Beothuk. Go to History Resources, then to *Canada: The Story of Our Heritage* to see where to go next.

Snippet

Red Ochre

Ochre is a pigment made of earth and other natural substances. The Beothuk covered their bodies with layers of red ochre from infancy on. The term *red Indian* comes from this tribe's practice. A major *ochring* ceremony occurred at least once a year. Red was a colour that many Aboriginal groups associated with supernatural powers. The layers of ochre may have also helped protect the skin from the elements and insects.

SUM IT UP

The dominant features of life in Lower Canada, the Maritime Colonies, and Newfoundland at this time are change, contrasts, and struggles. For most inhabitants of these colonies, the struggle to survive was daily and ongoing. Farming was essential, yet difficult. The economy was mostly resource-based, but people often suffered from a lack of resources. The population was growing rapidly; most settlers were first- or second-generation immigrants. This early phase of the Great Migration would be devastating to the original inhabitants and put the long-term inhabitants, like the French Canadians, in a difficult position.

Technology was transforming. Steamships and railways were significant advances, yet most people still did everything by hand. Fortunes could be made, and there were aspirations for a more "advanced" society that included universities, public schools, banks, and charitable organizations. On the other hand, sickness and physical injury played a large part in the colonists' lives. So did bad weather, fire, famine, and a host of other unpredictable disasters.

Despite the obstacles, each colony expanded, progressed, and asserted its own particular focus. British North America was still a collection of colonies, but the challenges they faced would ultimately unite them.

THINKING ABOUT YOUR LEARNING

1. Compare and contrast the early phase of the Great Migration with the Loyalist Migration. Consider why the settlers came, the hardships they faced when they arrived, and the impact they had on the receiving colonies.

2. There is a saying, "history repeats itself." Describe a condition in Canada today that reminds you of something that happened in Lower Canada or the Maritime Colonies in the early nineteenth century.

3. Play *Maritimes Charades*. Pick a person, place, or thing mentioned in this chapter and have a classmate guess who, what, or where.

APPLYING YOUR LEARNING

1. Create a *Trivial Pursuit*-type of game in which the questions and answers cover the developments in Lower Canada, the Maritime Colonies, and Newfoundland in the 1800s. Remember that in *Trivial Pursuit* there are different categories. Perhaps your categories

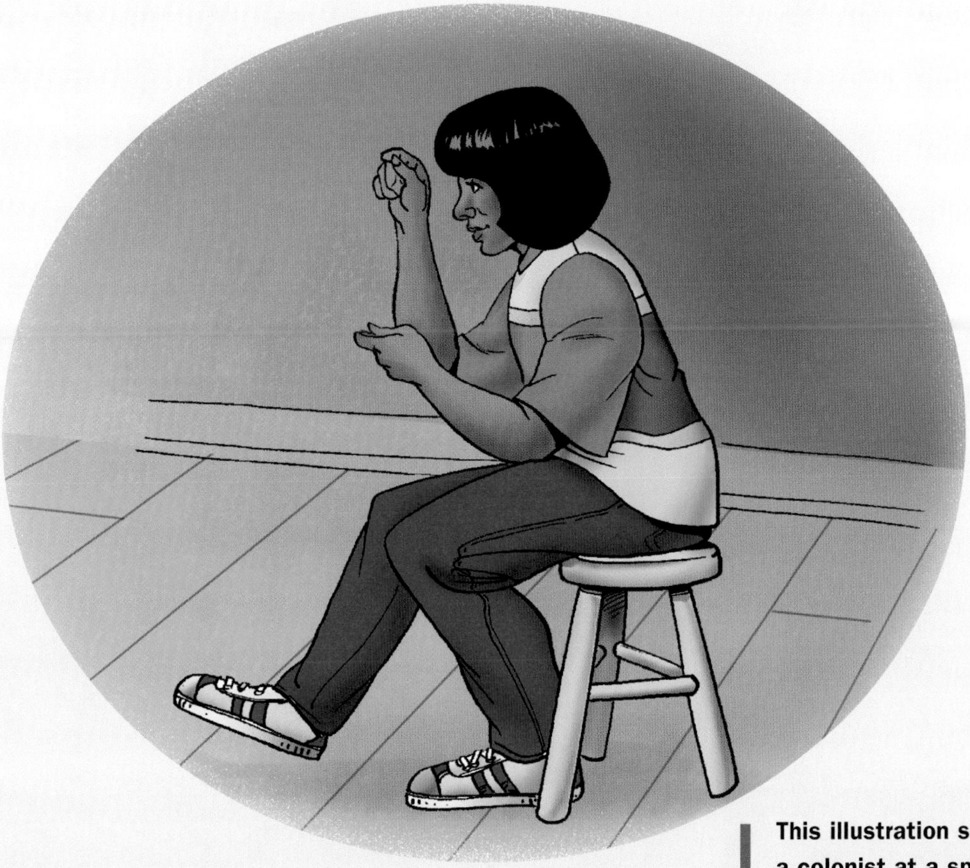

This illustration shows a girl miming a colonist at a spinning wheel for activity 3, Thinking About Your Learning, on page 234.

could include people, dates, places, disasters, and wild cards.

2 Continue to uncover the historical development of your own community. Focus on the developments from 1800 to 1835. Include a graph to show any changes in the population. Categories to research are: immigration, settlers' hardships, sickness, transportation, technology, and institutions.

3 Pick one of the people spotlighted in this chapter and prepare a television talk show interview with him or her. Consider preparation for the host, interview topics and questions, other guests, and possible audience participation.

4 If you could be any person mentioned in this chapter, whom would you be and why? Whom would you least like to be and why?

5 Design a totem pole representing five significant features during the time period of this chapter. (Suggestion: use a paper towel roll or a potato chip tin as a base.)

USING KEY WORDS

1 Make a *Word Search* puzzle using the key words and at least two other words you think are significant to understanding this chapter.

CHAPTER 8

Life in Upper Canada

1802

Thomas Talbot land settlements begin

1815

Population of Upper Canada reaches 95 000

1816

The Common School Act passed

1817

Formation of the Society for the Relief of Strangers

1819

- Bank of Upper Canada established
- Robert Gourlay banished

SETTING OUR FOCUS

The picture on the left shows a ship of emigrants leaving Liverpool, England, for British North America in the 1800s. The trip will be long and uncomfortable. Some emigrants will lose family members to disease on the way over. Some will arrive with a place to stay and money to get them established. Others will have to rely on good fortune and their wits to find employment. All will be faced with challenges.

During the first third of the nineteenth century, the population of Upper Canada quadrupled, from less than 100 000 in 1806 to over 400 000 by 1840. In this chapter you will examine why such a large number of people took part in a mass migration from Britain after the War of 1812 ended. You will learn about some groups and individuals from this time period. You will identify the hardships faced by these new settlers, and the repercussions their settlement had on life in British North America. Using a variety of sources, you will also try to understand something about the life of the early nineteenth-century settler in Upper Canada.

PREVIEWING THE CHAPTER

In this chapter you will learn about these topics:
• **the hardships of immigration**
• **some strategies used by early settlers to meet the challenges of life in Upper Canada**
• **life from a variety of perspectives — family life, economy, social life, institutions, transportation, and emerging towns**
• **a variety of sources for historical information**

KEY WORDS

bee
Canada Company
corduroy roads
Clergy Reserve
Crown Reserve
directed
  settlement
land baron
Reformers
shanty
squatters
Tories

1824
The *Colonial Advocate* started by William Lyon Mackenzie

1829
Welland Canal opens

1832
• Rideau Canal opens
• York riots
• Cholera epidemic

1834
• York becomes Toronto
• Population almost quadruples from 1806

This caricature (cartoon) was published in England in 1832. Titled *For Emigration. The Parting Hour*, it shows how some people viewed immigrants. How would you describe this couple? How would you rate their chances of success at farming?

THE GREAT MIGRATION

The mass migration of people to Upper Canada after the War of 1812 is known as the *Great Migration*.

After the war, there was a degree of anti-American nationalism, and new laws in Upper Canada prevented Americans from receiving land grants until they had lived in Upper Canada for seven years. This was discouraging to most Americans, though some settlers continued to trickle in.

Another result of the War of 1812 was a strengthening of the bond between Britain and the colonists of British North America. However, most people did not even think of leaving their home countries in the early nineteenth century — especially to travel across the Atlantic Ocean — unless they had a very good reason. The British government did not encourage emigration when the wars in Europe required a stable or growing population. Immigrants had come from Britain before, but not on the scale of the Great Migration.

After the wars, several conditions made life in Britain intolerable for many people. In fact, some saw emigration as necessary for their survival. A general economic depression across Britain caused high unemployment. After the war, many soldiers were looking for work. The onset of the Industrial Revolution meant that many workers were replaced by machines and that many smaller, family industries were replaced by factories.

In Ireland crop failures were so extreme that the choice for many people was to emigrate or starve. In Scotland the change from their traditional tenant-farmer system left many people without a house, a job, or even the traditional means of obtaining food: subsistence farming.

The British government made great efforts to encourage emigration to British North America. Here is one recollection of emigration propaganda from the day:

> . . . Canada became the great landmark for the rich in hope and poor in purse. Public newspapers and private letters teemed with the unheard-of advantages to be derived from a settlement in the highly favoured region. . . . But they never ventured upon a picture of the disgusting scenes . . . dens of dirt and misery, which would, in many instances, be shamed by an English pig-sty.

These words were written by author Susanna Moodie. Susanna and her husband, John, moved to the Peterborough area of Upper Canada in the 1830s. Her sister, Catharine, along with her husband, Thomas Traill, also lived in the same area. Both sisters found some fame in England from writing about their experiences as pioneers.

The Trip Over

Imagine a space about 28 m long and about 7 m wide. Now imagine 2-m square bunk beds two and three high down both sides of the space and down the middle. Place 250 men, women, and children into this space. How do you think they feel? How does the air smell? They had better not be too picky because the trip, under these conditions, will take at least six weeks!

At least there were bunks. Of course, four or five people would have to sleep in each one. If people were lucky, they might have been bunked with people they knew, but maybe not. People often did not bring enough food. As for water, the supply probably would not last. Since it was not clean to begin with, it was not much use anyway. Unfortunately, if a person travelled before the 1850s, they did not know the importance of clean water.

Diseases of all kinds spread like wildfire on these ships. Approximately one of every 28 people on their way to British

On the deck of an emigration vessel from Liverpool to North America, 1830s. What class of people do you think these passengers are? Why?

Susanna Moodie
THE RELUCTANT PIONEER

Quilting bees, barn raisings, the clearing of trees. At first glance, Susanna Moodie's writings seem what she intended them to be: well-written stories of everyday life. One hundred and fifty years later, those detailed observations take on a special significance.

Susanna Strickland was born in Bungay, England, on December 6, 1803. Like her sisters, she began writing at an early age. When her father died in 1818, the reasonably well-off family suddenly had no income. Much to their delight, the Strickland girls discovered that they could sell their writing without losing upper-class status for being employed. To contribute to the family finances, they wrote children's books, gift books, and articles for ladies' magazines.

In 1831 Susanna moved to London where she met Lieutenant John Moodie. They were married, and the following year Susanna had the first of six children. Realizing that Moodie's income as a half-pay officer and Susanna's earnings were not enough to support a family, they set out for British North America in July 1832 with the hope of a better life.

They settled near Cobourg and tried for two years to make a living at farming. Susanna, used to upper-class society, tried to keep her genteel ways and was resented for it by her pioneer neighbours. Unhappy, the Moodie family moved north of Peterborough, where Susanna's sister Catharine Parr Traill and brother Samuel Strickland lived. Over the next five years, they established a farm there successfully.

Although Susanna never really took to the pioneering lifestyle, it gave her plenty to write about. In 1839, after John Moodie was appointed sheriff of Victoria District, he and Susanna moved their family to the town of Belleville. In this more civilized setting, Susanna began writing about the trials of a settler's life.

From 1839 to 1851, she wrote stories for Montreal's *Literary Garland* and *British North America Magazine* and Belleville's *Victoria Magazine*. In the 1850s she wrote her two famous narratives of the pioneer way of life: *Roughing It in the Bush* and *Life in the Clearings*. She continued to publish in Canada, the United States, and England until the mid-1860s. After her husband's death in 1869, she moved to Toronto, which became her home until her death in 1885.

Although Susanna Moodie published many novels, romantic fiction, and documentary narratives, it is her chronicles of Canadian pioneer life that have endured. Her writings paint a vivid picture of the joys, hardships, and overwhelming challenges faced by the ordinary folk who flocked to Canada in the 1800s.

More people you could research are

Wilson Benson

The Mississauga

Susanna Moodie

Walter Riddell

Samuel Strickland

Catharine Parr Traill

North America died aboard ship. In the worst times of cholera, some ships buried many more passengers than that at sea. One traveller to British North America reported seeing more than 50 burials at sea on his way over. Here is one recollection from a voyage in 1832:

> We had the misfortune to lose both our little boys. . . . We were very much hurt to have them buried in a watery grave; we mourned their loss, night and day they were not out of our minds. We had a minister on board, who prayed with us twice a day. . . . There were six children and one woman who died in the vessel.

For those who survived the trip by sea, there would still be a long, exhausting journey over land to their destination in Upper Canada, assuming they had a destination. If they did not, there were usually some suspicious characters ready to take advantage of bewildered and weary newcomers with offers of passage inland or "connections" with land companies. Some of the travel could be done by boat, but eventually everyone would have to travel over land. This part of the trip was quite arduous, as roads were few and far between.

There were no roads connecting one settlement to another. Some of the settlements had laid down an interesting patchwork of **corduroy roads**: a Canadian invention of logs placed side by side to form a road. However, these were not much use to newcomers trying to reach a settlement.

Reflections

You have arrived at Kingston, York, or London, in Upper Canada. You survived the trip by sea and land. Now what are you going to do? Write a diary entry about your hopes, dreams, and expectations.

What would it feel like to drive over this corduroy road in a wagon?

In 1837 one Englishwoman reported that it took three and a half hours to travel an 11-km distance on a road between Hamilton and London! Even when a regular stagecoach line was established between York and Kingston in the 1820s, that trip could take four days, one way.

The Story So Far . . .

1 Imagine you live in Britain in the early nineteenth century. You are unemployed. You have a family, food is in short supply, and money is even scarcer. Make a list of the pros and cons for emigration to Upper Canada. What would you do?

2 Some historians compare the emigrants in the early 1800s and the conditions in Britain to those who seek refugee status, and their situations, today. Historians say that these immigrants were economic refugees. Make a chart to compare and contrast the Great Migration to the Loyalist migration. Does economic hardship fit into a definition of *refugee*? Explain your answer.

3 Design a poster the British government might have used to encourage emigration to British North America.

4 Create a visual representation of the trip from Britain to British North America. You could make a collage, mobile, or drawing.

TOWARD SETTLEMENT

Many aspects of pioneer life in Upper Canada in the early 1800s were similar to life in New France a hundred years before. People's main concerns were centred on the land: adjusting to the wilderness, clearing the land, and obtaining food, shelter, and clothing from it. Almost all immigrants to Upper Canada aspired to owning land. Many eventually attained this, but not for quite some time. They survived by a variety of means: renting land, labouring in towns, and saving. Often settlers took on a variety of occupations to make ends meet.

Directed Settlement

For about a ten-year period the British government provided a substantial amount of aid to prospective emigrants to Upper Canada. The settlements were called **directed** because, in addition to transportation and rations, the government gave land grants to heads of families of particular groups. For example, in

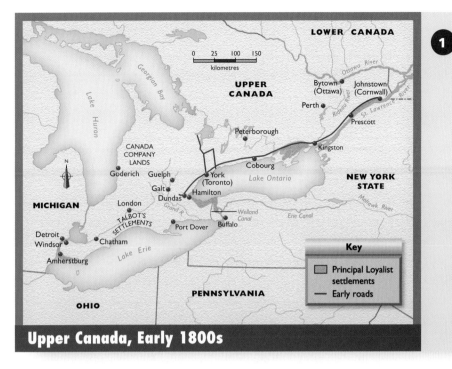

1 This map of Upper Canada in the early 1800s shows the major settlements of the time. What do you notice about the settled areas?

Upper Canada, Early 1800s

1816, about 1400 people had been transferred to the Lanark area, south of Ottawa. In 1820 the British government assisted 2000 Scots to migrate to the Rideau area in Ottawa. Most of the men in this group were unemployed weavers. A little later 3000 Irish immigrants were helped to settle in the Peterborough area. This process of government aid stopped in the mid–1820s.

Land Owners and Companies

Some individuals and companies managed to make a profit doing what the British government found to be too costly. The emigrants were assisted, but those helping them profited. The Talbot Settlement was one such settlement.

Companies also entered the business of land distribution. Since they could raise larger amounts of capital to begin with, they eventually outstripped and replaced the **land barons**. Land barons were individuals, like Thomas Talbot, who owned large amounts of land. In 1826 in Upper Canada, the **Canada Company** purchased almost all the **Crown Reserves**, land that was government-owned, and about half the **Clergy Reserves**, land owned by the church. Later, it also bought about 500 000 ha of land on the shores of Lake Huron. The Canada Company made a deal allowing it to spread the payment for this land over 16 years. Many critics at the time felt that the payment was not equal to the value of the land. The company did, however, settle large numbers of people on its land. The towns of Guelph, Cambridge, and Goderich trace their roots back to the Canada Company settlements.

Thomas Talbot
UPPER CANADA'S LARGEST LAND BARON

He was born in Malahide, Ireland, on July 19, 1771, but it was in Canada that Colonel Thomas Talbot was destined to make his mark. Because of his ambition and eccentricity, 30 000 new immigrants would settle a vast area of Upper Canada in less than 35 years.

By the time he was 12, Talbot was an officer in the British army. At 19, he was sent to Québec and, after travelling to Upper Canada, became secretary to Lieutenant-Governor John Graves Simcoe. A few years later he left the British army and officially immigrated to Upper Canada, building himself a cabin on the north shore of Lake Erie.

In 1802, through a land grant system that was often unfair, Talbot secured a deal to promote settlement. According to the deal, he was granted an initial 2000 ha of land in return for a promise to settle it with British rather than American immigrants. To each new colonist, he allotted 20 ha of land from his original grant, but for each colonist settled, Talbot *received* an additional 81 ha of land. He gained 61 ha for each new settler!

Talbot was very strict about the settlement requirements. As he distributed lots, he simply pencilled in the name of the new settlers on a township planning map. If they did not actually clear the land and build a house on it, Talbot would not legally transfer the ownership to them. He would even go so far as to "ungrant" land, erasing one settler's name from the map and pencilling in the name of another!

As a result of his requirements, the land he managed was more successfully settled than in some other areas. His eccentric habits, however, more than likely contributed to Upper Canadians' extreme discontent with the entire land distribution system, especially in the 1830s and 1840s.

Eventually Talbot had a huge estate of nearly 30 000 ha and control or ownership of hundreds of thousands more hectares in at least 28 southwestern townships. He was probably the largest landholder in Upper Canada. In return, he settled more than 3000 lots and helped develop a road system that stretched from Amherstburg to Niagara. He also helped establish one of the first medical schools, Talbot Dispensary, in the 1820s.

With age, Talbot's peculiar behaviour increased as his tolerance of people decreased. Eventually, he renounced society altogether and retreated to his estate. His eccentric, dictatorial methods had made him wealthy but left him alone. When he died in February of 1853, Upper Canada's greatest land baron left his fortune to the only people who would share his company: his servants.

More people you could research are

Robert Gourlay

Francis Bond Head

Anna Jameson

Anne Langton

John Graves Simcoe

Thomas Talbot

Aboriginal Land Surrenders

All British North American land was originally the ancestral homeland of Aboriginal Peoples. By 1815, before the Great Migration, the Aboriginal Peoples were outnumbered ten to one. After the start of the Great Migration, various Aboriginal groups were persuaded by the British government to make several land surrenders — much of what we know today as Southern Ontario. At the same time, the British government stopped offering large, one-time payments for land. Instead, it changed to an annual *payment in perpetuity* method which divided the total payment into small annual payments. This may not sound so bad until you examine the facts. Between 1818 and 1838, for example, over 5 000 000 ha of land was given up by the Aboriginal Peoples for payments that were supposed to equal £6653 annually. However, only £1400 actually came to the Aboriginal Peoples as cash; the remainder of the payment was made in "goods." These "goods" were not necessarily what the Aboriginal Peoples had bargained for. In one case, two-thirds of a payment came in the form of a stone church!

Here are some of the factors that affected the Aboriginal Peoples' lifestyle in Upper Canada during the early nineteenth century:

- Settlements ruined land for hunting.
- Settlements had separated Aboriginal groups from one another, so a united front was less and less possible.
- Traditionally, the Aboriginal Peoples in the area of Upper Canada had been treated as allies.
- This allied relationship was in contrast to the relationship between the American government and Aboriginal Peoples south of the border. In the 1830s and 1840s several thousand Anishinabe (Ojibwas) fled America for Upper Canada.
- Some Aboriginal groups, like the Mississauga, were convinced by the government that they should adopt a farming lifestyle in order to secure their lands.

In this picture, Hurons are tending crops. What do they appear to be doing?

The Aboriginal Peoples saw that when white colonists simply **squatted**, or cleared land that was not theirs and built homes on it, they were usually allowed to remain as long as the land was cultivated as a farm. As Sir Francis Bond Head, Lieutenant-Governor of Upper Canada, stated it to a group of Ottawas and Objibwas:

> . . .*An unavoidable increase of white population as well as the progress of cultivation have had the natural effect of impoverishing your hunting grounds . . . . If you would like to cultivate your land, it would then be considered your own property . . . . But uncultivated land is like wild animals . . . .*

The Story So Far . . .

1 List the challenges faced by the Aboriginal Peoples in Upper Canada at this time.
2 Rewrite the words of Sir Francis Bond Head in today's language. Respond to his message with a drawing, song, or poem.
3 Examine the sketch on the left. Discuss impressions you might have of the Objibwas from this sketch.

A sketch of Ojibwas at Coldwater, just north of Lake Simcoe in 1844. Notice the style of their clothing.

FIRST STEPS IN SETTLING

How do you feel when you are "lumped in" with a whole group and then described? Just as there is no one way to describe an average thirteen-year-old, there is no single description that would accurately sum up the pioneer experience in Upper Canada, though some experiences were common. Most settlers wanted land. Some were able to purchase it immediately or eventually, while others had to rent it. Some settlers stayed in towns, while others developed the wilderness. Some came as labourers and moved to wherever the work was, while others became entrepreneurs. Some made fortunes; some lost them. Look around your class. Are any two of you really alike? Neither were the pioneers.

What Settlers Said

If we look at actual reports from settlers of that time, we can gain some insight into their lives. In 1838 Catharine Parr Traill wrote:

Even a labouring man, though he has bought land of his own, is often, I may say generally, obliged to hire out to work for the first year or two, to earn sufficient for the maintenance of his family; and even so many of them suffer much privation before they reap their reward.

This was certainly the case for Wilson Benson. He published a slim book in 1876 entitled *Life and Adventures of Wilson Benson: Written by Himself.* In it he recalls his and his wife's trip, first to Québec and then overland to Brockville. On the way to Brockville most of their personal possessions were stolen. Upon arriving in Brockville, the Bensons had to go their separate ways to find work. He wrote, "My wife hired out to do general housework. However times were so bad I could not find a stroke of work to do."

For the next ten years Benson moved about continuously to find work — in shops in Kingston and Toronto, on a river steamer, and on inland vessels. Finally he and his wife purchased some land, but it is not clear whether they had raised or inherited the money needed for the purchase. Ultimately, Benson saw his life as a success. He wrote in his memoirs, "It is a source of extreme gratification. . . (to) have so largely contributed to the development of our country."

Once land was obtained, then the work began. John Howson described it this way: "After the trees have been felled, the most suitable kinds are split into rails for fences, and the remainder. . . burnt. After felling, dividing, and burning the timber. . . the stumps still remain. . . ."

Samuel Strickland, who worked with the Canada Land Company, gave this advice:

The emigrant should endeavour to get as much chopping done as possible during the first three years, because after that time he has so many other things to attend to, such as increase in stock, barn, and house building, thrashing, ploughing, etc. which of course, give him every year less time for chopping, particularly if his family be small.

Only one thing seemed sure: hard work, and lots of it, lay ahead for most prospective immigrants. One anonymous Scottish weaver said optimistically after immigrating to Canada in 1821, "Here. . . labour will give me. . . a fair prospect of independence." On the other hand, *The Church of Scotland*

In this picture, the settlers have just begun clearing the land and building a home. What would life have been like for them at this time?

David Alexander Fife

A FARMER'S PERSEVERANCE

Times were tough for immigrant farmers. Once they had finished the backbreaking job of clearing the land of trees, they were still at the mercy of the climate. Summers were short. Early frosts wiped out entire fields of wheat just days before harvest. Having worked so hard, many early Canadians, like David Fife, were not prepared to admit defeat.

David Alexander Fife was born in 1805 in Kincardine, Scotland. When he was 15, his parents and six brothers crossed the Atlantic to British North America. His family settled in the county of Peterborough in Upper Canada. Eventually he married and established his own farm nearby. Trying his hand at growing wheat, he planted the usual variety called *Siberian*, but lost much of his crop to frost damage and rust.

He wrote to a friend in Scotland, asking for a sample of spring wheat. In 1841 he received a handful of seeds originally from Poland. The next spring, Fife roped off a plot of land and planted the sample seeds, but only a few stalks grew. Then a cow broke into the plot and ate most of the small crop. Chasing the animal away, Mrs. Fife managed to save just three stalks of wheat.

The following spring, when his Siberian crop was sprouting, Fife planted the seeds from the three saved stalks. To his surprise, that wheat matured at the same time as the Siberian, even though it was planted much later. As well, the new wheat seemed free of the rust that badly affected most Siberian crops.

Convinced of the superior quality of the wheat, Fife spent seven patient years cultivating his crop and collecting the seeds for the next year's planting. Gradually he supplied seeds to interested neighbours. In 1849 one farmer produced enough to supply members of the local agricultural society with close to 300 bushels.

David Fife's experimental wheat, known as *Red Fife*, not only grew a better crop, but it also resulted in excellent flour when ground. By about 1860, Red Fife was the only variety grown in the area. Eventually it spread across Ontario, and into the northern United States and western Canada.

Farmers everywhere were thrilled to find this disease-resistant strain that matured about ten days earlier than other wheat. Previously plagued with frost damage and rust, the farmers were suddenly making a profit. Red Fife remained the primary wheat for many years and was largely responsible for Canada's emerging reputation as the "Granary of the World."

How did David Fife respond to the hardships of life in Canada? By rising to the challenge. His original handful of seeds improved the fortunes of wheat farmers all over Canada.

More people you could research are

Sir John Colborne

Alexander Drummond

David Fife

Jesse Ketchum

Jane Marion

Laurent Quetton St. George

Magazine in Upper Canada had this to say: "Thousands upon thousands in this vast uncultivated territory, [struggled] with hardships and penury of new settlements . . . years of constant toil."

The Story So Far . . .

1 Brainstorm a list of problems most immigrants to Upper Canada faced at this time. Make a list of problems you think immigrants to Canada face today. Create a graph, chart, or drawing to compare and contrast the problems of today's immigrants with those of the past.

2 With a partner, stage a debate on the topic: "Upper Canada: years of constant toil or a fair prospect of independence."

BUILDING A HOME IN THE WILDERNESS

Most first homes were built to look something like the one pictured here. The size could vary somewhat, but this first home, often called a **shanty**, was probably about the size of your bedroom. Do you share your bedroom? Lots of people do. Do you share it with your whole family? Try to imagine your entire family cooking, working, and sleeping in your bedroom!

Round logs, notched at the corners to fit into one another, formed the walls. Rocks were placed around the base for support. The roof was made of overlapping layers of elm bark or hollowed logs. Roofs were usually improved as the need arose.

Once the walls and roof were up, the ends of the logs were evened up by saw, and cracks were packed with wedges of wood. The spaces between the logs were filled in with clay or moss. Improvements that usually came later included a fireplace and a room added at the side or above, usually for more sleeping space.

Most settlers in this time period tried to make a floor. Often, logs that were split and then squared were used. Doors and windows were usually chopped out after the house had been built. Often, though, pioneers did not bother with windows in these first houses because they complicated construction, and the door and the cracks in the walls let in enough fresh air. Wooden doors were eventually made, but blankets were sometimes used instead.

In this drawing of a pioneer shanty, notice the construction methods being used and the task each family member is performing.

Many first-generation settlers lived in their original shanty for years, although most planned to build a more elaborate log house. If a settler, or the next generation of the family, were particularly successful, then a third home might be hoped for, perhaps one made of stone. Brick was not commonly used in the country until the mid-nineteenth century. The building materials that were available in the area also affected construction. For example, the Kingston, Brockville, and Bytown (Ottawa) areas had many limestone buildings because limestone was readily available. Towns like York, Cobourg, and London had many brick stores and homes.

The *Bee*

Co-operation with neighbours could help things get done. In Upper Canada, **bees** were a popular way for the immigrants to both get the work done and get together. In the Maritime colonies they called these gatherings *frolics*, a word that emphasizes the social aspect. In Upper Canada the bee, as in "busy as a bee," emphasizes the work aspect. For work accomplished for any one settler, it was understood that the favour would be returned. It was also understood that plenty of food and refreshment would be supplied.

Reverend William Proudfoot was the recipient of a three-day bee to raise his log house in June 1833. Out of respect for his position, he was not required to provide food or drink; the workers supplied it themselves. In his diary, he wrote:

> *Had I to give them their victuals and drink the raising would have cost an outlay of more than a frame house. Many of the people came for the sole purpose of drinking, and never once assisted in lifting a log.*

The social aspects of a bee probably meant a lot to people whose nearest neighbours might have lived 13 km or more away. After the work was done, there were often dances or parties.

Inside a settler's house we see a family eating a meal. What is the mother doing? What are the men in the background doing?

Snippet

The Corn-Husking Bee

According to the memoirs of Walter Riddell, who lived in Hamilton Township, husking bees were an opportunity for young people to get together and have some fun. Young men and women, probably in their teens, sat on alternate seats to husk corn. If a young man found a red ear of corn, he could kiss the girl next to him.

The Evidence Behind the Story

John Thomson was a retired naval officer who moved to Simcoe County in 1832. In 1834 he hosted a barn-raising bee. He kept a detailed journal. Its contents are very interesting, as the following entries reveal.

Saturday April 19, 1834: Sent off two hands to raise country to come Tuesday to get up the frame of the barn.

Tuesday, 22nd: A bad rainy morning; however, as people come forward we commenced. . . . It was with difficulty we got them persuaded to stay. . . . I sent for a fiddler and cajoled and flattered them. . .

Wednesday, 23rd: Began to put up the frame. . . . While the men were at supper this evening a half playful wrestling scuffle occurred. . . . He received some mortal injury, and, in the course of seven or eight minutes, expired. . . .

Thursday, 24th: Sent a warrant to the constable to call a jury by daylight . . . found a verdict of manslaughter. . . . Very cold day. . . . Had it not been for the detention as witnesses on the inquest I believe they would have all decamped by daylight. . . .

They have used a barrel of pork and one of flour. . . besides tea and sugar. . . .

Despite unfortunate incidents like the one at Thomson's place, bees did serve to get the big jobs done. They also provided a social life.

QUESTIONING THE EVIDENCE

1. In your own words, explain what happened at John Thomson's between Saturday, April 19 and Thursday, April 24, 1834.

2. Compare John Thomson's barn-raising bee to Reverend Proudfoot's house-raising bee. What impression do you get from the two experiences?

3. The *bee* has been romanticized over time so that people today tend to view it as a charming part of "the good old days." Depict the pros and cons of a bee in a visual way.

4. Historians often use diaries to understand what life was like. Explain the value of a diary as historical evidence. What would you check to be sure of a diary's value as historical evidence?

The Story So Far . . .

1 In a group, plan and build a model log shanty.

2 In groups, assign each member a different type of bee to investigate. The following is a list of some of the kinds of bees that were held in Upper Canada:

Hauling	Quilting	Butchering
Hay cutting	Corn husking	Paring
Fence building	Ploughing	Linen spinning
Preserving	Harvesting	Pumpkin harvesting

Have each member prepare a report on the bee and share the information with others, perhaps as a display.

3 From the information you have read, how does the romantic memory of bees compare with what they were really like?

CITIES AND TOWNS

The towns in Upper Canada grew rapidly during the nineteenth century. York, for example, grew from 12 cottages in 1795 to over 1000 homes and 100 shops by 1834.

Towns tended to grow in concentrated areas around a port facility. Kingston grew because of its large fort and its location at the junction of Lake Ontario and the St. Lawrence River. Before 1825 it was the leading town in terms of size and port activity, but that changed when canals were built. Toronto and Hamilton took over its trade activity when the Erie and Welland canals shifted shipping routes toward America.

Bytown, later named Ottawa, also grew as a result of its location on water. It developed as a timber-trade centre and was selected to be the headquarters for the building of the Rideau Canal. London was the one inland city that grew steadily.

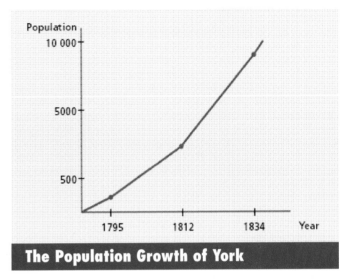

The Population Growth of York

Living Conditions

Paintings and drawings from the time being studied are often a good source of general impressions. Examine the following illustrations.

Painted by Elizabeth Frances Hale in 1804, the picture shows a tavern in the left foreground, then the houses of Duncan Cameron, William Baldwin, and William Allen, all prominent in business and government. In the distance are the government buildings, which were burned down during the War of 1812.

Life in Upper Canada **253**

This drawing by Thomas Young shows us King Street, Toronto, in 1835. Where did all the trees go?

Despite the pleasant appearance of King Street in Young's drawing, the growth of the cities and towns in Upper Canada also created the development of poor areas and rich areas. What is not shown in Young's drawing are the rows of small, crude sheds and huts where the working poor and the unemployed lived. There was quite a bit of poverty in York, and in 1817 a public-welfare agency was created. Eleven years later there was a Society for the Relief of the Sick and Destitute. By 1837, the government had established *houses of industry* to provide work in exchange for assistance.

Unsanitary conditions were synonymous with town life. This was particularly evident when the cholera epidemic struck in 1832. Orders were given to clean up the town and appoint a board of health, but it was too late. It is estimated that the death rate was close to ten percent of the entire population. The conditions that seemed to lead up to the epidemic would prompt many people to demand some improvement in their system of government.

Commerce and Institutions

Between 1815 and 1840, business was booming. Although many of the new immigrants were poor, there were some who were well enough off to start businesses, workshops, stores, and banks, which filled block after block in the rapidly expanding cities. The types of businesses found in the growing towns and in the countryside included shipping, construction, sawmills, tanneries, breweries, furniture makers, wagon manufacturers, soap processors, leather-goods makers, and saddlers.

The Working World

Most women worked hard on the home front. Many women were also employed outside their homes. The most common jobs for females were in the domestic service, such as maids, cooks, laundresses, companions, and governesses. This is known from the hundreds of advertisements placed by prospective employers in local newspapers. After the Great Migration began, there were also many advertisements posted by hopeful employees. Education was the second largest field of work open to women.

Some widows carried on family businesses, as did Catherine Chesney and Jane Marion. Chesney took out an ad in the *Upper Canada Gazette* on March 25, 1812, to inform customers that she would carry on her deceased husband's saddlery business. Marion also advertised in the *Upper Canada Gazette* when her husband died, hoping for continued patronage of his "baking business and keeping a house of entertainment." Advertisements also supply evidence that women ran their own businesses in the manufacture and sales of women's clothing and accessories, especially hats, and in the operations of inns, taverns, and boarding houses.

One hardship faced by many workers in the early nineteenth century was that their wages were decreasing. In 1818, female servants, for example, could expect to earn 20 to 30 shillings a month, plus bed and board. By the 1830s, the wage advertised in many newspapers was 15 to 20 shillings. There was little that workers could do about it. Workers were not very organized. Even when they were, the Great Migration provided an ever-increasing supply of labourers. Wages were also very low for young workers. Fourteen-year-old miners, for example, could make almost 3 shillings a day, but 12-year-olds were paid just over 1 shilling a day. The employment of children in many businesses and industries increased steadily in the nineteenth century.

Newspapers sprang up, many of them critical of the government, land distribution, and a seemingly unending stream of political favours. The newspapers represented political sides. Some, like William Lyon Mackenzie's *Colonial Advocate*, were for reform and were anti-government; others, like *The Patriot*, were for tradition and were pro-government. There were no real political parties until the 1840s, but the people who supported the British tradition were **Tories**, and those who favoured change and a more democratic government were **Reformers**.

One sign of a growing economy was the growth of banking. The Bank of Upper Canada received its royal charter in York in

Snippet

Poor Planning

Sometimes planning did not keep up with development. Funds were found to build the first Toronto General Hospital in 1820. The building fund came from a surplus of £4000 that had been collected by the Loyal and Patriotic Society to make medals. Unfortunately, all this money was used to build an expensive brick structure, and no money was left to equip or operate the hospital until 1829.

1822. This would become a controversial issue, for many people outside York resented its monopoly and domination of the economy. Also, the bank directors tended to be from an increasingly unpopular social elite.

The Good Old Days

Many people wish they lived in "the good old days," when life was "simple." How simple would your life be if you had to make everything yourself or, for variety, trade a few things with neighbours? Despite the growth of towns, the majority of people lived simply, which meant they were self-sufficient or just did without.

Snapshot

Making Maple Sugar

In the first half of the nineteenth century, there was not very much cane sugar imported into Upper Canada. Consequently, most farmers who had a sugar bush spent a few weeks every spring making maple sugar. It is estimated that during the 1830s and 1840s, the average family made about 45 kg of maple sugar each year. However, some families made as much as 450–1350 kg!

This picture shows some of the equipment pioneers used in the sugar bush. Often the area would be fenced off to prevent cattle from wandering in and either tipping the troughs or drinking so much sap that they made themselves sick and died! Pioneers created a maple sugar station in the following way:

1. They cleared the ground of underbrush, logs, and fallen trees.
2. At the centre of the bush they made a place for boiling the sap in a large kettle and built a large trough, usually a hollowed-out log, for storing the sap.
3. They inserted a wooden spout in a hole made in each maple tree.

4. They placed a small trough under each spout for the sap to drip into.
5. They boiled the sap down for hours over a fire tended day and night.
6. They poured the syrup into pans and moulds.
7. They let the syrup cool until it hardened into maple sugar.

The pioneers often made the sap that came at the end of the season into vinegar because it was less sweet and more acidic. Some found they could also make a good beer from the sap. The sugar-making season usually ended with a maple syrup- and maple sugar-eating bee.

Sickness and Health

Accidents, illness, and malnutrition were problems that plagued all the settlers. Doctors were few and far between, and even they did not understand the importance of basics like clean water. Many people in Upper Canada died from drinking contaminated milk. There was no refrigeration so food had to be preserved in other ways, especially for survival during the winter months.

Most illnesses were treated with home remedies, some of which made sense, some of which did not. Rose-hip tea and syrup was a popular remedy for many ailments. Many years later it was discovered that rose hips contain high levels of vitamin C. Garlic was also thought to be a general cure-all. Today garlic is believed by some to be good for thinning and purifying the blood, among other things. One interesting idea the settlers had about garlic was that a large quantity of it, mashed and rubbed on bald heads, was a cure for baldness!

Accidents were common, and so were injuries from them. Eliza Harrison, however, managed to survive a freak occurrence without a scratch. In 1833, near present-day Milton, Ontario, Eliza was hanging freshly washed clothes outside to dry. Suddenly a tornado ripped through the area, lifting both Eliza and the clothesline into the air. Witnesses claimed to have seen her whirling about above the treetops. Amazingly, the wind set her down unharmed, about three-quarters of a kilometre away!

Celebrations and Recreation

Although settling the land was difficult work, the pioneers did take time for a social life. Most people attended church. There was not always a church building, so services would be held in government buildings, stores, or private homes until one was built. The week's mail would often be distributed at the end of the service.

Almost every gathering turned into a social affair. Bees, weddings, auctions, elections, and even funerals would be celebrated with food, refreshments, and dancing, often for more than one day. Visiting was also popular, especially on Sundays and during the winter months. Sometimes celebrations of events were a bit late, but better late than never! In 1830, for example, settlers living in Goderich found out about the death of King George IV and the enthronement of King William IV two months after the fact, when the newspapers finally arrived. Everyone within a 15-km area came to celebrate!

This is an outdoor church service. Why do you suppose there are no children in this scene?

This is a country dance in Upper Canada. Dances were popular. They were one place where young men and women could meet and socialize with one another. Since the settlers' homes were often far apart, and school was not attended regularly, young people depended on social occasions to meet one another.

Curling became popular in Upper Canada in the 1820s. Curling clubs appeared in the 1830s with associations in Perth, West Flamborough, Niagara, Newmarket, Toronto, Dundas, and Milton. Since official granite stones were not always available, many early associations used blocks of hardwood instead.

Hockey and lacrosse, Canada's national sport, became popular after the 1830s. In 1838, in Beachville, Upper Canada, a game of baseball was played. Most of these games and sports were initially played by adult men. Skating was considered improper for women until the 1830s, but it was a popular winter activity.

Web Connection

http://www.school.mcgrawhill.ca/resources

Go to the web site above to find out more about the history of curling, lacrosse, hockey, or skating. Go to History Resources, then to *Canada: The Story of Our Heritage* to see where to go next.

Curling on the Don River. Sometimes these games went on all day, since many curlers travelled the entire night before to get there.

Immigrants also brought, from their home countries, popular games such as dominoes and checkers. Some games were invented, such as this one:

- Peel an apple, trying to keep the peel in one piece.
- Twirl it over your head and drop it.
- What letter does it look like?

That will be the first initial of your husband or wife to be, or so pioneers said.

The Story So Far . . .

1 In a group, create a graphic organizer to compare the pros and cons of the growth of towns in Upper Canada in the early 1800s. Share your results with the class.

2 Create an advertisement for a local newspaper in Upper Canada presenting your skills as a worker from this time period.

3 Research and present a report on one of the early sports or games played in Upper Canada during the early 1800s.

4 Learn a nineteenth-century dance and teach it to, or perform it, for the class.

SUM IT UP!

In this chapter you have had a glimpse of some of the elements that made the early 1800s in Upper Canada a period of transformation. There was a population explosion. Close to 300 000 immigrants came to Upper Canada from Great Britain between the years 1815–1840. While settlement expanded, the Aboriginal population shrunk. This dramatic transformation could not possibly take place without difficulties. There were problems of a personal nature for individuals struggling to survive, and there were growing pains for the community as a whole. Many social and political questions developed during this period that had not existed before. In the chapters to come you will examine some of the political aspects of this transformation.

You examined the hardships faced by the early nineteenth-century immigrants and learned about some of their coping strategies. You considered evidence from a variety of sources and tried to piece together the story of life in Upper Canada from a variety of perspectives. The story of Canada continues, but these roots and this background will continue to influence our country well into the next century and beyond.

THINKING ABOUT YOUR LEARNING

1 Imagine you want to present an idea to a television network for a realistic weekly drama about pioneer life in Upper Canada. Come up with a proposal to cover the following aspects:
- location and setting
- characters and characterization
- general plot developments
- a title for the show

2 Compose three questions about Canada as it is today that link back to this time period in Upper Canada.

3 Much of the advertising to attract emigrants to Upper Canada was not accurate or honest. Design a poster that "tells it like it was." Explain why this more honest approach would or would not attract settlers.

APPLYING YOUR LEARNING

1 Some of what is known about British North America from 1800–1830 is from newspapers. Examine the first section of a current newspaper and ask yourself the following questions:
- Overall, is it an accurate portrayal of your life?
- What would you add or take away to make it more representative?
- What, for example, do you think of the newspaper's portrayal of thirteen-year-olds?

2 Continue to work to uncover the historical developments of your own community. This time focus on Aboriginal Peoples, settlers' coping strategies, and "real" people.

3 Look at the drawing of *The Quilting Bee* by J. G. Laughlin, below. In groups, discuss what you notice about the people in the picture, such as their clothing, mood, activities. As a class, discuss what the picture tells us about the early 1800s.

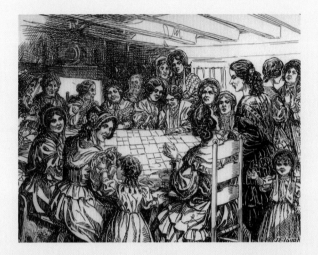

4 Plan a class or community bee that would be useful. Explain what work needs to be done and why a group could get the job done better than an individual could. Remember to plan refreshments and socializing.

5 Go back to the time line on pages 236–237. Choose one date and event that interests you most and prepare a report on it.

USING KEY WORDS

1 Use the Key Words and other words you think are significant to this chapter to create a Word Search puzzle. The key words are:
- bee
- Canada Company
- corduroy roads
- Clergy Reserve
- Crown Reserve
- directed settlement
- land baron
- Reformers
- shanty
- squatters
- Tories

Try it out on a classmate.

CONNECTING YOUR LEARNING

British North America

UNDERSTANDING CONCEPTS

1 Interview a member of your family, a friend, or a neighbour who has immigrated to Canada. Compile at least ten questions that will help you understand the difficulties faced by newcomers to Canada. Write down the questions and the answers you receive. Conclude with a paragraph stating your general impressions, the most interesting part of the interview, and how you think the recent newcomer's experience compares to the immigrant experience from the past.

2 Research a recent mass immigration to Canada. Compare this with the Loyalist migration, the migration of 1812, or the Great Migration, on the basis of the cause of migration and the effects in Canada.

3 Divide the class into four groups. Each group should use a map of the world for the following:

- One group should show the population in Canada from 1775 to 1812 and the countries of origin for its citizens.
- A second group should concentrate on the time period from 1812 to 1835.
- A third group should show the same data today in Canada. Check government census information.
- The fourth group should show the ethnic origins of the class. As a class, compare the four maps. What story do you get about the development of Canada? How does the development of your community compare to Canada's development?

DEVELOPING RESEARCH SKILLS

1 Using the "history repeats itself" principle, select a condition in Canada today that reminds you of something that happened in British North America in the past. Show this "then and now" comparison visually.

2 Some of what we know about these times comes from diaries and letters published after their authors' deaths. Overall, do you think these materials are a good source of history? Make a diary entry of your own for this day in history. Compared to the newspaper or other ongoing records, explain how you would rate your diary in terms of its value as an indication of your times.

3 A new millennium provides us with a focus for reflection.

Consider 1800 versus 2000. Prepare a television talk show to portray the main concerns of then and now. Include material for the host, interview topics and questions, guests, and possible audience participation.

COMMUNICATING REQUIRED KNOWLEDGE

1. Find a novel set in this time period of 1770 to 1835. Read it and prepare a book review. Did you enjoy the novel? Did it help you see the history? Were there parts that did not seem realistic, given what you know now? Design a poster to advertise the book.

2. As a class, work to create a living time line of this period. Using costumes, props, and a script, depict significant people and events in chronological order. Perhaps your class could arrange to perform your living time line for another class, or for an audience of parents/guardians.

3. Create a "recipe" for Canada. Write an ingredients list and instructions for "preparing." Illustrate your recipe.

APPLYING CONCEPTS AND SKILLS

1. Copy this mind map on a sheet of paper. List the challenges each group of settlers faced at this time. (Hint: Remember that there is more than one type of settler in each group.)

2. In the past, Canada was a haven for people seeking a better life. With a partner or in a small group, find out more information about the Underground Railway and prepare a visual presentation of its history. This presentation could be in the form of a large poster and oral explanation, or it could be a skit.

3. Go back to the investigation you did of your own community during the time period of this unit. Write a short story that provides an account of the challenges that existed and how the settlers in your area met them.

1815

1837

1841

Act of Union 1841

Conflict and Change

1848

POLLING PLACE

THE BIG PICTURE

These are some of the stories you will read about in this unit:

- Discontent grew in Lower and Upper Canada for many reasons, but the main source of conflict was how the colonies were ruled.
- In both colonies, there were people who urged change through non-violent means, but they could not keep discontented people from rebelling.
- After the rebellions, the British government joined Lower and Upper Canada, forming a single province.
- Canada and other provinces in British North America soon achieved more control of their government and more democracy.

Discontent in Lower Canada

1815

End of the Napoleonic Wars in Europe and beginning of emigration from Britain to Upper and Lower Canada

1822

Louis-Joseph Papineau stirs up opposition to a proposed union of Lower and Upper Canada

1825

First canal on the Lachine Rapids in Montréal begins to open the upper St. Lawrence River to shipping

1831

Québec's citadel completed

266   CONFLICT AND CHANGE

SETTING OUR FOCUS

"French Canadians should form their own country." That is the aim of the Parti Québécois, which has been, in recent years, the governing party in the province of Québec. Their quest for sovereignty, or independence, is the biggest topic of debate in Canada today. But it is nothing new. The Québec separatist movement began long ago, during British rule in Canada. The beginning of Québec nationalism can be dated from speeches made in the Assembly of Lower Canada in the period from 1815 to 1840. During that time, conflict between the British and the Canadiens, or French Canadians, led to rebellion. Pictured on the left is a view of the Château Saint-Louis, the seat of British government and the source of unrest in Lower Canada.

PREVIEWING THE CHAPTER

In this chapter you will learn about these topics:
- how a group of people who were not elected ruled Lower Canada
- how thousands of newcomers created conflict in Lower Canada
- why Lower Canada's British population grew wealthy while many French Canadian people lived in poverty
- how Louis-Joseph Papineau tried to reform the government of Lower Canada
- how conflict between the British Canadians and the French Canadians grew from discontent into rebellion

KEY WORDS

Canadiens
Château Clique
democratic
Doric Club
Fils de la Liberté
legislatures
Ninety-Two
  Resolutions
oligarchy
rebellion
Speaker
strike
Ten Resolutions

1832
Immigrants bring deadly cholera to British North America, and more than 6000 die in Lower Canada alone

1833–1837
Years of economic hardship in Lower Canada

1834
The Ninety-Two Resolutions propose sweeping reform of the government of Lower Canada

1837
- The British govern Lower Canada without consulting the Assembly
- Separatists stage huge rallies near Montréal. Papineau pleads for moderation. Fighting breaks out anyway.

View from Château St. Louis by Coke Smyth in Sketches in the Canada.

This painting shows a view of Québec from the ramparts of Château Saint-Louis. In those days the province of Québec was called Lower Canada. The city has been known as Québec since 1608. The governor of British North America and the commander-in-chief of its military force sometimes worked and lived in the château.

THE CHÂTEAU CLIQUE

When the British took charge of Québec in 1759, Château Saint-Louis was a wooden building. Damaged in the attack on Québec, the château was rebuilt several times. One of the governors who rebuilt it was James Craig. He planned a huge project: to make the city safe from attack. On top of Cape Diamond, a mighty fortress was started in the 1820s and finished in 1831.

The Americans had tried and failed to capture the capital of British North America in 1813, and the feeling was that they might attempt it again. There was also a concern that the people of Lower Canada might try to take over the British North American government. Québec's walled Upper City was the centre of military power in British North America. During the period 1815–1840, a garrison of about 1500 British soldiers lived in Québec City, many in family housing inside the walls. As many as 2000 troops massed there in times of tension.

Château Saint-Louis looked out on the great St. Lawrence River. Under British rule, Lower Canada was definitely open for business. Directly below at the Lower City docks, a forest of masts showed how trade was flourishing under the British. The table below shows how busy the port of Québec City became.

① How much did traffic increase between 1812 and 1834? By what percentage? Graph the increase.

Ships Cleared Through the Port of Québec	
1812	362
1823	609
1825	796
1832	1008
1834	1213

The wide St. Lawrence River was crowded with vessels. On the way to Montréal were ships from British ports, laden with imported clothing, furniture, machines, and luxury goods. On the way back to Europe, they carried the raw products of Upper and Lower Canada: fur, wheat, and timber.

Chugging along the river between Québec and Montréal were the new steam-powered, paddle-wheeled riverboats. They left sailing ships wreathed in their smoke. Steamboats, the first motor-powered vessels, were an invention less than a decade old at the end of the Napoleonic Wars in 1815. Another new sight was the huge log rafts that floated on the current to Québec City. Timber had become the biggest industry of Lower Canada.

In 1806 the French emperor Napoleon had blocked all British ships from docking at ports on the mainland of Europe. The blockade cut off Britain from the raw materials for its shipbuilding industry. Britain turned to Upper and Lower Canada and the Maritime province of New Brunswick. The amount of wood cut in the Canadas and shipped to Britain soon tripled.

Every spring, gigantic rafts of logs came down the Ottawa and St. Lawrence rivers to the mills and the port of Québec. This coloured engraving by W.H. Bartlett shows this event.

Joseph Montferrand

Brawling was a way of life for the lumberjacks of the upper Ottawa River Valley. Their job was dangerous. The men who did it worked hard — and played rough. A Canadien born in Montréal, Joseph Montferrand arrived in the Valley in 1827 when he was 25. Right away, he landed a job with Bowman and McGill, lumber merchants. On company land up and down the valley, workers felled trees all winter. When the ice melted in the spring, they floated the timber downriver to Québec City in rafts and booms.

The biggest and strongest men were placed in charge of the rafts. One of their jobs was to protect the crews from attack by other gangs seeking to take over their work — and to stop their own men from fighting among themselves. Montferrand was perfect for this job. He was agile, quick-witted, level-headed, and he towered over most men. He had been winning fights since he was a teenager and was a fierce defender of his people. No one dared insult a Canadien when Joseph Montferrand was around. Bowman and McGill offered to pay him handsomely.

It did not take long for Montferrand to prove his worth. In 1828 he had safely steered the company's timber rafts to Québec City. The crew threw a party to celebrate, but it was crashed by officers from a British ship. Montferrand asked the intruders to leave peacefully, but they were spoiling for a fight. Reluctantly he obliged. When it was over, every one of the British sailors required a doctor's care.

Word of this exploit spread like wildfire. The British were humiliated. One of their sailors was the Navy's champion boxer. He challenged Montferrand to a match. It was to be a battle of titans: the pride of the Canadiens against the British champion.

The British champion was as big and strong as Montferrand. Through 15 rounds, neither fighter gained the upper hand. In the seventeenth round, Montferrand pounded the British boxer in the ribs and knocked him out of the fight. The Canadiens in the large crowd went wild, but Montferrand refused the prize money. True to his generous nature, he wanted it used to pay his foe's medical bills.

Montferrand spent the next 20 years in the Ottawa Valley, where his exploits became the stuff of legend. English-speaking storytellers pronounced his name "Joe Mufferaw." As the tales were told and retold, exaggerations crept in and Big Joe Mufferaw became a giant to rival the legendary Paul Bunyan.

More people you could research are

Thomas Storrow Brown

Katherine Jane Ellice

Philip Henry Gosse

Charles Grece

Joseph Légaré

Joseph Montferrand

Who Ruled Lower Canada?

A feeling of discontent took root in Lower Canada. French-speaking merchants were ignored while the governor's friends were appointed to positions of power. The governor and senior officials gave work and support to their friends and even their own families. The **Canadiens**, or French Canadians, could not get contracts to sell the timber of Lower Canada or even to supply potatoes and other food to the logging camps. The Canadien business people resented the way things were done in the British colony. They began using the term the ***Château Clique*** to describe the governor's friends in Québec. *Clique* is a French word meaning "a group that excludes, or keeps out, other people." The *Château* was, of course, Château Saint-Louis, where the favoured few often met to conduct business or attend parties.

The Château Clique included a few dozen families of merchants, manufacturers, shippers, and financiers. Very few were Canadiens. They were *seigneurs* of country estates or ministers of churches who were friendly with the governor.

How British North America Was Governed

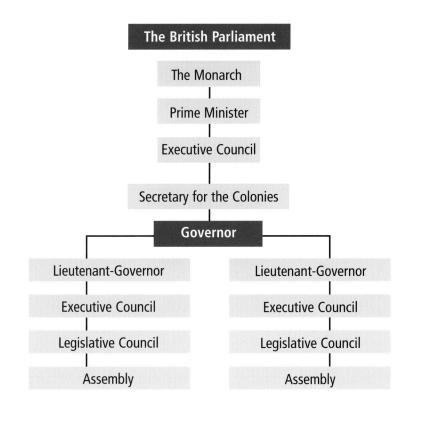

The ruler of British North America was the governor. He was appointed by the British government and lived in Québec. Most governors were members of the British aristocracy.

Upper Canada   Lower Canada

There were two ways the governor rewarded his friends that especially troubled the Canadiens. They might be appointed to the Executive Council, the governor's inner group of nine officials, or to the Legislative Council, the sixteen-member *upper house*. Legislative councillors were appointed for life. People in these positions had tremendous influence over the government of Lower Canada. They believed they had a right to power since they were wealthy, educated, and British.

Each province was ruled by a Lieutenant-Governor, also appointed by the British government. Lower Canada was different. The governor was also the ruler.

In each province, the governor appointed his advisors to an Executive Council. These prominent people helped the governor decide how to run the province and carry out the decisions.

Each province had **legislatures** — law-making bodies — that performed important duties. First, they made the laws by which the province was governed. Second, they reviewed the governor's yearly budget, or plan for spending. Third, they authorized the taxes that would supply the governor with the needed funds to run the government.

There were two legislative bodies in each province. The Assembly was **democratic**, made up of elected representatives controlled by the people. The Assembly elected its own leader, the Speaker. The smaller Legislative Council was made up of prominent citizens whom the governor appointed. Both legislative bodies had to approve laws and budgets before the government put them into practice.

The Story So Far . . .

1 Describe the different uses of Château Saint-Louis under British rule.

2 Construct a flow chart showing the steps involved in turning the forests of Lower Canada into wood products and getting them to market overseas.

3 What was the Château Clique? How did it work against Canadiens?

THE IMMIGRANTS

The port of Québec was bustling with another kind of cargo — human cargo. Beginning in 1815, peace in Europe opened the seas to travel once again. From 1816 to 1819, there were many incidents of factory and mine workers rioting in British cities. Farm workers gathered throughout the countryside to protest the low wages and the high cost of food. The government and the military came down hard on them. Emigration to Upper and Lower Canada began to increase.

The British government encouraged emigration to Canada. The merchants and builders needed workers for logging camps, canals, and factories in Canadian cities. The British also saw emigration as a way of increasing the British population of Lower Canada. They hoped the Canadiens would become a minority and their language, laws, and culture would gradually disappear.

Nearly 400 000 British people emigrated to the Canadas between 1815 and 1840. The table below will give you an idea of the increase in the number of immigrants during these years.

Arrivals at the Port of Québec from Britain				
Year	By Place of Origin			Total
	England	Ireland	Scotland	
1830	6 700	18 300	2400	27 400
1831	10 300	34 100	5300	49 700
1832	17 400	28 200	5500	51 100

1 Make a bar graph to show the numbers from each country in 1832. Where did most immigrants come from?

The Hardships of Immigration

People who wanted to make a new life in a new land faced hardship after hardship. Many emigrants had little or no money. They could not afford cabin fare, so they travelled in the open holds of timber ships that were returning to Canada. Crowded together, they endured life on the open ocean for six weeks or more.

This drawing by C.W. Jefferys shows emigrants on board a ship in the 1830s. How do you think the passengers are feeling?

Reflections

You have arrived in Québec with your family, from Ireland. Write an account of your first days. What would your family need to buy for a journey to Upper Canada? How would you earn enough money for the journey? Where would you stay while in Québec?

Most immigrant families were bound for the upper St. Lawrence Valley, Upper Canada, or the United States. But all immigrants had to stop at Québec, the port of entry. These newcomers faced another hardship. They were still far from their destinations, and overland travel was as challenging as the voyage across the ocean. Here is one account.

There is not one immigrant in five hundred who does not feel himself bitterly disappointed on his arrival at Québec. Instead of finding himself. . . on the very borders of his little estate, he learns with astonishment that he is still five hundred miles [800 km] from his transatlantic acres; and if he has no money in his pocket, he may probably have to encounter, in reaching them, more severe distress than he ever felt at home. . . .

Some 50 000 emigrants settled in Lower Canada during this period. Many of those stayed in Québec City to work in the mills and shipyards.

The Eastern Townships

Many immigrants settled in an area near Québec's border with the United States, known as the Eastern Townships. The Townships were first settled by Loyalists after the American Revolution. At first, few people came because there were no roads. Because the land is higher there, no navigable rivers run through it.

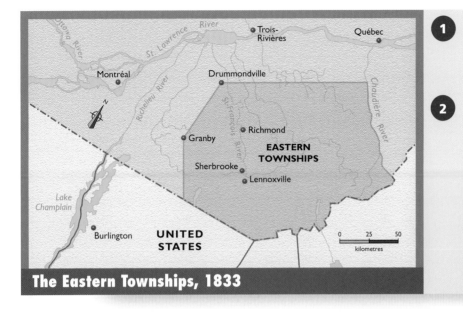

The Eastern Townships, 1833

1 Can you identify rivers that link the Eastern Townships with the St. Lawrence Valley?

2 Much of the townships lie in the hills above the flat valley. As a result, rivers could not be used to transport goods to and from the St. Lawrence Valley. Where do you think the roads would have been built to connect the townships with the outside world?

In 1833 the government of Lower Canada sold an area of nearly 350 000 ha to a developer, the British American Land Company. The developer lured settlers to the region with promises of beautiful countryside and easy farming.

The settlers did come. By 1844 more than 80 000 people had settled in the Townships. But they discovered how difficult it was to clear the land and how poor the soil was through much of the region.

This picture of farming in the Eastern Townships of Lower Canada was printed in a brochure published by the British American Land Company in 1836. In what ways could a picture make land look better than it really was?

Philip Henry Gosse settled with immigrant friends in the Townships in 1836. They looked forward, Gosse wrote in his journal, to "the peaceful and happy pursuits of agriculture." Within just two years, farming had become "a nightmare of profitless drudgery" to him. Soon he returned to England. How do you think Gosse felt at the end of his stay?

The settlement of the Eastern Townships became a big source of discontent in Lower Canada. The Canadiens resented the growing population of British settlers in the province. Worse, money from the British American Land Company went straight into the hands of the governor and the Château Clique, who used it to aid the merchants' development plans. Seeing this, the Canadiens in the Assembly of Lower Canada refused to supply any money to build public roads to the Eastern Townships. They also refused to allow the British settlers to elect any representatives to the Assembly and to have a voice in the government. The British settlers, in turn, grew more frustrated and angry.

The Rise of Montréal

You have seen how industry, trade, and commerce developed quickly in Lower Canada during this period. This trend was most apparent in Montréal. It became the centre of trade and transport for Upper Canada. People and goods had to go through Montréal whether they were bound west or east. In 1826 dredging the upper St. Lawrence River allowed ships with deep keels to get to Montréal. Many large ships began to sail past Québec and dock at Montréal.

Just west of Montréal, the St. Lawrence River forms a series of rapids that were unnavigable for larger boats and ships. But this was the age of canals. The first canal to be completed in Canada was the Lachine Canal in 1825, just upriver from Montréal. It was not a ditch at all; rather, a series of locks that helped boats get past the rapids. English-speaking business people in Montréal initiated the building of the Lachine Canal. They wanted to keep the trade of Upper Canada from going through the United States. The government

View of the Harbour, Montréal was painted in 1830. What kinds of ships and boats do you see? What kind of cargo is being loaded? What do you see on the shore between the ships?

financed these projects to promote more trade through Lower Canada, although French Canadian groups tried to block any spending of public money on canals. The British military also put money into canal-building. Can you guess why military leaders considered it their business to improve transportation between Lower and Upper Canada?

More than 20 years later, the last locks of the Lachine Canal were completed. The upper St. Lawrence was opened to ships bound for Upper Canada and the United States. The trade benefited the English-speaking merchants in Montréal.

Montréal was also becoming a manufacturing centre. Molson's Brewery, one of Canada's first modern industries, began making beer in 1786. In 1802 William W. Ogilvie exported the first shipments of flour from two mills. Montréal's first shipyard opened in 1806. Montréal was also the centre of Upper and Lower Canada's new banking industry.

As Montréal became larger and richer, it became more important than Québec City. More immigrants settled there than in Québec City or in the countryside. By 1820 Montréal's population already surpassed that of Québec City. The table below compares the population of the two cities between 1800 and 1851.

Population Growth of the Largest Cities in Lower Canada		
	Montréal	**Québec**
1800	6 000	8 000
1821	18 000	16 000
1833	31 000	27 000
1851	57 000	45 000

1 Between which years did Montréal's population surpass Québec's?

Montréal's English-speaking population became greater than the French-speaking population for the first time around 1831. French Canadian business people did not share in the city's growth, and their money was not in the new banks. As a result, in 1835 a group of Canadiens established their own bank, *Le Caisse Populaire* or The People's Bank.

The Cholera Epidemic

The summer of 1832 was British North America's biggest year for immigration up to that point. Hundreds of ships arrived in Québec, bringing as many as a thousand people a day to their new country. With them, unfortunately, came Asiatic cholera. The disease took a heavy toll on the Canadien population. It added to their discontent over the way Lower Canada was governed.

This picture shows the inspection and quarantine station of Grosse Île, on the St. Lawrence River east of Québec. Beginning in 1832, it was every immigrant's first stop in Canada.

The government set up a quarantine station in Grosse Île early in 1832, after British authorities warned that immigrants would bring cholera to the Canadas. Later, people wondered why the authorities did not stop the ships from carrying infected people. Their answer was that it was impossible to detect the disease in its early stages. This may explain why the quarantine station did not keep the cholera from spreading and may have actually helped spread the disease. Many people endured days of waiting on the island, and using the water for washing and drinking. They carried the infection, undetected, on to Québec and Montréal.

The outbreak in Lower Canada started in early June. People often died within a day of showing the symptoms. The few hospitals filled up with the sick and dying. Often the sufferers were taken to shacks lined with straw and left to die. As many as 100 people died a day, at a time when Québec still had less than 30 000 residents! Every day news from the quarantine station was signalled to the city. After feeding the growing panic, the station stopped spreading the news. In Montréal, it was worse: 149 people died on June 19 alone.

Snippet

Asiatic Cholera

Asiatic cholera is an infectious bacterial disease of the digestive system. You cannot get it from the air. Rather, the disease spreads through waters polluted with human waste that is infected with the bacterium. People get it from drinking infected water and eating infected seafood.

During the early stages of the epidemic, the governor did little to stop it or even to warn people of the danger. This made people more afraid. Then the authorities tried to devise ways of controlling the disease. Cholera outbreaks were often worst in the poorest parts of town. They searched for the source. Were people's living conditions responsible? The colonial government appointed health wardens to inspect the living conditions in people's homes and yards. If they found a lot of dirt and trash, they could order the building scrubbed down with lime or they would summon the city's firefighting equipment and turn the hoses on inside the home. They suspected that standing water harboured the disease, and they had ditches dug to drain the many pools and ponds in or between people's yards. The wardens could take people to court to enforce clean-up orders.

Légaré, Joseph, 1795-1855, Canadian, Cholera Plague, Québec c. 1832, oil on canvas, Purchased 1959. National Gallery of Canada, Ottawa

Joseph Légaré painted what he remembered about the 1832 cholera epidemic some five years after. What is the mood of this nighttime picture? What evidence of suffering and death do you see? Notice the fires burning in front of houses. Every evening from 6 p.m. to 10 p.m. the houses filled with smoke from pots of tar in the hope of killing the cholera bacteria. What would you tell people living in 1832 about how cholera spreads?

The cholera outbreak lasted into November. As many as 12 000 people died of the disease in the Canadas that year. The Canadiens loudly denounced the British policy of promoting emigration to Canada. They complained that the colonial authorities did too little, too late, to control the epidemic. Some believed the British actually encouraged emigration of Britain's urban poor to spread the disease to the French Canadian population.

1   Detail different circumstances that made people want to emigrate from Britain beginning in 1815.

2   In what ways was the rise of Montréal due to its location?

3   Write a letter to the governor pointing out the mistakes of the British authorities in dealing with the cholera epidemic.

SUBSISTENCE FARMING

The French Canadian people kept their culture intact during British rule. In the period we are studying, nearly 85 percent of the people of Lower Canada still farmed. But they paid a high price in preserving their system of farming. The average family of habitants was suffering in the 1830s, even without cholera. They were going hungry. Some habitants were forced off their land by debt. These circumstances added to their discontent with the British, especially when English-speaking residents were doing well. Were these problems also the result of British policies? The evidence points to other causes.

In the Parish of Château Richer was painted in 1830 by James Pattison Cockburn. How would you describe the parish from the details Cockburn supplies?

The original *seigneuries* were now 200 years old. Most habitants still practised subsistence farming, growing just enough to feed their large families. They rarely produced surpluses, whereas many British Canadian farmers grew enough to live on and enough to sell. The habitants fished and hunted to increase their food supplies. In spring they made maple sugar.

Earning the money to buy whatever they could not grow or gather kept the habitants employed through the long winters. Families who made furniture or clothing sold what they did not use themselves. They trapped fur-bearing animals and sold the surplus pelts. If there was any forest left at the back of their *seigneury*, they logged. Many habitants made potash and the more refined pearl cakes, which they sold to British manufacturers of soaps, bleaches, and dyes.

During this period, the population of Canadien society was increasing rapidly, as shown in the table below. In 1815 the French population of Lower Canada was about 288 000. The birth rate was very high, with more than ten children in the average family. By 1840 the Canadiens grew in number to about 600 000.

Population Growth in Lower Canada		
	1815	**1831**
Total	340 000	553 134
Living in cities	about 30 000	56 668

1. Did the percentage of people living in cities increase between 1815 and 1831? By how much?

2. What percentage of the population was French Canadian in 1815?

As the Canadien population grew larger and larger, farmers kept subdividing their lands among their children, according to *seigneurial* custom. Soon overcutting of timber in areas with growing populations caused shortages. By 1820 *seigneuries* around Montréal were reporting that they had no wood left for fencing or firewood.

The Mysterious Shrinking Crops

While the population was growing rapidly, the local food supply was shrinking. The staple of the Canadien diet was bread. Farmers harvested and ground their own wheat. But records of the older *seigneuries* of Lower Canada show that the production of wheat declined steadily after about 1800.

The Decline of Wheat Crops in Lower Canada		
	Annual harvest, in minots[1]	
	By Each Family	**On Each Arpent[2] of Land**
before 1802	100–200	6–12
1831	56.5	3
1840s	12	—

1 How much wheat, in *minots*, would you expect to have been harvested on each *arpent* of land in the 1840s?

1 *Minot:* A unit of dry measure equal to 36.4 kg or a little larger than a bushel.
2 *Arpent:* A unit of area equal to .342 ha

There were many British Canadian critics of French Canadian farming, and they often published their observations. Some pointed to the old-fashioned farming practices on the *seigneuries*. To maintain the fertility of the soil, the farmers needed to rotate crops from field to field, and to leave fields untilled after harvesting the crops. The soil was actually losing its ability to grow crops because the same crops were planted too often.

Observers pointed out other traditional farming practices that made for shrinking production. Habitant farmers used shallow ploughs, which did not mix the soil from top to bottom very well. This left the soil lacking the minerals needed for healthy crops. Other farming practices wasted nutrients. The farmers threw animal manure into the river instead of ploughing it into the fields to replace lost nutrients in the soil.

Some farmers tried growing new crops. As wheat crops diminished, many habitant families replaced bread with potatoes as the staple food in their diets. Over the long term, the soil's nutrients became depleted from growing potatoes in the same plots year after year, just as they had with wheat. Many farmers took to raising hogs and ate the meat. They grew oats to feed their animals. But each new product the habitants grew resulted in shrinking yields.

The following table suggests how farming shifted to new crops over time.

Snippet

A Little Ice Age

The weather did not help farmers either. Like most of the Northern Hemisphere, Lower Canada was in the grip of a Little Ice Age. Glaciers were advancing. Some years the growing season was so short that many crops were ruined. It was so cold in 1816 that people called it the year without a summer. Light snow fell all day on June 8. On August 21 it snowed heavily.

Cultivation of Wheat and Other Crops in Lower Canada

	Percent of total harvest		
	Before 1800	1831	1844
wheat	60–70	21	4.4
potatoes	—	46	—
oats	—	—	33

1 By what percentage did the wheat harvest in Lower Canada decline by 1844? (Assume that the wheat harvest was 60% of the total in 1800.)

2 What percentage of the total 1831 harvest would have been oats and other crops? What percentage would have been potatoes and other crops in 1844? What do you suppose the other crops might have been? Why do you think there are no figures for other crops?

At the same time, many farmers in Lower Canada were growing surpluses and selling them overseas. English-speaking farmers formed societies to improve farming. The habitant farmers did not join them. Few habitants spoke English, and even fewer could read it. There were other barriers. Families kept to their *seigneuries*, venturing to a neighbouring community only for a market or a dance or to attend church.

During this period, however, the outside world was coming into their communities. In some *seigneuries*, particularly around Montréal, English-speaking trade workers and business people moved in, bringing a cash economy to the habitant. Over time a whole cluster of shops, stores, and inns grew up around it. Many habitants got to know their English-speaking neighbours while buying their goods and services.

Farms in Crisis

Beginning in 1833, French Canada suffered five years of hard times. Swarms of insects devoured successive crops. In 1835 wheat stem rust, a fungal disease spread by the wind, killed the wheat crops. When crops failed, the habitants would have to buy enough wheat to ensure it would last for the winter. By 1840 wheat exports from Québec were half of what they were at the beginning of the century. Increasingly, Lower Canada relied on imported wheat from Upper Canada and the United States for its flour. But Upper Canadian wheat had become expensive. When wheat became scarce, its price went shooting up.

During this period, many habitants went into debt and lost farms that had been in the same families for generations. How did that happen? Habitant families owned their own land and could sell it. But the *seigneurial* system preserved some practices dating from the Middle Ages. The owner-farmers owed their *seigneurs* old-fashioned rents and fees. Some fees had to be paid no matter what the state of the household was. The habitants might also owe the *seigneurs* a portion of their working time. And if the owners did sell their farms, they had to pay yet another fee to the *seigneurs*.

The habitants had other obligations. They gave ten percent of their farm products to support the local Catholic priest and his parish. They also paid rent to the parish for pews in church, donated money to collections on Sundays and holy days, and paid fees for baptizing their babies, for getting married, and for being buried. During this time, when there were many deaths, the parishes became richer at the habitants' expense. Some habitants came to see the priests as non-productive members of their communities. Some developed an outright hatred of the Roman Catholic Church.

The need to buy staples became a trap that snared many habitant families. To survive, they went deeply into debt. If they managed to produce a surplus crop, they would not be able to sell it. Likely it would be claimed to pay off past debts. For some habitant families, the burden of debt became so severe that they lost their farms.

Many Canadien families migrated to the cities and joined the ranks of those seeking work on the docks or in the mills. They crowded into the Lower Towns of Québec and Montréal or into nearby newly cleared lands. Living conditions in either setting were very poor. Finding work in the logging, sawmilling, and shipbuilding industries kept many habitant families from starvation. Families began moving to the United States in search of better living conditions. Some ended up begging in the streets.

Katherine Jane Ellice painted this watercolour of the *seigneury* at Beauharnois in 1838. She was the daughter-in-law of Edward Ellice, one of the richest and most hated of the British *seigneurs*.

The Story So Far . . .

1 List the different factors causing the habitants' food supplies to "shrink" after 1800.

2 Construct a flow chart illustrating how a habitant family might lose their farm. In charting the order of events, be sure to show why events happened; in other words, show the link between causes and effects.

3 Imagine you are a recent immigrant to Canada today and you cannot write, read, or speak English. Make three columns, using the headings *Writing, Reading,* and *Speaking.* Under each heading, list some of the barriers and difficulties you would face if you, as this immigrant, were not able to read, write, or speak English. Can you draw any conclusions about how the language barrier might have affected French Canadian society?

A LEADER OF THE PEOPLE

The habitants found a champion in Louis-Joseph Papineau. He was the first of several leaders of the Canadiens to fight for independence. Papineau fought real battles but not on any battlefield. He fought them in the Assembly of Lower Canada. Along the way, he gained support from other groups, such as the Irish immigrant population.

The Assembly of Lower Canada was created in 1791 to meet popular demand for representative government. Citizens elected representatives to a Legislative Assembly that met to discuss and make decisions about how to rule. Elected representatives voted on how much money to collect in taxes, while a different group, the executive officers, proposed how it should be spent. Elected representatives also passed laws necessary for the executives to operate the government. The provincial election of 1792 was the first anywhere in British North America.

During British rule, however, the government of Lower Canada was not a democracy. The ruler was the governor, who was appointed by the British government and was usually a high-ranking person in British society. The governor did not have all power, since the British Prime Minister and foreign secretary instructed him at every turn. But he had the power to appoint his friends and family to government jobs. When a government is made up of a small group of people who are not elected, it is called an **oligarchy**.

The Assembly was the one part of the government of Lower Canada that was democratic. Modelled on the House of Commons in England, the Assembly of Lower Canada had 50 members. The Assembly sat in Québec in the old Bishop's Chapel, not far from Château Saint-Louis. After it burned down, a new Parliament building opened on the same site in 1834. It

Millicent Mary Chaplin painted this watercolour of the House of Assembly in Québec. She came from England to Québec in 1838 with her husband, a member of the Goldstream Guards.

was there that Louis–Joseph Papineau took the Canadien people down a new road. In defending their interests, he used the power of the Assembly to bring the government to a standstill.

Canadien Culture Under Attack

By the early 1800s, the Canadiens were beginning to feel that their heritage was threatened. First, some Montréal business people started to attack French culture. They questioned the Canadiens' rights to use their own language, follow their own laws in civil matters, and have their own Roman Catholic religion. It did not matter that these rights were protected by British laws: the Quebec Act of 1774 and the Constitutional Act of 1791. The British merchants told their friend, the governor, that the laws were a mistake.

Government officials did everything they could to help make Lower Canada a British society. The Canadien way was believed to be old-fashioned and a hindrance to economic growth. The British group tried to get rid of the French laws that governed business and property. They tried to get rid of the *seigneuries* so that farmland could be bought and sold on the open market. They attacked the Roman Catholic Church, too. Its economic power over the habitants gave the Church great influence in the life of Lower Canada. When public education was first established in Lower Canada in 1801, the government gave the responsibility to the Anglican Church.

Educated Canadiens turned increasingly to the professions, rather than going into business. Why?

Web Connection

www.school.mcgrawhill.ca/resources

Go to the web site above to find out more about how public schools developed in French Canada. Go to History Resources, then to *Canada: The Story of Our Heritage* to see where to go next.

Louis-Joseph Papineau
AN ETERNAL DISCONTENT

The cream of Lower Canadian society is dancing the night away at a ball at the magnificent Château Saint-Louis. As a *seigneur* and Speaker of the Assembly, Louis-Joseph Papineau is one of the guests. But he ignores the dancing and laughter. He is off in a corner, absorbed in a game of chess.

This scene was typical of Papineau. A reluctant politician, he was always pulled in two directions. He was a fiery speaker who could inspire audiences. Yet he was shy and liked the quiet of the countryside. He was a reformer and idealist who fought for the rights of Canadiens. Yet he believed in the *seigneurial* system. In fact, he became a *seigneur* himself.

People were challenging the old ways when Papineau was born in Montréal in 1786. Just a few years earlier, the American colonies had won independence from Britain. Though change was in the air, Papineau's own upbringing was very strict. He was the eldest of eight children. His father, Joseph, was a notary, *seigneur*, and politician. His mother, Rosalie, ruled the household with an iron hand. She was a devout Catholic who wanted her favourite son to become a priest.

When his parents enrolled him at a religious college in Montréal, young Louis-Joseph rebelled and had to leave. He was then sent to study with the priests at the *Séminaire de Québec*, which later became *Université Laval*. There he made a name for himself as a debater. What he really enjoyed, though, was reading. The books he chose introduced him to radical new ideas about democracy and individual freedom — ideas that his teachers did not like.

Papineau left the seminary in 1804, sure that he did not want to be a priest. He started training as a notary, who is someone who draws up documents, such as contracts. He soon grew bored and decided to study law instead. But he did not like this profession either.

Luckily people remembered his skill as a debater and orator. In 1809, when he was just 22, they talked him into running for a seat in the Assembly. He won the election and launched the career that would make him the first effective voice of his people.

For Papineau, the victory was double-edged. It gave him a chance to put into practice some of his beliefs. But it also meant that he would spend the next 45 years in the grip of what he called "the demon of politics." That "demon" would place him at the centre of events in Lower Canada. It would also draw him far away from the quiet life he longed for.

Other people you could research are

Pierre-Stanislas Bédard

James Craig

John Molson

William W. Ogilvie

Louis-Joseph Papineau

John Sherbrooke

Snapshot

I Want a Plamondon Portrait!

By the 1830s, Antoine Plamondon was the most popular artist in Lower Canada. Everyone who was "anyone" in Québec society wanted a Plamondon portrait. Louis-Joseph Papineau, for example, commissioned the artist to paint his own portrait, as well as that of his wife and daughter.

Like many artists of the day, Plamondon was also a skilled copyist. When clients liked a particular picture, they often asked the artist to make a copy, just as we might order extra copies of photographs today. Sometimes artists would make an exact copy; at other times they would change details in the picture.

In addition to making copies of his own paintings, though, Plamondon copied pictures by other artists. Today, this is illegal. It is considered forgery. In Plamondon's day, though, it was common. Papineau, for example, liked a painting by the Venetian artist, Titian, and commissioned Plamondon to paint a copy of it. Both Plamondon and Papineau were proud of the copy, which hung in a prominent place in Papineau's home.

Plamondon, Antoine 1804-1895, Canadian, Julie Papineau (née Bruneau) and her Daughter Ezilda, 1836. Purchased, 1974. National Gallery of Canada, Ottawa.

Snippet

Ezekiel Hart Barred from Assembly

In 1807 Ezekiel Hart was elected to the Legislative Assembly, but was barred from taking his seat. Why? Because he was Jewish. Hart was elected again in 1808. When he was barred a second time, he gave up on politics. It was not until 1822 that the Assembly passed a law giving Jews equal rights. The law made Lower Canada the first place in the British Empire to do this.

In Montréal and Québec, much of the business was conducted in English. The friends of the Château Clique controlled who succeeded in business and who did not. Some French Canadians became lawyers, notaries, or doctors. Others went into the newspaper trade or became scholars and teachers. Competition for work became quite keen in those professions as the supply of professional French Canadians outgrew the demand for their services within the French-speaking population. Educated Canadiens resented the restrictions that British control imposed on their careers.

Louis-Joseph Papineau took his seat in the Assembly just as a conflict flared up between the Assembly and the governor. It started with the question of whether judges and magistrates could also sit in the Assembly. The Canadiens said no: it was a conflict of interest. Judges and magistrates were appointed by the governor and most were British. In 1807 the Assembly passed a bill banning judges from the Assembly. The bill went to the Legislative Council, where the governor's friends turned it down. The Canadiens were angry. They passed another law banning judges from the Assembly in 1809. This time Governor James Craig used his power to dissolve the Assembly and force an election.

The Assembly was fast becoming a way for Lower Canada's French-speaking inhabitants to make their interests known and felt. The population of Lower Canada was at least four-fifths French-speaking during this period. Most members of the Assembly were Canadien, and their views carried the day. As with most representative bodies, the Assembly followed majority rule: bills required the support of more than half of those voting to be adopted. This trend reached its limit in the election of 1834, when 41 of 50 members elected were Canadiens of the same party.

In the Assembly in 1810, the Canadiens' voice was stronger than before. They continued to denounce the government's position. In February 1810 Governor Craig dissolved the Assembly. He arrested the leader of the Canadien Party, Pierre-Stanislas Bédard. Bédard was also an editor of the newspaper *Le Canadien*. The paper had been publishing criticisms of the government, arguing for more democracy. Governor Craig saw signs of treason in a silly little poem that was circulating in Québec and had been reprinted in *Le Canadien*. It called on people to tweak the noses of officials who were the friends of the governor. Craig had the presses seized. Even the printer was arrested. The postal service was stopped. The streets of Québec swarmed with soldiers, looking for signs of rebellion.

The crisis was called Craig's Reign of Terror. Why did it happen at all? Governor Craig was sure that a revolution was about to begin in Lower Canada. Many British soldiers and aristocrats had deep fears about democracy. One fear was that the colonists would rise up and overthrow the government as they had in the American Revolution.

Life returned to normal in Québec, but Craig's crackdown made a deep impression on young Louis-Joseph Papineau. He was angry at the way his people were pushed around. He was angry, too, at the Roman Catholic Church officials for siding with the governor against the Canadiens.

Soldiers on the streets of Québec were a common sight in the early 1800s.

The Struggle for Control

In 1815 Papineau was elected to represent the people in the Montréal West riding. That year he was elected Speaker of the Assembly. In representative bodies, the **Speaker** is the person who runs the meetings and keeps track of who has the right to speak in debates. Speakers are chosen from among the members and are not supposed to take sides. They prevent arguments from turning into more serious conflicts.

In Lower Canada, this rule did not apply. Papineau soon took Pierre-Stanislas Bédard's place as leader of the Canadien Party, the group with the most members in the Assembly. He continued to be Speaker *and* party leader for nearly 20 years. Papineau learned how to use the few powers of the Assembly to win wider gains. He used newspapers and public meetings to spread his message.

Louis-Joseph Papineau became the hero of the habitants, although he was himself a *seigneur* and defended the *seigneurial* system all his life. He felt *seigneuries* were a good way to organize society and that the Canadiens were destined to live on the land. Papineau also had a strong belief in the importance of following your people's traditions.

Soon another conflict arose between the Assembly and the governor. The issue was: who had control of government spending? Papineau argued that the Assembly should have the right to refuse its yearly funding of government programs if they would not benefit the people who paid for them. Without funds, the government could not operate. By himself, the governor did not have the power to tax. He could use some of the money the colonial government sent to run the army and other operations, but only the Assembly had the power to make new taxes. Papineau and his party wanted the Assembly to be able to look at all the governor's spending plans. They wanted to control government jobs, especially the positions to which the governor appointed his friends.

During the War of 1812-1814 and afterward, the government ran up some big bills. The governor paid off the debt by borrowing money from the treasury, which the Assembly controlled. When Governor John Sherbrooke presented the budget to the Assembly for approval in 1818, the government already owed the Assembly £120 000. Papineau seized the opportunity to make a deal: the Assembly would vote

British Governor James Craig tried to prevent an uprising of Canadiens in the Lower Canada Assembly.

for loaning the money if the governor followed the Assembly's advice on running the government.

Governor Sherbrooke was so grateful to have avoided a fight that he offered Papineau a seat on the Executive Council, the governor's inner advisory group. The governor's friends raised a great outcry against this idea and Papineau turned the offer down. What the Governor proposed in 1818 was the first step in a key reform called responsible government. When it was adopted 30 years later, the practice of selecting executive councillors from among the elected representatives became a cornerstone in Canada's democratic government.

Relations between the Assembly and the governor got steadily worse. For 14 years the Assembly refused to approve the government's budget, and the governor had to scrape together the money to operate. On the other side, the Assembly passed more than 200 bills that were rejected by the Legislative Council.

Radical thinkers of the *Patriotes* (as Papineau's party was called after 1826) began talking about a revolution. Papineau himself came to believe that the Canadiens' only hope of surviving was to be free of British rule. But he remained a moderate and said that violence was not the way to achieve their goal.

Finally, in 1834, Papineau and a group of *Patriotes* presented a list of **Ninety-Two Resolutions** to the Assembly. The resolutions called for sweeping reform of the government of Lower Canada, within the British parliamentary system. Among the Ninety-Two Resolutions were these:

- Members of the Legislative Council should be elected, not appointed.
- Patronage should be abolished. The governor should not make any appointments without the approval of the Assembly.
- Responsible government should be the rule. The members of the governor's Executive Council should be elected members of the Assembly.
- Judges should be independent of the government.

Soon after, there was a general election. The *Patriotes* got more than three-quarters of all the votes and won 77 seats; the British party had only 11. Would the governor and the British rulers not have to listen to the Canadiens' demands now?

Philippe Aubert de Gaspé
FIRST FRENCH CANADIAN NOVELIST

When 18-year-old Philippe-Ignace-François Aubert de Gaspé went to work as a journalist in 1832, it was an exciting time for political reporters in Lower Canada. The forces favouring responsible government were gathering strength and talk of rebellion was in the air.

Though Aubert de Gaspé's heritage was mostly French, he sided with the ruling elite. As the eldest son of a *seigneurial* family with deep roots in Lower Canada, he was happy with the status quo. This attitude was not unusual among *seigneurs*. It also was not unusual to find British Canadians siding with the *Patriotes*. Many of the English-speaking *Patriotes* were immigrants of Irish descent. Like the Canadiens, they were often Catholics who believed they had been wronged by the British. Edmund Bailey O'Callaghan was one of them. An outspoken supporter of responsible government, O'Callaghan was a doctor and newspaper publisher who had been elected to the Assembly. There, he had become Louis-Joseph Papineau's right-hand man.

Both Aubert de Gaspé and O'Callaghan were proud men with fiery tempers. As they rubbed shoulders in the hallways of the House of Assembly and argued in their newspapers, it is not surprising that their arguments turned to insults. When the insults turned to blows in 1835, though, Aubert de Gaspé was sentenced to a month in prison for assaulting O'Callaghan.

Once out of prison, the young man wasted little time in taking revenge. He placed a stink bomb in the House of Assembly, which was controlled by the *Patriotes*. The smell was so terrible that the building had to be evacuated. The authorities treated this prank seriously. When a warrant was issued for his arrest, Aubert de Gaspé fled to his family's *seigneury*. There he passed the time writing a novel titled *L'Influence d'un livre*. The *livre* of the title referred not to a book, but to the old French unit of money.

Though his book was the first French Canadian novel, critics were not kind when it appeared in 1837. One called it "a historico-poetic mish-mash." Aubert de Gaspé was crushed by the criticism. Because of the warrant for his arrest, he could not work as a journalist in Québec. Now, his novel was being ridiculed in the press. He decided to go to Halifax. There, out of reach of the arrest warrant, he licked his wounds and again found work as a legislative reporter. Sadly, his career was cut short when he died at 26.

His story has an interesting postscript, however. Twenty-two years after Aubert de Gaspé's death, his father, also named Philippe, published his own novel, *Les anciens canadiens*. An immediate success, the book is now considered the first classic of French Canadian literature.

More people you could research are

Millicent Mary Chaplin

Philippe Aubert de Gaspé

Edmund Bailey O'Callaghan

Antoine Plamondon

Philemon Wright

Protest Becomes Rebellion

In 1836 the old conflict between the governor and the Assembly was repeated. The governor submitted the budget and the Assembly refused to grant supply. This time the Assembly went further: it voted to go on **strike**. It refused to deal with the governor and councils until the government carried out the reforms the *Patriotes* had proposed.

The two parts of the government of Lower Canada were moving further and further apart. Early in 1837 the British government gave its answer to the Ninety-Two Resolutions. The Secretary for War and the Colonies, Lord John Russell, presented his answer in the form of **Ten Resolutions** to the House of Commons. They rejected all the *Patriotes'* demands. Soon the Governor, Lord Gosford, got new instructions from Britain. The government would not have to borrow money from the Assembly but could just seize the funds. Remember that the whole idea of creating the Assembly was to give the people of Lower Canada representative government. The British government now took that away.

Until now, the *Patriotes* had expressed their discontent in peaceful protest. They had tried to bring about reform in government. Now people started taking up arms, and soon their protest turned into a **rebellion**, an organized resistance against the government. There were different groups within the *Patriote* Party, and each was pulling in a different direction. Dr. Edmund Bailey O'Callaghan called the British seizure "robbery" and "plunder" and wrote in a newspaper that:

> *Our rights must not be violated with impunity.*
> *HENCEFORTH THERE MUST BE NO PEACE IN*
> *THE PROVINCE* — no quarter for the plunderers.
> *Agitate!* Agitate!! AGITATE!!! *Destroy the Revenue;*
> *denounce the oppressors. Everything is lawful when the*
> *fundamental liberties are in danger.*

The British government was denounced at public meetings. Soon the governor banned such meetings. In September a new group appeared in Montréal: ***Fils de la Liberté***, the Sons of Freedom. It was formed by some 500 young people. One of its organizers was an Irish radical, Thomas Storrow Brown. He claimed the club had been formed to protect the *Patriotes* from gangs of British supporters who beat people up during election campaigns. In fact, they wanted to overthrow the British rulers. Soon after that, a few local governments began electing their own magistrates and militia officers. They no longer accepted the authority of appointed officials.

Louis-Joseph Papineau speaking at Saint-Charles-sur-le-Richelieu. Judging from the crowd in the picture, what would you say the mood is?

In October there was a huge rally in the town of Saint-Charles-sur-le-Richelieu. Some 5000 people attended the meeting. Amid banners and flags, the *Patriotes* made their case for declaring independence from Britain. Papineau pleaded for moderation. He said that a peaceful way to defeat the government would be to boycott imported goods that carried duties. If people refused to buy such goods, the government would get less money. The people of Lower Canada could make their own goods. Papineau also suggested that they avoid paying duties by smuggling goods into the province. Papineau was still hailed as the leader of the *Patriotes*, but few people supported his stand now.

Things soon got out of hand. In Montréal, on November 6, the *Fils de la Liberté* clashed in the streets with a pro-government British gang known as the **Doric Club**. The British supporters wrecked a newspaper office and attacked Papineau's home. The *Patriote* supporters smashed the windows of an unpopular magistrate's home.

Governor Gosford had tried to bring in some of the reforms the *Patriotes* had demanded, but now he turned in the other direction. He imposed martial law, suspending the regular laws and using military courts. British troops stationed in the Maritime provinces and Upper Canada began marching toward Montréal. British Canadian volunteers formed militia units and began training. On November 12 Lord Gosford banned all public meetings. On November 16 he obtained warrants to arrest 26 *Patriote* leaders. The leaders fled to the countryside and pursuing soldiers were ambushed. Shots were fired, and the first casualties lay dead. Six days later, at the village of Saint-Denis, the first battle of the rebellion was fought. When the guns began to fire, Louis-Joseph Papineau was nowhere to be found.

The Evidence Behind the Story

Between 5000 and 7000 *Patriotes* took up arms in 1837. About half of those were habitants. The rest were Canadien labourers, tradespeople, business people, and professionals. Many more were sympathetic to the rebellion but would not endanger their families. Still more were unhappy about their condition but were unwilling to consider changing their society.

John McGregor, a Scottish traveller in Lower Canada in about 1830, made the following observations about the Canadien farmers.

> There is not probably in the world a more contented or happy people than the habitants or peasantry of Lower Canada. They are with few exceptions in easy circumstances; and they are fondly attached to the seigneurial mode of holding their farms. In all the settlements, the church forms the point around which the inhabitants born in the parish like to dwell; and farther from it than they can hear the ringing of its bell, none of them can be reconciled to settle. They are not anxious to become rich, but they possess the necessary comforts, and many of the luxuries of life. . . .
>
> Their mode of agriculture is clumsy and tardy; yet the soil, with the most negligent culture, yields abundance for domestic consumption, and something over the tythes [tithes] to sell for the purchase of articles of convenience and luxury. . . .

> Contented to tread in the path beaten by their forefathers, they in the same manner till the ground; commit in the like way the same kind of seed to the earth; and in a similar mode do they gather their harvests, feed their cattle, and prepare and cook their victuals. . . .

— from British America, published in 1832

QUESTIONING THE EVIDENCE

1. What specific observations can you identify in this passage that do not agree with what you have learned in this chapter?
2. Which of the following factors could have contributed to John McGregor's impressions of habitant life?
   - his country of origin
   - his attitude toward farmers
   - how many farmers he visited or talked to
   - which parts of the province he visited
3. How might the author have gained a different impression? How might his impression have changed in later years?
4. What conclusions can you draw about the accuracy of first-hand accounts? How can you be sure an overall impression is accurate? When should you be suspicious of such generalizations?

The Story So Far . . .

1. Draw and label a chart showing the different parts of the government of Lower Canada. Include as many details as you can. Try to show how the parts were connected.
2. What were the key practices of the government that the *Patriotes* wanted to reform?
3. How did Louis-Joseph Papineau become the leader of the *Patriotes*? How did he lose control of them?

SUM IT UP!

A number of factors contributed to conflict in Lower Canada. The province was ruled by a small group of the British governor's friends, known as the Château Clique. Their rule favoured British merchants and business people in Lower Canada, which bred discontent among the Canadiens.

Immigrants flooded into Lower Canada beginning in 1815. When newcomers brought cholera to British North America, thousands of Canadiens died. The Canadiens feared that the British were trying to kill their culture, and even the people, by encouraging emigration and doing little to stop the spread of cholera.

While the British population of Lower Canada prospered, many Canadiens lived in poverty. Habitant farming familes suffered hardship as their system of agriculture failed. Many families fell into debt and were forced to leave their farms.

Louis-Joseph Papineau became a leader of the Canadiens through his power over the Assembly of Lower Canada. Papineau tried to reform the government, arguing for more democracy instead of the rulership of a few appointed officials. When the colonial government began to rule without the Assembly, discontent swelled into open conflict.

THINKING ABOUT YOUR LEARNING

1. List the main reasons for the discontent of the Canadiens of Lower Canada.
2. What were some of the ways people in Lower Canada could express their discontent? Use specific examples where possible.
3. Was Louis-Joseph Papineau too old-fashioned to lead the *Patriotes*? Explain your thinking by referring to what you know about Papineau's life.
4. What did Governor Craig do that revealed his deep mistrust of the Canadiens?

APPLYING YOUR LEARNING

1. a) Form groups and choose a topic relating to Lower Canada during this period. For example:

   • how the Québec citadel was constructed
   • where streets and buildings were in early Montréal
   • early steamships of Lower Canada
   • how timber rafts were made
   • how a water-powered sawmill worked
   • how a *seigneury* was laid out
   • early newspapers in Lower Canada

   b) Make up questions to guide your research. Use some factual questions, some comparison questions, and some speculative questions. Locate eyewitness accounts and pictures. Keep notes and make drawings and charts.

   c) Decide with your group how to present your research findings, and then prepare and deliver the presentation.

2. Cholera outbreaks still occur in many parts of the world. Consult the cholera and

epidemic dysentery section of the World Health Organization web site. Find out where the disease is occurring and how many people are affected. Prepare a report that includes information on how travellers can avoid the disease.

3 Form two groups and take opposing views on the following quotation stated by Québec Bishop Lartigue in 1837: "A revolution [or rebellion] would be bought too dearly if it cost a single drop of blood."

Using the example of events in Lower Canada, present your arguments in the form of a debate. Afterward, vote to decide whether rebellion was justified.

4 Separatist or independence movements are as old as history itself. Here are some examples: the Swiss, the Scots, the Irish, the Americans, the Basques. How often do they succeed in breaking away? Choose one of the above groups of people or another case, and study its history. Find out what the people wanted and what they did to become independent. Present your findings. Compare the results. What factors contribute to the success of separatist movements? Why do they fail?

5 Construct a chart of events in Lower Canada during the period you have studied, using the example below as a guide.

EVENTS IN LOWER CANADA

1791-1837	Society	Building and Technology	World Events	Politics

Using point form, enter the events from the time line at the beginning of this chapter on your chart, under the appropriate headings. Now add as many events as you can from the text for which you know the dates.

USING KEY WORDS

1 Match the terms in Column A with the definitions in Column B.

Column A	Column B
a) legislatures	i) a group of young *Patriotes* that formed in Montréal
b) representative	ii) an exclusive group of the governor's friends
c) Assembly	iii) government by a small group of people who are not elected
d) Canadiens	iv) government reforms presented by the *Patriotes* in 1834
e) democratic	v) the leader of the Assembly
f) Ninety-Two Resolutions	vi) French Canadians
g) oligarchy	vii) Lord John Russell's response to the Ninety-Two Resolutions
h) Doric Club	viii) a democratic body in Lower Canada
i) Château Clique	ix) a group of pro-British youths in Montréal
j) strike	x) a violent uprising of the people against their rulers
k) Speaker	xi) a group's refusal to deal with authorities until proposed reforms are addressed
l) Ten Resolutions	xii) someone elected to speak for the voters in an area
m) *Fils de la Liberté*	xiii) groups made up of elected representatives controlled by the people
n) rebellion	xiv) law-making bodies

CHAPTER 10

Discontent in Upper Canada

1817
- First steamboats operating on Lake Ontario
- First road built between York and Kingston

1819
Robert Gourlay banished from Upper Canada

1824
William Lyon Mackenzie starts publishing *The Colonial Advocate*

1825
Canada Company established

1828
Reformers form majority in Assembly

SETTING OUR FOCUS

Fort Henry in Kingston, Upper Canada, during the 1830s. British ships sail by on the wide St. Lawrence River, seen in the foreground of this picture. Upper Canada was British all the way. Under the surface, things were not so peaceful. Founded by the same British law that created Lower Canada in 1791, Upper Canada was also ruled by a few individuals who were not elected. Upper Canada had a democratically elected Assembly, as did Lower Canada, and its Assembly also had little power. During the period from 1815 to 1840, thousands of immigrants flooded into both provinces from England, Scotland, and Ireland. Like the habitants of Lower Canada, the farmers of Upper Canada suffered through hard times while a few people prospered. Representatives in Upper Canada's Assembly demanded reform, as did those in the *Patriote* Party in Lower Canada, to little avail. In their frustration, there came a point when, as in Lower Canada, people took up arms.

PREVIEWING THE CHAPTER

In this chapter you will learn about these topics:
- the growth of the town of York into the City of Toronto
- the government of Upper Canada in the grip of the Family Compact and the conflicts that resulted
- canals, which improved transportation in Canada but were expensive, leaving little money to build roads
- settlers' discontent with the way townships were developed in Upper Canada
- the conflicts that developed over lands reserved for churches, the government, and schools
- William Lyon Mackenzie and other reformers who tried to change the government of Upper Canada

KEY WORDS

aristocracy
Family Compact
leveller
moderate
radical
reform
sedition
township
transship
wholesale trade

1832
Rideau Canal opens

1833
- York becomes Toronto
- Mackenzie elected as first mayor

1836
Robert Baldwin and other moderate reformers appointed to Executive Council, but soon resign

1837
William Lyon Mackenzie agitates for a new form of government in Upper Canada

THE GROWTH OF YORK

York, now Toronto, got its start as the capital of Upper Canada. Economic forces helped it grow into the province's largest centre. York's protected harbour was an important factor in the town's growth. Many small sailing ships worked on Lake Ontario, transporting people and goods to and from York. After the War of 1812, the new steamers quickly took over much of the trade. York was one of the major **transshipping** centres for goods and people bound to and from Western Canada, the area between lakes Ontario, Erie, and Huron.

Population of York/Toronto	
Year	**Population**
1813	625
1824	1 700
1834	9 252
1851	30 800

1. Compare these figures with those for Québec and Montréal in Chapter 9, page 277. Which town grew the fastest in the interval before 1851? (To find the average growth rate, first calculate the overall growth rate in percent. Do this by dividing the difference in population by the earlier number. Next, divide that by the difference in years — 17 for Toronto, 18 for the other cities.)

First-time settlers bought supplies and wagons in York. As a result, retail businesses flourished. Some businesses got rich at the settlers' expense. Gradually businesses in York began to take over the **wholesale trade** — the business of supplying goods to stores — from those in Montréal. The wholesale trade helped the town grow.

Most settlers stopped at government offices in York to apply for their land grants. Later, York was where land companies had their sales offices, including the biggest one, the Canada Company.

As the town became the centre of business for the province, it also became a centre of banking. The Bank of Upper Canada was chartered in York in 1821. It came to have a great influence on the province's economy.

This picture shows the entrance to York harbour, a busy shipping centre.

York also became a shipping centre for exports from Upper Canada. When the farmlands of western Upper Canada began producing wheat for export, the farmers transported their crops to the wharves at York, where they would be loaded on ships for the first part of the long trip to the ocean.

Settlers on the land lived in isolation, cut off from the outside world, surrounded by the gloom of the forest. Many laboured for years to get out of debt. They grew to resent the canal-building and other developments taking place elsewhere. A difference in thinking widened between townspeople and country people over how the province should be developed. Pioneering people also resented the "society" people: the leading families with their British ways, grand houses, and fine carriages. Resentment of Toronto's wealth and influence continue to this day, right across Canada.

The muddy town of York grew westward along the lakeshore. King Street was the main corridor of development. The new government buildings were on King Street West: Government House, the Lieutenant-Governor's residence and workplace, and the Parliament building, where legislators met from 1829 to 1892.

Reverend John Strachan advanced his career in the Church of England and had a powerful influence on the government.

The Real Ruler?

Near the Parliament building was a residence whose owner called it The Palace. For a time it was the finest home in York. Who lived there? An ordinary schoolteacher and priest, John Strachan (pronounced *Strawn*), and his family. Somehow, this ordinary person rose to prominence among the families of York. As well as having many admirable qualities, Strachan had a talent for creating hostility. He was domineering, spoke bluntly, and did much to inflame public opinion.

John Strachan was a schoolteacher in his native Scotland. He migrated to Upper Canada, set up a school, and began teaching in Cornwall, the heart of Scottish Upper Canada. Soon Strachan, a member of the Church of Scotland, switched churches. He was ordained a minister in the Church of England. In 1812 Reverend Strachan was appointed rector of the Church of England at York and chaplain of the garrison at Fort York. Critics later said Strachan joined the Church of England to advance his career.

Soon after moving to York, Rev. Strachan started teaching again. He founded the Home District Grammar School. In Rev. Strachan's day, the school was for boys only — and not just any boys. It trained the future leaders of Upper Canada. Strachan instilled ambition in his students and kindled a desire to uphold British traditions.

Some people said that Rev. Strachan was the real ruler of Upper Canada. As in Lower Canada, most of the government positions were filled by the friends of the Lieutenant-Governor. They guided his every decision. Behind closed doors they made decisions that affected every corner of the province. Rev. John Strachan was at the very centre of this elite group for more than 20 years.

By the time of the rebellions his influence had waned and he all but retired from politics. Rev. Strachan had another career in mind anyway. He worked for two decades to become the first bishop of York. He even travelled to England to use his powers of persuasion to get the appointment. His wish was granted in 1839. But Bishop Strachan did not earn any pay, and he had to meet all the expenses out of his own pocket! Bishop Strachan never forgave the archbishops for this slight toward him and Upper Canada. He refused to accept the successor who the Church of England appointed to be the next bishop of York. Instead, the congregation and clergy elected the bishop. This method has been used ever since.

The Family Compact

The group close to the Lieutenant-Governor came to be known as the **Family Compact**. A *compact* is a plot or conspiracy. Historians have discovered no plot in Upper Canada — just an iron rule by pro-British people. In every community the Family Compact was a fact of life. The Lieutenant-Governor appointed public servants throughout the province. Sheriffs, justices of the peace, judges, commanders of militia, clerks, registrars — all positions were filled by friends of the Lieutenant-Governor or of the British way. These officials could exercise considerable power over the lives of the ordinary people. The government handed out land, but the settlers went where they were told. They also had to satisfy the justice of the peace of their loyalty to the King. If they criticized an official's decision, they might be called disloyal and find doors to advancement closed.

Conflict arose in Upper Canada over the influence of the Family Compact, much as the Château Clique created resentment in Lower Canada. Many people felt powerless to make their lives better, and they blamed an unfair system.

The Story So Far . . .

1 Summarize what you have learned so far about Rev. John Strachan's character.
2 How is the conflict over the Family Compact in Upper Canada similar to the conflict that developed over the Château Clique in Lower Canada? How is it different?
3 Create a chart that illustrates the different ways York was a centre of government, business, and immigration for Upper Canada.

Richmond, George, British 1809-1896, Portrait of Sir Beverly Robinson, 1856 oil on canvas, 76.7 x 63.5 cm, Art Gallery of Ontario, Toronto On loan from John B. Robinson.

John Beverley Robinson, a former student of John Strachan, became the Attorney General and Chief Justice of Upper Canada and a member of the Assembly after 1820. He is an example of the people who made up the Family Compact.

THE IMPORTANCE OF TRANSPORTATION

Historian Donald Creighton called the colonial region that the British won from France "the Empire of the St. Lawrence." There, the fur trade was a thing of the past. The new economy was based on wood products and wheat. Immigrants were essential to its success.

The upper St. Lawrence was the weakest link in the long chain connecting Upper Canada to Britain. Not only was it full of rapids and other hazards, but Canada shared that part of the river with the United States.

1 The only route to Upper Canada was by way of the St. Lawrence River and Lake Ontario. Identify these two features on the map.

2 Use the scale and a ruler to measure the distance from Montréal to
a) Kingston, b) York,
c) London,
d) Amherstburg.

3 Assuming you could travel an average of 20 km a day, how long would it take you to reach each place?

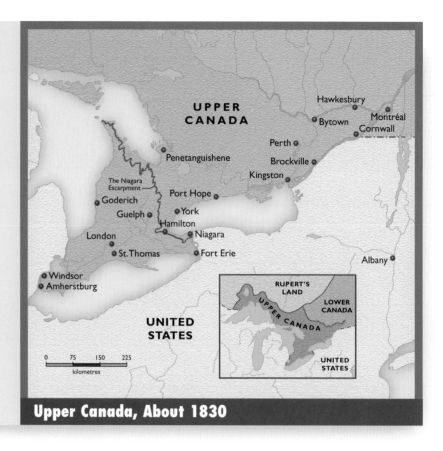

Upper Canada, About 1830

American forces had already tried to close the St. Lawrence to traffic during the War of 1812. From forts on their side, American guns had an easy shot at passing vessels. If there were another war and the Americans took control of the upper St. Lawrence, they could easily swallow up thinly populated Upper Canada. The United States was already far larger, with nearly 13 million people in 1830.

Another geographic obstacle was the Niagara Escarpment, including Niagara Falls. This long limestone cliff, 100 m high, runs across the middle of Upper Canada. In those days it barred all shipping between lakes Ontario and Erie.

South of the Great Lakes, navigable waterways made travel relatively easy. The state of New York commanded the southern shores of Lake Ontario and the east end of Lake Erie. New York was poised to challenge the Empire of the St. Lawrence for the trade of the whole Great Lakes region. Between 1817 and 1825, American workers dug the Erie Canal clear across the state. Canal barges provided a link between the ships that plied the Great Lakes and the riverboats that ran up and down the Hudson River between Albany and New York City. Situated on the Atlantic seaboard, New York City quickly became a main port for people and goods bound for the Great Lakes. The Erie Canal started a trade war.

Britain encouraged Canadian farmers to export wheat to Britain. The colonial government also allowed American goods to be shipped down the St. Lawrence without paying duties. These measures increased traffic through the Empire of the St. Lawrence. The Empire relied on the amount of goods and people that flowed up and down the St. Lawrence valley.

Britain resolved to do more to help build the Empire of the St. Lawrence. They got to work on overcoming the difficulties of travel on the great river.

The Canal Controversy

How could the Empire of the St. Lawrence keep its hold on the trade of the Great Lakes region? The constant threat of invasion by the United States required action, too. To defend Upper Canada, Britain's armed forces had to be able to move troops and artillery around the inland province. So Britain strengthened the transportation system connecting Upper and Lower Canada.

The British government decided to create a system of canals on two routes, so that vessels could travel between Montréal and Kingston without hazarding the upper St. Lawrence. Meanwhile investors raised enough money to build a canal that conquered the Niagara Escarpment. Gradually, the Empire could transport more trade goods and more people. The Lachine Canal, completed in 1825, opened up a little stretch of the upper St. Lawrence River to larger boats.

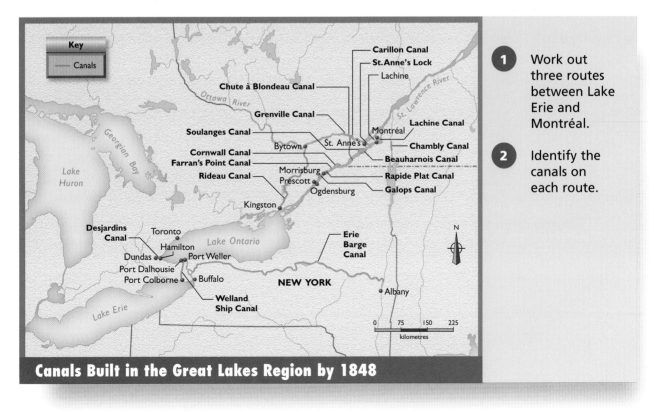

Canals Built in the Great Lakes Region by 1848

1. Work out three routes between Lake Erie and Montréal.

2. Identify the canals on each route.

Colonel John By designed and oversaw the building of the Rideau Canal. His disregard for cost caused serious problems for the citizens and the government of Canada.

The Rideau Canal

During the 1820s, workers constructed locks and canals at three places on the Ottawa River. Next, they created a new route between the Ottawa River and Lake Ontario. This was the Rideau Canal, designed by John By.

The Rideau Canal cost £822 000 — five times the budget! Colonel By built the canal without regard to price. He believed a bigger canal would pay for itself through increased shipments of cargo. He ignored the officials, both elected and appointed, who were supposed to control the cost. The magnificent locks were nearly forgotten in the scandal that erupted. The Rideau Canal cleaned out the imperial treasury for public works in Canada — although the British military continued to strengthen its line of fortresses on the U.S. border.

The human cost of building the Rideau Canal was enormous. Hundreds of workers died during its construction. Many died of a malarial fever.

As for By's vision, the Rideau Canal never did fulfil its promise. The canal attracted some upriver business, but shippers continued to use the St. Lawrence down river. The Rideau was never used for defence against American attack, either. It did provide the insurance of an all-Canadian route to Upper Canada.

The Welland Canal

The barrier posed by the Niagara Escarpment is dramatically evident at Niagara Falls, where water flowing from Lake Erie cascades down sheer cliffs before flowing on to Lake Ontario. All people and goods travelling between the lakes stopped at the escarpment. Within a distance of 50 km, they were unloaded from one vessel, transferred to vehicles that could handle the steep pathways of the escarpment, and transshipped a second time on the other side of the escarpment. The most-used route was through Queenston. In 1818, though, residents of the Niagara District petitioned the provincial legislature for a canal. A canal that linked the two lakes would add a huge shipping area to the Empire of the St. Lawrence.

The Welland Canal Company, incorporated in 1824, started raising money to build the canal. The builders, headed by St. Catharines businessman William Hamilton Merritt, used the waterway of Twelve Mile Creek between Lake Ontario and

St. Catharines. The plans kept changing, the alterations required new canals, and the locks needed constant rebuilding. The costs became enormous! Americans met some of the costs. However, time and again, the Welland Canal Company borrowed money from the government of Upper Canada, leaving the province deeply in debt.

Farmers living nearby used the Welland Canal to ship wheat, potash, and other products. Like other canals, however, it was a benefit mainly to the leading merchants of Upper Canada. The vast majority of farming families needed roads to get their products to market and supplies to their homes. Existing roads were mud holes for much of every year. People waited eagerly for freeze-up, when the roads and creeks would harden and they could start transporting goods by sleigh. The Welland Canal swallowed up money that could have been used to improve land transportation in the province.

The country people's discontent over the condition of the roads grew acute during the 1830s. The conditions added to their burden of resentment about the hard life of the settlements.

Web Connection

www.school.mcgrawhill.ca/resources

Go to the web site above to find out more about Canada's canals. Go to History Resources, then to *Canada: The Story of Our Heritage* to see where to go next.

The Story So Far . . .

1 Explain why the upper St. Lawrence River was so important to Upper Canada. Why was it also a big problem?

2 Was the government of Upper Canada wise to ignore the demands of ordinary farmers for roads? Using point form, compare canals and roads — both their benefits and their drawbacks. Be prepared to use your list to argue for canals or roads in a class debate.

3 On a map of central Canada, show the upper St. Lawrence and Ottawa rivers and the Rideau Canal. Use the map on page 305 to locate the major locks, and mark them on the map.

SETTLING THE TOWNSHIPS

A blanket of ancient forest once covered the entire region between lakes Ontario, Erie, and Huron. This old-growth forest disappeared slowly at first, then faster and faster.

Farmlands slowly emerged, revealing the checkerboard of settlement called **townships**. The townships of Upper Canada were designed and surveyed in the 1790s. Surveyors measured and laid out more than 300 of them. The colonial authorities wanted settlement spread thinly across the lands between the Great Lakes. What purpose do you think that policy served?

For a long time there were only a few towns. In 1825 Upper Canada had only three towns with more than 1000 residents: Kingston, York, and Niagara. Slowly, townships across the province filled up with people.

On this 1846 map of the Home District, the boundaries of the district are marked with thick lines while those of townships are marked with thin lines.

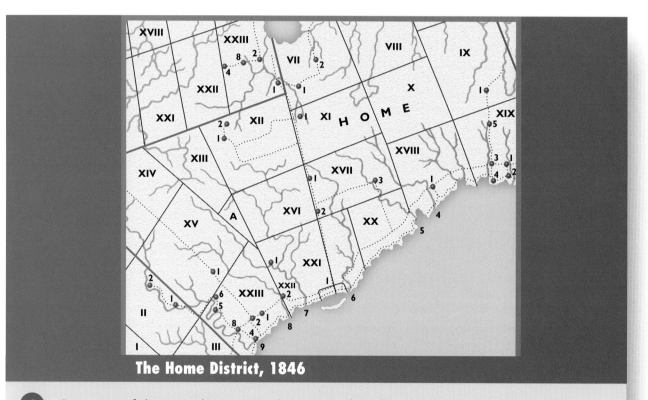

The Home District, 1846

1. On a copy of the map above, write the names of the following townships in place of the Roman numerals: XVI – Vaughan, XVII – Markham, XVIII – Pickering, XIX – Whitby, XX – Scarborough, XXI – York, XXII – Etobicoke, XXIII – Toronto.

2. Use a modern map of the Greater Toronto Area to locate the following places and features, and label them on your map. (On the old map, communities are marked with dots and Arabic numerals, roads with dotted lines, and rivers along the lakeshore with Arabic numerals.)
   • Markham Township: Richmond Hill (1), Thornhill (2), Markham (3)
   • Whitby Township: Oshawa (1)
   • York Township: Toronto (1), Yonge St., Kingston Rd., Don River (6), Humber River (7)
   • Etobicoke Township: Weston (1), Mimico (2)
   • Toronto Township: Cooksville (2), Port Credit (4), Streetsville (5), Credit River (9)

3. What conclusions can you draw about the way Toronto has developed since 1846?

The government of Upper Canada gave away land until the 1820s. It had to. Land was the province's only wealth at first. Giving it away was the only way to attract settlers. The government hoped that, over time, the land would bring a good price. As settlers cleared land, their improvements would make its value rise. If even a few families settled in an area, it became more desirable to newcomers. A new road, canal, or railway made the value of land in the neighbourhood shoot up.

Each settling family got at least 81 ha and up to 400 ha more. Settlers could choose the township they wanted to settle in, but it was up to the local authorities to assign lots. They issued *location tickets* to guide the newcomers.

The settlers who applied for a grant of land owned it, after they fulfilled some conditions. They had to clear a certain amount of forest. Before they received the deeds to their property, they also had to pay a fee. Immigrant settlers also had to swear an oath of allegiance to the British monarch. Later a law required settlers to maintain the roads bordering their properties.

From the start, the system of settlement grants was open to abuse. Some settlement grants fell into the hands of people who made oaths and promises but had no intention of settling. Rather, they would let the land sit and later sell it. These lots stood empty between the settlers' farms. Their wild state made travel difficult and kept communities from developing.

Log houses were every settling family's first home in the forest.

Anna Brownell Jameson was an Irish writer who came to Upper Canada for eight months in 1836–1837. She wrote an account of her travels, called *Winter Studies and Summer Rambles in Canada*. She wrote this about the drive to clear land:

> *A Canadian settler hates a tree, regards it as his natural enemy, as something to be destroyed, eradicated, annihilated by all and any means. The idea of useful or ornamental is seldom associated here even with the most magnificent timber trees. . . .*
>
> *There are two principal methods of killing trees in this country, beside the quick, unfailing destruction of the axe; the first by setting fire to them, which sometimes leaves the root uninjured to rot gradually and unseen, or be grubbed up at leisure, or, more generally, there remains a visible fragment of a charred and blackened stump, deformed and painful to look upon; the other method is slower, but even more effectual; a deep gash is cut through the bark into the stem, quite round the bole of the tree. This prevents the circulation of the vital juices, and by degrees the tree droops and dies. This is technically called ringing timber. . . .*

One day, Anna Jameson had a vision of Upper Canada's future. While travelling through the Talbot Settlement, near Lake Erie, she went riding and climbed a hill:

> *On the highest land I had yet stood upon in Canada . . . I stopped the horses and looked around, and on every side, far and near — east, west, north, and south, it was all forest — a boundless sea of forest. . . .*

> *. . . The present fell like a film from my eyes: the future was before me, with its towns and cities, fields of waving grain, green lawns and villas, churches and temples turret-crowned; and meadows tracked by the frequent footpath; and railroads, with trains of rich merchandise steaming along — for all this will be. . . .*

This view of Kingston, Ontario, in the 1850s affirms Anna Jameson's prediction.

QUESTIONING THE EVIDENCE

1. Why would Mrs. Jameson find it "painful" to look on tree stumps? Can we draw any conclusions about her attitude to settlers from this and other words in her description? Would you say she is on the side of the settler or the trees?

2. Anna Jameson's prediction that it "*will* be" has proven true. The area she was in is now near the heart of Ontario, with its population of nearly 11 million people. With all the forces working against it — the United States, geography, nature — the colony might have failed. What do you think made Jameson so sure of its success?

CONFLICT OVER LAND

Much of Upper Canada's surveyed lands was given away — but not to settlers. People who had served in the government or military were rewarded with large gifts of land. The government also set aside huge reserves for the clergy, the Crown, and schools. Each giveaway became a story of conflict.

Gifts of Land

Gifts of land were a reward to people for military service. Some of the richest people in the province were also rewarded for civil service.

The original idea was to create an **aristocracy**: an elite group of wealthy people whose children would rule the province. This practice was based on a British tradition. The British aristocracy got its wealth from owning land and the work of the people who lived on it. Governor Simcoe hoped land ownership would help to create an aristocracy of Upper Canada's merchants, bankers, lawyers, top public servants, and their families. Few had any interest in living on their land, but they welcomed the gift. They could hold the land and, when it became valuable, sell it.

These gifts of the best lands were spread out in townships across Upper Canada. Many of them remained unused, even after land started to acquire a price. When the children of the established settlers looked for land within their districts to begin their own farms, they had to pay more or move elsewhere in search of cheap land.

Often families of squatters moved onto absentee land-owners' properties and started clearing the back half. The squatters were usually able to acquire the land they occupied at a low price when the original owners sold it later. This, too, bred resentment among poor but honest settlers.

Land Reserves

Nearly one-third of every township surveyed in Upper Canada was set aside for the use of churches and the government. The Constitutional Act provided reserves of one-seventh of the total land in each province. It stated that "the rents, profits, or emoluments, which may at any time arise from such lands" could only be used for "the maintenance and support of a Protestant clergy." Lieutenant-Governor Simcoe set aside the same amount for the support of the government. In each township except the earliest ones on the Niagara Peninsula, the surveyors marked off and removed from the available land one-seventh of all lots for Clergy Reserves, and another seventh for Crown (government) Reserves. Together, these reserves amounted to nearly two million hectares. The government also set aside about 200 000 ha to support schools and universities. Like the lands belonging to distant owners, the reserves remained unused for decades.

1 **What is the total area of this township? The total area in the settlement? In Clergy Reserves? In Crown Reserves?**

2 **Clergy and Crown Reserves were set aside in each township, using this checkerboard pattern. Each rectangle represents an 81–ha lot. Why do you think Upper Canada used this pattern rather than making fewer but bigger reserves?**

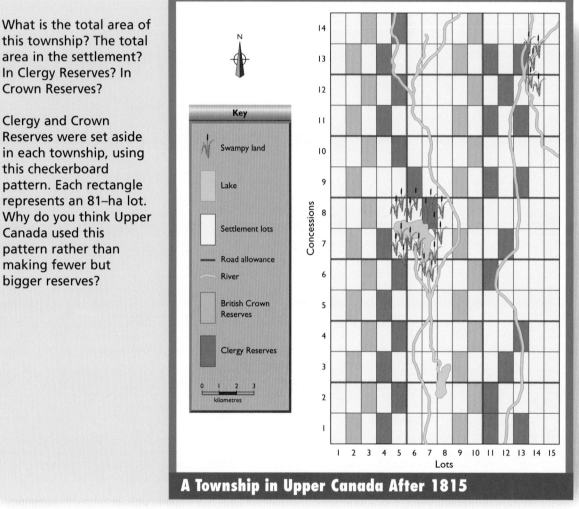

A Township in Upper Canada After 1815

The Reserves were established with the same high hopes of other land schemes. The churches and government thought that when the value of the land increased they would sell it for much-needed money. This plan did not involve taxation or rely on the approval of the Assembly. Were reserves a sensible way of covering costs without taxing the hard-working people of Upper Canada? Or was it a way for the government to spend public money without accounting to the Assembly? Clergy Reserves came under attack in the Assembly as early as 1817.

Land and Churches

Rev. John Strachan believed that the land set aside in Clergy Reserves belonged to the Church of England. He wanted to see the Church of England made the established church of Upper Canada — "an institution recognized and supported by the government." Rev. Strachan argued that the Church of England was needed to keep the province safe from the American threat. This was the threat, not of invasion, but of a gradual takeover by **levellers**: American settlers and others who urged more democracy for Upper Canada. Democracy is the system that gives everyone a say in the government through elected representatives.

For years Rev. Strachan used his influence to gain control of land reserves. In doing so, he managed to make many enemies. He was accused of manipulating the government for the benefit of his friends and followers.

While the Clergy Reserves were still just a checkerboard of lands, Rev. Strachan developed a scheme to form a company and manage the lands as rental properties. When it was discovered that Rev. Strachan ran the Upper Canada Clergy Corporation himself, it was disbanded.

Rev. Strachan went to England in 1824 and 1826. He asked the British government to allow the province to sell some of the Clergy Reserves. He stopped a deal that was about to sell all the Crown Reserves and half the Clergy Reserves to a British firm, the Canada Company. Strachan struck a new deal. Upper Canada could sell one-quarter of the Clergy Reserves, at the rate of about 40 000 ha per year. The proceeds went straight into Upper Canada's treasury. This scheme frustrated Assembly members who were trying to make the province account for all its finances.

Upper Canada's common school system, which the government created in 1816, owed a lot to Strachan's advice. Naturally when the government created a provincial board of education in 1823, Rev. Strachan was appointed to head it. He saw to it that the entire board belonged to the Church of England. The board administered the school reserves, a total of more than 100 000 ha of land spread out among the townships. After great public criticism, the board was abolished in 1833.

Another ambition of Rev. Strachan's was to create a university in Upper Canada. While in England in 1826, Strachan spent months hammering out a charter for King's College. The college was endowed with 91 462 ha of the best land from the Crown Reserves. Rev. Strachan tried to make sure that the university was operated by the Church of England. He was

Religious Denominations in Upper Canada, 1841

	Percent of Total Population
Church of England	22
Church of Scotland and dissenting Presbyterian sects	20
Methodism (4 sects)	17
Roman Catholic	12
Baptists, Quakers, Lutherans, Congregationalists, Mennonites, Tunkers (German Baptist Brethren), and all others	19
No religion, or did not respond	10

appointed its president. The governing council began selling land and was developing a building site in York. But after another outcry, the university was taken out of Rev. Strachan's hands.

John Strachan's attempts to use the Clergy Reserves to the benefit of the Church of England aroused great opposition. The Church of England, with just over one-fifth of the population as members, claimed all of the proceeds from the Clergy Reserves. The population of Upper Canada belonged to several Christian denominations, as shown in the chart on the left.

Once, in a speech, Rev. Strachan called the Methodist Church ministers ignorant, incapable, idle — and disloyal. He suspected that many Methodists secretly wanted Upper Canada to become American. Why do you think he held this view?

A young Methodist minister named Egerton Ryerson responded to Rev. Strachan's speech. Ryerson was born in Upper Canada of Loyalist parents. Rev. Ryerson was well-educated and, like most Methodists, he believed in the importance of education. Ryerson believed that the Clergy Reserve lands should be divided among the Protestant denominations. Rev. Ryerson went on to become an Assembly member and public servant. He was a lifelong foe of Rev. Strachan.

Representatives of other denominations made petitions to the governments of Upper Canada and Britain. In 1824, the Presbyterians were the first to claim a share of the Clergy Reserves. The other groups eventually won recognition. The Assembly passed a law in 1840 giving half the revenue from the clergy reserves to the Church of England and the Church of Scotland and the other half to be divided among other denominations.

Egerton Ryerson
THE OTHER REVEREND

The Methodist Church had struggled hard to become a presence in Canada but had met with much resistance from the powerful Church of England. So when Anglican John Strachan scorned Methodists, labelling them "ignorant traitors," his words brought their simmering resentment to full boil. Little did he know that this would cause a strong Methodist spokesperson to rise from among them.

Adolphus Egerton Ryerson was born March 24, 1803, a few kilometres west of what is now Port Dover. Growing up, he learned the value of education and was inspired to proceed with his own.

Ryerson's father, Joseph, was staunchly Anglican, but his mother, Mehetabel or Hetty, became a Methodist in 1816. This had a tremendous impact on her children. Four of the five Ryerson boys eventually became Methodist ministers.

Ryerson was a Methodist preacher, not yet a minister, when Strachan's speech prompted his written response. That letter spurred the Methodists' challenge of Anglican domination. Within four years, new laws were passed allowing denominations other than Roman Catholic and Anglican to own land, and recognizing the marriages and baptisms the Methodists performed.

But Ryerson's influence in Canada went beyond religious freedom. Religion and education, he believed, were the two most important factors in improving individuals and the society they lived in. He travelled to London, England, to raise funds for a school run by the Methodist Church. Upper Canada Academy opened in 1836 due, in large part, to his efforts. Defying British tradition, he promoted the idea that schools should be for those of any religious denomination, and that courses be taught in English rather than in Greek and Latin.

In 1844 he was appointed superintendant of education for Canada West to create a system of schools compulsory for youths from all levels of society. For a year he studied school systems in more than 20 countries in order to develop a public school system suited to Canada. He had a lot of input into the school act of 1871 that founded Ontario's elementary and secondary school systems.

In spite of early disagreements, Ryerson and Strachan had more in common than either cared to admit. When the two renowned men finally met in 1842, Ryerson was amazed to find that they agreed on many topics. When Ryerson died of pneumonia in Toronto in February 1882, it seemed that most of the country mourned him. In recognition of Egerton Ryerson's great contribution, the legislature adjourned so that its members, along with 3500 other citizens, could attend his funeral.

More people you could research are

Marshall Spring Bidwell

Robert Gourlay

Christopher Hagerman

John Beverley Robinson

Egerton Ryerson

Rev. John Strachan

1 Design an advertisement to attract settlers to Upper Canada. Include details about land grants and the conditions of ownership.

2 Outline the hardships immigrants to Upper Canada faced, in the order they would encounter them.

3 Why did the government of Upper Canada give land away? Summarize what you know about the different groups that received land through grants, gifts, or land reserves. How much did each get, and for what purpose?

4 What were some of the ways Rev. Strachan tried to control the land reserves? How would you evaluate his success in each case?

THE MOVEMENT TOWARD REFORM

The **reform** movement took longer to get started in Upper Canada than in Lower Canada. The Tory or pro-government people held control with an iron will. At first few people spoke out about the need to reform, or change, the government of Upper Canada. After the War of 1812, some grew determined to bring more democracy into the province. Reform leaders emerged in the Assembly of Upper Canada, but none had the knowledge or power of Lower Canada's Louis-Joseph Papineau. And whereas the *Patriote* Party was able to control the Assembly of Lower Canada, the reformers of Upper Canada could not win two elections in a row.

When historians traced the events leading up to rebellion, they identified Robert Gourlay as the person who started the movement toward reform.

The Beginning of Protest

In 1817 Robert Gourlay and his family moved to their property in Dereham Township. Seeking to encourage emigration from Scotland, Gourlay started to write a guidebook for people trying to decide whether to emigrate. It would show the hardships of Canadian life accurately. To get settlers' views on the subject, Gourlay published a questionnaire. One of the 31 questions asked: "What, in your opinion, retards the improvement of your township in particular, or of your province in general?" Many answers said such land policies as the Clergy Reserves prevented improvement.

Gourlay urged the Assembly to open a public inquiry to get to the bottom of the wrongs. He started a petition and proposed a convention to consider the need for reform. At that point, Rev. John Strachan talked to his friend, Attorney General John Beverley Robinson, the province's chief law enforcement officer. The government prosecuted Gourlay for spreading false information against the Lieutenant-Governor. Gourlay stood trial twice and was acquitted by a jury both times. Then Gourlay was arrested under the **Sedition** Act. The government could force people to leave the province unless suspects could prove they were not spreading disaffection, or unrest. When Gourlay refused to leave, he was arrested again, held in jail for more than six months, tried, and banished. He left the following day. The Lieutenant-Governor punished anyone who had shown any support for Gourlay.

Robert Gourlay published his book, *A Statistical Account of Upper Canada*, in 1822, and it was widely read. As a historical document, it is still useful. Gourlay's greater achievement was to stir the beginning of protest and reform in Upper Canada.

Moderates and Radicals

The movement for reform gained ground slowly. Its supporters included farmers, especially from isolated settlements in the West; merchants who wanted more trade with the United States; and Scottish and Irish immigrants. In the provincial election of 1828, reform candidates won more seats than the government's friends. Among the new faces in the Assembly was William Lyon Mackenzie, a feisty newspaper publisher in York.

In 1829 another newcomer to politics won a by-election in York and joined the Assembly. Robert Baldwin was born in York in 1804, into a family of politicians. His father, William Warren Baldwin, was an early leader of the reform cause. Baldwin believed in taking a **moderate** rather than an extreme approach to reforming the government. Like his father, he argued that the Executive Council should be made up of elected members of the Assembly, instead of being simply appointed by the Lieutenant-Governor. The Baldwins raised the same issues that Papineau and others did in Lower Canada. Who controls the purse strings? Who makes the laws? Should it be the friends of the Lieutenant-Governor who were appointed to the Executive or Legislative Council and given generous gifts of land? As in Lower Canada, moderate reformers placed high hopes in responsible government.

The Tory party took back control of the Assembly in 1830.

Robert Baldwin joined the Assembly in 1829 as a moderate reformer.

Lieutenant-Governor Francis Bond Head appointed reformers to the Executive Council, then ignored their advice.

Baldwin lost his seat and returned to law and family life. The reformers took control away from the Tory party again in 1834, but Baldwin did not run.

A new Lieutenant-Governor, Sir Francis Bond Head, arrived in Toronto the same month. Lieutenant-Governor Head was welcomed by the reformers. He promised to introduce changes, starting with appointments to the Executive Council. He invited Robert Baldwin, Speaker of the Assembly Marshall Spring Bidwell, and Dr. John Rolph to sit on the council. Almost at once, Head began to ignore the council's advice. The reformers soon quit. The Assembly voted to criticize Head. He retaliated by dissolving the Parliament. Another election followed.

The election campaign of 1836 was fought on the issue of loyalty, and it marked the beginning of the crisis that led to armed conflict within two years. As in Lower Canada, groups of **radicals** broke away from moderate reformers. The moderates believed in the gradual reform of parliamentary institutions, but the radicals wanted to bring in American-style democracy, with elections for many more positions.

A few radicals were prepared to take up arms to change the government. Lieutenant-Governor Head plunged into the election campaign. He branded both radical and moderate candidates as traitors. It worked. The Tory party won.

Snapshot

Voting a Risky Business

In the early 1800s, elections were rough-and-ready affairs. Because there was no secret ballot, bribes, threats, and violence were common. Strict rules governed who could vote. Only men who met certain property qualifications were eligible. Women were not allowed to vote at all. Voting often went on for a week or more. Because only one polling place was set up in each riding, many people had to travel a long way. For some people, voting meant being away from home for days.

On the first day, the candidates gave speeches from rough wooden platforms. These were often conveniently set up outside a tavern. Then the candidate and his supporters mingled with the crowd, trying to win votes. This sometimes meant inviting voters into the tavern and plying them with food and liquor. When a race was close and drink had flowed freely, it was not unusual for the supporters of opposing candidates to end up in wild brawls.

To vote, a man had to show proof that he was qualified. Then he mounted the platform and declared his choice for all to hear. If a man accepted the hospitality of one candidate and then voted for another, he was in for trouble.

Mackenzie Leads the Way

One day in 1820 a young immigrant from Scotland stepped off the deck of a steamer and onto a rickety wharf in York, Upper Canada, after working as a labourer on the Lachine Canal. From his small frame and few possessions, no one would have guessed that he brought a world of trouble with him. This was William Lyon Mackenzie — newspaper writer, politician, and champion of democracy. A fighter by nature, he took on the British Empire as his opponent. His cause was hopeless, yet democracy triumphed in the end. The question is, did he have anything to do with it?

Born in Dundee, Scotland, in 1795, "Willie" Mackenzie was raised by his mother Elizabeth. Together, they ran a combination store and library, while he apprenticed to different trades and started writing newspaper articles. In 1820 he came to Canada with family friend John Lesslie. They set up a store in York. Two years later their families came out, along with Isabel Baxter, 15, whom Elizabeth Mackenzie chose to be her son's wife. William and Isabel were married 39 years and had 13 children.

Mackenzie worked in business in Dundas and Queenston before starting a newspaper, *The Colonial Advocate*, "to influence voters in their choice of representatives in the approaching elections." The first issue came out on May 18, 1824. Mackenzie wrote this about Rev. John Strachan's hold on the government of Upper Canada:

> There never was an example in history of a great colony kept in awe for years, in daily terror of political annihilation, not by a powerful invader at the head of twenty thousand men, not by a plague or famine, not by a tyrannical prince. . . but by one single diminutive, paltry, insignificant Scotch turn coat parish schoolmaster.

Mackenzie's "plain truths" drew the anger of Rev. Strachan's supporters. In June 1826 a gang of 15 young men broke into the newspaper office and, in plain view of a law enforcement officer, took Mackenzie's press and threw it into Lake Ontario. Mackenzie sued the leaders of the mob — sons of rich Family Compact families, destined for power. The court awarded him £625. He was able to get a new press and pay his debts besides! The so-called Press Riot was the beginning of a ten-year campaign to silence Mackenzie. It did not work.

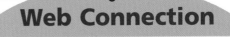

Web Connection

http://www.school.mcgrawhill.ca/resources

Go to the web site above to find out more about newspapers in Upper Canada. Go to History Resources, then to *Canada: The Story of Our Heritage* to see where to go next.

Mary Sophia O'Brien

STAYING LOYAL

Like many people in Upper Canada, Mary Sophia O'Brien and her family had no use for William Lyon Mackenzie. In her journal, O'Brien did not mince words. She called the Scottish-born radical a "tormentor of our peace."

O'Brien and her husband Edward were neither wealthy nor members of the inner circle of the Family Compact. Still, their loyalties lay with the government. Mackenzie's growing admiration for American-style democracy horrified them. "His decided Yankeeism has lost him many friends who once adhered to him as the friend of reform and the people," O'Brien wrote in her journal.

Besides, loyalty had its rewards. Memories of the American invasion during the War of 1812 remained strong in Upper Canada, and another attack by the United States was an ever-present possibility. To make sure that trained soldiers were on hand to defend the important fort at Penetanguishene on Georgian Bay, Lieutenant-Governor John Colborne decided to encourage former British officers to settle nearby. If an attack came, these former soldiers could be quickly called to defend the fort.

A well-educated and loyal former British officer, Edward O'Brien was the kind of settler Colborne hoped to recruit. In 1831 Edward was granted land in Oro Township on an arm of Lake Simcoe called Kempenfelt Bay. He was also given the job of recruiting more settlers for the area. Early in the spring of 1832, the O'Briens left their farm northwest of Thornhill and journeyed to Kempenfelt Bay. On a spot overlooking the bay, they built the shanty where they planned to live while they built a log house. As other settlers began arriving, the new neighbours pitched in to help one another.

Over the next few years, the O'Briens had more children, cleared their land, and built a large log house called *The Woods*. One visitor called The Woods "a perfect gem of civilization set in the wildest of natural surroundings." They also travelled frequently to Thornhill, where O'Brien's brothers still lived with their families. On these visits, the O'Briens heard — and worried — about the discontent that was smouldering in the townships north of Toronto. When the troops protecting the province were sent to Lower Canada in 1837 to help stop the uprising, O'Brien was alarmed. "Their absence has encouraged the unquiet spirits of the Home District. . .and particularly the townships on the line of Yonge Street," she wrote. "These men have, since the troubles [in Lower Canada] became serious, been in a regular but half-concealed course of training to break out." Her relatives lived in the heart of the Home District. If rebellion erupted, how safe would these government loyalists be?

More people you could research are

W.H. Bartlett

John By

Anna Brownell Jameson

William Hamilton Merritt

Mary Sophia O'Brien

Laurent Quetton de St. Georges

Mackenzie gathered petitions that convinced the British government to make Upper Canada recognize the rights of American aliens, many of whom had lived in the province for decades. Mackenzie was elected to the Assembly in 1828 and returned in 1830. Mackenzie goaded the Lieutenant-Governor's friends into expelling him from the Assembly — not once, but again and again. The law required a by-election every time a member was expelled, and the voters always returned Mackenzie. The first time it happened, a parade of 134 sleighs cheered him down Yonge Street to the Parliament building.

Soon Mackenzie began to differ with more moderate reformers. He began to advocate American-style government for Upper Canada. When the City of Toronto came into being on March 6, 1834, there were elections for councillors. William Lyon Mackenzie was elected. The councillors then voted one of themselves mayor (a system no longer in practice), and Mackenzie was their choice. Toronto's first mayor lasted only a year. Says one historian, "He was not the man to begin the reforms he demanded." Mackenzie left the business of the city undone. He was roundly defeated in the second civic elections.

Meanwhile, Mackenzie and other reformers were returned to the Assembly in the provincial election of 1834. Mackenzie took charge of a special committee to look into the need for reform. He wrote the Seventh Report on Grievances. Like the Ninety-two Resolutions of Lower Canada, this report made many demands. Here are three of the most important demands:
- responsible government
- a Legislative Council that was elected rather than appointed
- a curb on the Lieutenant-Governor's power of appointing his friends to public office

Mackenzie lost his seat in the loyalty election. By now he had a new job. He was the leader of Toronto's rebel underground.

Rebellion!

By this time many farmers were mired in debt, owing money to the land agency, the bank, and the shopkeepers. In 1837 there was an international panic. Creditors wanted to get their money out of loans. The government of Upper Canada itself was deeply in debt. As public works ground to a halt, the province went into an economic tailspin.

William Lyon Mackenzie
SOWING THE SEED OF REBELLION

By August 1837 Upper Canada was in turmoil. Frustrated by the slow pace of change, William Lyon Mackenzie was rallying support to reform the government. As the fiery politician carried the message to the townships outside Toronto, Samuel Lount of Holland Landing, David Gibson of Willowdale, and Jesse Lloyd of Lloydtown were often at his side.

The first rally was in Newmarket, north of Toronto. Two days later Mackenzie and the reformers arrived in Lloydtown. Founded by Lloyd, this King Township village west of Newmarket was a hotbed of anti-government feeling. In the meeting hall, banners proclaiming Liberty or Death greeted the radicals, who were cheered loudly.

It did not take long, however, for things to turn nasty. Word came that government supporters were planning to disrupt the next meeting in Boltontown, now Bolton, where reformers were not as popular. To ensure Mackenzie's safety, 50 young farmers from King Township mounted their horses and escorted him to the rally. As rumoured, the meeting hall was packed with Tories. They unfurled a banner emblazoned with their slogan, *No Surrender*. They yelled insults and shouted down the speaker who tried to read the reform proposals to the audience. When the insults turned to threats of violence, the reformers decided to finish the meeting at a private house, where they could control who attended.

This gave some hot-tempered Tories time to concoct an ambush plan. As the young men from King Township rode across a bridge toward home, a gang attacked them from behind and tried to drag them off their horses and throw them into the Humber River.

Mackenzie's account of the free-for-all that followed was reported in his paper, *The Constitution*. He said: "With rails, sticks and their heavy fists, [the men from King Township] made the blood flow very freely — and a number of the men whose insults we had borne with patience, lay groaning with pain. . . ."

To scare Mackenzie into calling off the rallies, some Tory newspapers threatened him with death. Furthermore, government supporters started trying to disrupt every meeting. Undaunted, Mackenzie carried on. From then on, though, the reformers made sure that their outspoken leader was surrounded by guards.

By the end of August, Mackenzie's meetings had served their purpose. A number of people across the province were rallying to the cause and calling meetings of their own. As fall approached and the leaves began to turn, change was in the air.

More people you could research are

Robert Baldwin

John Colborne

Sir Francis Bond Head

William Lyon Mackenzie

Peregrine Maitland

Dr. John Rolph

The rebel cause took hold, and people took up arms in settled pockets in the Home, Midland, Niagara, Gore, and London districts. In the summer of 1837, gangs of youths fought in the streets of Toronto. Radicals armed themselves in self-defence. Mackenzie turned up the heat with his demands. He organized a big convention to be held in Toronto. He published a model constitution for the State of Upper Canada.

In November 1837, British troops hurried from outlying posts to Montréal. Soon there were no soldiers left in Toronto. Sir Francis Bond Head thought little of the threat posed by William Lyon Mackenzie and the radicals. They put out the word to gather at Montgomery's Tavern on Yonge Street, north of Toronto. They planned to capture the city on December 7. Mackenzie assured them it would be easy.

Here is the testimony of one of the leaders, Samuel Lount:

> *I did not know of any intention to rise in rebellion for more than two weeks previous to the Monday on which the Assemblage [began] at Montgomery's. . . . I had no idea it was to be a rebellion. I was informed and led to believe that what we wanted could be obtained easily — without bloodshed. . . .*

The important thing in capturing the government, Mackenzie said, was to maintain the element of surprise. They had to assemble very quietly, so they would not attract attention. Would thousands of fiercely loyal, pro-British families surrender meekly? Did Mackenzie lie to his supporters?

Jeffreys, Charles Wilham, Canadian 1869-1951, Rebels of 1837 Drilling in North York, 1898, pen and ink on cardboard 45.7 x 36.5 cm, Art Gallery of Ontario, Toronto

Rebels drilling in North York in Autumn 1837. Many of the farmers of Upper Canada were angry enough to rise up in arms against their government. What made these people so unhappy? What did they want?

The Story So Far . . .

1   Identify the different kinds of people who were interested in reforming the government of Upper Canada. Who were their leaders?

2   Why were the reformers in Upper Canada slower in getting started than those in Lower Canada? Which elections did they win? Which elections did they lose?

3   What triggered the start of the rebellion?

4   Mackenzie tried to convince his followers that it would not be violent. How?

SUM IT UP!

In this chapter you looked at the conflicts that grew in Upper Canada. Most of the province's trade was with Britain. British supporters did better than those who criticized it. A network known as the Family Compact ran the government of Upper Canada. John Strachan, a teacher and Church of England minister in York/Toronto, had especially powerful connections.

Transportation projects created conflict. Because of the difficulty of travelling on the upper St. Lawrence River, and the threat of war with the United States, Britain spent heavily on canals. Upper Canada also invested heavily in the Welland Canal, joining lakes Ontario and Erie. Most farmers, however, needed roads, not canals. As the province's debts increased, so did the farmers' discontent.

Land was also a major source of dispute. Farmers grew frustrated at the way townships were settled. In giving away land until the 1820s, the government made sure settlers were widely scattered across Upper Canada. Other granted land sat unused while the owners waited for it to increase in value before selling it. Land reserved for clergy, Crown, and schools amounted to nearly a third of the surveyed townships. The Church of England benefited from these lands, but the leaders of other denominations argued for, and won, shares of the income from the reserves.

Conflict grew bitter over the need to reform the government of Upper Canada. Reformers and the Tory party took turns controlling the Assembly. When the Assembly passed reforms, other arms of the government vetoed the changes. Reformers argued for responsible government, but the Lieutenant-Governor would not change the system. Radical leaders took over from moderate reformers, and William Lyon Mackenzie set the province on the path of rebellion.

THINKING ABOUT YOUR LEARNING

1. How was the government of Upper Canada similar to the government of Lower Canada? How was it different?
2. Why was the construction of canals important to the British?
3. How much land did the government of Upper Canada set aside for churches? For its own use? What was their purpose?
4. How did these reserves become a source of discontent for settlers?
5. How did radical reformers differ from moderates in Upper Canada? Explain in terms of their goals and methods.

APPLYING YOUR LEARNING

1. In this chapter you learned about several methods people used to express their discontent and/or try to resolve conflicts. For example, they drew up petitions, published newspaper articles, or circulated questionnaires. Form groups and choose a social or environmental issue about which you are unhappy. Plan and execute a campaign to create change. Keep diaries of your experiences. Evaluate whether your campaign succeeded and why.

2. a) In small groups, choose one of the following research topics about Upper Canada or make up your own:
   - streets and buildings in the town of York
   - types of ships and boats used for transportation on the Upper St. Lawrence River and the Great Lakes
   - the main roads of Upper Canada around 1840
   - the Rideau Canal or the Welland Canal

   b) Make up questions to guide your research. Use some factual questions, some comparison questions, and some speculative questions.

   c) Decide with your group how to present your research findings and prepare and deliver a presentation.

3. a) Research the history of the township or district you live in (or the one nearest you). You may have to do some research in the county office. Try to find out:
   - when it was established
   - what its name was
   - the name of the district where it was situated
   - who settled there and when
   - what communities grew up there and when
   - any changes in its boundaries

   b) Make a map showing its layout and features.

4. Debate the following topic: "The Family Compact was just another name for good, orderly government."

5. Many of today's immigrants suffer from a condition called *culture shock*. Research the meaning of this term.

6. Make up a time line of important events in the world during the period 1815–1840, using, for example, Grun's *The Timetables of History*. Add important events from Upper and Lower Canada. Do you notice any similarities between events in Canada and elsewhere? Prepare a brief report on your findings.

USING KEY WORDS

1. On a sheet of paper, match the words with the names associated with them:

   a) wholesale trade
   b) aristocracy
   c) leveller
   d) compact
   e) reform
   f) transship
   g) township
   h) moderate
   i) sedition
   j) radical

   i) Robert Baldwin
   ii) John Beverley Robinson
   iii) York
   iv) Welland Canal
   v) John Strachan
   vi) Tories
   vii) Home District
   viii) John Graves Simcoe
   ix) Robert Gourlay
   x) William Lyon Mackenzie

Rebellion and Revenge

1837

- In November, rebels in Lower Canada win a battle, then suffer a series of crushing defeats

- In December, uprisings in Upper Canada are quickly put down. Rebel leaders flee to the United States

1838

- In January, raiders from the United States begin to terrorize border communities in Upper and Lower Canada, trying to spark an uprising

SETTING OUR FOCUS

The little village of Saint-Eustache is northwest of Montréal. On December 14, 1837, it was under attack by British troops and forces from Upper Canada. In the picture on the left, see the large building in the distance? What kind of building is it? Barricaded inside and in other buildings were dozens of *Patriotes*. They were outnumbered more than ten to one. Do you remember why the *Patriotes* took up arms? Was the cause worth losing their towns? Their lives?

PREVIEWING THE CHAPTER

In this chapter you will learn about these topics:

- **how the rebellions in Lower and Upper Canada were put down by British troops, militia, and volunteers**
- **how raiders crossed the border from the United States during 1838 and sparked another outbreak in Lower Canada**
- **how Lord Durham governed British North America as an autocrat, yet helped to bring more democracy to Upper and Lower Canada**

KEY WORDS

amnesty

autocrat

due process

Frères Chasseurs

habeas corpus

high
   commissioner

Hunters' Lodges

jury

legislative union

plunder

prosecutor

- In April, Samuel Lount and Peter Matthews
  are executed for high treason

- From May to October, Lord Durham is Governor General of British North America

- In November, the second uprising in Lower Canada occurs

1839

The Durham Report recommends union of Upper and Lower Canada, and responsible government (self-government)

THE FIRST UPRISING IN LOWER CANADA

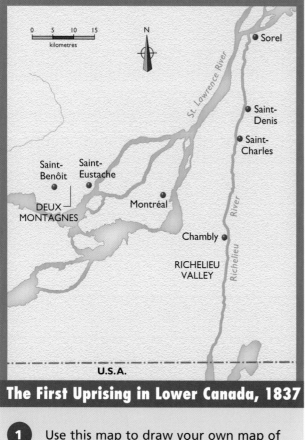

The First Uprising in Lower Canada, 1837

1 Use this map to draw your own map of the British troops and the sites of the three battles of the 1837 uprising.

Following violent clashes in Montréal in early November 1837, the government of Lower Canada issued warrants for the arrest of the *Patriote* leaders. In the first act of rebellion, Papineau and others first fled to the Richelieu Valley, where the rebel force was strongest. Wolfred Nelson barricaded himself in at his home in the town of Saint-Denis, a *Patriote* stronghold east of Montréal. Louis-Joseph Papineau and Edmund Bailey O'Callaghan then made their way under cover to Nelson's home and stayed there.

The *Patriotes* were not ready to form an army, let alone a government. The uprising was rushed. The *Patriotes* had used fear to persuade their neighbours to participate. Habitants who did not turn out to rallies and meetings woke up to find their barns burning. The crowds that gathered at night, however, vanished in the day. The *Patriote* army turned British Canadian landowners out of their homes and stripped their farms of food. They rode off with the owners' horses and saddles, and carted off the furniture. Bands of *Patriotes* roved the countryside looking for food, while other groups looked for guns. Later on the *Patriotes* paid a heavy price for their **plunder**.

The British commander-in-chief, Sir John Colborne, sent two detachments of soldiers to the Richelieu Valley. They were to close in on the rebel stronghold like pincers. One group marched east from Montréal to Chambly, a town in the Richelieu Valley, and waited. The second detachment took a steamboat from Montréal to Sorel, a town at the mouth of the Richelieu River. They marched south through the night to mount a surprise attack on Saint-Denis. They had an awful time of it. A crust of ice formed on the thick mud that covered all the roads. The soldiers' feet broke through the crust at every step, and they sank up to their knees in freezing-cold mud. The gun-cart wheels got stuck.

While they were struggling along, Lieutenant George Weir arrived at Sorel on a later boat. He carried an important message from General Colborne. The detachment was to slow down and wait for the others to march from the south. Taking a different road in the night, Weir soon forged ahead of the troops. *Patriotes* captured him and took him to Wolfred Nelson's headquarters. While being transferred by oxcart, he tried to escape, and the habitant guards killed him. They hid his body and hurried away.

At *Patriote* headquarters, Papineau and Nelson discussed what might happen after the coming battle. Just before the British arrived, Papineau fled south, away from the battle, with O'Callaghan. He later maintained that Nelson convinced him to leave. Papineau continued as leader of the *Patriotes* for a short time, but he lost his power at that moment and never regained it.

Soon the exhausted British troops came marching into Saint-Denis. Hundreds of *Patriotes* shot at them from a stone building. The British army could not penetrate the stronghold. Colonel Charles Gore ordered a retreat and the army withdrew to Sorel.

In celebrating their victory, the *Patriotes* imagined they were close to creating a democratic state.

Two days after the battle, the other British detachment marched north to Saint-Charles, where Thomas Storrow Brown, commander of the *Fils de la Liberté*, was waiting. He led fewer than 100 men. Here is an eyewitness report of what happened in the battle:

This picture shows British troops advancing on the town of Saint-Charles, November 25, 1837. How do you think the British crossed the river when the bridge was destroyed?

On arriving before St. Charles, Colonel Wetherel summoned the rebels to surrender. This was answered by a cheer of contempt. The gallant Colonel deployed his men, and instantly commenced an attack. . . . Most of the rebels ran, with the exception of about 50, who knelt down and reversed their arms, thereby intimating [signalling] that they surrendered themselves as prisoners. No sooner, however, did the troops advance to take them than the traitors opened a fire, by which a sergeant was killed and many men wounded. This act of treachery so exasperated the troops that the officers could not restrain their fury, and a general massacre ensued; and many were drowned in attempting to escape the enraged soldiery. The estimated loss of the rebels was about 300, killed and wounded.

The British troops returned from Saint-Charles with 30 prisoners. Gore's troops marched back to Saint-Denis with British Canadian volunteers and burned nearly 50 homes. Papineau and Nelson watched them burn from a distance, then rode south. Papineau hid at his sister's *seigneury* in Sainte-Hyacinthe. Two days later, British troopers knocked on the door, and Papineau had to slither along a ditch to escape. He crossed the border into the United States under the name Mr. Louis. Thomas Storrow Brown fled safely to Florida. Wolfred Nelson was captured near the border.

Events quickly took surprising turns. On December 4, a search party in Saint-Denis discovered the body of Lieutenant Weir. The next day, martial law was proclaimed in Montréal. The military was now in charge of the province's government and police. The authorities braced for the worst, fearing that the province might explode in violence at any moment. On December 7, volunteers and militia quelled an uprising in Toronto. In Deux Montagnes, an area north of Montréal, the *Patriotes* took a stand. Their leaders included Dr. Jean-Olivier Chenier in the town of Saint-Eustache and a Swiss officer named Amury Girod. Girod's party raided the Aboriginal village of Oka and stole a supply of rifles. While these were scattered incidents, the British expected worse to follow.

Web Connection

www.school.mcgrawhill.ca/resources

Go to the web site above to find more examples of *Patriote* flags. Go to History Resources, then to *Canada: The Story of Our Heritage* to see where to go next.

General Colborne waited in Montréal until his troops could march on frozen roads or rivers before heading for Saint-Eustache in the Deux Montagnes district. It was cold enough by December 13, and Colborne rode out at the head of an army of some 1300 troops. Mean-while, as many as 2000 volunteers from Upper Canada were making their way toward Deux Montagnes.

The final battle of the rebellion was fought the next day. The British approached Saint-Eustache by a back way. The surprised *Patriotes* panicked. Chenier and Girod herded many people into the church and the priest's adjoining house at sword point. "We have no guns!" they cried. "You will be able to use theirs," Chenier growled.

Volunteers plundered the village and burned it. Then they moved on to Saint-Benôit, destroying it, too, while General Colborne looked the other way.

Soldiers defeat a Patriote force at St. Eustache by burning the convent where they barricaded themselves. How would you describe the mood of the Patriotes? the British army?

Snapshot

In the deep cold of December 13, 1837, soldiers with the 43rd Light Infantry gave up the relative comfort of their barracks in Fredericton, New Brunswick. They began an overland march to Lower Canada in case reinforcements were needed to put down the rebellion. One company snowshoed up the Madawaska Valley and across to the St. Lawrence Valley. They spent Christmas on the march. In this painting, the soldiers are shown crossing the St. Lawrence River to Québec at the end of their journey. When they arrived, the rebellion was already over, but the festive season was in full swing.

The Story So Far . . .

1   Create a character sketch of Louis-Joseph Papineau. In your opinion, was he a hero, a villain, or a fool?

2   How did the weather influence the course of the rebellion in Lower Canada?

3   Give examples of how both the British military and the *Patriotes* practised plunder.

THE UPRISING IN UPPER CANADA

Dr. John Rolph was afraid it would be too late to attack Toronto on December 7, 1837. Rolph was secretly a rebel leader, but also a member of the government of Upper Canada. He knew what little protection the city had — for the time being. On December 2, Rolph changed the day of the uprising to December 4. When word of the change reached Samuel Lount's home at Holland Landing, Lount said, "I'm afraid that Dr. Rolph is going to be the ruin of us." William Lyon Mackenzie re-established December 7 as the date of the uprising. But the changes knocked the rebels' timing off.

More than a hundred rebels followed Rolph's orders and turned up at Montgomery's Tavern on Yonge Street on December 3. Their arrival aroused the attention of neighbours. On December 4 the rebels captured a spy near the tavern. Robert Moodie went to the tavern to rescue his captured friend and was shot dead off his horse. His companion escaped in a hail of bullets and galloped to the city to warn Lieutenant-Governor

Head, who sent messengers in all directions to get help.

The rebel leaders decided to attack at once. On the morning of December 5, they started to march south on Yonge Street. Soon they met Robert Baldwin and John Rolph, sent by the Lieutenant-Governor to negotiate a truce. Rolph whispered to Lount that an attack would still succeed.

Lount broke off and advanced toward the city, leading a few riflemen, followed by several hundred men armed with pikes and pitchforks. Near the city a nest of pro-government colonists fired on them, then turned and fled. The first line of rebels returned the fire, then dropped down to allow those behind to get a good shot. The people in the second line thought their comrades fell because they were hit and they all ran away!

The next day volunteers flooded into Toronto to help protect the government from the rebels. On December 7, an army of nearly 1000 of these volunteers assembled on Front Street and set off toward Montgomery's Tavern. The rebels staged diversions by burning a home and trying to burn the Don Bridge. As soon as the volunteer regiments approached Montgomery's Tavern, the rebels disappeared into the forest. The entire battle lasted all of 20 minutes. The pro-government force took many prisoners. The rebels suffered five dead and more than ten were wounded.

A search of the tavern turned up Mackenzie's bag, containing lists of all his supporters, real and supposed. The pro-government forces burned the tavern down. Meanwhile, as

Rebel soldiers marching down Yonge Street. From what you have read of the rebels so far, and from the details in this picture, what do you think was their chance of success?

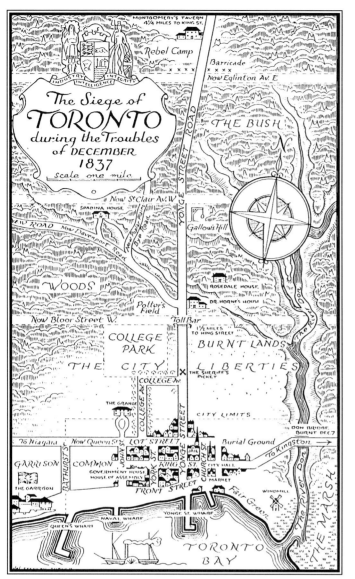

The Toronto area at the time of the rebellion. Montgomery's Tavern was just north of the Fourth Concession, now Eglinton Avenue.

many as 12 000 volunteers were making their way to Toronto in answer to the alarm. They and the militia fanned out across Home District looking for fugitives. Across Upper Canada people were on the alert for the missing rebel ringleaders.

Mackenzie made for the American border on the Niagara River. On the run for four days, he was recognized by many who could have turned him in and claimed the £1000 reward. Does that suggest anything about the situation in Upper Canada? As soon as Mackenzie reached the United States, he resumed planning a rebellion, as you will see.

Samuel Lount was not so lucky. He headed west and, with another man, tried to cross Lake Erie in a small boat. A farmer mistook them for rustlers and had them arrested.

Peter Matthews was careless. After his band of rebels set fire to the Don Bridge, killing the man who raised the alarm, he made his way homeward to Pickering Township where he was spotted. He asked a friend to hide him and turned in for the night, whereupon neighbours loyal to the government burst in and arrested him.

The day before the battle at Montgomery's Tavern, Dr. Charles Duncombe met with his supporters in the village of Sodom to plan an uprising in London District. Next day, Mackenzie's army was rumoured to have captured Toronto. Dr. Duncombe's supporters gathered in Sodom and began marching east, meeting with others at the village of Scotland. About 400 rebels gathered, planning to march northeast to Brantford, pick up support along the way, then continue east. News of Mackenzie's defeat reached Duncombe only on December 13. At the same time, he and his followers learned that Colonel Allan MacNab and 300 pro-government volunteers were marching from Hamilton to Brantford. More volunteers joined them the next day, and others were converging on Scotland. The rebels turned around. As nearly 2000 supporters of the government converged on them, Duncombe and his rebels made for the fields and woods in a desperate attempt to escape.

Samuel Lount

AN HONOURABLE REFORMER

When the dust of the 1837 uprising in Upper Canada had settled, two men in particular paid the price for the actions of a thousand rebels. One of these men was Samuel Lount. Unfortunately for the government, they had picked one of the most respected men in the area to label as a reformist villain.

Lount was the first child of Gabriel Lount and Philadelphia Hughes. He was born in Catawissa, Pennsylvania, on September 24, 1791, and lived there until 1811 when his family moved to Upper Canada. Samuel and his brothers settled on a farm south of Holland Landing, and in that town Samuel established a blacksmith business.

He married Elizabeth Soules of Big Bay Point on Lake Simcoe, whose family had come to America on the Mayflower. They began a family that eventually included seven children. Samuel worked hard and achieved moderate success but was better known in the region for his generosity. Always ready to assist incoming settlers, he was especially helpful to those with little or no practical knowledge of farming in Canada.

In 1834 he became Simcoe County's representative in the legislature of Upper Canada. When it was time for re-election in 1836, the government used dirty tricks to ensure Lount's defeat because of his reformist views. Lount and other reformist supporters became convinced that change would not take place using constitutional methods. They began holding meetings to discuss their options. Lount proposed the idea of a mass demonstration, and his blacksmith shop became the hub of the preparations.

After the failed march on Toronto on December 5, 1837, Lount fled west, staying with sympathizers or hiding out. Near Paris, he and two others found a boat and tried to cross to the United States. After two days of rowing, they were blown back to the north side and captured by a farmer, who thought they were simply rustlers.

On March 26 Lount and fellow patriot Matthews were tried in Toronto. Following the advice of lawyer and ex-Patriot Robert Baldwin, they pleaded guilty. Had they instead fought the charge and taken the case to a juried trial, public support may well have prevented a conviction.

Lieutenant-Governor George Arthur suggested that if Samuel turned in his co-conspirators, he would be spared. Honourable to the end, Lount refused to do that. He was executed on April 12 and buried without ceremony in Potter's Field. It would be another 55 years before a memorial marked the grave of this martyr to the reform cause.

More people you could research are

Robert Storrow Brown

Dr. Jean-Olivier Chenier

Amury Girod

Elizabeth Lount

Samuel Lount

Peter Matthews

Snippet

Daniel Conant's Brave Deed

Forty rebels who hid out for nearly three weeks near Oshawa were transported to safety across Lake Ontario by Daniel Conant in the schooner *Industry*. The ship became stuck in the ice far from the American shore. Despite falling into the water repeatedly, all survived their ordeal.

That was the end of the uprising in western Upper Canada. The militia rounded up some 500 suspected rebels. They invaded the families of arrested rebels, burned houses, looted farms, and tormented those said to have any sympathy for rebellion.

Meanwhile, Mackenzie addressed a large meeting of friendly Americans in Buffalo. By December 13, he was setting up camp on Navy Island, in the Niagara River, about 5 km south of Niagara Falls. Navy Island was Canadian territory. Supporters flocked to the island. Isabel Mackenzie left their children with her sister in Toronto and joined the refugees.

While the rebels enjoyed Christmas dinner on the island, Colonel MacNab's regiment set out for Chippawa. Some 2500 militiamen and volunteers massed on the Canadian shore of the Niagara River. In plain view, the rebels ferried people and supplies from the American shore in the steamer *Caroline*. The army remained there for more than two weeks without attacking the rebels. The last thing Upper Canada wanted was a border conflict with the United States.

Still, the loyal forces were infuriated to have rebels camped out on Canadian territory! On the night of December 29, Lieutenant Andrew Drew of the Royal Navy and a small party rowed across the river and boarded the *Caroline* on the American shore. After wounding the American captain, they woke the sleeping crew and herded them off the ship. Then they

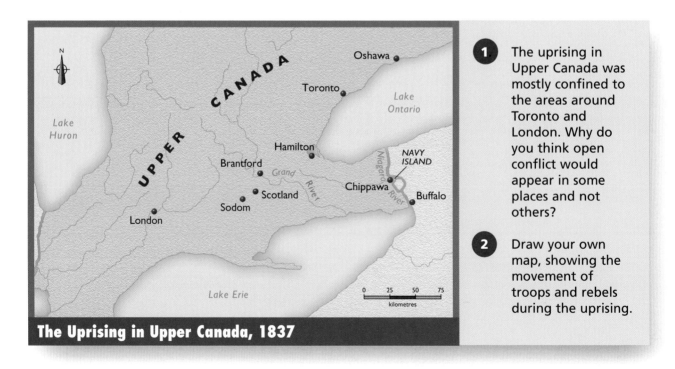

The Uprising in Upper Canada, 1837

1. The uprising in Upper Canada was mostly confined to the areas around Toronto and London. Why do you think open conflict would appear in some places and not others?

2. Draw your own map, showing the movement of troops and rebels during the uprising.

started fires on board. As the cry went up and people came rushing to the dock to stop them, Drew's party cut the *Caroline* loose. The blazing ship ran aground on an island near Niagara Falls and burned up. Even though Drew acted without orders, the American government was outraged. A British force had killed an American and destroyed American property! There was talk of war.

This painting shows the American steamer *Caroline* ablaze near Navy Island, Canadian rebel headquarters. Why do you think British naval officers set the ship on fire?

The Story So Far . . .

1 Make a time line of events in Upper Canada in December 1837.

2 Create police *Wanted* posters for Mackenzie, Lount, Rolph, and Duncombe.

3 How was the uprising in Upper Canada similar to the rebellion in Lower Canada? How were they different?

BORDER RAIDS BEGIN

Dr. Robert Nelson, a leader of the Patriot Hunters and the creator of Hunters' Lodges

Robert Nelson was a leader in a shadowy movement known as the Patriot Hunters. Groups of American republicans joined Upper and Lower Canadian refugees to form **Hunters' Lodges**, which were secret societies. Members used hand signals to communicate with others when in public. The Hunters and the French Canadian movement *Les Frères Chasseurs* (Brother Hunters) sought to free Upper and Lower Canada from British rule. As many as 40 000 people are estimated to have joined Hunters' Lodges during this period. They started the second uprising in Lower Canada.

Refugee Patriot Hunters following Mackenzie were still hoping to spark a huge uprising from the United States. The Patriot Hunters raised a little money for weapons and provisions and, more often, simply stole them. They were joined by Americans who considered British rule to be no better than slavery. Detroit, Buffalo, and other American border cities were hotbeds of rebellious activity.

United States President Martin Van Buren declared that his country was neutral and promised to arrest and punish raiders. Raiding parties were pursued by both American and Canadian forces.

A group called the Patriot Army of the North West staged the first of many raids across the Detroit River. Bois Blanc Island, near Amherstburg, was the base of a failed attack by a party of raiders on January 9, 1838. Raiders fired on the Canadian shore from a boat called the *Anne*, which ran aground and was captured by the militia.

In mid-February, William Johnston, a colourful figure known as Pirate Bill, joined William Lyon Mackenzie and others on Hickory Island, on the American shore near Gananoque. The Patriot Hunters were gathering for an attack on February 22, but only about 300 men responded. Kingston was a military stronghold with an active militia. The invasion was cancelled.

Web Connection

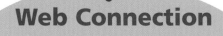

www.school.mcgrawhill.ca/resources

Go to the web site above to find more about Hunters Lodges, The Patriot Hunters, and *Les Frères Chasseurs*. Go to History Resources, then to *Canada: The Story of Our Heritage* to see where to go next.

William Johnston

PIRATE OF THE ST. LAWRENCE

For the first 30 years of his life, William Johnston was an ordinary early Canadian. Born February 1, 1782 at Trois-Rivières, he grew up on his family's farm near Kingston. He became a merchant and, like countless other merchants along the U.S. border, began smuggling.

Johnston's smuggling took him regularly to the United States. His wife and many of his friends were American. When the War of 1812 broke out, Johnston's ties to the enemy made his fellow Canadians uneasy. Charged with deserting from the Canadian militia, the smuggler was thrown in jail. To his further outrage, the government confiscated his property, which was worth about £1500.

Johnston escaped prison and journeyed to New York. He settled in the town of French Creek and demanded that the Canadian government reimburse him for his confiscated property. Their refusal fueled Johnston's hatred of Canada. Vowing revenge, he offered to help the Americans. For the rest of the war he was a spy and a raider who prowled the Thousand Islands with a group of like-minded comrades, terrorizing isolated farms and attacking small boats. He was as clever as he was treacherous, and every attempt to catch him failed.

After the war he remained in New York and continued smuggling. When the 1837 turmoil of the Canadian Patriotes arose, Johnston saw an opportunity to loot as well as defy the government and he grabbed it.

The 1838 attack on Kingston's Fort Henry fell apart, but Johnston planned another means of punishing his homeland. In May of that year, his gang looted and burned the steamer Sir Robert Peel, taking more than $100 000 in cash and valuables. Johnston claimed it was in retaliation for the Canadian attack on an American supply boat to the Patriotes. More likely, Pirate Bill simply loved to plunder.

In spite of rewards for his capture, Johnston continued to terrorize the St. Lawrence until November, when he was finally captured by American forces. A New York court found him guilty of murder and piracy but handed down a light sentence of a $250 fine and one year in jail!

Six months into his sentence, Johnston escaped again and turned up in Washington with a petition for his unconditional pardon, signed by friends and sympathizers. America's new president, William Harrison, granted the pardon, setting the infamous pirate free on the St. Lawrence once more. He returned to smuggling in French Creek. His extraordinary life ended in 1870 when he died at age 88.

More people you could research are

Charles Duncombe

Colonel Allan MacNab

William Johnston

James Moreau

Wolfred and Robert Nelson

Nils Von Schoutz

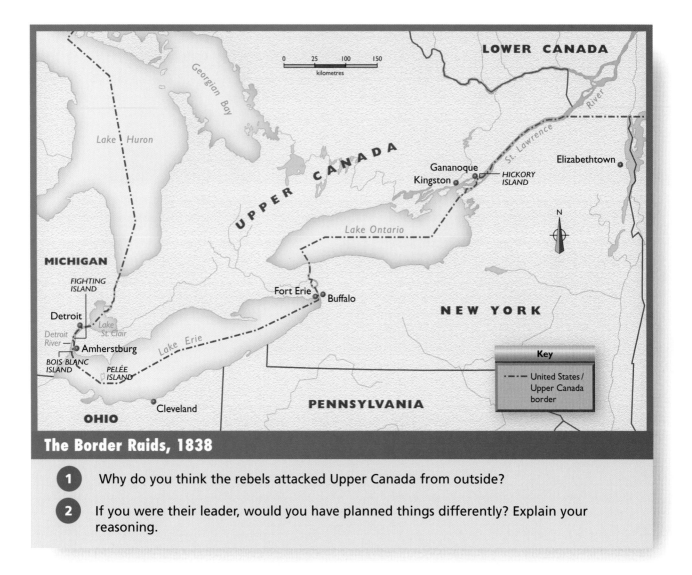

The Border Raids, 1838

1 Why do you think the rebels attacked Upper Canada from outside?

2 If you were their leader, would you have planned things differently? Explain your reasoning.

On February 23 a band of Patriot Hunters in Detroit joined with a larger force that had marched from Cleveland. Led by Dr. Charles Duncombe, they got into a skirmish with the militia on Fighting Island in the Detroit River and were forced to flee back across the frozen river. On February 25 there was agitation in Fort Erie on the Niagara River, while, in Elizabethtown, New York, Patriot Hunters stole more than a thousand rifles and three cannons. Dr. Robert Nelson, the brother of Wolfred Nelson, published a letter to rebels in Canada denouncing Louis-Joseph Papineau as a coward. On February 28 Nelson and a group of rebels crossed the American border to Lower Canada, declared Lower Canada an independent country, and returned to the United States.

The most serious raiding incident began on February 26 on Pelée Island, on the north shore of Lake Erie. More than a thousand rebels in the United States crossed the frozen lake on sleighs to gather on Pelée Island. They stole supplies from nearby farms until a combined force of British regulars and Upper Canada militia regiments attacked their island stronghold.

Besides killing and injuring quite a few people, the raiders harmed the cause they aimed to support. Upper Canada was so fearful of attack that a standing army remained there for three years. Pro-government citizens found it easy to blame the province's troubles on the rebels and their American allies. The militia and volunteers used the rebel threat as an excuse to continue terrorizing their enemies. Continuing the conflict also meant they received soldiers' pay and allowances. Many reform-minded families gave up and emigrated to the United States.

THE EMPIRE STRIKES BACK

Life was terrible for rebels captured in battle and for the many who were arrested on suspicion of being rebels. *Patriotes* captured at Saint-Charles were marched all the way to Montréal chained together in twos. They endured abuse from jeering crowds along the way. Rebels in Western Upper Canada faced similar treatment on a forced march to Toronto. The jails in both provinces filled up with suspected traitors: more than one thousand in Upper Canada, several times that in Lower Canada. Conditions in the jails, with their unheated rooms and lack of food, caused uncounted deaths. The prisoners of the Pelée Island battle endured over a year in jail before being brought to trial.

In both provinces, those who had been forced to take part in the uprisings were soon freed. Most of the people who just followed orders also went free. More than 300 remained in jail in Upper Canada; half that number in Lower Canada.

This picture was painted in the vicinity of Château Richer, Lower Canada. What do you notice about the seated figures? The standing figure?

In this illustration, Elizabeth Lount pleads with Lieutenant-Governor Arthur for her husband Samuel's life. Judging from the expression on Sir Arthur's face, do you think Mrs. Lount was successful?

Magistrates proceeded to charge the ringleaders and the people they suspected of murdering Weir and Moodie. In both provinces the pro-government population demanded the death penalty. They pushed the governors to make sure traitors hanged.

Because the uprising in Lower Canada was much more serious, the government's response was more severe — until it came to trying and punishing the rebels. Lower Canada remained under martial law until April 27, 1838. One of the outcomes of martial law is to suspend the law of **habeas corpus**. This law protects individuals, even those suspected of committing a crime, from the whims of the government. Under this law, the authorities cannot keep prisoners in jail without charging them with a crime and allowing them a fair trial — what is known as **due process**. A **jury** of ordinary people votes on the guilt or innocence of the accused, and makes its verdict only with the agreement of all members.

When the rule of martial law ended in Lower Canada, the law of habeas corpus should have been restored, but it was not. By proclamation, the law was suspended for two more months. No one dared to try the jailed *Patriotes*. The authorities in Lower Canada were afraid that jurors trying the rebels would vote along cultural lines: A British Canadian jury would convict, an all-Canadien jury would acquit, while a mixed jury would remain divided. With a divided jury, the accused would go free.

Lower Canada soon suffered an even greater fall from justice and democracy. An act of the British Parliament in February 1838 suspended the Constitution by which the colony had been governed since 1791. There was neither an Assembly nor a Legislative Council for three years. At first, a Special Council of 22 people appointed by the governor, the Earl of Gosford, made the laws needed to govern the colony. Because the governor had resigned and left Canada at the end of February, Sir John Colborne, the military commander of British North America, became the colony's overseer until Lord Durham arrived.

In Upper Canada, the government continued to function. Lieutenant-Governor Head was recalled after quarreling with the British government. His replacement was Sir George Arthur, who arrived in Toronto from Van Diemen's Land (now the

Australian state of Tasmania) on March 23, 1838, just as the first sentences on the rebels were being pronounced.

One of Sir George Arthur's first duties was to sign the death warrants for Samuel Lount and Peter Matthews. Lount, a blacksmith with a wife and children, played a major role in the December 5 attack on Toronto. Peter Matthews, the son of Loyalists and a leading reformer in Pickering Township, led the rebel group that burned a home and killed a man near the Don Bridge on December 7. Matthews and Lount had been tried before the Chief Justice of Upper Canada, John Beverley Robinson. The Crown counsel, or **prosecutor**, was the Attorney General of Upper Canada, Christopher Hagarman. The accused pleaded guilty to treason, and Robinson sentenced them to hang. The Executive Council, on which both the judge and prosecutor sat, received petitions bearing thousands of signatures, asking for mercy. The Executive Council upheld the sentence, sure that the pro-government population would create even more trouble if they did not.

Arthur heard the appeal of Samuel Lount's wife, Elizabeth, but would not stop the executions. The two men hanged on April 12, 1838, in front of the King Street jail. The gallows were near the windows of the other prisoners' cells.

A view of the jail and courthouse outside of which Samuel Lount and Peter Matthews were hanged on April 12, 1838. The hanging was intended to discourage those with rebel sympathies. Executions were considered public entertainment in the nineteenth century. Few people witnessed these hangings. Why?

While the pro-government Canadians shouted for more, the radical reformers made martyrs of the two men and muttered bitterly about the tyranny of British rule. Lieutenant-Governor Arthur, who had a reputation for being ruthless, was sickened by the conflict. Two days after the executions, Arthur made it clear he would not sign any more death warrants.

Elizabeth Lount described her exchange with Lieutenant-Governor Arthur in a letter she published in the Pontiac, Michigan, *Herald* on June 12, 1838:

> The day before my husband was executed, I, in company with a lady of Toronto, visited the Governor. . . . I told him I was the wife of Samuel Lount, and had come before him to plead for mercy. . . . Thirty-five thousand of his subjects also asked him to interpose his power and save my husband from the sentence of the law. I then kneeled before him on behalf of my husband. . . . He said he did not condemn my husband because he was guilty — "I do think," said he, "if Rolph and Mackenzie were here mercy would be shown to them. Two lives were lost at Montgomery's and two must now suffer."

QUESTIONING THE EVIDENCE

Interpret and discuss Mrs. Lount's report of Arthur's words that justify the death of two men.

1. Was Arthur saying that Lount and Matthews would not be hanged if they had Mackenzie and Rolph? Why would he say that?
2. Did he mean that Lount and Matthews did not have to hang? If not, why were they executed?
3. Discuss how public opinion can affect decisions on issues in your community.

LORD DURHAM ARRIVES

Lord Durham, the new governor, arrived in Québec in May 1838. He rode up to Château Saint Louis on a white horse amid general rejoicing. Many on both sides of the conflict prayed that he could heal their ailing land.

Lord Durham ruled British North America, including Newfoundland, for barely five months. Still, he is considered Upper and Lower Canada's most influential governor ever, although he left his stamp on our country with a report he wrote after leaving it. The Durham Report became the blueprint for change in the government of Upper and Lower Canada. What else would you expect from someone known as Radical Jack?

As **high commissioner**, Lord Durham was charged with studying "certain important questions" respecting "the form and future government" of Lower and Upper Canada. Durham's own government consisted of a council of five, three of whom he brought with him. He was, in other words, an **autocrat**, a person who has absolute power over his subjects. Was that to be Upper and Lower Canada's new form of government?

Soon after Durham arrived, Pirate Bill Johnston's gang was causing problems. On the night of May 30, 1838, as many as 40

John George Lambton, Lord Durham

A MAN FOR THE PEOPLE

The Canadas were a mess. Citizens were up in arms over the dictatorial government. The clash between French and British was escalating. Into this storm stepped the man given the monumental task of fixing it: John George Lambton, Lord Durham. Although Lambton knew little about Canadian affairs, he knew about conflicts between a government and its subjects.

Born in London, England, on April 12, 1792, John Lambton practically grew up in the British government. His father, William Lambton, was a wealthy coal-mine owner and a member of Parliament for the city of Durham. William was known as a radical, and after his death the education of seven-year-old John passed to guardians and relatives who held similar views.

Lambton spent three years at Eton College and served in the army from 1809–1811. In 1813, at 21 years of age, he entered the British House of Commons representing the County of Durham. He married the daughter of Lord Grey in 1816 and continued in the House of Commons until 1828, when he became a baron and took a seat in the House of Lords.

Lambton was "for the people" in more than just government. He supported the advance of education and provided his coal-mine workers with libraries and schools. He worked hard to improve working conditions inside his mines as well.

His father-in-law, Earl Grey, was elected Prime Minister in 1830, and his party, the Whigs, began to make sweeping changes in the British system of government. Lambton got the nickname "Radical Jack" for his significant role in shaping the Reform Bill of 1832. Respected by his political peers, he was also a hero of the common people.

In 1838 Prime Minister Lord Melbourne, aided by a personal appeal from the Queen, convinced him to go to British North America as High Commissioner and Governor-General. Lambton reluctantly agreed but made it clear that he required full power. Melbourne replied, "As far as I am concerned, and I think I answer for all my colleagues, you will receive the firmest and most unflinching support."

After Durham's unsuccessful mission to the colony, he returned to England and wrote the report which so greatly influenced Canada's future. On July 28, 1848, within 18 months of completing that report, Lord Durham died of tuberculosis, unaware that he would become known as one of the founders of the modern Commonwealth.

More people you could research are

George Arthur

John Colborne

Charles Gray

Christopher Hagerman

John George Lambton, Lord Durham

John Beverley Robinson

This illustration shows, in great detail, a British unit attacking a sailboat. Step into the picture. Imagine that you are a crew member aboard either the sailboat or one of the British rowboats. What emotions are you feeling? Fear? Anger? Excitement? What are you doing? Rowing? Firing the cannon? Giving orders? Communicating with the enemy? What are you saying? Are you thinking about who is going to win? Whether or not you will live or die? What will happen to you if the enemy catches you?

With a partner, decide on a role for each of you. Create a script, including stage directions, dialogue, and the use of props. Then act out the scene for the class.

bandits boarded the *Sir Robert Peel*, a steamer bound from Prescott to Toronto, when it was docked on the American shore. They awoke the sleeping passengers and crew and drove them off the ship. Then they towed the vessel into the river, looted its cash and valuables, set it afire, and rowed away. Johnston's gangs continued to harass farmers in the Thousand Islands.

More trouble was brewing along the Niagara River border. Patriot Hunter James Morreau led a party of 30 raiders across the border on June 11, and they holed up in tiny Short Hills. After ten days, a large force of militia captured many of the raiders, including Morreau. He was quickly tried and executed in July, but Lord Durham's intervention saved four of the others from hanging. The Patriot Hunters continued their raiding.

Lord Durham soon restored good relations with the United States over the raiding parties. He won over the British Canadian minority in Lower Canada. He agreed with the moderate reformers in Upper Canada on the need for change. However, within a month of taking office, Durham made a decision that would soon come back to haunt him.

Durham realized that *Patriote* leaders who had been in jail since the rebellion would not get a fair trial. He worked out a deal for some of the prisoners. Eight of the leaders, including Wolfred Nelson, would not have to stand trial if they confessed their guilt. Instead, they would be banished to a foreign land and would face the death penalty if they returned to British North America. There would be no deal for the ten men accused of murder and the 16 leaders who had fled the country, including Louis-Joseph Papineau. For the rebels who had simply followed the leaders, Lord Durham declared an **amnesty**, or official pardon, and had more than 125 released. The eight who confessed their guilt left Lower Canada for Bermuda on June 28, 1838.

When word of the deal reached Britain, the government's response was positive at first. But opposition members of Parliament objected that even a mighty governor could not punish people without a trial. The opponents brought the matter to a vote in Parliament and won. In September Durham received the news that his deal had been rejected. He was humiliated. They had taken away his authority to govern, except by force. He resigned at once and left British North America within two months.

Events soon confirmed Durham's concern about trial by jury. After the amnesty, in the trial of four men accused of murdering an informer, a jury of Canadiens freed all four. The British Canadian population of Lower Canada was outraged.

As for the eight lucky exiles in Bermuda, they soon hired a ship and returned to North America.

The Story So Far . . .

1 How were Patriot Hunters different from rebels? How were they similar?
2 What does *due process* mean? How is due process supposed to guard the rights of accused criminals? Point out ways it was not followed in bringing the rebels to justice.
3 Debate whether Lord Durham's deal was the only possible way to punish the *Patriote* leaders fairly.

THE SECOND UPRISING IN LOWER CANADA

A new rebellion started the day after Lord Durham's ship sailed away from Québec. The *Frères Chasseurs* had been busy recruiting new members since September, often by threat of harm. They were not all that secretive, running an office openly in Montréal. On November 2 many Canadien farmers walked away from their work. The *Chasseurs*' foot soldiers gathered in prearranged places. On November 3, a British Canadian farmer was murdered in La Tortue, southwest of Montréal.

Some of the 500–600 *Chasseurs* occupying Beauharnois decided to seize a supply of guns in the Mohawk community of Caughnawaga. They rode over and demanded the weapons. Sixty-four *Patriotes* were promptly captured by a much smaller group of Mohawks, most of whom were unarmed.

Meanwhile, on November 4, an army of *Frères Chasseurs* led by Robert Nelson crossed the border into Lower Canada from the United States. At Napierville, Nelson once again proclaimed the province a free country and himself its president. The *Chasseurs* were trying to ignite a ring of rebellion around Montréal and cut it off. When a band of 500 *Chasseurs* returned south to pick up a cache of arms near the border, an army of volunteers inflicted heavy losses on them at Vitman's Quay.

The rebels at Napierville began to disappear into the countryside. Canadiens abandoned the uprising and tried to show their loyalty. Nelson's army dwindled from 3000 to 800. He rode into the night, saying he was going for reinforcements. His officers suspected he was fleeing from the approaching

"November 7: The whole house is surrounded by *Guards*," Jane Ellice wrote in her diary. "I sketched some of them from the window — picturesque ruffians."

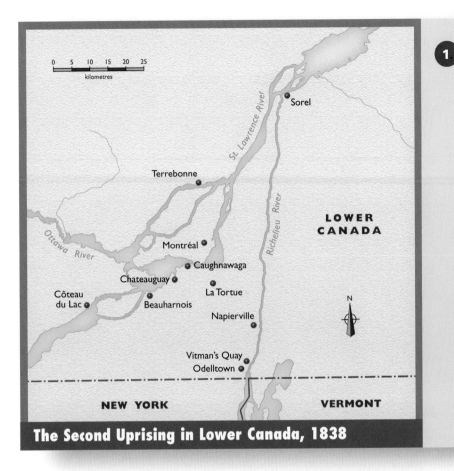

The Second Uprising in Lower Canada, 1838

1 The centres of rebellion in 1838 were different from those in 1837, yet they were also close to Montréal. Why do you think Montréal was the centre of *Patriote* activity?

battle. They overtook Nelson near the border, tied him up, and brought him back to make sure he led them into battle.

The *Chasseurs* were in deep trouble. Sir John Colborne proclaimed martial law again, and the army began arresting suspected rebels. A revolt in Terrebonne, north of Montréal Island, failed after the first arrests. The planned capture of Sorel by the *Patriotes* never got off the ground. And the Glengarry Scots were on the march. Fifteen hundred volunteers reached Côteau du Lac on November 8 and started crossing the St. Lawrence River, headed for Beauharnois. At the same time, General Colborne rode out, leading an army of 8000. They swept south along both sides of the Richelieu River, headed for Napierville.

The rebellion collapsed on November 9. The *Chasseurs* remaining at Beauharnois ran into a force of Highlanders on the road west. Nelson's force, marching south, engaged the volunteer army at Odelltown. President Nelson slipped away while 50 of his comrades died in the fighting.

General Colborne's force arrived at Napierville the same day and began burning the houses of suspected rebels. General Colborne soon ordered his soldiers to stop. Local resentment of

At the Battle of Odelltown, Lower Canada, on November 9, 1838, the *Patriote* rebellion was crushed, leaving a legacy of fear and mistrust.

the people's ill-treatment lingered for decades. The Glengarry Scots plundered Beauharnois the next day.

The next day, the Hunters started more trouble in Upper Canada. On November 11, nearly 400 American Patriot Hunters and Canadian refugee rebels crossed the upper St. Lawrence River near Prescott. Their aim was to capture Fort Wellington, take control of the river, and isolate Upper Canada. Pirate Bill Johnston provided boats, but the invaders came under fire at once, a boat got stuck, and Johnston vanished. Militia and regular troops chased half the rebel force into a stone windmill, where they barricaded themselves and for four days put on a brave show. They inflicted heavy casualties in the Battle of the Windmill, while suffering the loss of 30 men. When they surrendered, 160 rebels were taken prisoner. The prisoners had to be protected from the militia by the regular army.

The Patriot Hunters made one final mass attack as the curtain fell on 1838. Seizing a steamer in Detroit, raiders attacked Windsor, with loss of life on both sides. Hunter attacks continued for months, aiming simply to terrorize loyal Upper Canadians and their families. Was there any remedy for such hatred?

Snapshot

John A. Macdonald and the Rebels

Young John A. Macdonald was called to military service in Toronto in December 1837. He fought in the battle at Montgomery's Tavern. Within a year, however, he was acting as counsel for Nils von Schoutz, leader of the raiders accused of treason in the Battle of the Windmill. They lost, and his client was hanged. But that did not deter Macdonald from taking on the unpopular cause of the rebels. Less than 30 years later, he became the first Prime Minister of Canada. By the time he retired, his government had created the country that we know today.

What Became of the Rebels

Some 13 000 people are estimated to have been involved in the uprising of 1838 in Lower Canada — more than in the previous year and many times more than in Upper Canada. More than 800 were arrested and charged. As before, most of those arrested were pardoned and released. For the others, punishment was much more severe than before: execution, or hard labour in Van Diemen's Land.

Most of the people who started and led the rebellions got off without punishment. With a few notable exceptions, it was the everyday people, mostly farmers, who paid the penalty. Their families suffered greatly as a result. Many of the leaders who fled across the American border had the means to get by. Louis-Joseph Papineau and his family settled in Paris, France. William Lyon Mackenzie had to work for a living. He and his family moved to Rochester, where he spent a year in jail for encouraging Americans to attack Canada. Mackenzie and his family moved to New York City after four years of poverty, and became more prosperous.

In 1843 the Legislative Assembly of Canada passed a bill granting amnesty to most of the rebel refugees. Papineau returned and took up his previous professions: lawyer, politician, *seigneur*. William Lyon Mackenzie was not included in the amnesty. A special act of the legislature in 1849 lifted his banishment. Mackenzie and his family returned to Toronto the following year. Given a house by grateful citizens, he returned to the newspaper trade and ran for office again.

LORD DURHAM'S REPORT

What was wrong with Upper and Lower Canada? Why were the neighbouring United States flourishing, while the two Canadas were foundering? Did Upper and Lower Canada have the same faults or did they have to be treated with different remedies? During his brief stay in British North America, these questions troubled Lord Durham. His staff gathered information from colonists on all sides of the conflicts. Lord Durham completed his book-length report on the problems almost three months after he left the Canadas.

Reformers in both colonies told Durham that the government had been badly designed in 1791, with too much power at the top. The result was "a great degree of mismanagement and dissatisfaction." But Durham felt that "there existed a far deeper and far more efficient" reason for the conflict: "I expected to find a contest between a government and a people; I found two nations warring in the bosom of a single state; I found a struggle, not of principles, but of races."

Lord Durham paid little attention to the pro-government people of Upper Canada. For them the main problem was the radical beliefs of settlers with American ties. Lord Durham accepted the arguments of William Baldwin and Robert Baldwin that "local control" via responsible government would solve the unrest in Upper Canada. He also recommended abolition of the Clergy Reserves and other irritants.

Durham listened more carefully to the British Canadian minority in Lower Canada. They complained that the Canadiens had gained too much power by being able to control the Assembly. "Those who were not trusted with the management of a parish, were enabled, by their votes, to influence the destinies of a State." Durham felt that the Canadiens should have been introduced to democracy more slowly. The British Canadian minority, he wrote, "would never peaceably submit" to a French Canadian majority again. An artificial boundary between the two provinces made British Canadians a minority in Lower Canada. "Sooner or later the English race was sure to predominate even numerically in Lower Canada, as they predominate already by their superior knowledge, energy, enterprise, and wealth." Lord Durham emphasized the need to ensure "at once and for ever" that Upper and Lower Canada stayed British and urged the British to "abandon the vain endeavour to preserve a French Canadian nationality in the midst of Anglo-American colonies and states."

Durham's solution was to join the legislatures of the two provinces into one.

I believe that no permanent or efficient remedy can be devised for the disorders of Lower Canada, except a fusion of the government in that of one or more of the surrounding provinces; and as I am of the opinion that the full establishment of responsible government can only be permanently secured by giving these colonies an increased importance in the politics of the Empire, I find in union the only means of remedying at once and completely the two prominent causes of their present unsatisfactory condition.

Durham hoped that a **legislative union** would result in the gradual assimilation of the French Canadian people. His proposal went against the wishes of the majority in both provinces. The people of both Upper and Lower Canada were outraged at the idea of being yoked together by a single legislature. Their objections were ignored. At once, the Durham Report became the blueprint for change in Upper and Lower Canada.

The Story So Far . . .

1 Take the point of view of a Canadien and write a poem telling future generations what you want them to remember about the rebellions. Choose a title for your poem.

2 What two causes did Lord Durham identify for the conflicts in Upper and Lower Canada? Which was the more serious in his view? Why?

3 How would a legislative union solve the British-French conflict in Upper and Lower Canada, according to Lord Durham?

SUM IT UP!

Rebellion broke out in Lower Canada in November 1837. The *Patriotes* won a victory before suffering two crushing defeats. Smaller uprisings occurred in Upper Canada in December 1837 but were quickly put down by pro-government volunteers.

Samuel Lount and Peter Matthews were executed in Toronto in April 1838 to satisfy demands for punishment. In Lower Canada, the authorities were afraid that accused rebels would not get fair trials, so they kept them in jail. When Lord Durham arrived as Governor General, he made a deal whereby most of those in jail in Lower Canada were freed and a few of the leaders were exiled. The British government forbade Lord Durham's deal, and he resigned.

Raids on Upper and Lower Canada from across the American border were aided by Patriot Hunters or *Frères Chasseurs* and by pirates working in the Thousand Islands. These attacks made things worse for colonists on their side. The *Chasseurs* started a second uprising in 1838 and continued random acts of terrorism.

The uprising in Lower Canada in November 1838 was larger than the first one. British troops and colonial volunteers defeated the rebels. Following the rebellion, some convicted rebels were executed, while many more were transported to Van Diemen's Land to serve terms of hard labour.

Lord Durham's report suggested that cultural differences were the root of the conflict in Upper and Lower Canada. He recommended union of the two colonies as a way of removing the threat of French power. Over the long term, he wanted French Canadian society to assimilate with the British Canadian minority.

THINKING ABOUT YOUR LEARNING

1. Did Papineau start the 1837 rebellion in Lower Canada? Did Mackenzie start the rebellion in Upper Canada? If they did not, who, or what, did?

2. You are one of Lord Durham's research staff in Upper or Lower Canada. You know that the sources of conflict leading to rebellion include these factors:
   - building canals rather than roads (mainly in Upper Canada)
   - the Clergy Reserves: land that remained undeveloped yet claimed by the Church of England (in both Upper and Lower Canada, but a source of conflict in Upper Canada)

- Assembly votes vetoed by appointed legislative councillors or the governor (in both provinces)
- attacks on French language, laws, and religion (in Lower Canada)

Choose one of these sources of discontent and write a report for Lord Durham explaining how the conflict arose. Include your own theory on why it contributed to armed uprising.

3 Research one of these topics in depth:
- pirates of the St. Lawrence
- jails in British North America during 1815 to 1840
- rebels transported to Van Diemen's Land
- Patriot Hunters/*Frères Chasseurs*

APPLYING YOUR LEARNING

1 The rebellions in Upper and Lower Canada were the worst conflicts ever to occur within British North America. Did they have to happen? Could they happen again? How? Discuss.

2 Choose one of the following situations, find a real-life case that is in your local newspaper, and study the ways the conflict is resolved, if at all. Rate the participants for their willingness to resolve the conflict.

a) Land-use dispute (for example, a group of neighbours tries to rescue a heritage house from demolition)

b) Social conflict (for example, a group of downtown shopkeepers tries to keep "street kids" away from their doors)

c) Labour dispute (for example, nurses go on strike at hospitals to protest inadequate payment for their services)

d) Political strife (for example, a federal politician is criticized by a provincial politician over a decision to close a fishery that employs thousands of workers)

3 In teams, make up a time line that incorporates the important events of the rebellions of 1837 and 1838 in both

colonies. Decide on a visual way of showing which events happened in Lower Canada, in Upper Canada, and in the United States.

4 On a blank map of Northeastern North America plot the major movements, battles, and other events of the rebellions.

USING KEY WORDS

1 In groups, use as many of the words from Column A as you can in a meaningful paragraph. The definitions of the words appear in Column B for your reference. Read your paragraph to the class to see which group's is the most creative.

Column A	Column B
amnesty	a government pardon for past offences
autocrat	a person exercising absolute authority
due process	the requirement that a person be charged before being jailed and tried
Frères Chasseurs	French Canadian variety of a Hunters' Lodge
habeas corpus	a law protecting an individual's rights
high commissioner	one of Lord Durham's titles, the mission to research what was wrong with Canada
Hunters' Lodges	groups formed to overthrow British rule in Canada
legislative union	a fusion of two governments
jury	group of people who give a verdict based on evidence presented to it at a trial
plunder	robbery by an invading army
legislative union	the joining of the legislatures of Upper and Lower Canada

Chapter 12

Toward Responsible Government

1840
British Parliament passes the Act of Union

1843
Robert Baldwin and Louis La Fontaine resign from the government

1846
Britain adopts free trade

SETTING OUR FOCUS

A winter's day in 1848. High-stepping horses pull Montréalers to their appointments. The square is known as Place d'Armes. In 1644, French soldiers and Iroquois warriors fought a battle here, outside the little mission known as Ville Marie. The people in this picture are probably of neither French nor Aboriginal origin, though. Montréal has become a mostly English-speaking city. The large building with the pillars is the new Bank of Montreal headquarters. The canals on the St. Lawrence River, the railway to the United States, and Hugh Allen's new telegraph company all got their start with money from the bank.

The British way predominates in government also. When Lord Durham set out to solve Upper and Lower Canada's problems, who did he listen to? The merchants and bankers of Montréal, who were mainly British Canadian. The largest city in the Province of Canada is now the capital city as well as its financial and transportation centre. It is also emerging as a factory town.

Behind the scenes, however, something new is happening. French and British Canadians have banded together and used the British parliamentary system to win responsible government. In other words, Canadians are beginning to govern themselves. And it happened without a shot being fired — almost. How did they do it?

PREVIEWING THE CHAPTER

In this chapter you will learn about these topics:
- how Lower and Upper Canada were united as a single province
- how politicians from both regions worked together to reform the government
- what happened to Canada when the British Empire adopted free trade
- how responsible government began in British North America

KEY WORDS

free trade
Legislative Assembly
nationalists
opposition
patronage
party
repeal
riding

1847
Lord Elgin appointed Governor General of Canada

1848
Responsible government begins first in Nova Scotia, then in Canada

1849
The Rebellion Losses Bill tests the new system of responsible government

SURVIVAL THROUGH CO-OPERATION

Would Canadians ever take control of their own affairs or would they always remain, as jeering Americans called them, "slaves of the Queen?" After the rebellions, French Canadians wanted more than ever to break the British tie. They believed French Canada had a better chance of surviving on its own. A small number of Canadiens still wanted to overthrow the government by violent means. Most, however, believed that the less they had to do with British government or British Canadians, the better. Today they would be called **nationalists**. They believed in looking after the interests of their own people.

The majority of people in Upper Canada had a similar view, although they did not share the Canadiens' mistrust of the British. They were loyal to Britain. They wanted nothing to do with French Canada.

In both provinces, there were people who wanted to promote peaceful change. One such person was Louis-Hippolyte La Fontaine, a young lawyer who lived in Terrebonne, near Montréal. La Fontaine had represented the voters of Terrebonne in the Assembly of Lower Canada since 1830. La Fontaine hated violence and had a genius for compromise. He broke with Louis-Joseph Papineau and the *Patriotes* before the rebellion of 1837, yet he represented some of the jailed leaders of the rebellion in their efforts to get fair treatment.

When the new Act of Union — the proposal to join Upper and Lower Canada — came before the British Parliament in 1840, La Fontaine was opposed to it. He, too, wanted to see French Canada survive. As the details of the new government emerged, his mistrust deepened.

One cause of bitterness was the way the legislatures of Lower and Upper Canada were united. French Canadians were outraged at Lower Canada's share of the seats in the **Legislative Assembly** of Canada, as it was now called. According to the census of 1841, Lower Canada had about 650 000 people, compared with 455 688 in Upper Canada. Lord Durham had recommended that seats be shared according to the rule of representation by population. Since Lower Canada had 60 percent of the total population, it should get 60 percent of the seats. Instead, Lower Canada and Upper Canada each got 42 seats in the new Legislative Assembly. The 490 000 French Canadians felt cheated out of some of the seats they would have won through representation by population. What share of seats would Lower Canada have had under representation by population?

Louis-Hippolyte La Fontaine
A MAN OF MODERATION

Could Upper and Lower Canada successfully be joined? As the two provinces moved toward union, Louis-Hippolyte La Fontaine stepped into the foreground. He was not new to the battles between the French people and the British government. He had already played a role in the tumultuous events of the previous few years.

Louis-Hippolyte La Fontaine was born October 4, 1807, near Boucherville, Lower Canada. He was the son of a carpenter and the grandson of Antoine Ménard La Fontaine, a member of Lower Canada's Legislative Assembly from 1796 to 1804. A diligent law student, Louis-Hippolyte was called to the bar in 1828. He married Adèle Berthelot, the daughter of a rich lawyer in Québec. In 1830, 22-year-old La Fontaine was elected to the Assembly of Lower Canada.

Like many loyal French Canadians, La Fontaine was a *Patriote* under Louis-Joseph Papineau. Favouring compromise over force, however, he turned away from Papineau as the *Patriotes* became more violent. When Papineau issued the call to arms for the Rebellion of 1837, La Fontaine did not answer that call. Instead, he travelled to England to try, unsuccessfully, to solve the problem democratically. When he returned to Canada five months later, he was placed in jail as a French *Patriote* but was released shortly afterward. Later still, he served as a negotiator between the government and the eight imprisoned *Patriote* leaders exiled in Bermuda. This was a testament to his level-headedness.

La Fontaine was what many would describe as a model politician. He attended church regularly, and was a very upright and moral citizen. Although not an eloquent speaker, he was very persuasive. This logical and moderate man is said never to have lost his temper, despite the politically volatile times in which he lived.

La Fontaine and Robert Baldwin became best friends when Baldwin offered La Fontaine a chance to represent York District in the Assembly in 1841. La Fontaine returned the favour the following year by sponsoring Baldwin's candidacy in the French riding of Rimouski, which he won. They remained both friends and allies until Baldwin's death in 1858.

After serving as Attorney General of Canada East and premier of the united Canadas, La Fontaine left politics in 1851. In 1853 he became Chief Justice of Lower Canada and maintained this position until his death in 1864. Although he did not live to see the federated nation of Canada, his efforts to stabilize the country were recognized during his lifetime. In 1854 he was made a baronet by Queen Victoria and a papal knight by Pope Pius IX.

More people you could research are

Charles Bagot

Francis Hincks

Louis-Hippolyte La Fontaine

John Neilson

Charles Poulett Thompson (Lord Sydenham)

Denis-Benjamin Viger

Lord Sydenham, Governor General of Canada, 1841

Worse discoveries followed. English was the only language that could be used in the legislature and government. To French Canadians, the British government and its supporters seemed intent on killing their culture!

The French Canadian people also found that they would be responsible for Upper Canada's debts from such projects as the Welland and St. Lawrence canals. The new Governor General, Charles Poulett Thompson (soon dubbed Lord Sydenham), had made the Upper Canadians an offer they could not refuse. Taxes and duties produced by Montréal shipping and manufacturing would help to pay off Upper Canada's crushing debts. On the promise of this deal, the Assembly of Upper Canada had agreed to the union of Upper and Lower Canada.

Another matter that stirred loud opposition was control of **patronage**, or the power to appoint and pay public servants. The Act of Union gave this power to the Governor General and listed the pay that many officials would receive. Such appointments would not be open to review or refusal by the Legislative Assembly. Many people in both provinces wanted to make all government taxation and spending subject to review by the democratically elected representatives of the people.

The new union seemed to have no place for responsible government. Lord Durham had recommended that the new province should be self-governing in its own affairs. The British colonial secretary, Lord John Russell, had made this clear, instructing Sydenham to keep the Assembly's support at all times, unless its actions threatened "the honour of the Crown or the interests of the Empire."

The test of "responsibility," you will recall, was that the governor's advisors would have to be elected members of the Legislative Assembly and answerable to the Assembly. They would be the leaders of the party that could command a majority in the Assembly by vote, not because they were the Governor General's friends.

Lord Sydenham, however, appointed his friends and tried to make sure they were elected to the Assembly. He appointed Robert Baldwin, a lawyer from Toronto, to be solicitor general. Later Sydenham invited him to sit on the Executive Council, but it was just a token appointment.

Like most of his compatriots, Louis-Hippolyte La Fontaine began calling for a **repeal**, or cancellation, of the Act of Union. La Fontaine soon took a different view, however. What started him to change his thinking was a letter from Toronto newspaper editor Francis Hincks. This immigrant from Ireland started *The Examiner* in 1838 to promote the cause of peaceful reform.

Hincks was excited by the union of the two provinces. He believed that the new province of Canada could be of benefit to both French and British Canadians if they joined forces. Together, the reformers outnumbered the people who wanted to follow separate paths. The nationalists in the two provinces would never join forces and work together.

Soon after the Durham Report was published, Hincks wrote the first of many letters to La Fontaine. In it he wrote: "If . . . you are really desirous of liberal institutions & economical government, the union would. . .give you all you could desire, as an United Parliament would have an immense Reform Majority." Out of this small beginning would grow a powerful partnership. Francis Hincks and Robert Baldwin led the reformers in Upper Canada, while La Fontaine became the leader of reformers in Lower Canada.

Newspaper publisher Francis Hincks became one of Canada's outstanding politicians and, later, a builder of railways. He pressed for co-operation between reformers in the two former provinces of Canada.

Two Provinces Become One

The Province of Canada came into being on February 10, 1841. It had two parts: Lower Canada, which was now called Canada East, and Upper Canada, which was now called Canada West. However, people continued to use the old names for decades.

Governor General Sydenham called for elections to return representatives to the new Legislative Assembly. The elections began at the end of March and ran for three weeks. The elections stirred up great resentment. The reformers had to compete with the nationalists. The nationalist leaders in Canada East, John Neilson and Denis-Benjamin Viger, hoped to repeal the Act of Union. Their party did well in that election.

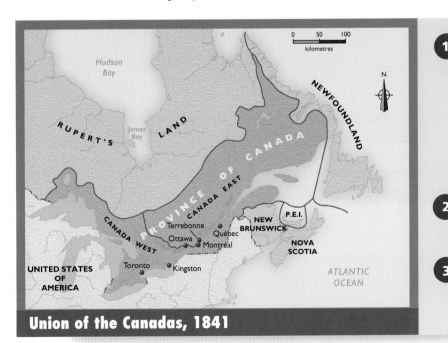

Union of the Canadas, 1841

1. Which of Canada's present-day provinces were included in the Province of Canada established in 1841? What were their names at the time? What were their previous names?

2. Which of the provinces shown on this map were not included?

3. Which present-day provinces were included in Rupert's Land?

Nationalist leader
Denis-Benjamin Viger
of Canada East

Louis-Hippolyte La Fontaine was one of many reformers who lost his election race. He lost despite having been his area's representative for eight years, and the fact that the French Canadian population of Terrebonne outnumbered the British Canadian population ten to one. As in several other **ridings**, or political areas led by a member of Parliament or of the Legislative Assembly, the election in Terrebonne was marred by the threat of violence. At least four people died in riots at polling stations. The Governor General shamelessly meddled in electoral politics to make sure his supporters won. An editorial in the *Montreal Herald* openly supported the meddling: "From the known character of the majority of the electors in Terrebonne, we doubt not La Fontaine would be returned if all the votes were polled; but it must be the duty of the loyalists to muster in their strength and keep the poll!"

Can you guess what the newspaper meant by "keeping the poll"? Before the election, La Fontaine had been warned that there would be thugs at the polling station ready to frighten off people who wanted to vote for their opponents. La Fontaine gathered 800 people and made for the only polling station in his riding. They were greeted by a hostile mob, better armed and ready to fight. La Fontaine decided not to fight. Not many of his supporters risked crossing the line to declare their vote.

After the election Baldwin insisted that some of the French Canadian reformers be invited to sit on the Executive Council. Sydenham refused and, when Baldwin pressed him, Sydenham removed him from the council. Sydenham's supporters rejoiced, thinking that Baldwin's political career was over.

On June 14, 1841, the Legislative Assembly of the new Province of Canada opened with great fanfare. The location was a converted hospital in Kingston, in Canada West. For the people of Canada East it was a very special day. For the first time in three-and-a-half years, their elected representatives could meet and discuss public business.

On that hot June day in 1841, only a few familiar faces turned up as members of the Legislative Assembly. Robert Baldwin was one of only six reformers returned from Upper Canada. Clearly it would be an uphill struggle for the reformers even to achieve a majority in the Legislative Assembly.

La Fontaine had to convince the French Canadian people to work within the new system.

A few months later, Baldwin invited La Fontaine to run for office in the Toronto area. Baldwin had been elected in two ridings, but he occupied only one seat in the Legislative Assembly. La Fontaine accepted the offer to run in a by-election held in September 1841. The following year La Fontaine took his seat in the Legislative Assembly, representing the voters of York District's fourth riding.

To the French Canadian people, Sydenham was just one more tyrannical governor forcing them to follow the British way. However, his government developed rules that put someone in charge of every department. Every decision followed a chain of command, from the Governor General down to the letter carriers and road-building crews. One of the features of responsible government is that an elected official is accountable for, or answerable to, the success or failure of government programs. Consequently, Sydenham is credited with helping Canada move toward responsible government.

Lord Sydenham's motto was *harmony*, but his personality, not the principle of responsibility, was what kept members of the Legislative Assembly working together. Sydenham was always able to influence and amend motions to keep a majority of the

Kingston was the first capital of the new Province of Canada. The selection of the garrison city on Lake Ontario was a compromise and it only lasted for three years. The Legislative Assembly voted to move the capital to Montréal in 1844.

Legislative Assembly on his side. The real test would be whether his hand-picked Executive Council would resign if the Assembly opposed its decisions.

Before it came to that, Sydenham died. He fell off his horse and suffered an infection in his leg that quickly spread. With his passing, the fortunes of the reformers began to change.

The Story So Far . . .

1 How did Francis Hincks convince Louis-Hippolyte La Fontaine to work within the parliamentary system?

2 You are a French Canadian citizen. Write a letter to the editor of a newspaper outlining your views on the united Province of Canada.

3 Design a poster for the election of 1841. First, choose which side you will represent. Who is your candidate and for what riding? Write a platform (program) and a slogan. Remember, in advertising, "less is more!"

ON THE WAY TO RESPONSIBLE GOVERNMENT

The next Governor General of Canada, Sir Charles Bagot, arrived in Kingston in the winter of 1842. In Britain, the winds of change had swept through the government since Sydenham's death. Following an election, a new government was in power in London.

Bagot's instructions were to draw French Canadians into the government of Canada. Bagot asked La Fontaine and other French Canadian reform members of the Legislative Assembly to join the Executive Council. La Fontaine insisted on having Robert Baldwin on the council as well. Bagot worked hard to avoid letting the reformers take total control of the Executive Council. He succeeded, but lost the support of the pro-government party in Upper Canada. They viewed La Fontaine as a dangerous traitor.

When the second session of the Canadian Parliament began in September 1842, a dramatic scene unfolded in the Legislative Assembly. La Fontaine rose to make his first speech since being elected. He spoke in French. A British Canadian member from

Sir Charles Bagot, Governor General of Canada, 1842

Canada West interrupted him, asking that he follow the rules of the Assembly and speak in English. La Fontaine replied in French. Here is a translation of part of his speech:

> *Even if I knew English as well as French, I would still make my first speech in the language of my French Canadian countrymen, if only to protest solemnly the cruel injustice of that part of the Act of Union which aims to proscribe* [that is, forbid] *the mother tongue of half the population of Canada.*

La Fontaine raised the issue of language rights again and again. He used the threat to Canadien culture as a rallying cry — and to keep himself in power.

On September 19, 1842, the Governor General announced the new Executive Council. Louis-Hippolyte La Fontaine was appointed Attorney General East, and Robert Baldwin was appointed Attorney General West. This practice of dual appointments continued as long as the Province of Canada existed. It recognized that Canada was really two separate and distinct provinces, each requiring its own administration. What a reversal this was! The whole idea of the union was to submerge French Canada in a British Canadian-dominated government. It now seemed that the French **party**, or a group with similar interests and aims, was in charge. In fact, the Executive Council was a coalition or temporary association of different interests.

As the leader of the dominant group in the Legislative Assembly, La Fontaine was able to pursue a fair deal for his people. He had the election laws changed, hoping to avoid a repetition of the violence that erupted in 1841. He had the capital moved to Montréal. He started negotiating for the amnesty, or pardon, of rebel leaders who were living in exile or prison.

The first La Fontaine–Baldwin ministry, or time of service under these leaders, lasted only a year. Early in 1843, Sir Charles Bagot resigned and died before he could leave Canada. His replacement was Sir Charles Metcalfe, who had been governor of Jamaica. Metcalfe was not used to making deals, and he soon undid the progress the government had made toward achieving responsible government. He did not consult with the Executive Council before making appointments. You can probably guess the result. On November 26, 1843, Baldwin, La Fontaine, and their supporters resigned from the Executive Council. The election that followed was even more violent than in 1841. Many reformers were defeated. For the next four years, La Fontaine had to be content with being the leader of the **opposition** party in the Legislative Assembly.

Metcalfe succeeded in luring members of the nationalist French Canadian group into the Executive Council, along with British Canadian Tories, as the pro-government party was beginning to be known. La Fontaine scorned his compatriots for teaming up with their rivals. To the reformers, responsible government meant maintaining unity within the party, not making coalitions.

As if there were a curse on the job of Governor General, Metcalfe soon died, and the fourth governor in as many years put on the robes of state. By the time Lord Cathcart, the new Governor General, left Canada in 1847, the British Empire itself had changed.

The opening of Canada's Parliament on November 28, 1844. Under the crimson canopy is Governor General Sir Charles Metcalfe.

Rosanna Mullins Leprohon
PRIDE OF ENGLISH AND FRENCH CANADA

In the midst of the French-British clash of government, Rosanna Leprohon was able to bridge the gap between the nationalities in a way politicians could not. An English woman living in French Canada, she found common ground with all of her fellow Canadians.

She was born Rosanna Eleanor Mullins in Montréal in 1829. Her father, originally from Ireland, was a prosperous merchant. Rosanna was educated at Montréal's Convent of the Congregation of Nôtre Dame. The nuns who taught her encouraged her to write.

While she was still a teenager, her first poem was published in 1846 in the Montréal magazine *Literary Garland*. After that, she became a regular contributor. Most of her poems expressed a high regard for the important work done by religious communities, as well as her sympathy for struggling immigrants. In 1847 the magazine published her first work of fiction in instalments.

Soon after, she began writing novels that the magazine published in instalments as well. The first was *Ida Beresford* in 1848, which was praised by fellow writer Susanna Moodie. That novel and the three that followed it, *Florence Fitz Hardinge* (1849), *Eva Huntington* (1850), and *Clarence Fitz Clarence* (1851), peeled away the glamour from England's fashionable upper class and depicted society life as cold and superficial. Although her writing was very popular, she had yet to produce her most notable work.

Then in 1851 something happened that changed the focus of Rosanna's writing. She married Dr. Jean-Lucien Leprohon, a physician whose ancestors had come to New France in the eighteenth century. They began a family that eventually included 13 children. A few years later, Rosanna's writing began to centre around French Canadian society with French Canadians as their main characters. First came *The Manor House of de Villerai* in 1859, then *Antoinette de Mirecourt* in 1864, and *Armand Durand* in 1868. The three stories of French society were popular among British Canadian readers. More surprising was that all three were quickly translated into French and were enjoyed by many French Canadians as well.

A popular writer of her era, Rosanna Mullins Leprohon continued to write poems, periodical articles, and another novel before her death in 1881. She has the distinction of being one of this country's first British writers to depict French Canadian life in a way that gained favour with all Canadians, regardless of their ancestry.

Other people you could research are

Elizabeth Bruyère

Sir John Franklin

Paul Kane

Jean-Lucien Leprohon

Rosanna Mullins Leprohon

THE END OF AN EMPIRE

Before the coming of the railways, the St. Lawrence River served as the passageway for immigrants coming into Canada. The great river also carried wheat, timber, and other products to the ocean for export to Britain. Foods and raw materials from Canada helped the British economy grow, and Canada absorbed some of Britain's growing population. Britain supported the "Empire of the St. Lawrence" by constructing canals and by encouraging exports of Canadian products through preferential tariffs — those tariffs maintained by British Corn Laws especially.

Preferential tariffs were one part of the old mercantile trade system, and trade monopolies were another. To promote the growth of the empire, Britain would award companies a monopoly on trade in a large area. For example, the Hudson's Bay Company had a monopoly on trade in Rupert's Land, the huge area that drained into Hudson Bay. Trading monopolies were enforced by Navigation Acts or laws. These acts controlled shipping in all the harbours of British North America.

Canada's sluggish economy showed that the mercantile system did not work very well. On top of that, Canadians quarrelled over how to develop their transportation system. In the bigger province, Lower Canada, the Assembly refused to help Upper Canada's economy grow. Shipping duties on products from Upper Canada had to be paid for them to go through the ocean ports of Lower Canada. Lower Canada also refused to help pay for canals that would open the upper St. Lawrence River to navigation.

The merchants of Montréal had told Lord Durham that there was a simple solution to this problem. The two provinces should be joined. It would be easier to build the economy of a single province with one legislature. Montréal, naturally, would remain the centre of the inland empire.

Uniting Upper and Lower Canada did promote the growth of the Empire of the St. Lawrence for a while. Soon, however, more trade began running through the United States than through Montréal. American tariffs began to give preference to wheat and other Canadian goods that were bound

Québec City in the early 1800s was a busy shipping centre.

overseas, as well as to foreign goods that were shipped to Canada. The Drawback Acts of 1845 and 1846 reduced duties the United States had previously imposed on goods going through its ports. Now farmers in Canada West could get a break when they shipped their wheat through American ports. Business people in Toronto liked the Drawback Acts because more goods passed through their city. How do you think the merchants and shippers of Montréal felt? They saw their business slipping away to American competitors. They tried to get the Navigation Acts applied to shipping on the Great Lakes.

In the middle of this struggle, famine stalked Britain. In 1846 a blight caused the entire potato crop to rot in Ireland. Thousands of people starved to death. Summer rain destroyed England's wheat crop. The weather that brought disaster to Britain meant a great opportunity for Canadian farmers. The export of wheat and flour rose dramatically in 1846.

But the farmers' success was short-lived. The disasters in Britain led to a crisis in their government. Prime Minister Sir Robert Peel searched for a way of feeding Britain's people. His government's solution to the crisis was to get rid of the tariffs that drove up the prices of food. The government thus repealed the Corn Laws. Soon it also repealed the Navigation Acts. The old mercantile system of the British Empire came crashing down. In its place a new empire emerged, one which was based on **free trade**. Whoever sold goods for the lowest prices would get Britain's business.

Canadian farmers and merchants felt betrayed. They had to compete with other countries, and the cost of shipping their products across the ocean made them more expensive. Many Canadian farms failed and many shipping businesses suddenly dried up. The newly opened locks on the St. Lawrence River sat unused. The Montréal docks were strangely quiet.

But changes in British and American trade laws were not the only causes of Canada's economic problems. Larger forces were at work. Beginning in 1847, a serious depression set in worldwide. This was worse than the depression that haunted Canada beginning in 1837. It lasted for four long years.

Also at this time, Canada was inundated with refugees, many from the Irish potato famine. Many immigrants brought cholera and typhus with them. Doctors had learned nothing about the spread of infectious diseases in the intervening 15 years. The horrors of 1832 were repeated, with even more deaths.

Reflections

You are a doctor working on Grosse Île in 1847. Irish immigrants arrive by the boatload every day. The toll that cholera and typhus takes among them is terrible. You have your own ideas about the way disease spreads, but you have few tools to work with. Government officials and other doctors ignore your methods. Write a few journal entries to show your work in a typical day.

Web Connection

http://www.school.mcgrawhill.ca/resource

Go to the web site above to find out more about the quarantine station at Grosse Île. Go to History Resources, then to *Canada: The Story of Our Heritage* to see where to go next.

Here is a chart showing the effects of the diseases.

	Immigrant Deaths at Grosse Île		
Year	Number of Immigrants at Port of Québec	Number of Patients and Burials at Grosse Île	
		Patients	Burials
1846	32 753	892	69
1847	90 150	8 691	5 424

Loyal Canadians felt abandoned by their parent country. For reform-minded politicians, on the other hand, the collapse of the British Empire provided a great opportunity.

The Story So Far . . .

1 Why did La Fontaine and Baldwin resign from Metcalfe's government?

2 What caused Britain to adopt free trade and abandon the "Empire of the St. Lawrence"? How did the change affect the movement toward responsible government in Canada?

This portrait of Lord Elgin was taken in 1848 by Montréal photographer Thomas Coffin Doane. It is one of the earliest photographs made in Canada.

RESPONSIBLE GOVERNMENT AT LAST

With the coming of free trade in 1846, Britain no longer had a stake in maintaining the Empire of the St. Lawrence. Its objections to responsible government vanished.

In January 1847, a new Governor General of British North America arrived in Montréal. James Bruce, eighth Earl of Elgin, was 36 years old. His wife was the daughter of Lord Durham. While Lord Durham was rich, Lord Elgin was not — his father had squandered a fortune. Lord Elgin was like Lord Durham, however, in his belief in responsible government.

At the end of 1848, during Lord Elgin's first year in Canada, the province had another election. This time, the reformers won 32 seats in Canada East and 23 in Canada West. The Tory members of the Executive Council resigned. Lord Elgin asked Robert Baldwin and La Fontaine to form a new government. He promised to support its decisions. In March 1848 Lord Elgin swore in the new government. La Fontaine was appointed Attorney General for Canada East. As the leader who had the

Thomas Coffin Doane
DAGUERREOTYPIST OF THE ELITE

The political face of Canada was not the only thing changing in the 1830s and 1840s. An important technological invention was about to revolutionize the recording of history and change the lives of artists like Thomas Doane forever.

Thomas Coffin Doane was born in Barrington, Nova Scotia, in 1814. He was an artist who made his living painting portraits in oil. It was fashionable for the wealthy to commission pictures of themselves and their families. Many customers even bought miniature portraits that they used as calling cards. For a competent artist like Doane, business was brisk.

This began to change on August 19, 1839, when the Institut de France in Paris made an exciting announcement: Louis Daguerre had invented a new process, daguerreotypes. This was one of the earliest forms of photography. The exposure time for a daguerreotype image was between 8 and 30 minutes — too long for a person to sit completely still. By the following March, however, improvements were made and a picture could be taken in just 30 seconds.

Daguerreotype portraits quickly became popular. Newly trained daguerreotypists travelled from town to town offering their services. Regular portrait artists began to lose business. How could their portraits compete with photographs that were ready in a fraction of the time? Like many artists, Thomas Doane decided he would have to learn this technique to survive.

In March 1843, Doane travelled to St. John's, Newfoundland, with another artist, William Valentine. The two men set up a makeshift studio at the local inn, and for a few weeks, made what were probably the first photographs in that province.

Eventually daguerreotypes progressed from a novelty to the norm. Permanent studios replaced temporary ones. Doane established a gallery in Montréal in 1846 and was soon photographing the city's elite citizens. Already successful, his status increased in 1855 when his work received an honourable mention award at a Paris exhibition.

Doane continued taking daguerreotypes until about 1865, when he retired from photography. For the rest of his life, he reverted to painting portraits, at first in Boston and later in New York, until his death in 1896.

Doane helped usher in a completely new artistic medium. Photographer of countless Montréal citizens, including Lord Elgin and Louis-Joseph Papineau and their families, his work provides us with some of the earliest accurate images of famous people in Canadian history.

Other people you could research are

James Bruce (Lord Elgin)

Thomas Coffin Doane

François-Xavier Garneau

John Alexander Macdonald

William Valentine

In this modern rendition of an election victory, Joseph Howe is carried on his supporters' shoulders. Nova Scotia was the first province in British North America to win responsible government, a month before the province of Canada did. Howe, a newspaper editor and politician, took up the reform cause in the 1830s. He was a member of the reform party when it was called to form a government in February 1848. He had worked for years to make responsible government a reality in the Maritime province. There, the change to responsible government was accomplished peacefully.

Snippet

Tories

The term *Tory* was originally used in Britain for a person of the party that favoured royal power and opposed change. During the American Revolution the term applied to those who wanted to remain under British rule.

larger following, he became the premier. Baldwin became Attorney General for Canada West and co-premier. The Governor General was no longer in charge of Canada's government. He was now simply the representative of the British monarch.

The achievement of responsible government still had to be tested. When the Legislative Assembly met in February 1849, La Fontaine introduced a bill to compensate, or repay, innocent people who suffered losses in Lower Canada during the rebellions. A similar bill, amounting to £40 000, had been settled in Upper Canada in 1845. What about the people of Lower Canada who watched helplessly as British soldiers burned their houses in Saint-Eustache, Saint-Benôit, and Napierville? What about those whose properties the Glengarry Scots looted? For many Canadiens the bitter feelings over their cruel treatment were just as strong after ten years. Justice demanded the victims be compensated. The total claims amounted to £100 000.

In the House of Assembly, there were brawls and fistfights while the Rebellion Losses Bill was debated. Loyal Tories accused the government of rewarding traitors. Finally, in April, the Assembly took a vote on the Rebellion Losses Bill. The reformers and French nationalists voted in favour of it, while the Tories voted against it. The bill passed. Would Lord Elgin follow the decisions of the Assembly or would he follow the advice of the Tories and veto it?

The Evidence Behind the Story

The Rebellion Losses Bill stirred opposition throughout the Province of Canada. This poster (abridged) appeared on the streets of Toronto before Governor General Lord Elgin visited the city.

PROCLAMATION!

Britons of the City of Toronto! — Britons of the Home District!

Shall the rank rebels be permitted to tell us (as they now do) that they will drive the bloody Tories out of the country? Up to your duty, and let us no more Slumber! [Lord Elgin] is expected to arrive in Toronto on the 20th. . . . And shall Elgin, who pardoned the scoundrels whose hands were red with the blood of Weir and Usher, and Chartrand, and our own gallant Moodie, Elgin, who spurned the respectful petitions, and mocked the hopes of 100 000 of the loyal hearts of Canada, and who wantonly and clandestinely sanctioned the Bill loading and grinding down us and our children with taxes for twenty years to come, to reward rebels and murderers — shall Elgin, who is now, from his garrisoned residence. . . be permitted to be welcomed by a gang of sneaking radicals, in the good old loyal city of Toronto? No! No!

. . .By the blood of the murdered Moodie, who fell a victim to the radicalism of Upper Canada — by all that we hold near and dear, we publicly and solemnly warn the individual who calls himself James Bruce, and Her Majesty's Representative in Canada, and his rebel partisans, against any attempt to outrage and insult the feelings of the loyalists of Toronto by making a party triumph of his visit to Toronto — that is, if he or they dare to come! He and they shall receive such treatment as their past and present conduct towards Canadian loyalists deserves. . . . Let your eggs be stale and your powder dry! Down with Elgin! — Down with the Rebels!

QUESTIONING THE EVIDENCE

1. **What are the author's views about the Governor General? What words and phrases convey the author's attitude? Would you take the author's words seriously? Why or why not?**

2. **What are the author's views about the Rebellion Losses Bill? What words and phrases tell you? What does the author say will be the consequences of the bill? Do you accept that as true? How could you evaluate its truth?**

3. **What do you think was the author's ultimate goal? How does it compare with your own view of the significance of Canadian political events of 1848–1849? What would have been the result if the author and others like her or him had been successful?**

M11588,
Attributed to
Joseph Légaré,
The Burning of the
Parliament Building in
Montréal (detail), ca. 1849, oil
on wood. McCord Museum of Canadian
History, Montréal.

Imagine you are a British Canadian resident of Montréal, loyal to the British Queen. You just heard that the Legislative Assembly has passed the Rebellion Losses Bill. Public money will be given to people who may have participated in the rebellions of 1837 and 1838. You have been waiting for years to see more money spent to improve transportation in Canada.

Or, you could assume you are a Canadien living in Saint-Eustache or Napierville. You had nothing to do with the rebellions but some of your relatives did. For that, General Colborne's troops burned your home. Scottish raiders from Upper Canada stole your horses and farming equipment. You have been waiting for compensation ever since.

Study the people in the foreground of this painting. What do they seem to be doing? Now, step into the picture. You are one of the people in the mob. How do you feel as you watch the Parliament buildings burn? Excited? Angry? Sweaty? Afraid? How do the people around you make you feel? What are you thinking about? Are you glad you participated? Will you get caught? Was it worth it? Talk with a group about this experience, then role-play a short scene depicting your participation in the burning of the Parliament buildings.

Lord Elgin signed the Rebellion Losses Bill into law on April 25, 1849. As he left the Parliament building, his carriage was pelted with rotten eggs. Barely an hour later, a mob of about 1500 people gathered at the Parliament building in Montréal. While the Legislative Assembly was still sitting, a British Canadian mob started throwing rocks through the windows. Eventually they set fire to the Parliament building, burning it to the ground.

The next day, a rioting crowd attacked La Fontaine's new, as yet unoccupied, home, and gutted it. For a week the mobs continued to spread terror. Lord Elgin's carriage was attacked again, this time with rocks. He feared for his life but he did not back down. From then on, wrote one historian, "Canadians. . . had to take the responsibility. . .for running their own affairs."

Snapshot

The Moving Capital

Montréal was supposed to be the permanent home of the Canadian government, but after the riots of April 25, 1849, the government took to alternating between Toronto and Québec. The Parliament building on Toronto's King Street was the centre of government until 1851, and again from 1855 to 1859, while Québec hosted the Legislative Assembly from 1851 to 1855 and from 1859 to 1865. Finally, when the Parliament buildings opened in Ottawa in 1865, that city became Canada's permanent capital.

The Parliament buildings in Ottawa, built in 1865

The Story So Far . . .

1 You are a newspaper reporter assigned to cover the burning of the Parliament building in Montreal on April 25, 1848. Write an account that includes the points of view of the mob, the people who passed the Rebellion Losses Bill, and the Governor General.

2 You are an advertising agent hired to sell the idea of responsible government to the people of Canada. Make up advertisements for print and voice media that explain what it is, how it works, and why it is better than the old system of government.

SUM IT UP!

The Act of Union in 1840 created the Province of Canada. Britain's intention was to assimilate French Canada, but the act's effect was the opposite. Under the union, reformers from the two former provinces formed an alliance. Led by Robert Baldwin, Francis Hincks, and Louis-Hippolyte La Fontaine, the reformers slowly took control of the new Legislative Assembly. At first the British government was unwilling to grant responsible government to the province. By 1842 the reformers convinced Governor General Sir Charles Bagot to admit their leaders into the Executive Council, an important step toward responsible government.

Soon the reformers were voted out of office, and they spent four years in opposition. Famine and other misfortunes in Britain forced the British government to adopt free trade and stop protecting its colonies in British North America. With this change, Britain's opposition to responsible government ended.

When the reformers were returned to power in 1848, Governor General Lord Elgin invited Baldwin and La Fontaine to choose the Executive Councillors from their party, which had again won a majority of seats in the Assembly. Their government was tested the following year, when the Rebellion Losses Bill passed in the Legislative Assembly. Although riots broke out in Montréal, Lord Elgin refused to intervene. The Executive Council was now independent of Britain, and Canada was self-governing in its own affairs.

THINKING ABOUT YOUR LEARNING

1. Construct a time line that shows Canada's progress toward responsible government in the 1840s.
2. Design a poster commemorating Canada's first responsible government under Robert Baldwin and Louis-Hippolyte La Fontaine.

APPLYING YOUR LEARNING

1. Research one of the following topics or choose one of your own. Create questions to guide your research.
   - the movement to establish responsible government in the Maritime provinces in the 1840s
   - revolutions to create more democracy in European countries in 1848
   - the potato famine in Ireland
   - the Governor General's job after the achievement of responsible government

2. Free elections are an important part of democracy. Stage an election campaign and vote in your class. Form parties that choose leaders to run. Nominate an independent committee to make up the rules for voting and to oversee the balloting. After the election, discuss how governments can make sure elections are free and fair.

3. The legislative union of Upper and Lower Canada lasted less than 30 years. In its place, Canadian leaders created a federal union. Each province had its own government, and a federal government took care of matters of common concern. This is how Canada operates today. How is federal union different from legislative union?

USING KEY WORDS

1. On a separate sheet of paper, write the answers for the blank spaces in sentences a–h, using the correct word or phrase from the following list.

free trade
Legislative Assembly
nationalists
opposition
patronage
party
repeal
riding

a) The Canadians who wanted to break the British ties were called _____.

b) La Fontaine called for a _____, or cancellation, of the Act of Union.

c) When Britain adopted a policy of _____, it had no reason to continue ruling British North America.

d) The reformers found they had a majority of seats in the _____.

e) _____ are political areas led by a member of Parliament or of the Legislative Assembly.

f) When the reformers lost an election they had to be content to be the _____ party in the Assembly.

g) In Canada, the _____ that holds a majority of seats in the legislature forms the government.

h) The people of Upper and Lower Canada opposed _____, or the Governor-General's power to appoint and pay public servants.

UNIT 3

Conflict and Change

CONNECTING YOUR LEARNING

UNDERSTANDING CONCEPTS

1 Describe the society and way of life of the habitants in Lower Canada in the period 1815–1848. Include details about their environment and surroundings, their property and work, the things they produced, their food, dress, habits, religion, education, and any other notable details.

2 Write a biography of a member of a family settling in Upper Canada, showing why they might have immigrated, how they got there, and what they had to do to get started.

3 In what way(s) did the rebellions of Lower and Upper Canada succeed?

4 How was responsible government different from colonial government? Consider the following points in your answer:
- the way the ruler was chosen
- the choice of advisors for the Executive Council
- the test or proof that Canada's government was responsible

DEVELOPING RESEARCH SKILLS

1 In a democracy, conflicts are resolved by non-violent means. Think about the conflicts you have studied in this unit. In groups, discuss the circumstances when people tried to settle their disagreements by violent means, and those when they used non-violent ways. Report to the class on the conclusions you reached about the causes of violence.

2 The government of Québec staged a referendum on sovereignty, or independence from Canada. The sovereignty side lost, but the result was very close. And the government wants to hold another. In groups, conduct an opinion poll of people living on your street or in your neighbourhood. In your poll, include questions asking people:
- Should Québec be allowed to separate from Canada?
- If so, should it be unilaterally or by negotiation?
- If by negotiation, with what conditions?
- If not, what measures should Canada take to keep Québec in Confederation? By offering special deals? By the use of force?

Compile the results of your poll and present them to the class with your interpretation of their meaning. Then discuss what it would mean for you and for Canada if Québec separated.

3 Compile a list of street names with historical associations in your community. Trace the origins of the names. Classify them according to origins — people, places, events, or other. Map and display your findings. (It is probably best to choose one neighbourhood.)

COMMUNICATING REQUIRED KNOWLEDGE

1 Write a letter to a sovereigntist student in French Canada, persuading him or her not to separate. Use your knowledge of history to make an argument in favour of co-operation and against separation.

2 Construct a one-page cartoon or storyboard to tell the story of an incident in the rebellions of 1837 or 1838.

3 This cartoon, published in the magazine *Punch in Canada*, pokes fun at the Rebellion Losses Bill. In 1849, thousands of people flocked to California to pan for gold. Canada was in the depths of a depression, with thousands of people out of work. What is the cartoonist's point of view toward the Rebellion Losses Bill? Translate the dialogue into modern language.

CANADA *versus* CALIFORNIA.

Hiram. 'Say Zeb! I'm off right slick away for California. My wings is grew, and my nails is mad for diggin'!

Zeb. California be bust!—Canada's the washin for me; I guess I'll squat there, where Government pays for Rebellion and no questions axed!

APPLYING CONCEPTS AND SKILLS

1 On November 11, 1947, Winston Churchill said: "Democracy is the worst form of government except all [the others]." Discuss the meaning of the quotation. Then make a poster or advertisement for democracy that uses the quotation. Include illustrations and text showing the different elements of democracy, such as free elections, representative government, executive responsibility, and so on. Display your work.

2 On a sheet of paper, complete the mind map on the right to show the connections between different forces at work in Upper Canada during the period of 1815 to 1840.

3 In some ways Canada is very similar to the United States; in other ways, it is strikingly different. In groups of three or four, discuss the traits that mark Canadians as different. Create a skit or play that illustrates the differences. Your skit could be about Americans paying a summertime visit to their Canadian cousins, for example.

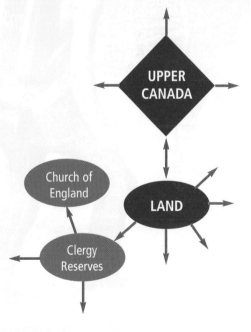

UPPER CANADA

Church of England

LAND

Clergy Reserves

The Story Today

SETTING OUR FOCUS

You have learned a lot about Canada and Canadians from the past. Remember Champlain, Count Frontenac, and Jeanne Mance? They helped to build the colony of New France. Laura Secord, John Graves Simcoe, and Colonel John By helped to build Upper Canada. There were many other builders, such as Mary Brant and other Loyalists, who came from the United States. They were followed by William Lyon Mackenzie, Louis-Joseph Papineau, Egerton Ryerson, and settlers like Susanna Moodie. In this chapter you will see how some of the people, places, and events that you learned about still have an impact on Canada today. There are many ways Canada reflects its Aboriginal, British, and French heritage, its role as a refuge for people escaping persecution, and its nearness to the United States. There are many aspects of Canada's story that we might highlight for their impact on the country today. We have chosen these five in particular. Our Canada Day celebration photograph can serve as a starting point for our learning.

On the left is a scene familiar to many Canadians — a Canada Day celebration. The people at this event are linked to many others who have come before them to build Canada and create the country's stories. These are the builders: Aboriginal Peoples, French colonists, British pioneers, American settlers, and immigrants and refugees from around the world.

PREVIEWING THE CHAPTER

In this chapter you will learn about these topics:
- **the effect Europeans had on the Aboriginal Peoples and what Canadians learned from them**
- **the influence the French heritage has had on Canada**
- **the influence the British heritage has had on Canada**
- **how Canada was, and still is, a safe haven for people from around the world**
- **the impact the United States had on Canada in the past and has today**

KEY WORDS

bilingual

Carnaval

descendants

motto

Québécois

referendum

safe haven

separatism

Members of Parliament display the new Canadian flag that was selected from thousands of designs in December 1964.

CANADIAN SYMBOLS

The Canadian Flag

It may seem hard to believe, but not very many years ago the maple leaf flag did not exist. Now you see it flying proudly from coast to coast. Our flag was first raised on February 15, 1965. The Prime Minister at that time, Lester Pearson, decided that Canada needed "a flag that is Canada's own, and only Canada's." What did he mean?

Until 1965, the Canadian flag had been either the *Union Jack* of Great Britain or the *Red Ensign*, which included a Union Jack. This is the flag of Great Britain, containing within it the flags of England, Scotland, Ireland, and Wales. Some Canadians were not happy about the flags that included the Union Jack because they did not originate in Canada. The government decided to hold a contest for the design of a new flag. Thousands of Canadians sent illustrations to the people in Parliament who were to choose the design. Canadians everywhere got caught up in the debate about the design of the new flag. It was an emotional issue.

We need our own flag, without British symbols on it. We are not part of Britain. We need a unique, Canadian flag.

What about the French Canadians? They don't want to be reminded of Canada's British heritage. Neither do all the Canadians from other cultures. They want a flag that is Canadian, not British.

We must retain the symbols of our British heritage on our flag. That's why we must keep the Red Ensign.

As you know, the maple leaf design was chosen for our flag. It was neither British nor French, but something new: Canadian. What other symbols convey our heritage?

The Canadian Coat of Arms

Look at the Canadian coat of arms. On it are many symbols from Canada's history. You will recognize some flags, flowers, animals, and other images. Take a closer look. With a partner, find and count the maple leaves. There are four. The maple leaf is an important Canadian symbol and is the centrepiece of the flag. Now find the lilies or fleur-de-lis. There are eight of them, including three on the flag on the right. They represent the French builders of the country, since the lily was an early symbol of France. Look for the lions. Six are visible. These and some of the other symbols represent our British heritage. You can see a Union Jack on the left, which is the flag of Britain.

Beneath the central lion you will see a shield with five separate sections. Three of these sections represent parts of Britain; a fourth represents France. Find out which three countries the British sections represent. The bottom section of the shield contains a common Canadian symbol, the maple leaf.

■ Canada's coat of arms

Now look at the bottom part of the coat of arms, beneath the shield. Here you will find some words on a banner, behind which are some leaves and flowers. These, too, represent our country's early builders. The Latin **motto**, or saying, *a mari usque ad mare* means *from sea to sea*. The leaves are the Scottish thistle and the Irish shamrock; the flowers are the English rose and the French lily. At the very top of the coat of arms, there is a crown that also represents our British heritage.

Now look at the three large animals on the coat of arms. Two are golden lions, representing our British heritage. One is a silver unicorn, a symbol of our French heritage.

The Story So Far . . .

1 Suppose you had an opportunity to design the Canadian flag. What would you include? Create a design and explain it.
2 A country's coat of arms includes many symbols. Create a coat of arms that you think represents Canada today.

LEARNING FROM THE ABORIGINAL PEOPLES

The very first peoples of what became Canada were Aboriginal Peoples. For thousands of years, they established themselves across this land, building communities, learning how to make the most of the resources of land and water, and passing on their learning to their children and children's children. From the eastern Atlantic coast to the western Pacific shore, Aboriginal communities grew and changed as the centuries passed. Some peoples used the resources of the forest: spruce, cedar, birch bark, elm, healing herbs, and edible plants. Others used the resources of the waters: fish, beaver, otter, and mosses. Many used the wildlife: elk, buffalo, and rabbit. When horses arrived in the 1600s, the Plains People had a new and wonderful addition to their culture. Now they could travel much farther more easily and carry bigger loads. Most bands in most parts of the continent were already involved in trading systems with other Aboriginal Peoples. Transportation routes were well established along the waterways that crossed the continent. Canoes of many designs carried people and their belongings and trade goods far from their home territories.

After many generations, the world changed forever for the Aboriginal Peoples: the first Europeans arrived. In what became Canadian waters, John Cabot and his sailors traded with the Aboriginal Peoples of the St. Lawrence River. Then came many centuries of contact between Aboriginal Peoples and Europeans, as the latter moved farther inland from their first landing sites along the Atlantic and St. Lawrence coasts. Soon, French settlers built settlements at Port Royal, then at Québec, Trois Rivières, Montréal, and beyond. Colonists came from the United States and Britain. The Aboriginal Peoples taught them many lessons in survival, trading, and transportation. In return, they got many diseases, a strange new religion, disruption of their lives, and new trade goods.

Remember the Aboriginal allies of Champlain, the Aboriginal trading partners of the French and British, and the role of the Aboriginal Peoples in war and peacetime during the time of New France and Upper and Lower Canada. What happened to the Aboriginal Peoples in the years that followed this period in time?

Today Aboriginal Peoples are dealing with the problems passed down from earlier generations, a result of their unfair treatment by non-Aboriginal Canadians and Europeans. They are working toward better health care in their communities, better education, better jobs, better homes for all who live in their communities. They are trying to maintain their languages and culture and feel pride in the value of their heritage in this country.

An Aboriginal person performs a dance at the Calgary Stampede in Alberta.

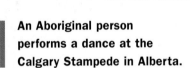

Web Connection

http://www.school.mcgrawhill.ca/resource

Go to the web site above to find out more about statistics of early Canada. Go to History Resources, then to *Canada: The Story of Our Heritage* to see where to go next.

The Story So Far . . .

1 Suppose you were to add an Aboriginal symbol to Canada's coat of arms. What might that symbol be? Where might it fit?

2 Discuss in class why you think there are no Aboriginal symbols on the coat of arms.

THE FRENCH CANADIAN INFLUENCE

The Canadian coat of arms includes symbols from three places: Britain, France, and Canada. As you learned in Unit 1: Early Settlement and New France, pioneers from France built New France into a thriving colony centred on the St. Lawrence River. The **descendants** of those habitants, voyageurs, and townspeople contribute to Canada in many ways today.

Bilingualism

One feature that sets Canada apart in the world is that it is officially **bilingual**, meaning it has two official languages: French and English. That is why signs, labels, packages, and instructions that originate in Canada appear in English and French.

"The Chip Wagon"© Carlo Italiano taken from Canadian Childhoods ©1989 Tundra Books Inc., selections from previously copyrighted works, all published by Tundra Books.

> Look at this painting from Montréal. Find evidence that it is winter and this is a bilingual community.

Many Canadians consider hockey to be part of our culture, whether in English, French, or another language. You may have read *The Hockey Sweater*, by Roch Carrier. Roch is an author from Québec who has written many stories about his childhood and his French-Canadian culture. *The Hockey Sweater* reminds us of some of the ways Canada is unique. It is a story about kids, hockey, the rivalry between two Canadian teams and their jerseys—and two languages.

When he was growing up in Québec, Roch and all his friends wore a sweater like their hero, Maurice Richard. He was an outstanding hockey player, and a star of the Montreal Canadiens. One day, Roch's Canadiens sweater had grown too small for him, so his mother ordered a new one from a catalogue. The order form was in English, Roch's mother was French-speaking, and she made a little mistake. To Roch, it was the worst mistake anyone could ever make. When he went to the post office to pick up his new sweater, a horrible surprise awaited him. The sweater was the blue-and-white Toronto Maple Leafs sweater, not the red-and-white Canadiens sweater. His mother had ordered the wrong one!

Roch was in agony, fearing the scorn of his friends. He felt ill having to wear the Leafs sweater. When he went on the rink to play, the other kids, the coach, and the referee all seemed to be against him. Roch thought it was because of his sweater. He lost his temper and was sent off the ice. In a church nearby, Roch said a special prayer. Read the book yourself to enjoy the surprise ending.

Holidays and Festivals

On June 24 each year, the people of Québec celebrate *Fête Nationale* — their national holiday. It is a chance for them to share in parades, picnics, music, dancing, and feasting. They celebrate the struggles and successes of early pioneers from France who built their communities. They remember the work of the early French explorers, the voyageurs and the coureurs de bois who paddled across the continent searching for furs, the settlers who built farms and towns, the missionaries who taught their beliefs and healed.

Today, Québec is home to 6 500 000 people, or one-quarter of Canadians. French is the first language for more than 80 percent of them. Their culture is unique, adding richness to the country's heritage. Many of these **Québécois** have worked hard to maintain their culture, heritage, and language. Sometimes this commitment to Québec culture causes conflict with other Canadians. One proposed solution has been **separatism**, or the policy of separation of Québec from Canada. Some political leaders in Québec have tried since the 1970s to remove the province from Canada and to form an independent country with links to Canada. In 1980 and again in 1995, the people of Québec voted in a **referendum**. This was a special vote to see how the Québécois felt about staying as part of Canada. Both times, a majority of people voted not to leave Canada. However, the issue has not been settled. Can French Canadians retain their distinctive culture and language across North America? Will Québec remain part of Canada? These

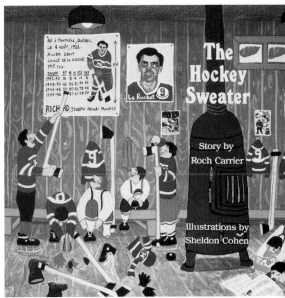

The Hockey Sweater by Roch Carrier, illustrated by Sheldon Cohen ©1984 published by Tundra Books.

Parade participants in a *Fête Nationale* celebration.

questions have been part of our country's history since the Conquest of 1759, Lord Durham's Report in the 1840s, and they still remain today. Meanwhile, Canadians of French ancestry continue to add to our country's stories.

French pioneers also had a big impact outside Québec. In Manitoba, the Voyageur Festival each year is a chance for people to celebrate the hard work and courage of the *Canadiens* and the Aboriginal fur traders who paddled their canoes full of fur along the lakes and rivers of the country. Many of Canada's Métis people are the descendants of these voyageurs and their Aboriginal wives. Tough and daring explorers and voyageurs set out from Québec for many parts of Canada.

Canada is a land of ice and snow and winter activities. The people of Québec City celebrate winter each year in February with the world's largest and oldest winter carnival. *Carnaval* is a ten-day celebration, with hockey, parades, a canoe race across the St. Lawrence River ice floes, feasting, and impressive ice sculptures. The first *Carnaval* was in 1894.

People cook and keep warm around a campfire during the Voyageur Festival in Manitoba.

This is one artist's version of Québec's legendary winter carnival. In this painting, called *Carnaval*, find the large snowman who is the symbol of the celebration. Find examples of French language on the signs. Find evidence that it is winter and that the event takes place in Québec City.

"Carnaval" © Miyuki Tanobe taken from Canadian Childhoods ©1989 Tundra Books, Inc., selections form previously copyrighted works, all published by Tundra Books.

There are many French Canadians who do not live in Québec. Many of them have special celebrations of their heritage. In New Brunswick, Acadians have a festival each July. They remember their ancestors, the pioneers in Acadia who were expelled by the British army in 1755. The Acadians who rebuilt their communities in later years enjoy this festival called Acadian Days.

The Story So Far . . .

1 Work with a partner to develop a question that will require your classmates to find evidence of a French presence in Canada. Your question might ask students to find a current news story involving French Canadians or to investigate local connections to French Canadian people or events from the past.

2 Find someone who is currently enrolled in French Immersion classes at school. Prepare some interview questions to ask the student. Use the 5 Ws (who, what, where, when, why) to help you learn why the student chose to attend French Immersion. Conduct your interview and present your findings.

3 Use at least one electronic source of information and at least one book to find out more about the Acadian people. Present your findings in either a newsletter or news magazine format.

4 Find out more about one of the following French Canadian communities today: Acadians, Franco-Ontarians, Franco-Manitobans, or French people in the Western provinces. Use the 5 Ws to organize your research. Present your findings on a bulletin board or other display board. Include information about cultural celebrations, special foods, favourite stories or legends, important leaders, music, art, and literature.

THE BRITISH CONNECTION

As you learned earlier in the chapter, Canada's coat of arms has many symbols of our country's British heritage. Look again at the lions, roses, thistles, shamrocks, and the Union Jack included in the coat of arms on page 383. They are a reminder for us of the pioneers who left their homes in England, Ireland, Scotland, and Wales to settle in what was to become Canada. Remember the Loyalists? They wanted to continue to live under a British system of government, so they left the United States in the early 1780s to settle here. Later, thousands of emigrants left Britain for this new country and a new life. They brought their system of government and law as well as their loyalty to the King or Queen.

Traditions

Today, there are features of Canada's laws, government, and language that remind us of our British heritage. We have a Prime Minister, a House of Commons, and a Parliament because early Canadians followed British traditions. English is spoken by most Canadians — another legacy of the British pioneers.

In the early days, many British pioneers had a keen interest in anything to do with royalty and they eagerly awaited royal visits. They constructed ceremonial arches to commemorate the occasions and to display local enterprise. This illustration commemorates the landing of the Prince of Wales at Halifax on July 30, 1860.

"The twenty-fourth of May is the Queen's Birthday." Many Canadian children used to know this rhyme well, for it reminded them of Canada's British ties. Victoria Day celebrates the birthday of the British Queen, Victoria. The first holiday was in 1845 in Upper Canada. Most Canadians now celebrate the May 24 holiday as the beginning of summer weather. In many communities, there are picnics, fireworks, and special entertainment, as people gather to celebrate upcoming summer fun and forget about the winter. Many people plant their flower and vegetable gardens that weekend.

There are many reminders of our British heritage in Eastern and Central Canada, from place names to street names. Every town seems to have a King Street and a Queen Street. Many schools are named after important British leaders or the royal family. Can you think of some schools in your neighbourhood or in places you have visited that were named after a famous British person?

As part of a Victoria Day celebration in 1868 in Canada, people in Ottawa watched a gun salute in front of the first Parliament buildings.

Pioneers

British pioneers had to struggle against many obstacles presented by the geography of our land. In order to become farmers, they had to cut huge trees, plant crops, fend off insect and animal pests, survive the harsh winters, build rough roads through the wilderness, and learn to live in a lonely new land. The foundation these early pioneers built lasted through many challenges.

Novelist Marianne Brandis' book, *Rebellion*, reminds us of the hardships British pioneers faced as they tried to fulfil their dreams in Canada. The book's main character, Adam, and his aunt Lenore, think about their first Canadian winter. They have just arrived in Upper Canada from England.

"But it's already October, and the thought of living for a whole winter in one of those shanties out in the woods, all by ourselves. . . !"

He knew exactly what she was seeing in her mind. . . .

The dwelling was a small shanty, with a roof made of hollowed half-logs laid overlapping like tiles so that the ones with the hollow upwards carried off the rain. It had a chimney made of mud plastered on some sort of framework, and it also had the luxury of a pane of glass in its single window. But it was even smaller than the cottages they'd lived in back home. . . .

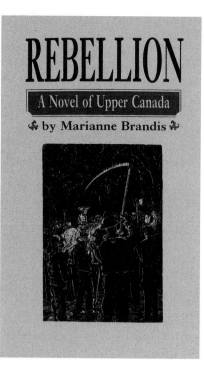

REBELLION
A Novel of Upper Canada
❧ by Marianne Brandis ❧

Aunt Lenore had said quietly, "Picture it in the winter, Adam, with snow."

Every emigrant knew that there was a lot of snow every winter in Canada. Would it be as high as the tops of those stumps? For a moment it was an attractive picture. If the snow were deep enough to cover the stumps, there would be a sheet of white around the two little buildings. The roofs would be laden with it. Smoke would curl out of the chimney into the blue sky.

And inside the shanty would be a whole family, already cramped for space but, in the winter weather, huddled even closer together to be near the fire. The floor would be damp and icy cold. Even by daylight, the room would be dim. There might not be enough food to eat, and water would have to be made by melting snow or found by hacking through the ice of a lake or stream. One crying baby, or one person with a bad cough, could drive the rest of the family crazy. And if there were worse illnesses, or other emergencies, someone would have to ride or tramp through the snowy bush for help.

"It's the loneliness, the distances," Aunt Lenore had said broodingly.

The Story So Far . . .

1 Sometimes people's surnames help us to identify their country of origin. Find the name *Smith* in your local telephone directory. *Smith* is a common English name. How many *Smiths* are there in the directory? How many centimetres does the name *Smith* take up in one column? Or, how many columns of the name *Smith* are there?

2 In your telephone directory, find all the names beginning with *Mc, Mac,* and *O'.* These people's surnames are of British origin.

3 Interview someone in your community who has a British heritage. Use the 5 Ws to help discover why that person, or his or her ancestors, chose to settle in Canada. Ask the person to name some features of Canadian life that they think are of British origin. Present your findings to the class.

4 On a map of your province, find some examples of place names that originated in Britain.

A Safe Haven

Political and Economic Refugees

In 1999 there were thousands of refugees from a place in Europe called Kosovo. They were people whose homes had been burned, who had watched family members or friends being marched away at gunpoint, who had been driven in terror from their communities into a foreign country. Then some of them were brought to another land — Canada.

The Kosovar refugees joined a long list of people who came to Canada to escape persecution and to find a **safe haven**, or place of shelter and safety. Before them had come, among others, Somalis, Hungarians, Guatemalans, Chileans, and, long ago, the Loyalists. The Loyalists were early political refugees who fled the United States for freedom and safety in Canada. Refugees who leave their homes for political reasons fear that they may suffer persecution or even death because of their beliefs. Some Loyalists were tarred and feathered, some had their homes and farms destroyed, and many had to flee to safety in Canada. Some refugees in later years came here for similar reasons.

Others were economic refugees. They came to find good jobs and economic well-being. Many people who came from Britain during the Great Migration in the 1830s were economic refugees. All hoped for freedom and safety in Canada, as well as the chance to have a better life.

These Kosovar children enjoy a Canadian summer activity, far from their war-ravaged homeland. The Canadian government and people wanted to ensure their safety and freedom from war.

Runaway Slaves

Barbara Smucker's novel *Underground to Canada* tells a story of two runaway slave girls. This passage helps us understand the feelings of a person seeking a safe haven. The main character, Julilly, is talking with her mother. Both are slaves in the United States.

> *Mammy Sally paused. She pressed her mouth against Julilly's ear. "This is secret talk I'm tellin' you now. Hold it quiet in your head and never let it out your mouth. There's a place the slaves been whisperin' around called Canada. The law don't allow no slavery there. They say you travel north and follow the North Star, and when you step onto this land you are free. . . ."*

Later, Julilly is talking with other girls who are slaves.

> *"This country is far away under the North Star," she whispered hoarsely. "It's run by a lady named Queen Victoria. She made a*

THE CLASSIC STORY
UNDERGROUND TO CANADA

BARBARA SMUCKER
With a new introduction by Lawrence Hill

law there declarin' all men free and equal. The people respects that law. My daddy told me that, and he was a preacher. . . ."

"How do you know where to find that North Star, girl?" she asked.

Liza answered with certainty and precision. "You look in the sky at night when the clouds roll back. Right up there, plain as the toes on my feet, are some stars that makes a drinking gourd." Night after night Julilly and Liza had been watching it when the stars hung low, sparkling and glistening.

"The front end of that drinking gourd," Liza went on, "points straight up to the North Star. You follow that. Then you get to Canada and you are free."

Web Connection

http://www.school.mcgrawhill.ca/resource

Go to the web site above to find current newspaper and magazine stories about refugees who have come to Canada. Go to History Resources, then to *Canada: The Story of Our Heritage* to see where to go next. Present your findings to the class.

You may have read or heard of this story. *Underground to Canada* is a thrilling and suspense-filled tale. The Underground Railway was a system that helped slaves escape to freedom in Ontario, Québec, and Nova Scotia. People risked their lives to flee their slave masters in the southern United States and reach safety far away in Canada. They did not find an easy life in Canada. They were victims of racist behaviour. But they were not slaves.

The Story So Far . . .

1 Design a research question that will help you learn more about one group of refugees who have found safety in Canada. Develop a research project and then carry out your research plan. Present your findings.

2 Read a history book about the experiences of African-American settlers in Canada. Share your book with a partner.

3 Read a novel or picture book about the Underground Railway. Share it with the class.

4 Songs called *Negro Spirituals* were often filled with coded language that helped runaway slaves escape to freedom in Canada. Find some music relating to the Underground Railway and share it with the class.

CANADA'S BIG NEIGHBOUR

One of the things that makes Canada unique in the world is our relationship with our neighbour, the United States. Not only is the United States a world superpower, it is also the country that shares our border from the Maritimes across the country to British Columbia. Thousands of Canadians and Americans cross this border each day to work, shop, and visit. Thousands of trucks, planes, and railway cars also cross it each day, carrying products from farms, forests, and factories back and forth. If you ate an orange recently, it was probably grown in the United States. If you watched a movie recently, it was probably made in the United States. If you read a magazine, listened to music, or watched a television show, they might also have come from the United States.

The U.S.–Canada border is the world's longest undefended border. This border crossing shows travellers returning to Canada from the United States over the bridge at Niagara Falls, Ontario.

The American Influence

The presence of the United States as our neighbour has had a huge impact on our history. During the era of New France, colonies in what became the United States were rivals of the French for land and trade. You remember the Loyalists. They left the United States to come to a country that remained British. You also remember William Lyon Mackenzie. His rebellion carried a threat of American forms of government that most Upper Canadians rejected. The Underground Railway existed to help people escape from slavery in the United States. You can probably think of many other examples from this text of the impact the United States has had on our history.

Some Canadians feel that the United States is like an elephant and Canada is like a mouse. When the elephant moves, the mouse has to be careful. Canadians depend on Americans to buy our products and, in turn, we enjoy many American products. We are also linked in the defence of North America. But that "elephant" sometimes seems enormous.

There are many stories involving Canadians and Americans, since we share the continent of North America. Canadian novelist Janet Lunn has written stories that explore the history of our connections with our American neighbour. In this passage from *The Hollow Tree*, the story's main character, Phoebe, learns what happens to a local family that is loyal to the British King. It is during the American Revolution in Vermont.

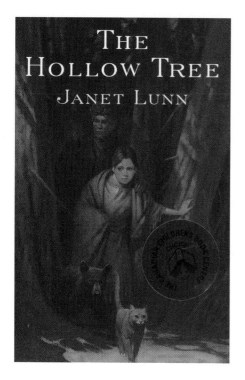

THE HOLLOW TREE
JANET LUNN

. . .Suspected Tories had been robbed, imprisoned, or turned from their homes to make their way, if they could, through the deep wilderness to find refuge in British strongholds. Some, it was said, to take ship to Halifax, in Nova Scotia. . .where the rebellion had not taken hold, or to head up the river to Canada. . . .

Then, very early one clear, cold October morning not long after the first light snowfall, when the sun had only just risen over the flaming red of the maple trees, the quiet of the village was shattered by sounds of shouting. Jed and Noah rushed outside to see what had happened. . . .

"We don't need the likes of traitors like you in our God-fearing village!" It was Elihu Pickens. . . . He was pulling Deborah Williams through her front doorway. . . .

The Williams's cart, the ox harnessed to the front, was pulled up to the front door. Moses Litchfield and Hiram Jesse were shoving the four small Williams children, wide-eyed with bewilderment, into the cart. With one hand Deborah clung to her door jamb. . . .

"No!" she cried. "You can't set me out of my own house. Where will we go? We'll starve!"

"Starve if you must," jeered Elihu Pickens, "that ain't no never mind of ourn. We been generous. We let you have a sack of beans, a sack of flour, and a cooking pot. . .and blankets and such so's you won't up and freeze. . . .You can be legal up there. . .in Canaday or Novy Scotey or wherever you fetches up."

In the novel, Deborah's husband, John, had disappeared a few months earlier, and many people believed that he had gone to join a Loyalist regiment or was spying for the British. Thousands of Loyalists just like Deborah Williams settled in British territory north of the United States.

Canadians do not always agree about issues that concern our country. Sometimes these issues involve our connections with the United States. For example, an issue of concern to National Hockey League hockey fans is that the small-market teams in Canada cannot afford to pay players huge salaries. Richer teams in American cities seem much more able to pay these salaries. Some Canadians fear that our teams will not be able to compete in the National Hockey League and may fold. Some Canadians think the government should help out.

Hockey is Canada's sport. If we don't have some Canadian teams in the NHL, it will be a huge loss, a blow to our national pride. The government of Canada should be providing tax breaks and funding to help keep the NHL teams in our country. Otherwise, the NHL will be all-American. We can't have that.

That's ridiculous. Professional hockey players make far too much money anyway. Why should my taxes go toward paying rich athletes? If the fans don't buy tickets and the owners have promised to pay the players so much, that's the owners' problem. Why should Canadians who are not hockey fans help to pay for this nonsense? Who cares if the NHL becomes all-American? Not me.

The Story So Far . . .

1   There are many issues that concern Canadians in terms of our relationship with the United States. Research to find different points of view about one of the following topics:
  • Can American companies purchase Canadian movie theatres and prevent Canadian films from being shown?
  • Can American magazines be produced more cheaply and flood into Canada so that Canadian magazines can not compete with them in Canada?
  • Will the popularity of American television shows prevent the survival of Canadian television shows?

2   List at least ten direct connections you have with something originating in the United States. These could include such things as music, television shows, food, clothing, or vacation spots. Compare your list with that of your classmates. Create a class graph or table to show the connections. Which item has the most connections?

3   At the beginning of this chapter, you designed a coat of arms. Do you want to keep the same design or make changes? Draw any changes on paper and explain why you made them to the class.

SUM IT UP!

Think of Canada's history as a tapestry, having different threads and strands. From the earliest days of Canada's story, many strands have been woven into the Canadian tapestry. They have shaped the country's past and present. In our Canadian tapestry there is a strand for Aboriginal Peoples. There is a strand for the French, and another for the British. The United States is represented as a fourth strand. These strands are joined by another, representing Canada as a safe haven for refugees. There are also many strands depicting the contributions of the people who have come from all over the world, throughout the ages, to make Canada their home. The tapestry would have to be large to include all the themes and stories of Canada's heritage: its vast geography, its varied landscape, its climate, and all the peoples who have added to the country's richness.

When you began this text, you learned that Canada was a unique place on this Earth. Our artists and athletes, our land, our governments, and our people are among the features that make Canada a place that many people want to call home.

THINKING ABOUT YOUR LEARNING

1 Write a letter to someone who lives in Asia, Africa, or Europe, telling them about Canada. Explain why there are two official languages, why refugees have come here, and when. Include some information about the impact of the United States on Canada.

2 Explain the difference between a political refugee and other immigrants to Canada.

3 Why do you think some people in Québec want to separate the province from Canada?

APPLYING YOUR LEARNING

1 Find out how refugees can find safety in Canada today. What is the process for a refugee to enter Canada? You could interview someone from Immigration Canada or your local member of Parliament's office to find out. Report your results to the class.

2 Find information about the Parti Québécois. What is the aim of this political party? Why do some Canadians object to this aim?

3 Find examples of American influence in your school and community. List as many examples of American products as you can. Some possibilities are: food, clothing, movies, magazines, footwear, sports equipment, logos. Create categories for the lists and group the items by category. Which category has the most items?

4 Make a poster, mural, or quilt showing these strands of the Canadian tapestry: Aboriginal Peoples, French heritage, British heritage, safe haven, influence of the United States. The map of Canada quilt, shown in this photograph, was created by students as a heritage day project.

USING KEY WORDS

1 Make a puzzle for the class, using as many of the Key Words from this chapter as you can. The Key Words are:
- bilingual
- *Carnaval*
- descendants
- motto
- Québécois
- referendum
- safe haven
- separatism

5 Create the front page of a newspaper. Write a story for this page about one of these topics: Aboriginal Peoples, French heritage, British heritage, safe haven, or the influence of the United States.

Glossary

A

aboiteau a valve device used to hold back waters along Bay of Fundy to assist Acadian farmers working in tidal flats

amnesty an official pardon for crimes committed

archives a public storage place for important personal and government historical papers and other records

aristocracy a small group of wealthy people

armistice a formal agreement between governments, in wartime, to stop fighting between their armed forces

assimilate to absorb a group of people into another group's culture

autobiography a person's history, written by that person

autocrat a ruler with absolute power over the people who are ruled

B

bee a gathering of pioneer neighbours to get a job done, such as building a barn

bilingual able to speak two languages, for example, French and English

biography a person's history written by someone else

C

calèche a carriage pulled by horses in New France

Canada Company an organization whose purpose was to bring settlers to buy land in Upper Canada

Canadiens French people of New France, later Lower Canada

capitulation an official document of surrender between two armies

Carnaval Québec's annual winter carnival

carriole a sleigh with runners that was pulled by horses in New France

castor gras literally, greasy beaver, or the fur of a beaver that became supple when worn by a person. It was highly valued by European fur traders.

cens a tax paid by a habitant to his or her *seigneur*

censitaire a habitant who rented land in New France

census an official count of people. Census information includes such things as numbers of people, animals, farms, factories, workers, immigrants, and so on. The main purpose is to count numbers of people.

Château Clique a small group of influential people who appeared to rule Lower Canada. They met at the Château Saint-Louis.

cholera a very infectious bacterial disease that killed many immigrants crossing the Atlantic Ocean to North America by ship. A serious epidemic killed many people in Upper and Lower Canada.

civilian a person caught up in a war who is not a member of the armed forces, for example, women and children during the War of 1812

Clergy Reserve land reserved for the Church in Upper Canada

coalition a coming together of groups for a special purpose

compensation in this usage, payment for losses suffered during the American Revolution

Confederacy an organization of groups so that they can support one another

conflict a struggle, contest, or fight

congés permits for official trips each year given to licensed fur traders or voyageurs

corduroy road a road made of logs laid side by side, common in Upper Canada

corvée work performed by a habitant on the *seigneur's* land

coureur de bois literally, a runner of the woods, or a fur trader in New France

Crown Reserve land owned by the British Government

culture the beliefs, customs, arts, and institutions of a particular people, community, or nation

curé a parish priest in New France

D

decapitation in this usage, the removal of the leaders of the society of New France

democratic a government by the people or their elected representatives

deportation the forced removal of a person, or group of people, from a country

depression a period of job shortages, low wages, bankruptcies, and economic troubles

descendants people in a family who have a common ancestor

directed settlement a colonial settlement that received special help, such as transportation, food, and land grants, from the British government

displaced people who are forced to move away from their home communities

Doric Club a gang of people who supported the British government and the Château Clique in Lower Canada

dowry a large wedding gift of money, goods, or produce from the bride's family to the groom

due process following the rules of the law

E

economy the organized way in which people in a country work, generate wealth, and spend money

elected assembly a governing body made up of representatives elected by voters

emigration the act of leaving a home country to move to another country

engagé a person hired to work for three years, after which they owned a plot of land to farm

entrepreneur a person who starts a business, usually involving financial gain and the risk of financial loss

expel to remove by force

F

Family Compact a small group of pro-British leaders in Upper Canada who ruled the colony

les filles du roi literally, *the daughters of the king*, or young women who were sponsored by the King of France to leave France to marry pioneers in New France

Fils de la Liberté literally, *sons of freedom*, or a group of people in Lower Canada who wanted to overthrow the British rulers

free trade when a company that sells for the lowest price gets the business; in other words, there are no preferential tariffs between countries

Frères Chasseurs French Canadian *Patriotes* who wanted to end British rule in Lower Canada

G

genocide the deliberate destruction of a racial or cultural group of people

government document an official document issued by a government, for example, licences, passports, visas, immigration entry documents, and social insurance cards

great coat a large, heavy, woollen coat worn by British soldiers

guerrilla warfare warfare using surprise attacks and ambushes rather than planned battles

guild an organization of skilled craftspeople, for example, silversmiths

H

habeas corpus the Latin term for a law protecting an individual's rights, whereby prisoners cannot be held without being charged with a crime, cannot be held without trial, and must be tried fairly

habitant a farmer in New France

habitation a dwelling. Champlain built a large habitation at Québec to house himself, his sailors, and pioneers, their belongings, animals, and food. The habitation was also a fortress.

heritage the stories, art, music, buildings, and ideas passed down to the present from earlier generations

high commissioner a person appointed by a government for a special task, for example, Lord Durham

Hunters' Lodges secret societies of rebels trying to overthrow British rule in Lower Canada

I

immigration the act of moving into a new country

industrial revolution a period of great and rapid change during which many jobs became obsolete, were redefined, or were created. People became factory workers operating large machines, rather than farm workers using hand tools.

industry a business, especially one in which something is manufactured

institution an organization created for a public or social purpose, for example, a church or a school

intendant an important government official in New France, responsible for the day-to-day running of the colony and for controlling the fur trade, industry, justice

interviewee a person in an interview who is being asked questions for information

interviewer a person in an interview who asks the questions and records the answers

J

Jesuits members of a Roman Catholic religious organization. Many came as missionaries to New France.

jury a group of people who hear evidence and pronounce a verdict of guilty or not guilty in a trial

L

land baron a person who owns a very large amount of land

la survivance survival of the culture of French Canada, especially in Québec

Legislative Assembly the group of representatives elected to the legislature of a province

legislative union the joining together of the law-makers in Upper and Lower Canada into one legislature

legislature a group of people having the duty and power to make laws

levellers people who wanted more democratic rule for Upper Canada

libel publishing false statements that would damage a person's reputation

lods et ventes taxes paid by habitants in New France

Loyalists people who supported the British side during the American Revolution. Many came to settle in British North America.

M

maritime near the ocean

martial law short-term military rule

martyr a person who suffers or dies defending his or her beliefs

mercantilism a trading system in which a colony provides cheap raw materials to manufacturers in a "parent" country. Manufactured products are then sold to colonists at a profit.

mercenary a soldier who fights in a foreign army for pay, not for the country

mess a group of soldiers organized for eating and sleeping

metissage the marriage of an Aboriginal woman and a French fur trader

migration a mass movement of people to another place, either inside a country or to another country

military rule government by the army

minutemen rebel soldiers on the American side during the American Revolution who were ready to act on a minute's notice

missionary a person who works to convert others and change their beliefs, especially religious beliefs

moderate a less extreme, slower approach to reform or change in Upper Canada

monopoly sole control of something, such as the right to trade in furs

motto words that are part of a heraldic crest, such as Canada's Coat of Arms

mutiny rebellion against authorities, for example, sailors refusing to obey their captain

N

nationalists people who look after the interests of their own people

Ninety-Two Resolutions a list of suggestions for reforming the government of Lower Canada to make it more responsible to the voters and the members of the Legislative Assembly

O

oath a sworn statement promising to do something

oligarchy government by a small group of unelected people

opposition the political party not in power

P

parish a district with its own church and priest in New France

parliamentary system a system of government by means of a legislature with elected members who make laws

party a political group with similar interests and aims

Patriotes people in Lower Canada during the 1820s and 1830s who were against British rule and who rebelled to gain responsible government

Patriots people in the United States who supported independence from Britain during the American Revolution

patronage the power to appoint and pay public servants

personal interview a conversation in which a person shares information with another person, who asks questions and keeps track of answers

plunder violent robbery to obtain food, guns, and other goods

prosecutor an attorney who presents the Crown's case, for example, the government against Samuel Lount and Peter Matthews after the Rebellion of 1837 in Upper Canada

Q

Québécois a person from Québec, especially one who is French Canadian

R

race a group of people who share the same biological characteristics

radicals people in Upper and Lower Canada who wanted a democratic government, with elections for many government positions

raids swift, sudden attacks made during a war, usually with a small number of attackers

rebellion organized resistance against a government

Recollets members of a French religious order or group within the Roman Catholic Church

referendum a vote from all eligible voters to answer a question. People in Newfoundland voted in a referendum in 1949 to join Canada. People in Québec voted in a referendum in 1980 and again in 1995 not to separate from Canada.

reform change

Reformers people who wanted to change the government in Upper and Lower Canada to make it more democratic

refugees people who flee from a war across an international border into another country

repeal to cancel something, for example, the Act of Union in 1841 in Upper and Lower Canada

responsible government government in which elected representatives of the people make the laws

riding a political area led by a member of Parliament or of the Legislative Assembly

rivalry competition

Royal Government rule by a King or Queen

S

safe haven a place where a person fleeing persecution is safe from harm

sedition promoting the overthrow of the state

seigneur a landowner in New France

seigneurial **system** the method of landholding in New France

separatism the beliefs and actions of people, especially in Québec, who want to separate their province from the rest of the country

shanty a small, rough shack, often a pioneer family's first home

Speaker in representative bodies, the person who runs the meetings and keeps track of who has the right to speak in debates

squatters people who take over a piece of land or a house that is not theirs

strike organized refusal to work

T

Ten Resolutions a list of statements from the British government refusing the demands for responsible government in Lower Canada

tithes gifts made to the Church. *Tithe* means *tenth*, so people in New France sometimes gave one-tenth of their earnings to the Church.

Tories people who did not favour changing the government of Upper and Lower Canada and who supported the British system of government

township a division of the land of Upper Canada by surveyors

transship to transport people or goods from one form of transportation to another; for example, to move people or goods off a lake-going ship and carry them by coach on land in Upper Canada

V

voyageur a fur trader, canoeist, and traveller along the lakes and rivers of North America

W

War Hawks Americans who wanted war with Britain before 1812

wholesale trade the business of supplying goods to stores

**Credits**

C-070006; **page 211** NAC/ C-003904; **page 214** NAC/C-010364; **page 215** NAC/C-005968; **page 217** NAC/C-0002873; **page 218** Toronto Reference Library MTL 2040; **page 220** NAC/AP C-12649; **page 223** NAC/C-00017; **page 224** NAC/C-003368; **page 225 top** NAC/C-011230; **bottom** Special Collections & Archives, James A. Gibson Library, Brock University, Photo by Lesley Bell, Slide Curator; **page 226 top** NAC/C-073674; **bottom** John Ross Robertson Collection, Metropolitan Toronto Public Library, JRR-1625; **page 227** Public Archives of Nova Scotia N-0132; **page 228 left** Corbis-Bettmann; **right** Library of Congress; **page 229** NAC/PA-124022; **page 231** Photograph courtesy of the Royal Ontario Museum © ROM; Courtesy of Provincial Archives of Newfoundland and Labrador A17-10; **page 232** Courtesy of Provincial Archives of Newfoundland and Lebrador (PAN L#A17-10) **page 236** NAC/C-011364; **page 238** NAC/C-004987; **page 239** Toronto Reference 004987 Library MTL 1787; **page 240** NAC/C-7043; **page 241** Archives of Ontario S-17349; **page 244** NAC/C-122927; **page 245** Archives of Ontario S-7696; **page 247** NAC/C-002401; **page 249** NAC/C-44625; **page 251** NAC/C-001707; **page 253** NAC/C-34334; **page 254 top** NAC/C-1669; **bottom** Archives of Ontario; **page 256** NAC/C-011401; **page 257** NAC/C-073696; **page 258** John Ross Robertson Collection/Toronto Public Library T-15727; **page 259** Archives of Ontario S-837; **page 261** NAC/C-013999; **page 264-265** NAC/C-003653; **page 266** NAC/C-040164; **page 268** NAC/C-001021; **page 269** NAC/C-040201; **page 270** Reprinted from *Mythical Mufferaw* by Bernie Bedore, illustrations by Allen Lutes, by permission of Quarry Press, Inc.; **page 274** NAC/C-073435; **page 275** NAC/C-114135; **page 276** NAC/C-001043; **page 278** NAC/C-120285; **page 279** National Gallery of Canada, Ottawa; **page 280** NAC/C-012491; **page 284** NAC/C-013370; **page 286** NAC/C-000828; **page 287** NAC/C-005435; **page 289** NAC/C-013647; **page 290** NAC/C-024888; **page 292** NAC/C-014256; **page 294** NAC/ C-073725; **page 298** NAC/C-000510; **page 301** NAC/C-040175; **page 302** Metro Toronto Reference Library; **page 306** NAC/C-003753B **page 309** NAC/C-023633; **page 310** NAC/C-003208; **page 315** NAC/C-007964; **page 317** NAC/C-005962; **page 318 top** NAC/C-18789; **bottom** NAC/C-073707; **page 322** NAC/C-005434; **page 326** NAC/C-000392; **page 331** NAC/C-006032; **page 329** C-000395; **page 332** C-115872; **page 333** NAC/C-013988; **page 334** Archives of Ontario; **page 337** NAC/C-020976; **page 338** NAC/C-108292; **page 341** NAC/C-040177; **page 342** NAC/C-004785; **page 343** NAC/C-001669; **page 345** NAC/C-011228; **page 346** NAC/C-001029; **page 348** NAC/C-13392; **page 350** NAC/C-000161; **page 351** NAC/C-005331; **page 356** NAC/C-000048; **page 359** NAC/C-01854; **page 360** Archives of Ontario; **page 361** NAC/C-003160; **page 362** NAC/C-006070; **page 363** NAC/C-002393; **page 364** NAC/C-005655; **page 366** NAC/C-00315; **page 368** NAC/C-041388; **page 370** NAC/C-008642; **page**

372 NAC/C-073708; **page 375** NAC/C-010978; **page 379** NAC/C-92205; **page 380** Winston Fraser; **page 382** NAC/PA-142624; **page 383** Canadian Heritage; **page 385** Kim Stallknecht/Ivy Images; **page 387 bottom** Winston Fraser; **page 388 top** Henry Kalen/Ivy Images; **page 389** Ivy Images; **page 390** NAC/ C-024369; **page 391** NAC/C-2837; **page 392** *Rebellion: A Novel of Upper Canada* by Marianne Brandis, published by Porcupine's Quill in 1996; **page 393 top** CP Picture Archive, Michael Lea; **bottom** From *Underground to Canada* by Barbara Smucker. Copyright © 1977 by Clarke, Irwin & Company Ltd. Reprinted by permission of Penguin Books Canada, Ltd.; **page 395** CP Picture Archive, Harry Rosettani; **page 396** From *The Hollow Tree,* Copyright © 1997 by Janet Lunn, Used with permission of Alfred A. Knopf Canada, a division of Random House of Canada Limited; **page 399** Ellie Deir.

Text Credits

Page 17 "O Siem" © 1994 Aglukark Entertainment Inc. and Chad Irschick; **page 391-392** *Rebellion: A Novel of Upper Canada* by Marianne Brandis, published by Porcupine's Quill,1996; **page 393-394** From *Underground to Canada* by Barbara Smucker. Copyright © 1977 by Clarke, Irwin & Company Ltd. Reprinted by permission of Penguin Books Canada, Ltd.; **page 396** From *The Hollow Tree* by Janet Lunn, 1997. Reprinted by permission of Alfred A. Knopf Canada.

▲

◄ *National Gallery of Canada, Ottawa*

Index